SAINT-JUST

SAINT-JUST, MEMBER OF THE CONVENTION

SAINT-JUST

COLLEAGUE OF ROBESPIERRE

BY

EUGENE NEWTON CURTIS

PROFESSOR OF HISTORY
GOUCHER COLLEGE

MORNINGSIDE HEIGHTS: NEW YORK
COLUMBIA UNIVERSITY PRESS
1935

TO
BLANCHE O'NEILL CURTIS

PREFACE

This book aims to give a fully documented account of a remarkable individual, who played a pivotal part in a remarkable
period. It strives also to interpret his personality and to estimate
the value of his services to France. The first aim is objective,
the second subjective. Some readers will hold to the one and
despise the other, according to varying tastes and predilections.
I personally feel that a biography which lacks the facts is merely
fiction and that a biography which is nothing but facts is merely
source material.

One of the valuable features of the book as originally conceived was to have been that it had no preface. Why take up
space spoiling the reader's fun by telling him what it is all going
to be about? The insertion of this page should not be held a
weak surrender to convention. It is rather due to the require-
ments of human gratitude, in which spirit I wish to acknowl-
edge the helpful suggestions as to form made by Dr. Ola Eliza-
beth Winslow and as to French idioms by Dr. Louise Cléret
Seibert, the kindness of Dr. Charles Downer Hazen in reading
the entire manuscript and of Dr. James T. Shotwell in reading
portions of it, the courteous aid of Mr. L. H. Dielman in the
making of photostats, the constant and invaluable counsel of
my wife.

E. N. C.

Baltimore, Md.
June, 1935

CONTENTS

CONTENTS

ILLUSTRATIONS

SAINT-JUST

I

THE VILLAGE RADICAL

RICHELIEU had his Gray Cardinal, Robespierre his Saint-Just. But there was nothing gray, nothing misty or self-effacing about Saint-Just. That bright, vivid figure flashed like a meteor across the last years of the Revolution, illuminating and destroying. In less than two years Robespierre's most trusted disciple had forced his way to the front, so that men gave ear to him not as the mouthpiece of another, but because his own thoughts had become important. Even earlier this handsome youth had compelled attention by the eloquence of his speech, the versatility of his interests and the driving power of his will. Many striking figures emerged out of the whirlwind of that Revolution; none was more dramatic or significant than Saint-Just.

His roots were in the soil. Generations of prosperous northern farmers lay behind him, sturdy and self-reliant, a world removed from the crushed, complaining peasantry of tradition. They came originally from Attichy in the present department of the Oise, then moved to Morsain in the Aisne. Here in 1715 his father, Louis Jean was born, the eighth of nine children.

Louis Jean showed signs of independence; he struck out for himself by leaving the farm and entering the army. Perhaps, with four older brothers, he had no choice in the matter. At any rate, he advanced as far in the service as a plebeian could in those days, becoming a cavalry captain and *chevalier de Saint-Louis*.[1] When past fifty and on the way to being an old soldier he married Marie Anne Robinot,[2] twenty years his junior, who had grown up in the historic little city of Nevers in central France. They settled in the neighboring village of Decize, the headquarters of his regiment, where on August 25, 1767,[3] their oldest child, Louis Antoine, was born. His full

3

name was Louis Antoine Léon Florelle; in later life he used his surname only.[4] Grandfather Charles, who had for years lived at Nampcel, managing the adjacent seigneurial estate of Morsain, died at the age of ninety-one and Louis Jean inherited the post. So he left the army for the farm and made his way back to the family home in 1768. In that year a daughter was born, Louise Marie Anne, and in 1769 another, Marie Françoise Victoire. The younger girl was Louis Antoine's favorite sister.

The little family was comfortably off; beside the income of the Morsain stewardship, Louis Jean had military pensions as captain and chevalier. It may not be fanciful to trace the son's later interest in agricultural and in military matters to his father's absorption in these two things. When the boy was nine, his family made a new home in Blérancourt, another village not far away.[5] Within a year Louis Jean died, leaving his widow at least enough to pay for her son's education and to set aside a sufficient dowry for her daughters.[6]

The lad was enrolled at the collège of the Oratoriens, Saint-Nicolas de Soissons. "An old man of Coucy," a fellow-student at Soissons, later thought he remembered that Saint-Just was a disagreeable boy, but a hard worker. Tacitus and Plato were his favorite authors. This is interesting if true; the conciseness of Saint-Just's oratory may have owed something to the sober austerity of Tacitus, the idealistic fancies of his *Fragments* something to Plato's *Utopia;* the whole of his prose and poetry are there. His career at Soissons is said to have closed abruptly in consequence of a schoolboy mutiny at the Spartan régime in force. Saint-Just, one of the ringleaders, was detailed to set fire to a school building, under cover of which all were to run away. Caught in the act, he refused to name his accomplices. Being then confined on short rations, the tale goes on, he threw a portion of the food out the window, saying grandly, "Go, recount to the principal what you have seen and tell him that Saint-Just, foreseeing more violence to come, hardens himself to support it with courage." Whereat the collège, with less foresight, expelled its most distinguished alumnus.[7]

4

As a matter of fact, we have no knowledge that Saint-Just's Soissons life ended so tragically. On the other hand the book is still preserved which he received on August 16, 1781, at a distribution of prizes, inscribed in monkish Latin: "SOLEMNIBUS collegii Suessionensis sacerdotum ORATORII DOMINI JESU ludis, Agonothetis clarissimis Viris Majore et Consulibus, maximo ordinum omnium applausu, ingenuus Adolescens LUDOVICUS SAINT-JUST, auditor in 5ª meritus est 1ᵘᵐ interpretationis et 2ᵘᵐ thematis Praemium." [8] In testimony of which the fathers affix the seal of the congregation. It is pleasanter to think of the ingenuous adolescent beaming down the aisle, prize under arm, than of the bad boy expelled for arson and impertinence. And we have the documents on our side. Leaving Soissons, with or without final honor, Louis returned to Blérancourt.

The province in which he lived was southern Picardy, which fell within the *gouvernement* of the Île-de-France. His section of it, now the department of the Aisne, is one of the leading agricultural and industrial areas of France. But for miles and miles, the land not under the plow is heavily wooded and studded with high, rocky plateaus, which rise sharply above the sea of forest, capped with an ancient fortified city like Laon, or a powerful medieval castle like Coucy. There was much here to stir an ardent imagination. The *gouvernement* itself was the very kernel of the kingdom, which grew out of it as out of a nucleated cell and bore its name. At Noyon, the city nearest Blérancourt, Charlemagne and Hugh Capet had been crowned kings of the Franks and there John Calvin was born. With his fatalism, his strong will-power and his recognition of the need for a close-knit social order, Saint-Just was a sort of Revolutionary Calvinist. At Soissons, the city of his formal education, Clovis had beaten the Romans and ruled; there was the old capital of Neustria. There is documentary evidence from his own writings that the boy dwelt much on these things. They might have turned him into a stubborn reactionary. They seem to have given him a zest for emulation. He would like to try his hand at ruling men too. And as these first kings (and the

5

theologian as well) had found they could clutch power only by overturning the governments of their day, he, like them, became a revolutionist.

As for his home village, it was a quiet little place in the woods, well removed from city clatter.[9] Behind the house lay a considerable garden, at whose end on the edge of a brook stood the famous hornbeam. From 1787 to 1792 Saint-Just spent much time reading and writing under the tree. It was his habit to set three tables equipped with writing-materials at equal intervals along an arbor. He would walk up and down, sometimes declaiming aloud and, as his ideas crystallized, would jot them down at the nearest table. In the evening, he would gather up and coördinate the notes on the three tables.[10]

There was in him an intense energy, a burning desire for self-expression. The arbor was well enough but, intellectual though he was, he could not live by the interior life of brain alone. Blérancourt frankly bored him. Two episodes, in flat contradiction to the later tempo of his life, arose from this sense of repression, the curious adventure with his mother's silver and the Thorin affair. Like other ascetics he had first to sow his wild oats.

On a September night of 1786, some bystander may have noticed a nineteen-year-old boy hurrying along with an awkwardly shaped bundle under his arm. It contained a silver bowl, a silver goblet, four silver cups, a pair of pistols and other objects. The boy was bound for Paris, where he duly arrived, put up at an inn and disposed of most of the silver. Wild with alarm, his mother turned for help to the Chevalier d'Evry.[11] A few days later she was able to hand over to him an extraordinary epistle, purporting to be written by a physician, who informed the lady that her son was working so hard that his blood was "calcinated"; he must stop studying, live on milk and vegetables and keep well covered at night or he would die within a year. The writer was glad to explain that the boy had taken the silver (now regrettably nearly all gone) to pay his doctor's bill. Saint-Just's address was artfully slipped in, together with the

6

suggestion that his mother write tactfully urging his return. D'Evry had no difficulty in divining that the letter was a forgery; the boy, nearing the end of his resources and having had his fill of Paris, was trying to save his face. Truly an ingenuous adolescent! At least he had the grace to be ashamed and to be sick of his lark within a week. But he was not to get out of it so easily. At Mme. Saint-Just's request, d'Evry had her son arrested and examined by Chenu, *commissaire* at the Châtelet. The boy broke down and confessed everything. Being asked what he proposed to do when the money was gone, he said that he had intended to get a place in the guards of M. le Comte d'Artois until he was big enough to enter the Gardes du Corps. Though he acknowledged the accuracy of the report of his examination when read to him, he refused to sign it; that personal pride of his forbade. The upshot of the matter was that through a provisional order by de Crosne, lieutenant general of police, regularized later by a *lettre de cachet* signed by the king himself, Saint-Just was placed early in October in the combination prison boarding house of Dame Marie at Picpus, there to reflect upon his sins. It is an odd circumstance that his first contact with the royal circle was an order for his imprisonment, following hard on his expressed desire to enter the king's bodyguard. Perhaps his antipathy to the monarch whose name he bore began then and there.

Mme. Saint-Just, though "much tranquilized" by the arrest, expressed herself to d'Evry as greatly hurt by her son's indifference, which ultimately caused her to fall ill. However, a series of letters in February and March indicates that the culprit has repented and is going to study law. Arrangements are made for him to enter the service of Maître Descharmes, *procureur* at Soissons, as second clerk. The family is overjoyed. By the middle of April, this kindly and apparently successful imprisonment, so characteristic of the paternalism of the old régime, came to an end.[12] Out of it emerges the figure of a mother who, if not strong, had more character than has commonly been attributed to her. After the reconciliation, she and her son remained deeply attached. If he owed his vigorous independence to his father, it is to his mother that one must trace his gentler qualities, his melancholy, courtesy and whatever pity for humankind he possessed.

After a few months at Soissons under Descharmes, Saint-Just flung himself into the study of his new profession with all earnestness, matriculating at the law school of the University of Reims. He passed his first examination September 24, 1787, his baccalaureate February 14, 1788, and his licentiate in law April 15.[13]

At the end of this adventurous eighteen months, six of which were passed under sentence of the law and the remainder in preparation for its practice, Saint-Just returned to Blérancourt. It had all passed like a dream and the old narrow routine closed in on him again.

The vital force of this lad, penned up in a remote village and seeking vivid experiences, was bound to find an outlet. It has been asserted that the next turn of the wheel cast him into a wild series of sexual excesses with the wives and daughters of the villagers.[14] While this is without proof, there was unfortunately at least one irregularity, the Thorin affair.

An attractive girl with red hair, named Thérèse Gellé, the daughter of a notary, lived in the village.[15] She was an energetic, passionate creature, somewhat older than Saint-Just, with whom she fell in love. Her ardor was vigorously returned. But obstacles arose in the shape of his youth and lack of fortune; the girl was married by her family in July, 1786, to François Thorin, son of the *receveur de l'enregistrement* at Blérancourt. Unanimous local tradition makes Saint-Just the lover of Mme. Thorin, as he had been of Mlle. Gellé. The secret was probably pretty well kept as long as Saint-Just remained in Blérancourt. He did not take her away with him. On the contrary she remained with her husband until July 25, 1793, when she left him for Paris.[16] It was on September 2, 1793, a year after Saint-Just's departure, that his intimate friend, Thuillier, wrote him from Blérancourt:

8

I have news of the Thorin woman and you still pass for having abducted her. She is living in the Hotel des Tuileries, opposite the Jacobins, rue Saint-Honoré. It is important, to efface from public opinion the slander which has been implanted in the hearts of honest folk, that you do everything possible to keep the esteem and honor which you had before this abduction. You have no idea of all this, but it merits your attention. Adieu, my friend, it is mail-time; do for your friend what you have promised him.

To which Saint-Just replied:

I received your letter yesterday. I have just opened it as I am endlessly busy. Where the devil have you dreamed what you say about citizeness Thorin? I beg you to assure those who talk to you about it, that I have nothing to do with this matter. I have no time to write you at greater length. . . . Would it please you to be administrator of purchases and food-supply for the army? Write me about it. You have been recognized as having the qualities, the necessary integrity and intelligence.

Adieu, if the story you have told me is repeated to you, you will please bear witness to the truth. I am going, I think, one of these days, to the armies.[17]

The last line of Thuillier's letter has been absurdly interpreted, "break off your intrigue with Mme. Thorin." It clearly means, "get me a government job." If, indeed, fascinated by Saint-Just's glory, she had followed him to Paris, Mme. Thorin must have been disappointed. He was too busy with politics to blow up the old flame, so the lady stayed only briefly, appearing again in Blérancourt October 8. This date is fixed, to be sure, by her husband's suit for divorce against her, with which she was in hearty accord. The cause was incompatibility and Thérèse agreed that she was determined "to remain the least time possible, wife of the said Thorin."[18] The divorce was granted July 9, 1794.

There is no proof that she denounced anyone to Saint-Just, that on his way to the scaffold he sought a last look from her, nor that she returned to the village after Thermidor and lived an evil life there. By that time she had been a long while in Blérancourt, obscure, poor and unreproached. The arrest of

9

Thorin, October 25, 1793, has been wrongly attributed to Saint-Just's vengeance.[19] Letters written by Thorin senior to his imprisoned son prove that the latter was denounced by one Monneveux and that the father had actually written "our fellow citizen" Saint-Just to use his influence in the prisoner's behalf.[20] In any event, Thorin regained his freedom in April, 1794, three months before the fall of Saint-Just. No, he was not quite a Galahad. Perhaps that would be too much to expect of a lad as handsome and eager, who read Rousseau and was bored with Blérancourt. It is clear from the story of Thérèse that he was at least as attractive to the girls as they to him and small wonder. But neither was he a Don Juan.

During this period when the physical tides of life flowed strongly, Saint-Just's intellectual energies were by no means in abeyance. Not far from his home rose the massive towers of Coucy-le-Château, with that stirring inscription over the donjon gate,

> N'y Roi, n'y Duc, n'y Prince je suis,
> J'y suis le Sire de Coucy.

There was a spiritual kinship between him and those old hawk-like feudal barons of Enguerrand, who revered no ranks of peerage, trusting only in the strength of their right arms. And so it is not surprising that Saint-Just spent many months studying the annals of the château and collecting notes for a monograph which was never written.[21]

His first venture in the literary field appeared anonymously and without a publisher's name in May, 1789.[22] It consisted of two thin volumes. The following announcement appeared in Number 6 of Camille Desmoulins's paper, *Révolutions de France et de Brabant:* "Organt, poem in twenty cantos, with this motto: *You, young man, have you said farewell to good sense?*"

Not much can be said for this long-drawn affair as a work of art. It is a burlesque epic, purporting to narrate certain adventures which befell the army of Charlemagne in his campaigns against the Saxons. There are endless battles between evenly matched hosts of heroes, wars between devils and angels, noble speeches of Satan in council. It was not Milton, however, but rather Voltaire who furnished the model for *Organt*.[23] In that clever and dubious satire, *La Pucelle,* the old cynic made sport of patriotism, religion and morality or what passed for them in the officialdom of his day. The poem was part of his long war against hypocrisy and became immensely popular, creating indeed a specialized literary type, imitated by budding authors. The fact that Saint-Just was following a recognized convention takes much of the point from the savage criticisms of those who have labeled *Organt* "one of those dirty books that are sold secretly" and have regarded it as evidence of an incurably licentious imagination.[24] There is, to be sure, the fact that the hero, Organt, illegitimate son of a bishop, is obviously meant to be Saint-Just himself and that a fair share of the poem concerns itself with his amorous adventures. Nor can one blink the point that in the rape of the nuns and other episodes there are passages of unbelievable coarseness. The young author quite frankly defends libertinism on theory. If hideous death destroys all beauty and life is but a dream, let us at least dream that we are happy, he advises. Fully granting the vulgarity of conception and imagery, one remembers the eighteenth century and *La Pucelle,* one recalls the restless, rebellious spirit of this young villager and one wonders whether a good deal of it was not written purposely *pour enrager les bourgeois.* It is so foreign to his later spirit that it seems from another hand; it appears rational to think of it as the work of a rather smart, rather impudent boy who wrote with his tongue in his cheek, trying to make a sensation by being as daringly naughty as he could, but who knew better and was not really so bad as he liked to have people think.

Aside from the question of Saint-Just's sexual morality, the poem takes on added significance from the standpoint of the political and social thinker he was to become, who may be traced here in the making. Were he king of the world, he says, all would be different; the insolent would be cast from their seats and timid innocents exalted; he would weigh in equal balance obscurity, greatness, poverty and rank. He would be surrounded by no armed guards, but by human hearts. If his neighbors should declare war, he would say to them: "Listen, good folk, have you no wives and children? Instead of steeping the earth in blood, return to their embraces; lay aside these terrible weapons and like us, live at peace." His happy people would grow rich with their own wealth without profaning the rights of others; they would flourish under the shadow of wise old laws, which he would never violate.

In this passage and many others Saint-Just has expressed his horror of war. He has a gloomy and rather fine picture of the Temple of Memory, of which Pride is the ingenious builder, dwelling there under the happy name of Glory. It is built of the somber vapor of famous deeds on earth and crimes brought forth by war. Glory is seated on shameful laurels, holding a few dusty twigs in his hand, with which he seeks to turn aside the blazing glare of the torch, whose terrible and incorruptible justice illuminates the emptiness of his heart. His hands and lips are bloody, his eyes haughty and menacing; about him profane incense swirls, through whose cloud the idol appears, adored by fools. There are placed all those vile conquerors, vaunted by us, cursed in their own day; those cruel gods, whose fame is permeated by blood, tears and smoke.

Yet one cannot miss the significance for Saint-Just's own future, of the line in which Organt is made mouthpiece of the traditional French maxim:

Le Rhin lui seul vous protège contre eux.

There is also a curious presage of the ultrademocratic military policy followed by Saint-Just during the Alsatian mission, in the speech wherein Nemours declares that cowards often hold a general's place, far from danger and close to glory, where like the gods they can be victorious without risk.

Le plus beau poste est celui du Soldat
Bravant la mort dans le feu d'un combat.

So he shows his sense of justice and deep-seated pity for the under dog. This pity doubtless passes into a Rousseau-like sentimentality when old Hirem releases the wicked Iramin on the ground that "il a peut-être un père."

Not content with ridiculing the social system in general terms (as in the elaborate figure of Asinomanie, where asses render judgment in Parlement, lecture in the university and preach from the pulpits), the satirist becomes daringly concrete.[25] The case of the stolen halter, over which the asses hold court, is a reference to the affair of the diamond necklace; the adventures of the Duc de Brissac and Mme. du Barry are burlesqued as well as a duel between the Comte d'Artois and the Duc de Bourbon. That there might be no mistake the author added a key, identifying his chief characters. Closely as this touched the throne, the venturesome young Juvenal did not stop there; with ferocious invective and under the flimsiest disguise he attacked the king and queen themselves. Most violent perhaps is the passage in Canto XVI, where the guardian angel tells Organt how much he pities France which tyrants rule.

> L'Etat faiblit, et les lois sans vigueur
> Respectent l'or du coupable en faveur.
> Dans ses écarts la Reine forcenée
> Foule, mon fils, d'un pied indifférent,
> Et la Nature, et tout le peuple franc.
> Son avarice, et cruelle et prodigue,
> Pour amasser, par-tout cabale, intrigue,
> Dissipe ensuite, et, sans s'embarrasser,
> Crache le sang qu'elle vient de sucer.
> Cruel vautour, dont la faim irritée,
> Du peuple entier fait un vrai Prométhée!

Meanwhile, the laborer with weakened arm vainly digs the soil; he returns home at night to find his wife in despair, their cabin pillaged.

> Et qui l'a fait? dit l'époux plein d'effroi;
> Et qui l'a fait? qui l'a voulu?—Le Roi!
> Le Roi, mon fils; sa funeste indolence
> Ignore, hélas! les malheurs de la France.

De noirs tyrans écrasent ses sujets
Et sa faiblesse épouse leurs forfaits.
La Cour n'est plus qu'un dédale de crimes,
Des traces d'or tiennent lieu de fil;
L'honneur s'y vend au coup le plus subtil.

There are plenty of other references to the feeble king and his wicked consort.[26] There are also more general accounts of court corruption. Such is the picture of the palace blazing with a million torches, whither men come from every land in search of the arts, good taste and happiness (he does not really conceal the name under the brazen abbreviation "V . . . le"), but where courtesans, "whitened sepulchres," sell their favors; where Envy walks with haggard eyes, side by side with Pride, Coquetry, Intrigue, Impudence and Devotion, careless of famished rhymers and virtue sighing beneath its rags.

Faithful to his master Voltaire, Saint-Just saw the Church as an essential part of the dreadful machinery of power which crushed men down. Outstripping him, Saint-Just comes out for atheism. It is rather suggested than openly stated, but it is the obvious inference of the couplets,

Dieu sommeillait sans sceptre et sans couronne,
Sur le dernier des degrés de son trône,
Le cou posé sur un broc de nectar;
Et cependant les rênes de la Terre
Erraient sans guide et flottaient au hasar.

One of the most remarkable parts of the poem is the materialistic account of the world's origin, given in the eighth canto, suggesting in the thousands of years which the author requires an anticipation of the theory of evolution.

On the whole, *Organt* suggests precocity rather than immaturity. Yet its extravagances in language, in metaphor, in obscene fancy and in moral condemnation place it definitely in the class of juvenilia. Perhaps the author realized this; the one-line preface is disarmingly modest.

J'ai vingt ans; j'ai mal fait; je pourrai faire mieux.

The value of *Organt* is as a study of origins; it is source-material in the strict sense. Here in the making is the lover of freedom in thought and conduct, despising the hypocrisies and corruptions of established monarchy and established religion, quick to sympathize with those oppressed, seeking reality.

From the standpoint of the authorities he had written a scurrilous libel. Once more de Crosne, lieutenant of police, sought his arrest, though without identifying thief and poet. It may even be true that Saint-Just took refuge at a friend's house in Paris. The royal order for the confiscation of the poem was issued June 10, 1789, and it is known that Saint-Just was in the city during the attack on the Bastille (*Esprit de la Révolution,* Part I, Chapter III). But the police had no luck in tracing the author and found few or no copies of his work in the bookstores.[27] Apparently not many were sold. Two years later, Saint-Just felt it might be a handicap to his political career and tried to withdraw it; its republication in 1792 under the title *Mes Passe-temps ou le nouvel Organt, par un député à la Convention Nationale* may even have been the work of an opponent.

Saint-Just made only one more venture in belles-lettres, a little one-act comedy called *Arlequin Diogène,* apparently written in 1789 or 1790.[28] Once more an absurd fantasy cloaked serious criticism of a bankrupt régime. The financier, the ambassador and the fop are convenient pegs on which to hang his general conclusion that monarchy is a false system and that the law will do anything for the rich. The idea was absorbing him increasingly.

Thereafter Saint-Just was through with literature as such. He found more arresting ways for expressing the vital energy of his nature than in libertinage of fact or fancy, more direct and forceful methods than through rhetorical verse for building a better France out of the crumbling ruins of the old.

II

THE LOCAL POLITICIAN

FTER the completion of *Organt,* Saint-Just visited
Paris where he met Camille Desmoulins, who
greeted him without much enthusiasm and
agreed to announce the poem in his newspaper.[29]
But the rushing sweep of national affairs soon drove thoughts
of Charlemagne's wars into the dustbin. The poet found himself far more interested in politics. He attended several sessions
of the National Assembly and of the Jacobin Club and returned
home aglow with a kindling enthusiasm. His deep dissatisfaction with things as they were was felt also by the new governors
of France, who were translating it rapidly into a whole new
series of epoch-making laws. There was work to be done and for
the first time in French history it was possible to do it. Here
was a new and fruitful outlet for Saint-Just's repressed vitality.
One's passion need not be mischievous or sterile; it would be
a man's work to help make a nation's dreams come true. And
to those strong enough to ride on the whirlwind and direct its
course would come the intoxicating fulfillment of creative
leadership.

Saint-Just became in his community the chief advocate of the
Revolution. On February 21, 1790, all the inhabitants took the
civic oath, swearing fidelity to law, king and constitution, at
that time the slogan of advanced reform. After the village
authorities, the Saint-Just family signed first.[30] When it came
to translating generalized aspirations for liberty and equality
into concrete desires, the French peasantry found themselves
chiefly interested in land. An unparalleled opportunity presented itself when the Assembly confiscated the domains of the
Church. The council of the Blérancourt commune was occupied from March to May, 1790, with taking inventories of the

16

convent of the Feuillants, calculating its revenues, issuing decrees and letters patent concerning ecclesiastics, making perquisitions in the château of Blérancourt. In all this, Saint-Just's advice and aid were asked by the commune, which entrusted him with various delicate duties.

His fellow townsmen must have come to place a high estimate on his intelligence and skill in these difficult affairs, for in April he was chosen as their delegate to the assembly of Chauny, where the departmental "county seat" was to be selected. The towns from which the *chef-lieu* was to be picked were Soissons, the old local capital, and Laon. The electors of Blérancourt directed their delegate to work for Soissons. Here for the first time he tasted the sweets of leadership, though on a tiny scale; he was the chosen spokesman of his fellows, though they told him what to say. It was a graceful, if a youthful, little speech.

My age and the respect I owe you [he began] do not permit me to raise my voice among you, but you have already shown yourselves indulgent to me. I have been denounced, I have been envied the glory of serving my country; but if malice had succeeded in tearing my body from my fatherland and from you, it could not have torn away my heart. It is before your eyes that I shall perform my first feat of arms; it is here that my mind is being exercised in the use of liberty, and this liberty which you enjoy is younger still than I. The will of my constituents and the rigor of my mission force me to take sides in the quarrel which divides you; compelled to choose but one, my conscience belongs to one alone, though my heart to both; young as I am, I must watch for wise examples that I may profit by them and if anything has touched me, it is the moderation which you have shown on both sides in your discussions this morning.

His argument, which followed, did not prevail; the vote went to Laon.

Soon after he wrote one of the most interesting letters in his brief correspondence.[31] It is the only letter to Camille Desmoulins, with whom he appears to be on friendly, though not on intimate terms. The date, superscription and place of writing are all lacking.

17

Monsieur,

If you were less busy, I would go into some detail about the Chauny assembly, where there were men of every stamp and every caliber. In spite of my being under age, I was received. The sieur Gellé,[32] our colleague at the bailliage of Vermandois, had denounced me. They threw him out bodily [*par les épaules*]. We saw there your compatriots MM. Saulce, Violette and others, from whom I received much kindness. It is needless to tell you (for you do not care for stupid praise) that your home-folks are proud of you.

You knew before I did that the department went definitively to Laon. Is it a good, is it an evil for one or the other town? It seems to me that it is only a point of honor between the two towns and points of honor amount to very little in almost any connection.

I went up on the platform, I worked with the purpose of letting daylight into the county-seat question, but I accomplished nothing; I left loaded with compliments as the ass with relics, having moreover this confidence, that I may be among the rest of you in the National Assembly.

You had promised to write me, but I foresee clearly that you will not have the time. I am free at the present moment. Shall I return to you or shall I stay among the stupid aristocrats of this region?

On my return from Chauny, the peasants of my canton came to meet me at Manicamp. The Count of Lauraguais was very much astonished at this rustic-patriotic ceremony. I led them all to his house to pay him a visit. They told us that he was in the fields, so I copied Tarquin; I had a stick with which I cut off the head of a fern that happened to be near me beneath the château-windows, and without saying a word, we turned on our heels.[33]

Farewell, my dear Desmoulins. If you need me, write to me. Your last numbers are full of excellent things. Don't be annoyed if I tell you that Apollo and Minerva have not quite abandoned you yet. If you have some message for your Guise people, I shall see them again in a week at Laon where I am going to make a trip on personal business.

Goodby again, glory, peace and patriotic rage.

Saint-Just.

I am going to read you this evening, for I know your last numbers only by hearsay.

There was still a probation to undergo in village affairs, however, before Saint-Just was ripe for national service. The electors of the Chauny district met in Blérancourt, May, 1790,

to choose judges, but disorder caused the meetings to be transferred to Chauny. Saint-Just, who was not present, wrote his
friend Thuillier in this imperious fashion:

You will move that before adjournment an address be made to the
Department, demanding that the next session take place at Blérancourt. You will have this address in readiness as soon as you have
read it and you will have it signed in duplicate. Here it is, you will
not write it yourself.[34]

Evidently Saint-Just was feeling more and more the divine right
and the responsibility of leadership.

It cannot be denied that he craved opportunities to exercise
his indwelling sense of authority. Chances for distinction did
not come often in Blérancourt; on so lowly a pedestal one had
to stand tiptoe, straining upward, if one were to be seen at all
above the crowd by those in Paris, whose attention one so badly
wanted. Fortunately Saint-Just was quite tall in mental stature
and that helped. A curious chance gave him such an opportunity, which he seized avidly. Some conservative members of
the National Assembly had protested a recent decree refusing
to declare the Catholic Church to be the state religion. A
package containing thirty copies of this protest was sent to
Saint-Just by some luckless person who apparently knew of
him only as a local leader without troubling to ascertain his
opinions. This fact in itself attests the progress Saint-Just had
already made, for he held no local office at the time. He at once
requested a special session of the municipality. The action
which they took is spread on the register of the borough of
Blérancourt as follows:

This fifteenth day of May, 1790, the municipality of Blérancourt
being convoked in extra session, François Monneveux, *procureur* of
the commune, took the floor and said to us:

That on the eleventh of the present month there was addressed
to M. de Saint-Just, elector in the department of the Aisne and living in the said Blérancourt, a package containing thirty copies of a
leaflet entitled *Declaration of a part of the National Assembly on a
decree rendered April 13, 1790, concerning religion;*

19

That to this enclosure was attached a letter filled with odious maxims, engaging him to employ the credit which he possesses in this region on behalf of religion, sapped by the decrees of the National Assembly, and to propagate the document contained in the enclosure.

At this point, the Assembly with a single cry demanded the letter and M. de Saint-Just. The latter was requested to come to the Assembly; he [did so and] read the letter which he had personally denounced to the *procureur* of the commune.

The whole Assembly, justly revolted by the abominable principles which the enemies of the Revolution seek to circulate in the popular mind, resolved that the Declaration should be torn and burned on the spot, which was done that very instant; and M. de Saint-Just, his hand over the flaming libel (*la main sur la flamme du libelle*) took an oath to die for fatherland and National Assembly and sooner to perish by fire like the document he received, than to forget this vow. These words brought tears to all. M. the mayor, with hand over the fire (*la main sur le feu*), repeated the vow with the other municipal officers; he then congratulated M. de Saint-Just, saying to him: "Young man, I knew your father, your grandfather and your great-grandfather; you are worthy of them. Continue as you have begun and we shall see you at the National Assembly."

Signed: Honoré, mayor; Monneveux,Thuillier, Sr.; Charbonnier, Dutuilly, J. B. Cappeton and Thuillier, Jr., secretary.[35]

This extract from the register, together with a few opening and closing sentences, was reprinted as an address and sent to the Constituent Assembly, before which it was read. Strange as this occurrence is, an even stranger story grew up about it. A correspondent of the Jacobin Club, writing in 1793, said that like Mucius Scaevola, indifferent to pain, Saint-Just plunged his hand into the flames of the brazier while taking the oath. It was because he was moved to admiration at this heroic gesture that the mayor congratulated Saint-Just as he did.[36] The extract from the register shows that if Saint-Just played the part of Scaevola, so did the mayor, for whom the same expression is used. The gesture was really painless, but theatrical enough for all practical purposes.

A like effort to impress himself on the minds of those who counted is the letter that marks the beginning of his contact with Robespierre. This stands as a milestone in his life. There is no conventional salutation.

Blérancourt, near Noyon, August 19, 1790.

You who sustain the tottering fatherland against the torrent of despotism and intrigue, you whom I only know like God, by miracles; I address myself to you, monsieur, begging you to join me in saving my saddened village. The town of Coucy has had the free markets of the borough of Blérancourt transferred to itself (so runs the rumor here). Why should the towns swallow up the privileges of country districts? Soon the latter will have nothing left but the *taille* and the imposts! Please support with all your talent an address I am sending by the same mail, in which I demand that my heritage be added to the national domains of the canton, that my native village may retain a privilege without which it must die of hunger.

I do not know you, but you are a great man. You are not only the deputy of a province, you represent humanity and the Republic. So act, if you please, that my demand be not despised.

Saint-Just,
Elector in the department of the Aisne.[37]

Whether Robespierre answered this letter is unknown, but it shows how early Saint-Just conceived that great admiration, which was destined to bring him in so short a time both fame and death.

It seems singular in view of his theoretical dislike of war that the most permanent office held by Saint-Just in these early years was in the National Guard. There was no thought of military aggression in this body, however; it was simply the citizen's organized duty to preserve order in a troubled time. His brother-in-law, Decaisne, was elected colonel of the Blérancourt Guard, February 7, 1790; Saint-Just became lieutenant colonel, June 6.[38] In this capacity he led a delegation of nine to effect a "federation" with the adjoining commune of Vassens and so had his share in the revolutionary fad of the hour.[39] Later at Chauny he was chosen as honorary commandant of the canton to go to Paris for the national Festival of Federation on July 14. This time he was there neither as a fugitive thief nor a writer of seditious verse, but as the duly elected representative of his fellow citizens, one of thousands of Guardsmen from all over France, sitting with the National Assembly and the highest dignitaries of the land and swearing a common allegiance to nation, law and king.

The mood of the occasion on which he next saw the king differed profoundly from the joyous optimism of July 14, 1790. It was nearly a year later, June 24, 1791, that the district of Chauny sent an armed detachment to Soissons *au-devant du roi*. This royal escort was not to do him honor; it was a prison guard. Already the shadows were closing in on Louis, who was being brought back from Varennes, a virtual captive in disgrace. Saint-Just was a member of the detachment.[40]

Trees of liberty began to sprout in the enriched revolutionary soil. At the Blérancourt planting (March 13, 1792), Saint-Just was hospitably prominent. He informed the Guardsmen, assembled in hollow square, that he had at home the bust of Mirabeau and invited all to follow him "in search of it." They obediently trooped to Saint-Just's house, the bust was placed on a table and brother-in-law Decaisne made an appropriate speech, recorded in the municipal register.[41]

In one connection after another Saint-Just's popularity is manifest. When the local Guard was reorganized in February, 1792, he was made captain of a company and when soon after, a staff election raised him to lieutenant commander, "la compagnie dite de Saint-Just" continued to bear his name and sent him to the Federation at the district *chef-lieu* as its representative.

The other capacity in which for weary months Saint-Just served his commune was as its lawyer in a long controversy with the local *seigneur,* M. de Grenet. The matter is of interest as an example of change in local public opinion toward the landed gentry and of how Saint-Just changed with it. Originally respected and often liked as they were, clashing interests and growing radicalism led to bitter estrangement. The case in point arose from the fact that Grenet had planted a part of some 150 acres of pasture, wood and marsh which the commune claimed as common lands. In October, 1790, an arbitration seemed possible. Grenet chose as his agent the notary Gellé; the commune chose Saint-Just.[42] At this stage of affairs Saint-Just reports to the communal assembly a generous proposal from the *seigneur,* suggests that it send him a message of gratitude and attachment and labels his offers "the pure result of the goodness of his heart." A year later the tone is angry and hostile. The friendly arbitration has fallen through and Saint-Just has become the official advocate of Blérancourt in a court action. The brief which he drew up is technical, closely reasoned and to the layman seems convincing. Only once the sense of social justice forces itself indignantly through the mass of detail; this single sentence shows how public feeling in France had developed within a year.

Thus the commune of Blérancourt has found itself driven off its properties and no other rights have been urged against it than those of force; the plowman has lost half his herds; woods without value and barely growing on the rocks have replaced pastures, ditches dug about these woods have prevented the approach of the legitimate proprietor, whom despotism has repulsed from his own lands; the richest of the inhabitants was also the most greedy, the most discourteous, the least generous; he cut down plantations, closed rights of way, despised agriculture, and when the reign of laws revived the hopes of the inhabitants, a thousand tricks were tried to frighten and deceive them; he offered 3,000 francs for the plantations, they are worth 12,000.

So as writer, citizen-soldier, town-lawyer, the man grew stronger in the respect of his fellows. Some disliked him, others envied him, most followed him. He was incontestably the local leader, for all that he was so young. The time seemed ripe to try his wings in a longer flight. There was to be a new Assembly and in a moment of quixotic unselfishness, the old Assembly had decreed that none of its members should be eligible for reëlection. Here was a chance for new men.

III

ENTRANCE UPON THE NATIONAL STAGE

N PRACTICAL politics Saint-Just had won his spurs. But this was not enough for a Frenchman of the eighteenth century. In those days they took their political platforms seriously. Saint-Just built an unusually solid one. It was called *L'Esprit de la Révolution et de la Constitution de France*. It contained the most subtle and fine-spun speculations in political theory as well as definite ideas on what was happening in France. Perhaps people would forget his poetry. Perhaps they would elect him to the Legislative Assembly.

The *Spirit of the Revolution* appeared in an octavo volume of viii-174 pages in 1791, published by Beuvin at Paris.[43] On the first page there was printed as a sort of motto, this quotation from Montesquieu: "If I could bring it about that everyone should have new reasons for loving his duty, his prince, his country, his laws, that everyone might better realize his good fortune . . . I would think myself the happiest of mortals." This sets the tone for the whole work, which is in the main satisfied with things as they are, in marked contrast to most of Saint-Just's other writing. Here he points with pride, elsewhere he views with alarm. The years 1790 and, to a less degree, 1791 mark a kind of lull in the fury of the Revolutionary storm. Indeed with the adoption of the Constitution of 1791 and the formation of a limited monarchy most people felt that the Revolution was finished. It is in this mood of finality, the goal well reached, that *L'Esprit de la Révolution* was conceived. There is no doubt that it fitted in with what people felt at the moment more perfectly than an unsettling, critical book would have done. It was good political strategy. There is no reason, however, for regarding it as insincere. Granted that

24

Saint-Just was a young rebel when he wrote *Organt* and a radical revolutionist in 1793-94, there is no more inconsistency in his having passed through an intermediate, moderate stage than in the relative quiet of France between the Bastille and the Terror. People change.

Europe is marching with great steps toward its revolution, and all the efforts of despotism will not stop it. . . . The Revolution of France is not the work of a moment, it has its causes, its sequence and its goal: this it is which I have sought to develop.

So ran his introductory sentences. The author is judging an achievement, quite unaware that the web is but half woven and that he is to be one of the master weavers. In his essay there is that ephemeral quality which inevitably characterizes contemporary history.

In the historical chapters, which contain an admirable thumb-nail sketch of the causes and early days of the Revolution, there are many shrewd estimates of character. Later in life, Saint-Just did not show himself particularly happy in this field. He misjudged some of his associates woefully. It may have been so because his emotions and ambitions were engaged. Here where he is more detached, he is more successful. The king and queen for instance, though sharply criticized, receive much fairer treatment than in *Organt*.

Louis reigned like a private citizen; hard and frugal for himself alone, brusque and feeble with others; because he thought of good, believed he was doing it. He put heroism in little things, weakness in great; drove M. de Montbarey from the ministry for having secretly given a sumptuous repast, saw with complacency his whole court pillaging the finances, or rather saw nothing, for his soberness had only made hypocrites; soon or late, however, he knew all, but he piqued himself rather on passing for an observer than on acting like a king. In so far as the people . . . saw that Louis was being deceived, . . . it cherished him through hatred of the court. . . .

Marie-Antoinette, deceived rather than deceiving, light rather than perjuring, devoted entirely to pleasures, seemed not to reign in France but at Trianon.

The Comte de Provence "had for sole virtue a fairly good wit," Necker "put less of virtue than of pride in saving France." Lafayette, whom he lampoons without directly naming him, is "a naïve courtier, vain with simplicity." Mirabeau, on the other hand, seemed comparable to that ancient worthy who presented himself naked, club in hand, at the council of a Macedonian king. Saint-Just particularly admired his delicate art of laughing at slanders and his wise dissimulation.

The brisk account of the fall of the Bastille has several points of interest: it proves that he was present on that occasion, it shows that in 1791 he had a horror of public violence and it contains a curious prediction regarding America.

I know not whether one has ever seen except among slaves, the people carrying the heads of the most odious persons on the ends of lances, drinking their blood, tearing out their hearts and eating them. . . .

Some day one will see and perhaps more justly this frightful spectacle in America; I have seen it in Paris, I have heard the joyous cries of the unbridled populace, which played with fragments of flesh, shouting "Long live liberty, long live the king and M. d'Orléans."

The spectacle seems on the whole to have alarmed Saint-Just; terrorist though he became, he was always a disciplinarian, whom chaos offended.

The bulk of the essay is devoted to theory. These passages are less tangible, more disconnected; it is hard to get one's teeth in them. Many pages naturally deal with the new constitution, which the author justifies philosophically by comparison with the practices of antiquity and with particular reference to the classical division into monarchy, aristocracy and democracy, all of whose advantages he finds happily combined in France.

Is it not splendid to see how everything has taken shape within the structure of the monarchical state, which the legislators have judiciously chosen as the form of a great government; democracy frames the constitution, aristocracy makes the laws, monarchy governs!

So all is for the best in the best ordered of worlds.

A long and rambling section deals with social institutions. Here among others are chapters on the noblesse (absurdity of hereditary honor), education (there isn't any, but there will be; it should teach modesty, politics and war), youth and love (prudery accompanies vice), divorce (he disapproves), marital infidelity (he opposes the double standard), women (among truly free peoples, they are free and adored), the army (the regular soldier is in reality a slave), the National Guard (dangerous, but necessary for order), French religion and theocracy (the countries where the Gospel has remained pure have become republican), priestly religion ("France has not demolished its Church, but repolished its stones"), monks ("ferocious virtues make atrocious morals"), and the Federation (though at first sight admirable, it was the work of a few popularity-seekers and was intended to revive enthusiasm for the king). Though the organization is defective, many of the ideas are fruitful. Even at this early stage, a clearly marked personality with a definite body of opinion is beginning to emerge.

The part devoted to political institutions is likewise a catch-all. One is struck by the passages which set forth views in sharp contrast to those he later held. He cannot pardon Rousseau, great as he was, for permitting the death penalty; he defends the *assignats*, for if you establish public confidence in the laws, you may make money of leather or paper and it will be more solid than gold; in twenty years Paris will be no longer the center of the kingdom, because the nation's resources will be in commerce and in agriculture.[44]

His view of international relations bears no trace of militarism, soldier though he was in effect to become. France, he says, by renouncing conquest, has purified the love of country.

A people which loves conquests, loves only its glory and finishes by contempt for its laws. It is fine to take arms only in defense of liberty; he who attacks that of his neighbors, cares little for his own.

He agrees with the Assembly's ruling that peace and war should be deliberated in the legislative, declared by the executive authority. Permanent embassies are a vice; they are always ready for conspiracy and harmful to good relations. Sharp words follow for the Family Compact with Spain and alliances in general; war in Europe is a sport and greedy kings use men like race horses. Somewhat surprisingly he denounces the Nancy mutiny; one must not confound insubordination with love of liberty. The navy, colonies, commerce and wealth all link together, but superfluous products should be subject to internal taxation, that luxury may come to the relief of agriculture. As France has been unified by the disappearance of tolls, so free trade will break down national barriers. In time there will be only human beings; in that day, those wise and simple men will look on us as we do on the Vandals and the Huns. At the end comes the dictum:

When all men are free, they will be equal; when equal, they will be just. Honesty will follow of itself.

Like most of his contemporaries, Saint-Just was a great admirer both of Montesquieu and Rousseau. Here are the checks and balances of the one, the popular sovereignty of the other. But as the Constitution of 1791 was made by men swayed chiefly by the ideas of Montesquieu, so in this early essay devoted to its praise, it is Montesquieu's influence that prevails. This is true in style as in thought. Saint-Just too is concise, epigrammatic, a lover of antitheses. So dense and closely packed is his thought that its brevity leads to obscurity. Indeed the darkness seems sometimes inherent in the thought itself; the young writer in his effort to be clever is oversubtle and defeats his end. Likwise there is a discontinuity and lack of logic in the development. One chapter follows another with no particular reason; within the chapters, sometimes, brilliant sentences are strung together like a necklace of bright stones, with no more contact than the sayings in the Book of Proverbs. It has even been guessed that the book was made by joining together fragments, stray ideas that had come to him from time to time in the course of his reading. This would be consistent

28

with his method in earlier days when he set his tables along the garden arbor, and later when he wrote the *Fragments sur les institutions républicaines*. But there is enough unity in this essay to make one think that he wrote the body of it as a single piece of work for a definite purpose, his candidacy for the Assembly. Into this structure it may well be that he wove bits of theory and observation from his scrapbook. And for all its weaknesses the work is full of shrewd comment, penetrating ideas, pregnant sayings.[45]

Like every author he is eager to see his book in print and writes from Blérancourt, February 18, 1791, to his publisher, Beuvin, at the Palais-Royal:

Lazybones, where are your promises, why don't I hear from you? If, like you, I were placed under an arcade, where so many sorts of creatures pass by; if, like you, I had a lively life, I feel sure that the uselessness which sometimes overwhelms me here would be less oppressive. . . . I am isolated here like a saint and a saint's life is a sad life. Write me every week if you have time and hurry up your printer.

He thinks that he would like to edit a newspaper until he became twenty-five.

I am bored and this continual work in solitude torments me. Besides, I should like to be in Paris to frequent the libraries, which I can no longer get along without.[46]

The book came out at last. It was successful, but a technicality kept its author from his goal. The citizens of Blérancourt were gathered on August 23 in their primary assembly to draw up the electoral list for the canton. As his name was called, Saint-Just arose to reply but was interrupted by three citizens, his old enemy Gellé and two others, who objected that he was not yet twenty-five and hence ineligible to vote; they desired that he be asked to withdraw from the assembly. This was an unexpected blow. No one but Gellé had seriously opposed his political activities in the past; a lively campaign in favor of his election to the Legislative Assembly had been conducted and many promises of support received; his book had shown maturity. He seemed to his fellow citizens so eminently their logical choice that the protest was unanimously defeated except for the three votes. Inasmuch as a prophet ordinarily fails to be honored in his own country, this was a decided compliment. It was nothing more, for the law was on the other side. The case was appealed to the district of Chauny, whose *procureur-syndic* energetically denounced the action of the electors; the district and the department directories in turn declared Saint-Just's ineligibility.[47]

He swallowed his defeat as best he might and proceeded to wait until he grew older. A letter in October to Garot, a notary and family friend, asks for the loan of certain law books which he needed for legal business.[48] Apparently he had settled down to work.

December 9, he wrote a charming letter to his new brother-in-law, Adrien Bayard, who had married Marie less than three weeks before.

I did not know, my dear brother, that the indisposition of our sister was continuing; mamma had told us that she left her on the highroad to recovery. Take care that the water and the raw air of your mountains be not the cause of her trouble. I advise you to make her take a great deal of milk and not to let her drink water.

I cannot tell you precisely when I shall be able to come to see you; I am rushed with business and the days are now very wet and short. However between now and Christmas I shall have the pleasure of embracing you both.

If you discover that the air is bad for your wife, send her to us for a little while; she has no doubts about the tender affection with which she will always be received by us. I hope that her marriage will not separate us and that we shall not forget, on either side, the sentiments which ought to unite us. Write to us, both of you, from time to time, and especially do not keep us in ignorance between the present and the moment when I shall start to see you, as to the course of my sister's sickness. I can hardly wait to see her in order to reassure myself. Keep your young wife gay and be especially watchful that she may not feel any domestic unhappiness of the sort that she would not dare confide to you. The idea which I have conceived of your family makes me believe that they will tenderly love this new sister and new daughter. Make her sovereign after you, but a gentle sovereign; that is the way I look at it. You are the sort to take the place of everything in the world for her; but love does not console for *amour-propre* and you know what the *amour-propre* of a woman is. She will make you happy, I hope and am convinced. I shall not espouse her grievances against you; you are both equally dear to me, and in all circumstances I shall show you the heart of a brother and a good friend. Adieu. Kiss your dear wife, kiss her from time to time for me, so that she may remember that I love her and may return it to you.

I am your brother and servant

Saint-Just.

At Blérancourt, this December 9, 1791.

P.S. I beg you to present my respects to Madame Hannotier and to M. the curé and to your family which I love like my own.

Everyone sends greetings and we are all well.[49]

But beneath this calm there was storm. There is no doubt that Saint-Just was bitterly disappointed at his failure, though it was obviously no fault of his and was soon to be remedied. A letter written from Noyon to Daubigny at Paris, July 20, 1792, gives our next knowledge of him. He was very despondent. He begs his dear friend to come to a festival and predicts a great political future for him. For himself, he is afflicted "by a republican fever, which devours and consumes me." He is sending Daubigny's brother *"la deuxième"* (perhaps a second copy of his *Esprit*) and asks him to pass it on to Lameth and Barnave.

You will find me great some day. It is unfortunate that I cannot stay in Paris. I have a feeling that I can soar above the rest in this age. Companion of glory and liberty, preach it in your sections, let peril inflame you. Go see Desmoulins, embrace him for me and tell him that he will never see me again; that I esteem his patriotism, but that I despise him because I have penetrated his soul and he is afraid I will betray him. Tell him not to give up the good cause and recommend it to him, for he still lacks the daring of great-hearted virtue. Adieu; I am above misfortune. I will bear everything but I will tell the truth. You are all cowards; you have not appreciated me. My palm will rise none the less and perhaps obscure yours. Infamous creatures that you are, I am a rogue, a rascal, because I have no

money to give you. Tear out my heart and devour it; you will become what you are not now; great! . . .

O God! Must Brutus languish forgotten, far from Rome! My decision is made meanwhile: if Brutus does not kill the rest, he will
kill himself.

It would be unfair to take this outburst of homicidal and sui-
cidal fury too seriously. The notion of self-slaughter is a symp-
tom of adolescence and moroseness, partly real, partly assumed,
an inevitable characteristic of the Byronic type of genius. Besides, the letter was never sent.

Fortunately for Saint-Just the Legislative Assembly did not
last long. Within a year the National Convention was summoned. Now at last he was of age. Once more he plunged into
all the excitement of a new election. A letter to Garot denies
indignantly that he had called on a certain Bigot to electioneer
for votes. He did go to see Bigot's brother, but stayed only five
minutes and called only to see his new godchild.[50]

Propaganda in his behalf is said to have been made by the
Paris clubs. The departmental electors met at Soissons, September 2, 1792. Saint-Just, the youngest present, was made
secretary of the provisional bureau, then on the fourth, president of the first bureau, organized to count the vote. On the
fifth he was elected by 349 votes out of 650 and became fifth
representative from the department of the Aisne. (Condorcet,
a rival, came through with greater difficulty.) The presiding
officer introduced him to the assembly. His youth and serious
air, his self-confidence and evident intelligence evoked general
applause. The minutes of the election state:

M. the president said a few words about his virtues which were beyond his years. M. Saint-Just in his reply revealed to the whole
assembly his entire gratitude and the greatest modesty; he further
took a vow to maintain liberty and equality, and the ringing of
bells announced his nomination.[51]

At last, the goal. Saint-Just wasted no time in self-congratula-
tion. We have only a hasty note to Bayard from Soissons, September 9, stating the bare fact of his election and asking the

privilege of using Bayard's apartment for a couple of weeks; [52] there is also a brief letter of thanks to Garot and a promise to be useful to his friends.[53] Twice only he returned to Blérancourt, once to complete the sale of a piece of property at Nampcel,[54] once to see his mother. He had outgrown Blérancourt. Now for better or for worse he belonged to France.

IV

THE KING'S TRIAL

HEN he reached Paris, September 18, 1792, Saint-Just was less than a month past his twenty-fifth birthday and the youngest member of the Convention.[55] He took up his abode in the Maison des États-Unis on the rue Gaillon.[56]

He was a handsome and a striking figure. Of average height, strongly proportioned and healthy, he had a large head covered with masses of thick, light hair; his eyes were blue and alert, though small; [57] his features of sculptured regularity; his lips firmly compressed; his color overpale. His expression was habitually severe, even scornful, his manner cold, his carriage rigid. Those who saw him and describe him comment to a man on his pride and his beauty. His voice was strong though husky. To some he seemed preoccupied, suspicious, to others melancholy. Like Robespierre he dressed with extreme care. The portrait reproduced here as frontispiece was made by his landlady, a gifted artist; after his execution she sold it to the widow of Le Bas, fearing to keep it. It represents Saint-Just in a light blue coat closely buttoned over his chest with gold buttons; the coat collar mounts high in the back and in front is the great white cravat mentioned by every observer. Usually he wore this close under his chin, which seemed to force his head up stiffly. Desmoulins with his diabolical cleverness later made the famous analogy, "One sees in his bearing and his attitude that he considers his head the cornerstone of the republic and that he carries it on his shoulders with respect and like a Holy Sacrament." To this, legend makes Saint-Just reply: "He says that I carry my head like the Holy Sacrament? By God, I will make him carry his like Saint-Denis!" [58] Everything about him was scrupulously careful, even dandified; it

34

was his habit to wear a boutonnière of white flowers clustered about a red carnation. In contrast, his mode of life was simple. He lived on eighteen livres a day, the regular salary paid members of the Convention.[59] He had no more after election to the Committee of Public Safety; the enormous increase in labor was compensated only by honor and a dubious security. Into his duties as member of the Convention, Saint-Just flung himself with whole-hearted, single-minded energy; light pleasure had no further loan of his body, nor literature of his mind; he was consecrated entirely to the serious task of government.

The first tangible record of him is at the Jacobin Club.[60] Here he made a speech, October 22, which gained considerable attention. From the very beginning of the Convention, there was bad feeling between the Girondins, who drew their strength from the provinces, and the Mountain, basing its power on Paris. Saint-Just was an ardent member of the latter group. Alarmed at the September massacres and fearing perhaps for their personal safety, Kersaint and Buzot, Girondin leaders, started a debate on the disorders and murders of the time. They wanted an investigating committee and an armed guard for the Convention, drawn from all the departments. This plan was broached September 24, only three days after the Convention opened and was vigorously discussed during the following month. The Mountain maintained that such a guard was quite needless.

It was on this subject that Saint-Just made his bow at the Jacobins. He opposed the plan as separating the Convention from the people, with which it was properly identical. He announced himself less afraid of an armed populace than of an organized body of armed men with ambitious leaders. Even anarchy was preferable to slavery. He felt that the proposed force was dangerous and useless. Paris would mistrust it. The true solution was republican unity and virtue, giving "new life to laws that devour anarchy." Saint-Just had an almost superstitious belief in the power of laws to accomplish miraculous results, even to the changing of human nature.[61] In its

35

issue of October 24, the *Journal des débats et de la correspondance de la Société des Jacobins* mentioned this speech by "a young citizen, deputy to the Convention, Sinjeu," [62] alluded to the wealth and originality of his ideas and promised to print the argument in full. This was not done, but by direction of the society the speech was printed in pamphlet form. [63]

The departmental guard was dropped, but 16,000 Fédérés, as they were called, came to Paris without legal sanction. As the uninvited Fédérés began to filter into the city, feeling rose still higher and on November 4, Saint-Just spoke again at the Jacobins "on suspicious armaments." He did not know what stroke was in preparation, he said, but certainly the whole city was agitated. Paris was gorged with soldiers on the eve of the king's trial and at the moment when Robespierre was under fire. Meanwhile the foreign danger was at an end. "What a government it is, planting trees of liberty on the scaffold and placing death's scythe in the hands of the law!" Though Saint-Just had definitely adopted the Mountain's policy on most matters, such as the supremacy of Paris and the king's guilt, he still opposed violence and capital punishment.

This is all we know of his activity in the Club. Only three months a member, he was elected president for the fortnight and was in the chair at the sessions between December 19, 1792, and January 1, 1793. At most of these meetings debate centered on the king's trial and the wickedness of the Girondins.

For the king of the French was now on trial for his life. He was a kindly, good-natured soul who had tried to make things better, though he had done so neither consistently nor tactfully. The rôle of revolutionary king bewildered him; his mind was too set to change into new patterns. He was definitely old-style and that would not do in a new age. He seemed sly and crooked, the pathetic defense of the weak. He would fain clean his house if he could, but it annoyed and perplexed him when men began to tear it down about his ears, expecting him to look pleased as he moved his chattels into the few rooms left standing.

The popular leaders, who were less concerned to understand the king's psychology than to have a government they could trust, removed him from throne to prison. When after August 10, successful revolutionists began poking about in the empty palace, they unearthed papers that seemed to them treasonable. The king must be tried.

A plan of procedure was brought in and with Hérault de Séchelles in the chair, discussion of it opened, November 13. The first question taken up was *Le roi peut-il être jugé?* This debate on inviolability is the first of three phases into which the discussion falls. Morisson, a Girondin, began, speaking in favor of banishment. The first representative of the other side was Saint-Just. It is interesting to speculate why he was put forward, for it is hardly likely that he sprang to his feet spontaneously. In these first days at least, however it may have been later, Robespierre and his group must have given the word. Was it just because he had never spoken before and was so young and handsome that out of sheer curiosity the Convention would listen as they might not to a seasoned veteran? Quite likely, but it must also have been because his backers had heard him at the Jacobins and felt sure the impression would be favorable. They judged rightly, for he spoke with savage power that bit deeply and was not forgotten. With that first speech, he took rank among the leaders.

He awoke attention with his opening sentence.

I undertake, citizens, to prove that the king may be tried; that the opinion of Morisson, which defends inviolability and that of the committee, which would have him tried as a citizen are alike false, and that the king must be tried under principles which derive neither from the one nor the other.

The committee on legislation had not gone far enough, he felt.

The sole purpose of the committee was to persuade you that the king may be tried as a plain citizen; but I tell you that the king should be tried as an enemy, that we have less to try him than to fight him, and that, since we are no longer under the contract uniting Frenchmen, the forms of procedure are not in the civil law, but in the law of nations. . . . Some day people will be astonished that in the eighteenth century, we are less advanced than at the time of Caesar; then the tyrant was immolated in the midst of the Senate with no other formalities than twenty-three dagger blows and with no other law than the liberty of Rome. And today we respectfully conduct the suit of a man, assassin of a people, caught in the act, his hands in blood, his hands in crime!

The people are too timid, he continued; what must one not fear who sees the ax trembling in their hands and beholds them, from the first day of their liberty, respect the memory of their chains? In a rather intricate argument he sought to show that the social pact is a contract between the citizens and not with the government (thus replacing the time-honored feudal contract by the doctrine of Rousseau) and that Louis, not a party to this contract, cannot be judged as a citizen. That would be a tyrant's last stroke indeed, to claim the right of judgment by the laws he has destroyed.

As for me, I see no middle ground: this man must reign or die. . . . He oppressed a free nation; he declared himself its enemy; he abused the laws: he must die to assure the repose of the people, since it was in his mind to crush the people to assure his own. Did he not, before the fight, pass his troops in review? Did he not take flight instead of preventing them from firing? What did he to stop the fury of his soldiers?

It seems needless to point out how grossly unjust was this version of August 10, when the king's guard were the attacked, not the aggressors, when Louis took refuge in the Assembly on the advice of its leaders, and when he sent his troops a written order to cease firing. It should be said, however, that this distorted version was not peculiar to Saint-Just, but constituted one of the prosecution's main charges.

The argument mounts higher and higher. Not only has the king done wrong; even before his crime the people had the right to drive him out, for no constitution can bind citizens against a king. Then comes his daring climax. The real heart of the matter is not that the king was a bad king, not even that the people can change their government when they choose, but that royalty itself is "an eternal crime."

No one can reign innocently: the folly is too evident. Every king is a rebel and a usurper.

Louis cannot be judged by a court like a citizen, for he is not a citizen. He could not vote nor bear arms before his crime; by what abuse of justice would you make him a citizen in order to condemn him? A man loses his citizenship by crime, would Louis gain his? It was not necessary to secure popular sanction of a death sentence [and here as in the matter of August 10, Saint-Just's argument seems tricky and mean]; not even the act of the sovereign people, he maintains, can force a single citizen to pardon him, each would still have the right of Brutus toward Caesar; on the other hand, should the Convention acquit him, then a referendum would be necessary, for no act of the magistracy can be binding on the sovereign.

He ends on his high note.

Louis has fought the people and been overcome. He is a barbarian, a foreign prisoner of war. . . . He is the murderer of the Bastille, of Nancy, of the Champ-de-Mars, of Tournay, of the Tuileries: what enemy, what foreigner has done us greater harm? [64]

There is in this philippic the cruel injustice of the young; a mellower mind would not have pushed invective to the point of sophistry. So, by overstatement of the royal guilt, he weakened his argument. To no considerate judge was Louis the murderer of the Bastille, or of Nancy, or even of the Tuileries. The fairness of the *Esprit de la Révolution* is absent here. But the pith of the argument matched to a nicety the mood of France. *On ne peut pas régner innocemment.* Wild as the generalization is, for the case in point it had one supreme merit. The whole question was taken out of the juridical into the political sphere, where indeed it belonged. To judge Louis as a murderer was folly; that charge would collapse before any court not already prejudiced. In sober fact, it was not Louis at all who was on trial, but the institution of kingship. That case

39

was already prejudged, for France had determined to shake off monarchy; poor Louis, no doubt an inefficient king, had to suffer because by his inefficiency he had turned the stomach of France against the institution he embodied. Now he was little more than a lay figure, an effigy king, who must die to demonstrate a principle and clear the field for the classic republic of antiquity. The merit of Saint-Just is to have sensed the heart of the whole cause so clearly. With remarkable intuition, he pierced through to the essential marrow of the matter. Unfortunately, he did not limit his argument purely to political expediency, but obscured it with exaggerated and unprovable charges of a judicial nature against Louis as an individual. One may retort upon Saint-Just the very charge he brought against the committee on legislation, "that it had not developed all the consequences of its principles." It would have been sounder and kinder and in the end stronger to have attacked Louis's weakness and unreliability even to the point of treachery than to have called him tyrant and murderer; then to base the argument on the nation's need of a strong, liberal government to save its new-found freedom from clustering foes. But when all is said, it was a remarkable achievement for a youth of twenty-five. His somber eloquence made a deep impression. The journal *Le Républicain* caught up the phrase *On ne peut pas régner innocemment* and lauded its creator to the skies.

It is thou, Saint-Just, who announced so simply this great eternal truth! It is thou who hast proved it with no less energy at the tribune of the National Convention! We invite all those who wish to have a just and precise notion of the important question relative to the judgment of the former king of the French, to read the opinion of Saint-Just on this subject; they will find there much reasoning, profound views and that legislative philosophy so needful to those who must draw up the social pact of a great nation.[65]

Two more speakers were heard, after which the debate was adjourned until the middle of November. At that time it was decided to close separate discussion of inviolability and the first phase of the proceedings came to an end.

The second phase was a general debate on the whole subject of the trial. December 3, Robespierre made his famous motion that the king should not be tried, but that the Convention should decree that "Louis XVI, traitor to the nation, enemy of humanity, shall be punished with death on the spot where the defenders of liberty perished August 10." This was substantially the idea of Saint-Just carried a stage further. The Convention decided, on Pétion's motion, that it should try the king.[66]

Preliminaries were accordingly arranged. Barbaroux read a list of the king's crimes (December 12).[67] Discussion followed. The Convention decreed that the commander of the Paris National Guard bring Louis at once to the bar. Once more the list of crimes, now in its final form, was read. The president of the Convention was authorized to conduct the examination. It was forbidden to make any motion, any sign of approval or disapproval while the prisoner was at the bar. Someone nervously suggested that it would be a fine thing and would put the king in his place, if when he was announced they should be discussing some question of public welfare and should keep him waiting awhile. One can almost feel the tension; they had never judged a king before. Almost at once the doorkeeper announced that Louis Capet was at the door and awaited their pleasure. The little self-important plan to make him wait was forgotten; the old instinctive respect for royalty, ingrained by habit of a thousand years, asserted itself. Word went forth to bring him in immediately.

Some humane person had suggested that it would be cruel to make him stand during the examination. So a large upholstered chair was brought and the king sat in it, a doomed man already, sitting there and gazing somewhat stupidly at hundreds of hostile faces in what used to be the *salle des spectacles* of his palace. Barère, the president, asked him many questions. He did not know, he could not tell. It was ordered that he be returned to the Temple.

While these arrangements were in process, Buzot once more

complicated matters by moving (December 16) that Philippe Égalité, the former Duke of Orléans, and all the Bourbons be banished. This clever stroke was strictly intended to embarrass the Mountain, which Égalité had shrewdly if ignobly joined, hoping to conceal himself in radical sheep's clothing. After some discussion, Thuriot (Mountain) adroitly said that he felt the national interest was in accord with Buzot's motion. But everybody must be convinced. "Saint-Just has told me that he had some new ideas to offer you on this subject; I yield him the floor and request that he be heard." Saint-Just then spoke.

"Citizens, I too demand the eternal exile of all Bourbons and death for the one among them who sets foot on our territory. . . . Brutus drove out the Tarquins to assure the liberty of Rome; as for me, I do not know whether among us the Tarquins are not being driven out to give place to other Tarquins." (*Applause on the extreme left.*) *Several members:* "That's the right word." (*Murmurs in the center.*) *Saint-Just:* ". . . I abhor the Bourbons; I demand that they all be driven out, except the king who must remain and you know why (*Applause and murmurs*) ; but I am suspicious of all haste where there are no laws and no settled order of things. There is an attempt at this moment to link the fate of Orléans with that of the king; it is to save them all perhaps, or at least to soften the judgment of Louis Capet."

Several members: "No, no!" *Saint-Just:* "I demand that the constitutional committee present between the present time and the judgment of the king, the Rights of Man and the constitutional act of the republic; then I demand that the Orléans family withdraw the following day." (*Applause.*)

This is an excellent example of Saint-Just's style in spontaneous oratory. He seems no less ingenious in conception, fertile in imagery and fluent in language than in his set speeches. His proposition was not carried out. After a violent discussion, the whole matter was put off until after the king's trial.

On December 26, the king was brought in once more. His counsel did his best. The king declared his innocence of wrong. It was decreed that the speeches be printed. What was to be done next? Some wanted an immediate vote on the question of guilt, some adjournment of the whole matter for a period, some discussion. Saint-Just secured the floor and asked permission to open the discussion. "Several members," who had favored an immediate vote, learning that he wanted to speak, demanded that he be heard. Already they had found he was worth listening to. He felt, he said, that an immediate reply to the defense was important and as he had foreseen a part of their case, he asked permission to refute it. Several members insisted on adjournment; Bourdon wanted to hear Saint-Just. A vote was presently taken; adjournment seemed carried; after much argument it was reconsidered and unanimously resolved to discuss the verdict at once, all other business being set aside. Best have it over.

So starts the third phase of the trial, the debate on the decision. Saint-Just, the second speaker before, is the first now. It was December 27. The speech, though twice as long, is only half as striking as his previous one. He began,

When the people was oppressed, its defenders were proscribed: O you who defend him whom a whole people accuses, you cannot complain of that injustice! The kings persecuted virtue in the shadows; we judge the kings in the face of the universe!

This, he reminded them, was in his eyes an act of needless generosity. Then, point by point, he reviewed the events of the last few years, from the time when the Assembly by destroying the power of the privileged orders left the king a tyrant with no opposition. (This statement incidentally is a remarkable anticipation of Tocqueville's famous theory.) Everywhere Saint-Just found evidence of the cunning hypocrisy of the king, who did his best to sabotage each reluctantly conceded reform. "If he is innocent, the people is guilty." On no account should there be a referendum.

Citizens, if you permit the appeal to the people, you will be saying: *It is doubtful whether your murderer is guilty.* . . . Citizens, crime has wings, it will spread through the empire, captivate the ear of the people. O you, depositaries of the public morals, do not abandon liberty!

43

Then, summoning all his strength to convince his auditors,

This day will decide the Republic's fate; it is dead and done with, if the tyrant stays unpunished. . . . Men say, the revolution is over, you need have no further fear of the tyrant, . . . but, citizens, tyranny is a bush which the wind bends low, but when it passes, the bush rebounds. . . . The revolution commences when the tyrant comes to his end. . . . The fatherland is in your midst, choose between it and the king, between the exercise of the people's justice and the exercise of your personal weakness. . . . Truth burns silently in all hearts, like a lamp glowing in the tomb. . . . Not without effort does one gain liberty; but in our position it is no time to fear, it is time to conquer and we shall know how to triumph! No consideration can stop the course of justice; it is the companion of wisdom and of victory.

It is the speech of a prosecuting attorney. The man's mind is made up and he seeks with passionate ardor to convince others. He was a judge in this case, but there is nothing judicial in his argument. Nor was there indeed in the speeches that followed. It was impossible in this case of King vs. People to rule out of the great jury those who had not formed an opinion. The trial was a solemn farce, the formalities of even-handed justice with her scales were there, but the balance was already weighted. Better perhaps to have frankly faced this fact, to have recognized that opinions were fixed beyond the power of argument to sway them and to have adopted the summary procedure outlined by Saint-Just and Robespierre in their first speeches.

Thirty arguments were made in the Convention between December 28 and January 5, and 102 other orators were given leave to print.[68] On the seventh the discussion was ordered closed and a week's interval allowed for reflection.

The vote was taken January 15, 16, 17 and 19. Four times the roll was called. First came the question of guilt. "Is Louis Capet guilty of conspiracy against the public liberties and of attacks upon the general security of the state?" Saint-Just voted "Aye." The second roll call was on the question: "Shall the verdict of the National Convention against Louis Capet be sub-

44

mitted to popular ratification: yes or no?" Saint-Just like many others gave his reason:

If I did not hold from the people the right to judge the tyrant, I should hold it from Nature. No.

On the sixteenth, at six o'clock in the evening, the third and fatal roll was called. It lasted twenty-five hours without interruption. The question ran: "What penalty has Louis, former king of the French, incurred?" Saint-Just replied: "Since Louis XVI was the enemy of the people, of its liberty and happiness, I conclude for death." All through the night and the succeeding day, the roll droned on. The sun rose and marched down to its setting, while sleepless men doomed a king and ended an era.

One chance only was left. "Shall execution of the verdict on Louis Capet be postponed?" The foreign situation was in mind. Saint-Just said, "No." The vote was closest of all. Those who loved the old ways or feared the new, those moved with pity for poor, baited Louis, weak but not evil, those made timid by the thought of France alone against the world in arms, closed in together for one last desperate effort. The effort failed. The five-day tension was over. The exhausted Convention went its way and the king, his.

V

THE FARMER IN TOWN

OR centuries regulation had been the accepted economic policy. At first the guilds, then in mercantilist times the central government told the artisans of France what they could make and how they could make and sell it. Well enough in early days. But when capitalism had produced a strong commercial and manufacturing class, there crept in a growing resentment at these swaddling bands that fettered growing industry. With Adam Smith and the French Physiocrats the directly contrary doctrine of laissez faire became the theoretical rationalization of this desire on the part of rich men to grow richer. The new teaching became that of the best minds. Economic liberty was fused with political and ecclesiastical liberty in the general ideal of freedom which, touched with the fire of intense longing, blazed up quickly into so great a flame that the old palace was swept away.

The Revolution in its first phase was dominated by this spirit. All barriers of privilege were brushed aside. The natural rights of man must have free play. Liberty took precedence over Equality and Fraternity. Here was the giant Gulliver bound to the earth by Lilliputians and seeking to break his bonds.

When Saint-Just entered the lists, the situation was altered. France had been moving steadily to the Left. The Convention had been elected by universal suffrage. The nation was at war. The currency was inflated. Food was scarce. Prices were high. All of these were factors tending to restrict the free action of the individual. The safety of the state had become the supreme law. Men had to sacrifice their rights in the interest of the community. Ultimately this way of thinking prevailed completely and out of it came the Terror. Matters were not yet at

46

that pass in the fall of 1792 when the Convention assembled. The two philosophies, that of individualism and that of social control, were still strongly held and battled with one another like the twisting currents when two rivers meet.

The Girondins had become the champions of individualism. On the Left in the previous Assembly, they sat on the Right in the Convention. Though they were not personally rich and prosperous, the well-to-do conservative classes instinctively rallied to their support in default of better. The Girondins battled conscientiously for freedom and the right of each man to his way of life.

Social control had its most active proponents in the Enragés, led by Varlet and Roux, who wished the government to enforce use of the *assignats* at face value and to fix a maximum price on food. From the red Enragés, the color scheme of the Left wing faded to a more or less pronounced pink. The Commune or city government of Paris under Chaumette and Hébert was red indeed, but of a somewhat duller shade. The main body of the Mountain was paler still. But in contrast to the Girondins, representatives of the merchants, they felt themselves the advocates of the working class and in contrast to the uncompromising individualism of the former, they leaned increasingly, though with a certain irresolution, toward government interference in some form. This tendency was furthered by the fact that they drew their strength from Paris, while the Girondins were chiefly provincials.

Since there was little cohesion within the Mountain, it is not surprising that Saint-Just took a markedly independent line in the matter of economic policy. It is astonishing, however, to find Robespierre's lieutenant, a member of the more radical element (though not the most radical fringe in the Mountain), espousing economic doctrine closely akin to the individualism of the Girondins. The reason is to be sought partly in his love of freedom, not yet stifled by power nor political necessity, partly in his rustic origin, and partly in a singularly penetrating analysis of France's economic ills.

47

The fullest exposition of his views was made in connection with the crisis of October-December, 1792. In spite of a good harvest, there was little grain on the market, food riots were numerous, both in country and town, and the Convention was flooded with petitions to take some action in the matter. On November 3, a formidable decree in twenty-five articles was proposed by the joint committees of agriculture and commerce, calling for requisitions of grain by the municipalities on the basis of declarations by all farmers of the amount of grain in their possession. Three days later a letter came from the Girondin minister Roland, pleading for free trade as the proper cure and inclosing a copy of the Executive Council's reassuring proclamation of October 30 that there was plenty of grain; restrictive laws would only hamper its circulation.[69]

The issue between the Girondin policy of laissez faire and the committees' policy of requisitions was now clearly joined. No one was yet ready for the maximum except the Enragés.

November 16, the subject was once more taken up; two Girondins opposed the committees' project; two Mountain men upheld regulation, as did the first two speakers (both Mountain) on the twenty-ninth. In this debate the Girondins were much more unified; the Mountain, while desiring some form of control, seemed unable to agree on any one plan, that of the committees receiving up to that time no support at all.

At this point Saint-Just arose.[70] He began bluntly: "Citizens, I am not of the committee's opinion: I do not like violent laws about commerce." For him, the unsatisfactory condition of business was due to the political chaos and was bound to continue until things settled down into some sort of order. Free trade was indeed the mother of abundance, but times were not normal and English remedies, though bearing the sanction of Adam Smith's great name, were inadequate. He realized that the French solution must be in terms of the French problem. Then, grasping the nettle firmly and fearlessly with both hands, he announced the unpalatable truth that some had not wit to see and others had not dared to say.

What has upset the system of the grain-trade in France since the Revolution is the unregulated emission of the symbol of wealth.[71] All our wealth in specie and land is represented [by paper money]; and all this wealth is nothing in commerce because it does not enter into consumption. We have a great deal of paper money, but very few goods. The legislator ought to calculate all the products in the state and bring it about that the symbol represents them; but if the capital basis [*les fonds*] and the product of this capital are both represented, the balance is lost and the price of goods must increase by half. One should not represent the capital basis, one should only represent its product.

Saint-Just would thus limit the issuance of paper money to an equivalent of the value of consumable goods.

Meanwhile, he went on, luxury [always a factor of prime importance for French industry] has been abolished; the currency has been increased by half, while commerce has been diminished by half. "If that continues, the currency will finally be worthless, our exchange will be turned upside down, our industry dried up, our resources exhausted; nothing will remain to us but the ground, to divide and devour." A Cassandra prophecy of remarkable acuteness!

He was obviously irritated by the commotion which the city authorities made over the food supply; he dreaded the much more lasting hardships which would follow an inflated currency. His associates seemed to him shortsighted; to relieve a temporary ill, they would create a far more grievous one; their remedies were palliatives, they overlooked the real causes of the trouble. In one sentence, he contemptuously dismissed the situation out of which the present debate had arisen. "I shall not speak of the provisioning of Paris; it is an affair of police, which does not concern economics."

Saint-Just's friends on the Mountain were always talking about the troubles of the workers and he did his fair share of it on other occasions. But just now his sympathies were enlisted in behalf of a class which made little appeal to his party. "I do not know what so many merchants live on!" he exclaimed. "They cannot subsist much longer: I think I see in the interior of these houses families sad, in desolation; it is impossible for people to remain long in that situation." At a time when few radicals thought of the merchant class except to denounce them as profiteering monopolists, this breadth of human sympathy and depth of economic insight does Saint-Just honor.

With the remark that the artisans who used to live by satisfying the demands of the rich for luxury are also idle, and the not quite accurate but pungent epigram, "Misery brought forth the Revolution; misery may destroy it," he returned to his consideration of the nature of French commerce. He wondered if it were possible to cut it down from a commerce in luxuries to a trade in bare necessities. It was a desperate outlook, he felt; a great class thrown out of work, no chance to compete successfully with the Dutch and the English, nothing to export, a currency not considered respectable abroad—it looked as if France would have to give up commerce. But surely they did not want to live like the Scythians or the Indians! Their climate and their temperament unfitted them for idleness or a pastoral life, but that was exactly what they were headed for without knowing it. Saint-Just's clear analysis of an economic depression and of the doleful, narrow outlook for a society based on what contemporary parlance calls "autarchy" is applicable to conditions a century and a half after his day.

Turning from commerce to agriculture, he pointed out that inflation, which had destroyed commerce, was also responsible for the deficiency of grain, for the simple reason that saving and banking money had ceased to be attractive since money itself ceased to have stable value.

The deficiency in grain comes from nothing else. The farmer, who does not want to put paper in his treasury, sells his grain only with regret. In any other kind of trade, people have to sell to live on the profits. The farmer, on the contrary, buys nothing; his needs are not in commerce.

Somebody had complained of the luxury of the farmers. He would not decide, he said, whether luxury was or was not a good thing in itself, but it would be a mighty fortunate thing if the farmer did love luxury; then he would have to sell his wheat. The country seemed to him faced by an unhappy dilemma, either the encouragement of luxury trades or the enactment of violent laws requisitioning the farmer's grain. Liberty makes war on morals, so to speak.

The legislator then must bring it about that the farmer will spend or will not object to amassing paper, so that all the products of the soil may be put on the market and balance the symbol [*i.e.*, money]. Finally, it is necessary to equate the symbol, the products, the needs: there lies the secret of a sound economic administration.

This pregnant saying was the heart of his speech. While less thoughtful men were cursing the peasants as a race of avaricious profiteers, who must be forced to sell whether they would or no, Saint-Just looked at the situation with calm realism and put his finger on the fundamental vice in the situation, the excessive emission of paper money, bound to depreciate. The Parisians could not understand the peasants. But he was not a Parisian. Before him, as he spoke, there may well have passed a vision of the waving fields around Blérancourt; he may well have seen the weather-beaten, anxious faces of his rustic constituents, whose battle for the communal lands he had once fought against the Sieur Grenet. It was as one who knew the farm that he pointed out how war had destroyed the flocks, that fertilizer was thus lacking and that some day they would have to encourage the farmer deliberately to divide his land and time between grain and flocks, for the ultimate advantage of the former and for the resultant trade in leather and wool.

Only when the country had settled down to normal, constitutional living would economic abundance be possible. He knew hardly any provisional remedies. But meanwhile, it would be folly to issue more *assignats* on the security of the *émigrés'* land, adding that to the national domain and sending prices higher yet.

We cannot honorably pay our debts with this worthless money. . . . Tyranny will rise avenged and victorious from the midst of popular uprisings. . . . The farmer's sanctuary will be violated, perhaps the hope of future harvests destroyed and we shall be the jest of Europe.

In these terse lines, Saint-Just sums up the inexorable economic cycle. Inflation, a bankrupt social order, Communist insurrection, Fascism, loss of personal liberty were all for the future and for other lands, but though he used other terms he saw and set forth accurately the inevitable sequence.

He produced a decree in six articles.

That the property of the *émigrés* be sold, that the annuities be converted into contracts, serving to repay the debts.

That the land tax be paid in kind and stored in public granaries; that steps be taken to recover arrears.

That instruction be given on the free circulation of grain; that it be placarded in all the communes of the republic.

That the National Convention declares that the circulation of grain is free in the interior and fixes the death-penalty for exportation.

That a law be passed which we lack, concerning the freedom of river-navigation and a popular law placing freedom of trade under the safeguard of the republic itself, according to the genius of the republic.

That the principle be laid down that capital security [*les fonds*] may not be represented in commerce.

If matters went on as they were going, he concluded, in six months liberty would be no more.

By unanimous vote the speech was ordered printed. The Girondins in particular were delighted.[72] The decree finally passed by the Convention did little more than forbid the export of grain and safeguard its free circulation in the interior by severe penalties. How far Saint-Just contributed to this result by weakening the faith of his party associates in regulation, it is impossible to say.

The Convention's solution was not definitive. Had Saint-Just's advice been heeded and the flood of *assignats* been checked, the situation might have been improved. As it was, it went from bad to worse. In February, 1793, the Paris working class made another effort to secure the scale of maximum prices. On the eleventh, the president of the Convention received a letter from "the delegates of the united sections of Paris," requesting the privilege of presenting a petition on the food situation. The following day they were reluctantly received. In the name of Paris and the departments they demanded a maximum of 25 livres on every sack of grain weighing 250 pounds. Furious objections were raised on all sides at the deputation's daring to speak in the name of the departments. Who then represented the people of France, they or the Convention? Where were their credentials? To the general surprise, Marat led this movement of indignation, asserting that the whole business was a put-up job and that he recognized aristocrats in the deputation. Cries arose that the deputation be arrested. They were called on to give their names. Thrown on the defensive, Claude Hendelet, their spokesman, explained that they were a committee of the sections, who had been working on the food problem for months and that they had received the support of the *fédérés* from the departments. Before they had been admitted that morning, they had talked with several deputies, Hendelet continued. "Murmurs" arose from the Convention. Several members on the Right called out: "This is the nub of the question: go on, go on!" They were eager to catch some member of the Left in collusion with this dangerous group. "One of them," proceeded Hendelet, "told us that we should demand of the Convention that it occupy itself at once, dropping all other business, with the drawing up of a law on the food supply for the whole republic." At once bedlam. "The name of the member who spoke to the petitioner!" they shouted. Hendelet, hesitating an instant, stammered: "I am told that he calls himself Saint-Just, but I don't know him." Saint-Just immediately rose to his feet. He was in an ugly predicament, apparently implicated in a suspicious attempt to bully the Convention, which was too much for even Marat. Thuriot (Mountain) tried to help him by demanding whether the petitioner had shown Saint-Just the whole petition, "for he [the petitioner] is still bluffing the Assembly with it." [73] Without waiting for an answer, Saint-Just hastened to explain.

When I entered this assembly this morning, a petition from the forty-eight sections of Paris was being distributed, in which I was mentioned disadvantageously.[74] I was in the *Salle des conférences,* where I demanded of him who was to be the spokesman whether I had been at fault in the estimation of the authors of the petition: he told me, no, that he regarded me as a very good patriot. I asked what measures he intended to propose: a person handed me some black wheat and told me that there was a lot of that kind unloaded at the port Saint-Nicolas. I said to him: "Whatever your position may be, I urge you not to act violently: calm yourself and ask for a general law. If the Convention adjourns your proposition, I will ask for the floor and I will follow the thread of the views I have already presented." Citizens, I said nothing more.

This explanation demolished the incident, which received no further attention. Knowing Saint-Just's hostility to interference with free trade, it was ridiculous to expect that he would involve himself with a movement for extreme regulation. As for the deputation, it had overreached itself. Marat demanded that those who composed it be handed over to the Committee of General Security and that the Convention pass to the order of the day, which was so done.[75]

There is no mistaking the fact that Saint-Just favored a policy of economic freedom for normal times, nor that he clung to it even in a period that was far from normal. His own utterances and his unpopularity with the Enragés attest it.

Only once, in August, 1793, did Saint-Just propose regulation wholeheartedly. The needs of the army commissariat, at that moment before the Convention, seemed to him to require a more drastic policy than he normally favored. Here were united two of his favorite subjects, the army and the question of food supply. In the name of the Committee of Public Safety and of the committee of purchases, he made a report, August

9, 1793, proposing that all farmers owning over five acres of arable land be required to deposit in granaries for army use one quintal for every acre, to be paid for at the maximum rate for June. Richer landowners must give more according to a sliding scale. There is no record of any action on the plan.[76]

But whatever the fate of this decree, the tide had already set in strongly toward regulation of food prices, not only for the army, but for the population at large. The Enragés would not be denied. The widening disparity between prices and supplies brought the whole working class of Paris to their support. The pressure was too great to be resisted. If the Mountain wished to retain leadership of the Left wing, it must make concessions to the extremists. It capitulated. May 4, a maximum price for wheat was decreed, to be fixed by each department for itself. A whole series of popular movements during the summer forced the Convention to grant the national maximum of grains, September 11, and finally the general maximum on articles of prime necessity, September 29.[77] Concerning the principle of the maximum, Saint-Just retained his opinion. He is said to have called it "a famine project" conceived abroad in a spirit hostile to the Convention. Robespierre apparently thought likewise.[78]

Two days before the tariff of maximum prices was published in Paris, Saint-Just reiterated his well-known financial views in the great speech of October 10, which launched the Reign of Terror. He congratulated the Convention for having withdrawn 1,800,000 livres from circulation, and warned that if instead of economy and financial pressure on traitors, they issued more *assignats*, they would merely play into the hands of their enemies. The rich would be able more and more to entice the farmer from his plow by offering him high wages and the crops would shrink still further. When foodstuffs were taxed a third, a fourth, a half of their former price, an equivalent amount of paper should be canceled. At the present value of money, the state was actually losing half the value of the lands it sold. As for the maximum, it had not been a success so far. Rich people disregarded it and paid higher prices to get what they wanted. The markets ceased to be supplied because of the avarice of those who sold; the price of food had been lowered, but food was scarce.

"The avarice of those who sold." A year had elapsed since his speech of November, 1792. Had he so far lost touch with the peasant point of view as really to accept current Parisian suspicions? Or had the maximum actually corrupted the farmers? In any case the system seemed to him a failure. Nevertheless matters had now gone too far for retreat toward individualism, and Saint-Just, speaking for the Committee, proposed a still more drastic system of regulation as the only possible remedy. The needs of each department would be estimated and guaranteed; the entire surplus would be subject to requisition. The law must be enforced at all costs.

In the radical legislation of 8 and 13 Ventôse (February 26, March 3) 1794, Saint-Just placed on the statute books a scheme for a vast transfer of property from the rich enemies of the Revolution to its poor supporters. This was not communistic as it has erroneously been called; it was calculated merely to shift the possession of wealth into different hands. It confiscated the riches of the government's enemies to build up the fortunes of its friends, as Henry VIII created a Tudor nobility out of the lands of the Church. It was a war measure, emancipating the poor as Lincoln emancipated the slaves. The measure had social importance, but it was probably thought of primarily in terms of partisan advantage. In any event, it was an exceptional proposition for revolutionary times and no part of Saint-Just's general economic policy.

Saint-Just was no doctrinaire. The foregoing account of his flexible policy shows that he realized fully that circumstances alter cases. In normal times he would unquestionably have favored freedom of commerce. The most complete exposition of his views is in the speech of November, 1792. There he put his finger on the real cause of high prices, the inflated paper currency. Had it been possible to check that inflation as he

56

advised, relatively normal economic conditions might have returned. But such a course is not easily checked. The war enormously increased the government's need for ready money and
the *assignat* fluttered down and down until it disappeared into
the abyss forever. Together with a worthless currency and
mounting prices, there went the ever more menacing demands
of an impoverished and emboldened populace and, to complete the legislator's distraction, the outbreak of counter-
revolution and the wild fear of traitors and spies on every
street corner. When to the ever-present menace of profiteering
there was added the further peril of deliberately hostile price-
manipulation, conditions had become so abnormal that government regulation was inevitable. The pressure of events
gradually forced Saint-Just to abandon his original position.
In changing his policy in harmony with changed conditions,
he showed the versatility of a real statesman.

No doubt the Mountain was not at heart in favor of the
maximum. Very likely it was not carried out so wisely or successfully as it might have been. But 1793 was not 1917. The
thing was still experimental. It probably held prices down to
some extent. It certainly kept France from falling under control of the Enragés. In their hands the Revolution would have
perished.

VI

HOW TO BUILD AN ARMY

HILE the French Revolution brought rich gifts to posterity in terms of freedom from inherited privilege and an enlarged respect for the individual, it marks also the starting point of one of the greatest evils of modern times, nationalized warfare. Had there been no Revolution, there would have been no union of Europe against France, no need for the *levée en masse,* no Bonapartism, no national armies to resist it; not only would Europe have been spared almost a quarter century of continuous fighting, but the World War if it had come at all would in all likelihood have been waged on a far lesser scale and humanity would not now be weighed down by the burden of colossal armaments. One of the saddest declines in moral idealism is that slow but steady descent from the declaration of the Constituent Assembly in 1790, "The French Nation renounces the thought of undertaking any war with the object of conquest" to Napoleon's proclamation to his army in Italy six years later,

I will conduct you into the most fertile plains in the world. Rich provinces, great cities will be in your power, there you will find honor, glory and wealth.

One of the countless personal tragedies which always accompany a period of bloodshed, was the sweeping up of Saint-Just into this vortex of war. The generous young pacifist became one of history's greatest terrorists; the author of the lines on the Temple of Memory in *Organt* began to specialize on problems of military reorganization. He did so without developing the militarism of the professional soldier; war was for the moment the most urgent civic duty and he saw terrorism as a necessary

58

adjunct of war. He kept the vision of a better day within his heart. But he survives in the memory of men almost solely because of the blood that he spilled.

Saint-Just spoke twice in the Convention on technical army problems. Both speeches give evidence of careful study and minute acquaintance with the questions involved. Both show his ability to see matters of detail in proper perspective, as affording opportunity for putting into practice a general constitutional theory.

Early in its career the Convention took up the matter of reform in the administration of the war department, where graft was running riot. Sieyès, in the name of the newly created Committee of General Defense, presented a report on this subject. Saint-Just spoke, January 28, 1793. The report, he thought, proved that existing disorder was not the minister's fault, but that of poor organization. If instead of examining the real nature of the evil, they were to content themselves with making scapegoats of individuals, intelligent men would avoid the public service, he warned. It seemed to him that the weakness of the Executive Council was not really favorable to liberty; ministers lacked necessary legal powers; hence they must needs act arbitrarily or not at all. The minister of war, in particular, was completely devoid of authority over his subordinates. In proof of this statement, Saint-Just entered into a searching analysis of departmental machinery, explaining the actual methods by which contracts for uniforms were handled, horses purchased, payments for supplies made and foodstuffs bought. Over none of these important branches of his department did the minister have any real authority or any accurate means of finding out what was actually going on. The result was incalculable waste and corruption. To remedy this, Saint-Just approved Sieyès's proposal of a single disbursing bureau for the whole department.

The other chief point had to do with the minister's position in the general scheme. Care must be taken to keep that official and the Executive Council, of which he was a member, from becoming too strong. Acts of force which compromise the lives of citizens and public prosperity should be decided on only by the sovereign people. "The people has no interest in making war." But war gives the executive power a thousand chances of usurpation. The military power should be in the hands of the legislative branch, rather than of the Council as Sieyès had planned.

He found opportunity to inveigh once more against paper money on the ground that financial order underlies military order. Even though obligations were being paid in this way, "it makes us resemble those savages who, as Montesquieu says, cut down the tree to gather its fruits." For the rest, he regarded the situation optimistically, provided they all stood together. He proposed that the minister of war be immediately responsible to the National Convention and be separate from the Council.

The speech illustrates Saint-Just's instinct for efficiency, his hatred of corruption and militarism, his preference for legislative over executive authority. In his distrust of the Executive Council, he was really tilting against a windmill, for with the establishment of the Committee of General Defense its power was already on the decline. On the other hand, when the Committee of Public Safety held France in the hollow of its hand, he seems to have quite lost his fear of executive usurpation. Circumstances alter cases. But doubtless he would have pointed out that the emergency required unusual action, that after all the Committee of Public Safety was created by the Convention and that the legislative power remained in supreme control. It must be regretted that in the frightful maelstrom of party hatreds into which the Revolution presently plunged, neither Saint-Just nor anyone else held fast to the sane ideas on the folly of seeking scapegoats for defeat, which he here laid down. The cry of "Treason" was never more monotonously reiterated than in the later years of the Revolution.

Despite the continuous defeats suffered by French arms during the reign of Louis XV, a considerable advance had been made in military theory at the end of that reign and important practical reforms introduced under the rule of his successor. There was unfortunately one retrograde step, destined to have far-reaching results. A royal decree of 1781 provided that every candidate for an officer's commission must prove his possession of sixteen quarters of nobility.[79] The emigration of nobles which began immediately after the fall of the Bastille was thus an emigration of officers. By 1792, two-thirds of the 9,000 officers of the line had left the army. There was considerable sentiment in the country for discharging all the remainder, but an oath to the Constitution was deemed sufficient to insure their fidelity. Meanwhile the lower ranks were honeycombed with disaffection. The men distrusted their officers and mutinies were general. The army was reduced to far less than normal strength and was no longer a trustworthy fighting machine.

It was the king's flight to Varennes that awakened the legislators' eyes to the need of drastic action. A decree was passed June 21, 1791, creating a volunteer army from the existing National Guard. The men were to elect their officers from among those with previous military experience, the battalion of ten companies to choose its staff. Some 97,000 volunteers were raised in this fashion to supplement the 155,000 of the regular army. No doubt the principle of election was adopted in part out of distrust of the ministry of war and in part because the Assembly was wedded to the principle of popular choice, whether it concerned deputies, judges, priests or officers. In practice, it resulted in the choice of the most popular and the readiest talkers, nor were these army politicians the best qualified to enforce discipline. Narbonne, minister of war, and many generals wished to incorporate the volunteers into the regular regiments, but the Assembly refused, fearing to strengthen the force at the king's disposal. There was a feeling that while the regulars belonged to the king, the volunteers were devoted solely to the nation and would be an effective bulwark against possible reaction. In spite of these defects the volunteer army of 1791 did excellent service and made possible the victories of Valmy and Jemappes.

Before these victories of late 1792 had been secured the invasion of France was in progress and the alarmed Assembly called for 74,000 new volunteers on May 5 of that year. The principle of electing officers was maintained. In July a third call was issued, the country being declared in danger. A step was taken toward conscription by applying the plan of requisition, by which the National Guard of each canton was to meet and choose a sufficient number of men to satisfy the local quota. The volunteers of 1792 do not seem to have been up to the standard of 1791. They were more turbulent and had received less drilling. Again the generals implored fusion of volunteers and regulars in the same regiments, but the Legislative Assembly was no readier than its predecessor for this proposal. To increase the confusion, the volunteers of 1791 began to return to their homes in December, 1792, as was their legal right.

In February, 1793, war was declared on England and Holland. Clearly something drastic had to be done. The Convention's committee on war drew up a complicated bill in 58 articles, furnishing a thorough plan for reorganizing the army. It proposed to raise 300,000 men, one-third for the line and two-thirds volunteers. The principle of amalgamation was embodied in the bill. The infantry was to be formed into demibrigades, composed each of a battalion of former line regiments and of two battalions of volunteers.[80]

The bill was introduced February 7; discussion opened on the eleventh; Saint-Just was the third speaker. He came to the defense of amalgamation and of election, which had been attacked by the Girondins and by Barère. The idea of competition between different corps which Barère had suggested, had some point under the monarchy when the corps were small and sought only to please the king, he said; the situation had entirely altered now that there were two corporations of 200,000, whose rivalry might lead to civil war and thence to usurpation and military government. He felt that the matter was urgent; defeat or victory held danger for the state until the army was unified.

Most of his remarks dealt with the principle of election, which he discussed on an a-priori basis as though it had never been tried. He rehearsed the opposing arguments, that election would weaken and divide the army, disgust its chiefs, sap discipline, but these difficulties did not seem to him insurmountable. Election should be limited to corps officers. The private soldier was a better judge than anyone else of the conduct, courage and character of those with whom he had lived. To choose his leaders from among them was his electoral right [*droit de cité*]. Saint-Just thus based election on the right of self-government. He felt also that to leave so many appointments in the hands of generals or of the executive power, was to strengthen them unduly and to take a step toward monarchy. On the other hand, it would be dangerous to permit soldiers to elect generals or the staff; a whole army cannot deliberate; these highest officers should be chosen by the people or its legitimate representatives. To establish a republic, it was desirable to take from the people the smallest amount of power. The only considerations were the liberty of the people, the right of the soldiers and the restriction of all powers hostile to the spirit of popular independence. The antechamber of ministers must cease to be a market place for public employment.

He deprecated the committee's proposal to increase the pay of volunteers who had served more than one campaign, a plan which did not seem to him worthy of a soldier's pride. He looked forward to the time when difference in rank would not be marked by distinction in pay. A republic must rest on frugality and virtue.

He wished the committee had, in the same wise spirit, proposed views on recruiting. He desired further that the committee's bill be put to vote with this amendment, that its execution be suspended in armies too near the enemy.[81]

There is no denying the high plane on which the argument is made, though there occasionally creeps in a false note in the braggadocio temper of the times. It is also clear that Saint-Just, usually so practical, paid little heed to the teaching of experience in his discussion of military elections. Admitting these defects, there was much shrewd common sense and a fine civic spirit in the speech. It was also effective. In spite of opposition by the generals and the Girondins, the committee's plan was carried, thanks it is said to the Mountain and especially to Saint-Just.[82] The Convention adopted both the principle of amalgamation and of election, though the former was not carried out until the following winter. The former principle, at least, was not without effect on the final victory.

After 9 Thermidor there was found in Saint-Just's office at the Committee of Public Safety a small manuscript volume bound in red morocco, bearing the date 1793 and entitled *Notes militaires*.[83] The book contains forty-three miscellaneous items, apparently made by him in July and August of that year to aid him in his work as a member of the Committee. Here are, for example, a summary of the size of each French army, the latest news from the Armies of Brest, of the Alps and Italy, of La Rochelle, a note of supplies received at Metz, a detailed account of the munitions at Cambrai, the exact strength of the Army of the North, showing those in hospital, on leave, etc., an estimate of the provisions necessary for a besieged fortress with a garrison of 12,000 (he had Lille in mind) and a note on the proper use of these supplies. An item of interest in view of his mission to Alsace is a report on the siege of Landau. The booklet illustrates the careful study he gave to military matters and his desire for exact knowledge. Here are no bombastic sentiments, only statistics and concrete information. In singular contrast, he wrote in pencil on the first page, two lines: "He sees the human heart and searches out its spirit" and "Love is the quest of happiness." Who shall say which part of the book bears truer witness to the essential man?

VII

CONSTITUTION-MAKING

URING the period of the Terror, France was under the supreme authority of the National Convention. It was not technically a legislative assembly, though it fulfilled the functions of such a body during the three years of its existence. In theory, however, it had been called into being to give France a new constitution; it was a constitutional convention. With the suspension and arrest of the king, the executive was vacant except in so far as it was temporarily provided for by the Provisional Executive Council of ministers. Since there was no longer a monarchy, the Constitution of 1791 which had created a limited monarchy was already obsolete.

Exactly a week after the republic had been established, the Convention decreed (September 29, 1792) that a constitutional committee be created. Consequent upon this action, a committee of nine was elected by the Convention, October 11, consisting of Sieyès, Thomas Paine, Brissot, Pétion, Vergniaud, Gensonné, Barère, Danton and Condorcet. Barbaroux subsequently replaced Brissot. Though the gap between Girondins and Mountain had not yet become impassable and though the latter then considered several of these men sympathetic with their point of view, the committee would clearly be controlled by the Girondins. To check their influence, Danton proposed the creation by the Jacobin Club of an auxiliary constitutional committee. This was done October 19, by the election of Collot d'Herbois, Billaud-Varenne, Robespierre, Danton (thus a member of both committees, but apparently doing no work on either), Chabot and Couthon, all strong Mountain men. Subsequently at an unknown date, the Jacobin committee was almost entirely changed by the retirement of all except Billaud-

Varenne and Robespierre, and the addition of Saint-André, Robert, Thuriot, Bentabole, Anthoine and Saint-Just. After Condorcet, chairman of the official Convention committee, had read his report, February 15, 1793, Anthoine denounced it at the Jacobins (February 18) and proposed that the Club's committee be increased by a third and instructed to present a report within a fortnight. The motion passed and Dubois-Crancé, Collot d'Herbois, Anacharsis Cloots and Couthon were added to the committee.[84]

We know nothing further of the Jacobin committee; two of its members ultimately had a share in drawing up the constitution and may have begun their studies on the project at this time, but as a group it failed to function. Nor do we know much of what went on within the Convention committee. It has been conjectured that while Condorcet was the author of the bulk of its proposed constitution, Barère drew up the Declaration of the Rights of Man and some portions were the work of Gensonné and perhaps others.[85]

The Condorcet draft, which had been four months in the making, provided that each department was entitled to one deputy for every fifty thousand of population and that each citizen should vote for the whole department delegation. It also created an executive council of seven ministers, to be elected by the entire nation. The council was thus based on an independent and more extensive mandate than the legislature, where each member represented only a small area. This document, though in many respects democratic, was badly received by the Mountain for partisan reasons. Factional feeling was constantly increasing and they would have none of a Girondin constitution. Problems arising out of the conduct of the war absorbed so much time and energy that it was easy to defer consideration of the project for many weeks. Finally delay was no longer possible and on April 15, 1793, the Convention resolved to devote every Monday, Wednesday and Saturday to this question. Thus began the great constitutional debate, which continued intermittently for over two months.

66

Discussion was at first not limited to the Condorcet draft. Scores of rival projects rained upon the bewildered Convention. Among these was one by Saint-Just, who presented his plan April 24. When confronted by an emergency, no one could find more pungent, biting words nor set them together in clearer or compacter form. But on an occasion of this kind when nothing immediate was at stake, he was likely to adopt the profound, philosophical air so dear to the intellectuals of his day and to shroud thoughts none too clear in cloudy verbiage. In this vein, he introduced the exposition of his constitutional principles by a rambling sociological discourse, obviously inspired of Rousseau.

He began with a pair of his favorite antitheses.

All tyrants had their eyes on us when we judged one of their kind; today when by a gentler destiny you meditate on the liberty of the world, the peoples, who are the true grandees of earth, contemplate you in their turn.

You feared the judgment of men when you made a king die; that cause interested only your pride: the one you are about to take up is more impressive; it concerns your glory: the constitution will be your reply and your manifesto upon earth.

He was assuredly optimistic about the welcome this constitution would receive, predicting that the day it was adopted, Europe would demand peace; internal factions, crushed, would bend beneath the yoke of liberty; the citizens would return to their workshops and the republic's peace would make kings tremble. Did he deceive himself with this grandiloquence? It is hard to credit, yet many eighteenth-century revolutionaries, clear down to Napoleon Bonaparte, coupled the dreamer with the realist, and Saint-Just was no exception.

Somewhat more soberly he set forth the need of a vigorous government, particularly in time of war. On the other hand (and here the mind of Rousseau begins to move the tongue of Saint-Just) every people is naturally virtuous and should not be forced, but rather gently and wisely led. Social order is in the nature of things; give man laws suited to his nature and

67

he will cease to be unhappy and corrupt. The social precedes the political order; the former concerns relations between the men of a single society, which are naturally those of peace; the latter deals with relations between nations or rather those who govern them, which are sometimes those of war. From these premises Saint-Just argued that tyranny arose when a government applied against its own people the force properly used only against a foreign enemy. It was the business of the constitution to guard against such tyranny, likely in the future to be subtle rather than violent and all the more dangerous.

He then passed to a discussion of the nature of legislation, which might take the form of precepts or laws. The former he believed inadequate. In the time of the monarchy the principles of behavior were excellent, but they failed to influence conduct. This portion of the speech is more confused and disconnected than the first part, to which it seems at times contradictory. He hardly makes clear why human nature, so naturally good, should under the monarchy have become so debased, nor is it obvious why, if virtue be innate, precepts are insufficient. In all this introduction, much play is made with the names of Lycurgus, Solon, Minos; the great law-giver idea always intrigued him.

Finally he came down to definite criticism of the Condorcet project. It contained more precepts than laws, more powers than harmony, more motions than democracy (referring perhaps to the innumerable elections provided in this document, which the laboring class could not afford the time to attend). Then, suddenly dropping obscure generalizations, he grappled with the heart of the problem. In a dozen words, he skillfully laid bare the essential structure of the committee's scheme. "Here is its plan: a *federal* representation which makes the laws; a *representative* council which executes them." By this he meant that the legislature, whose members represented local areas, had a federal character (the Mountain, pluming itself on its devotion to a unified republic was constantly accusing the Girondins of federalism); the council, on the contrary, was the only representative organ of the whole nation, since it was elected by the entire people. The legislature, as a mere representation of departments, was in reality a congress. He objected also to the council's being composed of executive ministers for then the council would be the minister of its own will; its vigilance as against itself would be illusory. There, briefly stated, were his cardinal criticisms on the ground of constitutional theory, the remainder of the speech merely elaborated them. In such a plan, the council (named by the sovereign people as a whole) would constantly gain power over the legislature (whose members merely represented their departments); it would work out into a patriciate, clearing the way for a return to despotism.

The proper arrangement should be just the reverse. Let the legislature, guardian as it is of the unity of the state and supreme depositary of the laws, be elected by the entire people. Let the council be chosen in any other way suitable to make clear its subordination. The general will must be the majority of individual wills and thus expressive of their material interests; so the general interest is ascertained. The whole people is the unit, not any territorial fraction; the general will is indivisible; the legislature and the law represent this unity. The council should be a body intermediate between the legislature and the ministers; it may well be elected by the departments to mark its subordinate position and because its acts are not representative acts. Montesquieu, no less than Rousseau, still held his devotion. The English cabinet, a council of ministers, would have shocked Montesquieu and Saint-Just alike, if either had realized the extent of its power. But Condorcet's plan was still more repellent, for at least the English cabinet is a part of and subordinate to Parliament. Unity of the nation, separation of governmental powers, the supremacy of the general will guaranteed by the supremacy of the legislature and by the method of its choice—such were Saint-Just's constitutional principles.

If his previous speech had been turgid, his plan for a con-

69

stitution which followed was lucid and concise. Instead of an elaborate Declaration of Rights, he opened with a handful of "Fundamental Dispositions." They declare that a constitution is merely the application of legitimate rights and duties; that government officials are not above the citizens; that the latter are inviolable and can only be constrained by law; that foreigners, the good faith of commerce and treaties, hospitality, peace and sovereignty are sacred; that the fatherland of a free people is open to every man on earth; that legitimate power resides not in men, but in laws. This admirable little statement forms a marked contrast to the excessively detailed declarations then in vogue.

The constitution, which is in two parts, starts with a general view of the government to be established; France is an indivisible republic, whose deliberative assembly represents the entire nation; all officials are temporary; there is a National Assembly, an Executive Council and ministers; local administration is exercised by directories and communal councils; all the above officials except members of the Assembly are mandatories, not representatives, and are to be chosen by secondary assemblies, not by the people.

Since the nation is a unit, the departments, arrondissements and communes are maintained purely for administrative convenience. The vote is the privilege of every man who has reached the age of twenty-one and has lived a year and a day in the same commune; it must be exercised under penalty of fine. When a voter has become twenty-five he is eligible for office. In line with his principle that the National Assembly represents the entire people, Saint-Just provides that every citizen is to vote for one representative, the 341 receiving the most votes throughout the republic being elected for a term of two years without right of reëlection until the lapse of an equal interval. In a similar spirit, the Assembly is required to deliberate as a whole on all propositions, though it may name a committee for some special report. The Council (chosen by secondary electoral assemblies) is further subordinated by its non-national character; one member would represent each department. The term of office and the interval before reëlection were to be a year longer than for the Assembly. The Council was in theory an executive body, having the duty of carrying out the Assembly's decrees, of proposing and conducting war, proposing peace, preparing a tax budget, coining money, regulating commerce, corresponding with foreign governments and the like. In view of its size, it must needs act through the ministers whom it elects and who must function separately; though having a consultative voice in the Council, they cannot be present when it deliberates. Provision is made for a referendum if the Council considers any decree of the Assembly contrary to the Declaration of Rights (whether the Fundamental Dispositions or some other document is not clear) or if a constitutional change is involved. Local government is provided by a *procureur-syndic* and a directory for each arrondissement and a "council of communities" for each commune.

Two-thirds of Part II concern the judicial system which is conventional enough except for one striking chapter "On Public Troubles," characteristic of the naïve side in Saint-Just's make-up. Every two years six aged men, well-known for their virtues, were to be elected, whose duty should be to appease seditions.

These aged men are decorated with a tricolored scarf and a white plume; when they appear equipped with their insignia, the public keeps silence and arrests any who continue the tumult; the public takes the aged men for arbitrators. If the trouble continues the aged men shall announce that the law is in mourning. Those who insult them are considered wicked and lose their citizenship. In case of grave violence, the directories and mayors of communities may summon the armed force. They do not retire until the mob is dispersed. . . . If an aged man is assassinated, the Republic puts on mourning for a day and all labor shall cease.

A merciless terrorist, a driving organizer, a keen analyst in debate this boy was, but a poet too, dwelling sometimes in cloudland.

The last three chapters contain miscellaneous provisions. Universal military service is required. There is no generalissimo; in triumphs, generals march behind their armies; no army may surrender without infamy. The French people declares itself the friend of all other peoples; it respects treaties and flags religiously; it offers refuge in its ports to vessels from all the world; it offers an asylum to great men and virtuous unfortunates from any land; its ships protect at sea the ships of foreigners in storm. Exiles for liberty's sake are welcomed; homicides and tyrants are alone excluded. The French people will never take arms to enslave or oppress any other. It makes no peace with an enemy in possession of its territory. It makes no treaties except for the peace and happiness of nations. And with a final flourish, "The French people votes the liberty of the world."

Twice again, Saint-Just participated in the constitutional debate, both times on questions of local government. The first was May 15, in reply to a Girondin effort to strengthen the departments which had been bulwarks of conservatism, and to create large communes so as to swamp urban radicalism by attaching extensive rural areas to the towns. Saint-Just raised the usual reproach of federalism and pointed it with an astute prophecy of civil war across the sea.

That confederated state is indeed not a republic; furthermore the legislators of the New World have left a principle of dissolution in their work. One day (and may it be far distant) one state will arm against the other, the representatives will divide and America will finish as a confederation like that of Greece.

It was on the theory of national unity that the Vendéan war was being conducted; the sovereign was maintaining its domain intact against the usurpation of independence by a part. For these reasons he opposed giving any form of government to the departments, recurring to the scheme of smaller administrative units embodied in his constitutional draft.

It may be pointed out that however accurately Saint-Just

forecast the future action of the South in the United States, he was in reality concerned with the future action of the South in France. Already the Girondin departments were threatening revolt; within a month they had begun civil war. His views regarding local organization did not prevail and the department was made a political entity in the final draft of the constitution. It is possible, however, that inasmuch as Saint-Just had a considerable share in this final draft and since it became strategically important to present a plan which would mollify the enraged and insurgent departments, he may have withdrawn his theoretical objections.

With the cognate question of a maximum population for municipalities, he had greater success. The subject was raised by Louvet, who proposed a minimum of 200 and a maximum of 40,000 on May 22. In the lively debate which was stirred up by this obvious thrust at the domination of Paris and which spread over three days (May 22, 24 and 27), fifteen speakers participated, the Girondins and the Mountain being of course sharply divided over what was really a life and death question for their respective parties. Some notion of the leadership Saint-Just had already won and the respect in which his intellectual ability was held is gained from the remarks of one Guffroy, the fourth who spoke. He deplored the lightness and haste which seemed to characterize the constitutional debate; there seemed to be no reflection, no maturity of thought.

Except for the plan of Saint-Just, we have not a single good constitutional project. . . . Saint-Just told you a truth which you have not sufficiently realized; society must be so regulated that wherever any group of Frenchmen is found, they will carry out the promise of the solemn contract; that is why he wanted to see the French not divided, but so organized into a society that even though the whole French people were suddenly transported out of its territory, each individual might carry out his promise to help the others and exact like aid from all the rest.[86]

Three speakers were heard on each side during the first day's debate and after Lehardy had opened the subject on the second day (May 24), in favor of a maximum population, Saint-Just was heard for the negative. He spoke briefly, regretting once more than the fundamental bases of government had not first been laid down before details were discussed. Europe, he feared, was not finding in these debates that high level of thought it had a right to expect. He found it hard to understand why after the Convention had deliberately adopted the territorial rather than the personal division, they now proposed to divide the population of municipalities. They could not do that (except for convenience in voting) without dividing society, for the voice of a town was a single voice. Brushing aside the niceties of political theory, he boldly laid bare the real point of the whole argument in a passage famous for its eloquence.

You fear the immense population of certain towns, of that of Paris; that population is not redoubtable for liberty. O you who divide Paris, without intending it you oppress or partition France! . . . But when Paris is in commotion, there is an echo that repeats our cries; the whole of France repeats them. Paris did not blow up the spark that fired the Vendée; she hastened with the other departments to extinguish it. Let us then not accuse Paris and instead of dividing and making it suspect to the Republic, let us in friendship repay that city for the ills it has suffered in our behalf. The blood of its martyrs is mingled with the blood of other Frenchmen; its children and the rest are inclosed in the same tomb. Does each department wish to take back its own corpses and to go its separate way?

Let not the country fear the town, he pleaded; cities are no greater threat to rustic cabins than are the mountains to the valleys, which they protect from storm. He closed with the principle that municipal administration cannot be legitimately divided and demanded that in every town, irrespective of its size, there be a single municipality or, as he preferred to call it, a *conseil de communauté*.

On the twenty-seventh, another Mountain speaker, Philippeaux, gave further evidence of the impression made by Saint-Just's reasoning. "One of the speakers who preceded me in this tribune," he said, "told you with much good sense that you were reversing the proper order of things, by seeking to create a municipal government on a geographic basis." Harking back to an expression of Saint-Just's, Philippeaux proposed to divide the citizens into "tribes" of tens, hundreds and thousands. While nothing came of this, the proposal to divide large cities was dropped.

By reason of the pressure of other business and by reason of deliberate delay on the part of the Mountain, the debate had dragged so slowly that at the end of the month only the Declaration of Rights and six articles of the constitution had been passed, substantially reënacting the status quo. But now the menace of a great Girondin departmental revolt became so acute that in alarm the Mountain resolved to push through a fundamental statute so reasonable as to cut the ground from under the rebellion. On May 29, Barère, in the name of the Committee of Public Safety, proposed to add to that committee five members who should be charged with the task of presenting to the Convention as quickly as possible a constitutional draft reduced solely to such articles as must be made irrevocable in order to assure to the republic its unity, indivisibility and liberty, and to the people the exercise of all its rights. This motion the Convention passed. The following day, Cambon reported that the Committee had selected Hérault-Séchelles, Ramel-Nogaret, Couthon, Saint-Just and Mathieu; it sought the Convention's confirmation of its choice, which was immediately granted.[87]

These five worked apart from the rest of the Committee of Public Safety, of which they were at first only *adjoints* or associate members. The labors of the second or Mountain constitutional committee were as rapid as those of its Girondin predecessor had been leisurely. The fall of the Girondins left no further reason for delay. Enemies later spoke of the result as scrambled together (*bâclée*) in a few days by a few young men. Haste was mandatory by the terms of their appointment; their model lay before them in the shape of Condorcet's draft, whose essence they unblushingly appropriated, making such changes as their party allegiance or previous reflections dictated. The subject was by no means new to them, as in the case of Saint-Just at least has been amply proved. What share in the result is properly attributable to the several members of the committee, there is no means of knowing. Saint-Just in his denunciation of Hérault (11 Germinal, year II) asserted directly that while the latter managed to make himself the reporter, the others did the work. The manuscript is in Hérault's hand at any rate, both for report and constitution, nor can too great weight be attached to Saint-Just's statement under the circumstances in which it was made. While the committee was at work, Hérault sent a hurry order to the keeper of public documents for a copy of the laws of Minos, "which ought to be contained in a collection of the Greek laws," on the ground that the committee had urgent need of them. It has been suggested that the polished, ironical Hérault was too well-informed to have made such a request seriously; he was probably ridiculing someone on the committee with a propensity for quoting the classic lawgivers, perhaps Saint-Just. If this view is correct, there may have been more friction in the committee than Hérault's report would indicate.[88]

The five presented the result of their efforts to the Committee of Public Safety at its evening session, June 9, where the project was read and on the following morning approved. The same day, June 10, Hérault-Séchelles made his report to the Convention, dwelling on "the touching unanimity" that animated the committee.[89] When he had finished, Robespierre praised the project highly and moved that it be printed on placards and circulated and that discussion start at once. The motion was seconded by Barère, who had been on the first committee, but had proposed the formation of the second. This plan, he said, "short, clear and precise, in a veritably crystalline style, in the style of the Twelve Tables" proved the progress they had made and augured well for stability and peace.

The motion passed without dissent; the fall of the Girondins in the Convention a week before had eliminated the opposition.

The modifications of the committee's draft in the course of the ensuing discussion do not concern the rôle of Saint-Just, who took no part in this debate, though he doubtless had a share in the subsequent revision by the committee. The constitution was adopted June 24 and ratified by plebiscite during the first week of July.

Can one approximate Saint-Just's influence in the committee? [90] To begin with, there are certain characteristics of style, coupled with an emphasis on certain favorite ideas which suggest that even though, as Aulard says, Hérault held the pen, the thought and even the language may have been furnished in part by others. Reference has been made to Barère's delight at the brevity of the document and the clear precision of its style. If any two qualities distinguish Saint-Just's composition at its best, they are these two. His epigrammatic terseness and clarity excited admiration among his colleagues.

Early in his report Hérault sounded the keynote of the committee's plan. The sovereignty of the people and the dignity of man were ever before their eyes, he said. No one can read attentively the three speeches made by Saint-Just during this debate without being struck by the parallel. The sovereign will was indivisible and supreme, man was innately virtuous; on these two cardinal principles Saint-Just's whole structure was reared. No doubt they both go back to Rousseau, the patron saint of the Mountain. No doubt the whole committee was soaked through and through with this type of thinking. But without claiming any especial originality for Saint-Just here, it is at least fair to surmise that he had something to do with the emphasis on these two points.

For the sake of brevity, the committee had "severely restrained themselves from the pleasure" of introducing into the constitution articles relative to social institutions. So Hérault informed his hearers. One naturally thinks of Saint-Just's in-

77

terest in this subject, which was to be the theme of his *Fragments*.

Passing beyond these generalities, which are necessarily incapable of proof, more satisfying evidence of influence may be found in the concrete provisions of the constitution.

For article 18 of the Declaration of Rights, abolishing the legal relationship of master and servant, Saint-Just was directly responsible (cf. Chapter III, Article 3 of his own proposed constitution).

In expounding the chief ideas of the committee's plan, Hérault had emphasized the care bestowed upon the principle of representation. Though the machinery here set up differs somewhat from Saint-Just's scheme, they both spring from the same idea. The importance of breaking down territorial barriers and making the Assembly an expression of national unity rather than a representation of local areas, a principle set in the forefront of Hérault's report, formed also the burden of Saint-Just's speeches of April 24 and May 15. It was almost his hobby; its violation was one of the chief items in his indictment of the Condorcet draft.

Hérault's corollary follows that for the purpose of distinguishing between representatives sprung from and formulating the national will, and functionaries (mere agents for carrying it out), electoral assemblies rather than the people at large should choose the latter. This again was one of Saint-Just's pet ideas, as may be gleaned from his speech of April 24. Thus both the committee's Chapter VIII and Saint-Just's Chapter VIII establish secondary assemblies on the basis of one elector for every 200 voters. Other details differ, but the thought is the same.

While the Executive Council was a smaller body in the committee's plan than in Saint-Just's and was somewhat differently elected, yet here too the common groundwork in political theory is the same. Saint-Just in his speech of April 24 and Hérault in his report stressed the same points; the Council were only agents, not representatives, and must not be popularly chosen or they become dangerous; they must not be a group of ministers, but intermediate between them and the Assembly. Nowhere is Saint-Just's influence more marked than here.

The sanctity of municipalities and the duty of preserving them intact was set forth by Hérault in the report as an argument against the large commune or cantonal municipality projected by Condorcet. Saint-Just's speech of May 24 was directed against the opposite peril, the administrative division of large cities. Both sprang from the common principle that a community is a natural unit, irrespective of its population, and should not be artificially increased or decreased.

Finally a comparison of the sections on foreign relations in the committee's draft and in Saint-Just's leaves small room for doubt as to the common authorship of both. The former comprises four brief articles. The French people declares itself the friend and natural ally of free peoples. It does not meddle with the government of other nations; it does not permit them to meddle in its own. It protects foreigners banished from their homes for liberty's sake; it refuses asylum to tyrants. It makes no peace with an enemy in possession of its soil. All but the second of these are taken almost word for word from Saint-Just's Chapter IX. The idealism and essential pacifism of that chapter, blended indeed with a certain defiant nationalism, are characteristic of his thinking.

Whether Saint-Just was the chief author of the Constitution of 1793 or not, no one has a right to say. That he had an important part in its composition seems evident.

This document was destined never to be put into effect. Perhaps it would have been impracticable, even in times of peace. Its executive provisions were weak. A sterner, more centralized government was needed in a time of war and revolution. But it was not a failure for all that. It fulfilled its immediate purpose; the insurgent departments, finding guarantees for their future safety in the referendum, the loose Executive Council and in liberty of worship, received it with enthusiasm and were speedily pacified.[91] Enclosed in its "ark," it stood before the Convention as a perpetual reminder of human rights and the transitoriness of terrorism. For years it was a palladium of liberty. Unless one postulates an unproved cynicism, it shows that the men who were so soon to set up a bloody, despotic power, looked forward to a fairer time when the folk, self-ruled, would live in harmony and peace.

VIII

THE MOUNTAIN TRIUMPHS

ITTER partisanship was the Achilles heel of the French Revolution. This incurable evil festered into a running sore of suspicion and hatred, developing into the great plague known as the Terror, which decimated the ranks not only of the Revolution's enemies, but of its friends as well. Unfortunately, personal and political quarrels were intensified by social and economic differences, nowhere more so than in the contest between the groups known as Mountain and Gironde. There were other vital disagreements. The Mountain's centralizing policy, its vigorous ruthlessness, its growing radical dictatorship were the antithesis of the Gironde's belief in decentralization, its pseudo-legalism, its liberalism. Temperamental clashes played their part. But the climax came when by the destruction of more conservative groups, the Girondins became the champions of the commercial middle class, while the Mountain identified itself increasingly with the interests of the poor.[92] At a time when economic legislation was destroying old financial values and creating new ones, this opposition grew desperate. Around the Girondins clustered the flying remnants of the beaten parties of the early Revolution; ex-royalists and men of wealth took the garb of moderate republicans, while in the Mountain camp the ultraradical fringe, the Enragés and Hébertists were constantly urging the main group to sponsor advanced social legislation and were partially successful in forcing it to do so. Thus the Girondins were dragged back by an unsought association with the past, the Mountain pushed forward toward a social revolution for which it was not entirely prepared. Through the divergent pull of these more or less unwelcome allies, the gap between the main parties steadily widened.

Curiously enough these real differences were rarely alluded to in the Convention or the Jacobin Club. Here ridiculous charges of royalism and treasonable conspiracy flew back and forth between the two groups. Most of the great convictions under the Revolution were obtained on just these flimsy grounds.

With growing bitterness the factions grappled and swayed throughout the winter of 1792 and spring of 1793, the Girondins gradually slipping and weakening. Though they had a normal majority in the Convention, they lost the Executive Council; the great Committees of Public Safety and General Security were manned by Mountaineers. The high cost of food which the Girondins refused to check by law and the failure of the war, sharpened by the treason of their general, Dumouriez, completed their ruin. The extremists organized the working-class sections of Paris and a central revolutionary committee was established at the Éveché; hoarse-voiced spellbinders exhorted their hearers to rise as on August 10 and sweep the traitors out; the circle was closing in around the doomed party. They fought with dogged determination, but their moment had passed. On June 2, under the guns of Hanriot and his eighty thousand men, the twenty-nine leading Girondins and two ex-ministers were ordered under arrest, to be confined in their own homes. A tale sprang up that Saint-Just generously offered to go to Caen, a Girondin center, as hostage for the safety of the prisoners and that Couthon and Danton made a similar offer, but the Convention records show no such proposal.[93] Had he gone, he might have encountered Charlotte Corday, the would-be Jeanne d'Arc of the Girondins, for this was her home.

The proletarian victory in Paris had an immediate repercussion in the provinces; during the month of June the "federalist" revolt burst into flames in North and South alike, while the Vendéans had long since enkindled the West so that a great crescent of hostile departments surrounded the capital on three sides. Feeling was further embittered by the escape of most of the imprisoned Girondins from their light confinement or their evasion of the decree of arrest and their flight to the provinces, where they assumed leadership of the revolt against Paris. Though it became ultimately necessary to destroy this movement by force of arms, a moral offensive was first undertaken against it. Herein lies the reason for the haste in completing the constitution, thanks to which the military repression of the bitter-enders, which took place mainly in July and August, was effected more easily than had at first seemed possible.

In accord with this policy of mingled force and kindness, the Mountain determined to take definite steps against some of the Girondin leaders while showing mercy toward the majority. A committee was created, June 15, consisting of Saint-Just, Delmas and Cambon, to unify all measures relative to the operations and needs of the army against those in rebellion. On the following day, the Committee of Public Safety decreed that a report be made to the Convention on the arrested Girondin deputies, appointing Saint-Just and Cambon for this purpose. June 19, the Committee gave Saint-Just sole charge of the report. Whether this signal honor was the reward of his brilliant work in connection with the constitution or was based on his record in the Convention or in intimate party discussions, cannot be known. In any case, it indicates the ascendancy he had acquired in the assembly and the confidence of his associates in his ability. This was the first of those great philippics by which he achieved fame as the Mountain's spearhead against its opponents. He read his report to the Committee June 24; it was discussed, amended in certain particulars and adopted July 2, then read to the Convention July 8. The document is known as the "Report on the 32 members of the Convention detained by virtue of the decree of June 2."

Saint-Just's speeches, particularly his denunciations, rarely follow a logical outline. In this case, he launched forth at once with the monstrous and unprovable charge that the Girondins had a scheme, organized by General Dillon, to restore the dauphin, a calamity from which the country had been saved only by their arrest. He proposed, he said, to begin at the beginning and to follow the story straight through, not seeking to have anyone condemned for his opinions nor regarding all under arrest as equally guilty, for most of them were only misled.

Before starting his historical survey, he focused attention on the personality of his chief opponent, Brissot, whom he savagely attacked as a General Monk, a man who defended the monarchy and the republic alternately; who pretended misery while living in the palace of Saint-Cloud; pretended delicate health while all the time he was pulling the strings of empire; pretended gentleness and simple natural affections while he was rejoicing at his enemy's murder on September 2; [94] a man who had a nice appreciation of everyone's point of view and interest and used it as bait to draw them toward his own goal. Too suspicious for accomplices, he had only friends who conspired with him, led astray by their weakness and pride rather than by malice. He had finesse, not courage. The portrait Saint-Just drew of Brissot was quite as much of a caricature as the portrait the Thermidorians later drew of Saint-Just.

From this point on, the attack proceeds roughly in chronological order. Before August 10, the Girondins were strong monarchists, Saint-Just declared, favoring dethronement only to clear the way for a usurper; some preferred the Duke of York, others the Duke of Orléans. The charge that their royalism continued after that date he sought to prove with more ingenuity than ingenuousness by asserting that in order to preserve the throne they merely suspended the king instead of deposing him at once. So Cromwell showed respect for kingship, lest the notion of one-man rule be undermined.

Proceeding to the opening of the Convention, Saint-Just paints a picture of idyllic harmony, broken sharply by the belated horror of the Girondins at the September massacres. Everything had quieted down when they started declaiming against anarchy, with the result that the Convention was plunged into discord. Saint-Just charged unwarrantably that this pretended emotion was just a blind under cover of which they hoped to restore the throne. He granted that the massacres were deplorable, but inquired who were more responsible, the Girondins who were in power or the Mountain who were not?

Accusers of the people, no one saw you on September 2 between the assassins and their victims. Whatever inhuman men spilled this blood, you must all answer for it, you who allowed it to be shed.

Having scored a distinct point by retorting the characteristic Girondin argument against themselves, Saint-Just passed to the period of their control in the Convention. He leveled his guns first on Brissot's war policy, whose real object, Saint-Just charged, was to divert attention to foreign affairs, to restore the first constitution on the plea that a strong government was necessary, and to save the king by scaring folk with the peril of an English and a Spanish war. The attack then switched to Dumouriez, favorite general of the Girondins. This man, who had turned traitor, said the speaker, was in the habit of calling those now under arrest the healthy part of the Convention. When these were accused of being his accomplices, they smiled; dissimulation smiles, innocence would have been afflicted.

Whatever period or individual Saint-Just discussed, he always managed to lead up adroitly to his major contention: the Girondins had never ceased to be monarchist. He read part of a letter written by d'Estaing and found on Gardien, suggesting that the death sentence might be commuted and the king escorted to America by Thomas Paine. For all that, Saint-Just would have his hearers respect Paine, who had helped liberty in the other hemisphere and was deceived by others. In like manner, he linked the federalist revolt with a criminal plan to blind France for the sake of reintroducing the crown, a plot worked out at Saint-Cloud, he charged, where Mme. Brissot was lodging in the palace of the ex-queen. "Were they innocent, who began a civil war?" he queried sharply and quoted the Girondin Isnard's threat, "They will search to find on which bank of the Seine Paris used to stand." Now the Girondin uprising had nothing to do with royalism, but Saint-Just was on firmer ground when he charged his opponents with aggressiveness. They had assuredly begun to attack the Mountain soon after the Convention started and Isnard's grandiloquent boast was characteristic of an attitude. But the question of war guilt is always double-edged and the Mountain had its share of responsibility.

After exposing in great detail the alleged plot alluded to at the beginning of his report, Saint-Just denounced by name the leaders of the armed revolt in the various departments, dissecting their individual personalities scathingly. He closed with an eloquent peroration, which struck once more the note of mingled justice and mercy.

Pronounce now. You must differentiate among those now under arrest: the majority were deceived and which of us can flatter himself that he has never been? The true culprits are those who fled and you owe them nothing more, for they are desolating their fatherland. It is the fire of liberty which has purified us, as the boiling of metals drives the impure scum from the crucible. You could not save the country with them: leave them alone with the crime which they wished to commit. They complained of anarchy, they plunge us into it; they have troubled the peace of the good country-folk while you were making the laws: let the people choose between rebels who make war and you who assuage its ills. They shall not share with you the world's love. They complained of a will to divide the republic, they are dividing its tattered remnants; they say that members of the representative body have been outraged, they outrage it in its entirety; their opposition to the Vendéan brigands was lukewarm, today they summon France against you and find arms to combat its laws and destroy its empire! . . . Proscribe those who have fled to take up arms; . . . proscribe them, not for what they have said but for what they have done. Judge the rest and pardon the majority: error must not be confounded with crime and you have no love for severity. . . . I have painted the conspiracy: may fate grant that we have seen the last storm of liberty!

From the documents in possession of the Committee of Public Safety, he drew an indictment under seven heads, forming the basis of the projected decree. The indictment charged a conspiracy against the republic, an attempt to restore the dauphin, a redoubling of these efforts since the constitution had been completed, a plot to murder part of the Convention, an effort to kindle civil war between North and South, a seizure of public funds and declaration of independence by certain administrations at the end of May, open and still-continuing rebellion in three departments. For these reasons he presented a decree declaring Buzot, Barbaroux, Gorsas, Lanjuinais, Salle, Louvet, Bergoing, Biroteau, Pétion traitors and royalist rebels,[95] while Gensonné, Guadet, Vergniaud, Mollevault and Gardien were charged with complicity; Bertrand was completely exonerated and the rest pardoned as "more deceived than guilty." The decree was voted without discussion, partly on that day, partly on June 28. The committee on legislation was directed (July 29) to draw up acts of accusation at once, but for political reasons the government's delay continued and it was not until October 24 that the trial took place with its foregone sequel six days later. The list of those actually tried and executed differs considerably from that in Saint-Just's decree.

This report did not go unchallenged. At least three detailed replies were made, though they reached few readers. The two most important were by Brissot, who had fled immediately after the coup d'état of June 2 and tried to gain Switzerland, but was arrested a fortnight later at Moulins. Transferred to a Paris prison, he wrote, probably in July, his *Réponse au rapport de Saint-Just,* a fifty-page document in its printed form, wherein the charges against him are answered point by point. Early in October, Amar of the Committee of General Security read another report against the Girondins, whereupon Brissot wrote twice as long a reply as before, in which he referred again to some of Saint-Just's charges. This apologia was never finished.[96]

Brissot's first reply brought out the major points that the supposed Dillon plot had been demolished by Desmoulins and in any case had nothing to do with the thirty-two who were under arrest at the time it was supposed to have been formed; that the department revolts were due to this very arrest and were republican in spirit; that he personally had talked against monarchy as early as 1785; that any utterances of his in 1792 were non-applicable, since at that time everyone was at least officially royalist; that the (Mountain) committee of surveillance was in complete control of Paris during the September massacres and could have stopped them. He branded as a lie his supposed regret at Morande's escape and made plain that his wife's stay at Saint-Cloud was in two rooms formerly belonging to one of the concierges, from which she moved as soon as criticism was heard. In all this he was on firm ground; less so when he denied his party's responsibility for the war. After all, he summed up cogently, why should a plebeian want to restore monarchy, when he can have more influence in a republic? The idea that he had sold out was refuted by his poverty.

The third reply was anonymous. It was a pamphlet of thirty pages, published at Caen, July 13, only five days after the Committee's report had been read and only two days after it could have reached Caen. This hastily compiled document was called *Observations sur le rapport de Saint-Just contre les trente-deux proscrits, par une Société de Girondins.* For a good while it was thought to have been by Louvet; even Mme. Roland had this notion. It was in reality the work of Salle.[97] Instead of the earnest, serious refutation undertaken by Brissot, Salle used a very light touch, seeking to discredit his adversary by sarcasm and ridicule. He addresses him as "Monsieur le Chevalier de Saint-Just" and "Monsieur le ci-devant." The unprinted proofs, says Salle, seek to show that we are federalists and royalists, which seems to embarrass you no more than was the very Holy Inquisition embarrassed when it demonstrated to the damned *philosophes* that they were at once heretics, atheists and deists. "So you tell us, Monsieur le Chevalier, and we must believe you; for you realize that no one could conscientiously contradict a man who proves what he asserts like you by saying that he has left his proofs in the Committee of Public Safety." The defendants are in some perplexity to know who the king is for whom they have conspired; apparently they are in favor of Louis XVI, Orléans, Sr., Orléans, Jr., the son of Marie Antoinette, the Duke of York and King Roland. In similar vein Salle travesties the other charges of Saint-Just, concluding with a threat of imminent punishment at the hands of an aroused nation.

It seems difficult to deny that the attack shrivels into insignificance when confronted by the defense. Brissot, in particular, has proved his case, even though in a few instances he went too far. The truth is that the Girondins were not monarchist in 1793 and the charge was thoroughly disingenuous. It was easily demolished by bringing out discrepancies in fact and date as Brissot did. Probably it was because he realized the weakness of his argument from a legal standpoint that Saint-Just enveloped it in purposed obscurity. The vague, inconsistent statements, the innuendo were all intended to throw dust in his opponents' eyes. It is significant that most of his denunciations are in just this vein.

The fact is that the real case against the Girondins, as at a later date the real case against Danton, was purely political. These men must go, not because they were traitors or guilty of conspiracy. They had to go, partly because they were personal enemies of their accusers and partly because these latter conscientiously believed that the safety of the state required it. They must go, because they were guilty of inefficiency, of lax and careless government, of hesitation at a time when quick and vigorous decision was imperative, lest the republic perish. And in this sense the Mountain were probably right or at least sincere. The legal justification for their action was largely eyewash and they knew it, no doubt, as well as anyone. One could be more certain, if the times had not been so full of hysterical and groundless suspicion. The report is weak in facts, it was strong in effect, because the logic of events was on its side.

IX

RULING FRANCE

F THE guillotine and the Marseillaise symbolize the Revolution's savage fury against its foes within and without the land, if social legislation bears witness to its pity for its own children, the brain center which planned and coördinated these and all other activities when the great struggle had come to a white heat was the Committee of Public Safety. It is true that from 1789 to 1793, the Revolution's tendency was toward decentralization, until half of France made war on Paris in the interest of local home rule, and even the Mountain embodied its best notions of an ideal government in the weakly organized, ultrademocratic constitution already described. But facts could not be bent into support of theory and the new ship of state, built so carefully and launched so proudly with fluttering of bright banners and thunder of a multitude's acclamation, was deemed unseaworthy in the furious tempests that prevailed without ceasing, and never left port. Yet until the Revolution closed, men did not lose hope that some day she would put to sea.

Long before the constitution was even finished, however, it became clearly necessary to establish, if only for a short time, a stronger government than was afforded by the Provisional Executive Council. This Council was continued, but in a subordinate capacity. In addition, the Convention created two great bodies. One, the Committee of General Security, had charge of the political police; it began in October, 1792, and lasted through the Revolution, practically all of the time under control of the Mountain. The other, the Committee of General Defense, begun in January, 1793, was to conduct the war. Its membership was partly Girondin, partly Mountain, but it was a failure and yielded in April to the more compactly organized

90

Committee of Public Safety, controlled by the Dantonist wing of the Mountain. When "the Committees" are alluded to in Revolutionary parlance, Public Safety and General Security (lesser in importance) are meant.

How on May 30 Hérault, Ramel, Couthon, Saint-Just and Mathieu were added to the Committee of Public Safety as associate members for the purpose of producing a new constitutional draft has already been set forth. By June 5, these men had become tacitly accepted as full members of the Committee for all purposes. Saint-Just, Cambon, Berlier and Couthon were assigned to the first subcommittee, that on general correspondence.[98] This met "in the hall where the constitution was discussed" (a familiar spot for Saint-Just) and was instructed to open and register all dispatches and to make an analysis of all matters requiring prompt attention, for action by the full Committee that very day. Similar daily reports were required from the five other subcommittees. It was further decided on the fifteenth that all measures relative to the operations and needs of the army serving against the rebels be coordinated by a special subcommittee, consisting of Cambon, Delmas and Saint-Just.[99] The next day the Committee appointed Saint-Just and Cambon to draw up the report on the Girondins under arrest. On the seventeenth, the Committee proposed to the Convention that two of its members, Lindet and Saint-Just, together with two others, Lejeune and du Roy, be sent into the departments of the Eure and Somme to quiet the disaffection there; while the Convention was discussing the matter, a deputation came from the Eure pledging fidelity to the government and the proposal fell through. This was the first of seven missions for which Saint-Just was selected, though not all were carried out. June 18, more specific rules of procedure were adopted: the subcommittees were to meet every morning at six and to sit no later than two in the afternoon; at that hour the full Committee should assemble to discuss their reports; it must also meet at eight in the evening to consider matters of public safety; proposed decrees should be discussed only by the general Committee; six members might draw up propositions for Convention action, but to issue a Committee decree (*arrêté*) required two-thirds of the membership. Letters were read on the nineteenth from Vergniaud and Brissot urging an immediate report on their arrest; the report was fixed for the twenty-first, Saint-Just being placed in sole charge of it. Correspondence subsequently arriving relative to the whereabouts of escaped Girondin deputies was referred to him. As previously stated, the Committee listened to the report on the twenty-fourth and adopted it with some changes, July 2. Together with the rest of the Committee, he signed various decrees relating to the conduct of the war. The only other opportunity for more independent action came on July 9, when the Committee voted to propose to the Convention that the task of drawing up laws implementing the Constitution be intrusted to the members added on May 30. This was never carried out, for two days later the first Committee came to an end.

The important position held by Saint-Just during the brief forty days in which he was a member of this body is apparent from the foregoing summary of his activities. It is all the more remarkable in view of the fact that the Dantonists and the Center so completely dominated the Committee.

But the country had lost confidence in the leadership of these groups. Danton had failed in his effort to negotiate peace with the foreign powers. It was felt that the Committee's attitude was defeatist and lacking in resolution. The war was going badly; the government had not come to grips with the provincial rebellion; supply departments were honeycombed with graft; the army was inadequately provisioned and had lost its morale; discouragement and indecision reigned everywhere.[100] Led by Marat, the Left groups of the Mountain hammered the Committee daily in the press and in the clubs all through late June and early July. Bourdon de l'Oise and Chabot attacked the existing Committee at the Jacobins July 8 on the ground of its lack of energy. Both desired a practically complete change of membership, but Chabot would make exceptions.

Undoubtedly [he admitted] there are within it some men who would do well if they had good associates. We ought to leave there Jeanbon Saint-André, Saint-Just and Couthon, who have been proved and tested, whose patriotism and integrity are known by all France.

The remainder he wanted replaced by open ballot, for from a secret vote they might expect a Committee a hundred times worse than the first.[101] In consequence of all this, the Convention finally resolved to change the personnel of the Committee, which was done July 10, the ballot being viva voce. Jeanbon Saint-André and Barère received 192 votes, Gasparin 178, Couthon 176, Hérault Séchelles 175, Thuriot 155, Prieur de la Marne 142, Saint-Just 126 and Robert Lindet 100. Robespierre replaced Gasparin, July 27. Carnot and Prieur de la Côte d'Or were added August 14; Billaud-Varenne, Collot d'Herbois, Danton and Granet September 6, though the two last-named did not accept. Thuriot resigned September 20, leaving twelve who were reëlected monthly. The only change before the ninth Thermidor was the fall of Hérault, who was guillotined April 6, 1794, and not replaced.[102]

This was the second or great Committee of Public Safety, that band of determined men, who by herculean labor simultaneously carried through a Reign of Terror, conducted a successful war against half Europe, crushed two armed rebellions covering the larger part of France and found time for all manner of social and economic reconstruction. There were giants in those days. Nothing of the kind has since been seen except in contemporary Russia.

If the country had faced crises in January and April calling for centralized control, the situation was still more desperate in July. The second Committee came none too soon. Both in its powers and its policy the strong hand was soon apparent. The country had in effect given it the instruction *salus reipublicae suprema lex* and intrusted it with a fund of fifty millions to expend as it saw fit. By more and more drastic measures the Committee purged the civil administration and the army

93

of leaders suspected of lukewarm interest in the Revolution. Like Oliver Cromwell, it realized that a military force must be inspired by some sort of highly emotional idealism if it is to be daringly courageous; in place of royalist enthusiasm and aristocratic spirit, Cromwell found religious zeal an adequate substitute and created the Ironsides. The Committee utilized revolutionary fanaticism for a similar purpose and with similar success. The army that drove the invader finally out of France was made up of convinced republicans. There were henceforth to be no compromises with principle, no halfway measures; very simply and literally the alternative for all concerned with this great enterprise and particularly for those intrusted with leadership was to be victory or death.

The only opposition to this drastic policy was expressed by Thuriot, Lindet and Gasparin and sometimes by Barère, the skillful opportunist. Long after, when Jacobinism was out of favor, Barère tried to paint himself as quite out of touch with his colleagues of '93. "I was obliged to pass my best years in the Committee of Public Safety, which in my thought I often called 'the lion's den' because the National Convention in composing it had condemned me to live there close to Robespierre, Collot, Saint-Just, Couthon." [103] It is not apparent that those were his emotions at the time. For the rest, Gasparin lasted little more than a fortnight, while Thuriot was out less than a month later. Thuriot resigned, Barère tells us, because he was constantly at odds with Saint-Just and Robespierre over the violent measures which these two never ceased proposing.[104] Lindet had little interest in politics and Barère soon adapted himself to the new situation. The accession of the party chief, Robespierre himself, and of the two fanatical terrorists, Billaud-Varenne and the ex-actor Collot d'Herbois, decidedly stiffened the Committee's rigorism.[105]

The second Committee like its predecessor subdivided its work among its members, though our information on this point is less exact than that concerning the arrangements of the first Committee. By a resolution of September 23, 1793, the

Committee voted that each of its members should be attached to a department of work, but the departments are not indicated. It is believed that there were at least three bureaus, dealing respectively with correspondence, the execution of laws and "action." Saint-Just is said to have been intrusted particularly with constitutional legislation,[106] but the decrees signed by him fail to bear this statement out. His reports of October 10, 1793, and April 15, 1794, as well as the posthumous *Fragments* show, however, that his early interest in this field was a continuing one. From the internal evidence of signatures to decrees it has been deduced that Barère and (at first) Hérault specialized in diplomacy, Carnot, Saint-Just and Prieur de la Côte d'Or in army matters, Saint-André in the navy, Lindet in food and supplies, Billaud-Varenne and Collot d'Herbois in correspondence. Prieur de la Marne was usually on mission, Robespierre and Couthon signed very little, having a sort of roving interest in every field, particularly in affairs of politics and police. After referring to the paucity of Robespierre's signatures, the same authority declares that Saint-Just has left even fewer traces in writing or in the form of signatures, the only resolutions in his hand dealing with the army or with orders of imprisonment. That these statements are not entirely correct will appear from a detailed examination of the decrees themselves. There is reason to reject Carnot's classic division of the Committee into the "politicians" (Robespierre, Saint-Just, Couthon, Billaud-Varenne and Collot d'Herbois), responsible for the Reign of Terror, and the "workers" (the remaining members) occupied solely with the constructive labors of their bureaus. The signatures to political decrees indicate no such division and those who signed them knew what they were about.[107]

During the days when the republic seemed tottering, the Committee worked with feverish intensity. Members took turns at snatching a little sleep on mattresses spread on the floor of the meeting room, while the rest labored on. The belated wayfarer crossing the Seine at any hour of the night saw the lights gleaming from the lofty windows in their Louvre pavilion, while the city slept. More than 10,000 decrees poured from that famous green room; over 500 pieces of business had to be dealt with every day.[108]

Of this great mass of legislation we have not more than 394 decrees signed by Saint-Just. It must be remembered, however, that he was absent from the Committee, October 18–January 5 during the mission to Alsace; January 23–February 11, May 2–31, June 10–29 during the three missions to the North; a total of 151 days or five months out of the twelve (July 29, 1793–July 27, 1794) during which we have decrees bearing his signature as a member of the second Committee. Again, as the Committee's most brilliant speaker, he was constantly being intrusted with the preparation and delivery of important reports to the Convention. It is furthermore entirely probable that the list of decrees mentioned does not exhaust those in which he had a hand. Many decrees are unsigned by any of the Committee. The register usually gives a list of those present at each meeting, but these lists are extremely inaccurate. Frequently decrees are signed by members not mentioned as present, while conversely the attendance record sometimes includes those whom we know to have been elsewhere.[109] Nor is the inaccuracy confined to the roll call. The register contains no decrees, for example, on February 20 or July 2, yet decrees were passed on both dates and have been preserved.[110] But there is no doubt that the bulk of the Committee's ordinances bearing Saint-Just's signature are still extant and that what we have is sufficient to indicate the fields of legislation in which he had a major interest.

To most of these decrees several signatures are attached, making it difficult to detect the source of the idea therein expressed. A greater presumption of authorship may be made in the case of decrees signed by a single member. There are sixty-nine such decrees signed only by Saint-Just and often written in his own hand. Forty-seven of them are matters of police, eight deal with the army, five with public subsistence, five with appropriations, four are miscellaneous.

Twenty-two of the police decrees contain orders of arrest, one being for Saint-Just's boyhood acquaintance, the ex-count Lauraguais, who among other things had secured a judgment against the municipality of Manicamp for having cut a tree of liberty from his woods. The episode of Saint-Just cropping the fern beneath the count's château window comes irresistibly to mind (page 18). Of the twenty-five police decrees not concerned with arrests, eleven tend to centralize the administration of justice (five by removing prisoners or cases from the departments to Paris, six by ordering citizens to appear voluntarily or to be brought by local Paris committees of surveillance before the Committee of Public Safety for examination); five are orders of liberation (including "citizeness Brogui, schoolmistress at Blérancourt, district of Chauny, aged eighty, patriot arrested *malàpropos* by virtue of a decree of the representatives of the people, Saint-Just and Le Bas"). A decree is devoted to each of the following purposes: the dispatch of a representative to Nancy to purge it of suspects, the dispatch of another to the department of Mont-Blanc on the trail of counterfeiters, an investigation of crooked police agents, a report demanded on measures taken to unearth an assassin, prompt examination of a citizen under arrest, an investigation of a suspect, solitary confinement for a prisoner, the dismissal of a mayor for appropriating gifts made to the volunteers, the restoration of an acquitted citizen to his former office.

Each of the army decrees concerns a different subject: representatives Lacoste and Mallarmé must return at once to their posts with the Armies of the Moselle and the Rhine; two members of the commissary department are ordered to the front to make a complete inspection of stores and to report on abuses; an adjutant general, suspended by mistake, is restored to duty; a paymaster-general is dismissed; General Desjardins is to command the Army of the Ardennes and the right wing of the Army of the North under Pichegru, while General Charbonnier returns to Paris; the salaries of Gateau and Thuillier (boyhood friends of Saint-Just) are regulated while they are on mission; the Committee wants an interview with an officer temporarily in Paris; a workman named Henry Plaisant is to be intrusted with the first dispatch for the Army of the North to give him means for returning to his post with that army and is to be paid 300 livres for his services and postal expenses during the time that he was attached to the representative Saint-Just. In view of his own later Alsace mission, special interest attaches to the fact that it was he who on October 6 wrote the instructions for Lacoste and Mallarmé: they are invested with all power to requisition arms and National Guards from the surrounding departments; they are to dismiss and replace suspected generals and other agents and send them to Paris; army paymasters are to hold at their disposal such sums as the representatives shall deem necessary for public safety; all power is given them to save Landau and the Wissembourg lines, to arrest traitors, provision the armies, requisition superfluous clothing and blankets for the troops and buy arms and munitions. Within the month he was to use like sweeping powers himself.

All five of the decrees relative to public subsistence have to do with the provisioning of Paris. Three of them direct the immediate release of carts loaded with flour for the capital, detained at various points; one requires the national treasury to hold 3,000,000 livres at the city's disposal as a loan; one orders the mayor to give a daily report of the arrival of supplies and also to make an inventory of stores on hand.

Two of the five decrees on appropriations provide for the expenses of dispatch couriers, one fixes the salary of court stenographers at 2,000 livres, one sets aside 600 livres for the secretary of the representatives to the Army of the North, while the fifth gives 2,000 to an agent of the Committee.

Of the miscellaneous decrees, one suspends special taxes levied by representatives on mission in the departments, as interfering with the collection of regular taxes; one demands the name of a newspaper editor; a third appoints a new member of a Paris revolutionary committee; a fourth congratulates a rural district for its zeal in selling national lands and sending men to the army.

So much for the decrees signed by Saint-Just alone.

Considering now the total number of decrees bearing his signature, whether alone or with other members of the Committee, they fall into these groups: police, 132; military, 106; appropriations for other purposes, 30; public subsistence, 30; correspondence, 22; miscellaneous, 74. There is inevitably some overlapping.[111]

Of decrees dealing with police matters, 59 or less than half are orders of arrest. As will be observed from the table in Appendix III, about a sixth of these belong to the single month of March (explicable in part by the great political struggles against Hébertists and Dantonists) and one-half to July. The figures for July cover only the first twenty-five days, after which with one exception Saint-Just signed no more decrees. It must not be assumed that because in less than a month he signed more orders of arrest than during the whole preceding year, the youth had suddenly gone mad with blood lust. This was the so-called "Great Terror" for which Saint-Just was by no means solely responsible. The increase was also in large measure due to a new department of police, with which he was closely identified. But on the other hand the tremendous jump in the number of such decrees, whether signed by him or by others, was the chief factor in his party's fall. A third of the remaining 73 police decrees are orders of liberation; 14 are centralization measures. A written report is called for twice a day on the state of the prisons and the conduct of prisoners; a rural delegate to the Festival of Federation, having had his pocket picked, gets his fare paid home; articles needed for a prison hospital may be confiscated from the homes of *émigrés;* the public prosecutor is authorized to employ spies; the maximum wage is to be enforced against certain disgruntled woodworkers; search is to be made in Paris prisons for a prisoner who seems to have vanished—these are typical of the remainder. A decree of February 21, suppressing the Revolutionary Tribunal of Strasbourg, has some importance in connection with the Alsatian mission.

Of the decrees dealing with military matters, 88 relate to the army, 17 to the navy, one to both. The bulk of the former may be classified as follows: supplies, 30 (muskets, metal for cannon, saltpeter to be dug out of cellars, horses, fodder, grain, cattle, improved transport wagons, etc.); appointment of generals and lesser officers, 10; troop movements, 8; regular or special reports demanded, 8 (including a daily report from commanding generals and a detailed report of troop movements with tables and maps every decade); workmen, 5 (exempting coal miners, musket-makers and tanners from military service, while a previous decree exempting necessary farm laborers is repealed because of abuse). Among the more interesting of the others are the following: dismissal of a cruel hospital clerk who had wantonly kept sick and wounded men standing on pretext of making out hospital tickets; a courier service of thirty men established, as soon as one reaches an army with dispatches from the Committee, another is to leave the army with dispatches to the Committee; propaganda (the *Journal officiel* to be circulated among the troops); dismissal of the so-called revolutionary army, with incorporation of men from this force into the regular service; two hospices for slightly wounded and convalescent soldiers established at Paris; a secret decree levying a contribution of 60,000,000 in specie on Belgium and requiring 630 hostages from among the most wealthy, besides exacting 3,000 horses, 1,000 wagons and the disarming of all the inhabitants.

Naval decrees have to do with the hastening of ship construction and repairs; fleet movements; provision for an armed guard on Channel fishing boats; speeding up the delivery of supplies; the provisional suspension of sale of Danish and American prizes pending a report; an order that no special officers' quarters above the deck be included in the new frigates, etc. The curve of frequency in military decrees differs entirely from that of police measures. February and March are the two especially busy months, with April not far behind.

Most of the decrees granting appropriations authorize the payment of special agents; others repay damages, reimburse expenses or give rewards to various citizens. Two grants go to the band of the Paris National Guard for musical purposes (one of these sets aside 33,000 livres, for which the band must produce every month a symphony, a hymn or chorus, a military march, a rondeau or quickstep and at least one patriotic song, forming a volume of fifty or sixty pages, of which 550 copies must be printed for the Committee, to be distributed by it for use in civic festivals and the improvement of public spirit). In about half the cases, sums are definitely appropriated from the 50,-000,000 placed by the Convention at the Committee's disposal; in other cases, the national treasury or one of the ministries is ordered to pay the beneficiary. February and July are the important months.

Fourteen or nearly half of the decrees on public subsistence concern the provisioning of Paris. Couriers are sent to places where grain is available; two boatloads at Saint-Valéry-en-Somme are requisitioned; a sloop full of wheat, wrecked at the Rouen bridge, is to be salvaged; potatoes are to be planted in the Tuileries and Luxembourg gardens; Cambon is to audit the accounting of 31,000,000 advanced to the city at various times; Paris, being considered in a state of siege, is to be supplied at national expense. Four decrees concern purchasing agents in Switzerland or Germany; three approve contracts and arrangements made by the *Commission des subsistances;* two deal with requisitions (one in the newly conquered Palatinate); two with the provisioning of communes other than Paris; one each with the sale of wines seized in the Palatinate, with the rehabilitation of neglected coal mines, with the purchase of 50,000 stockfish, with the sending of an agent to investigate the destruction of potential supplies in the departments of Marne and Ardennes, and with a special exemption from law in favor of certain tanners. Most of these date from August and the following spring; there are none after April, 1794.

As for the Committee's twenty-two letters, the majority (twelve) relate to military affairs. They deal with such subjects as the transfer of recalcitrant officers; a general's complaint that his letters have not been answered; instructions regarding the siege and treatment of Lyons (in which the principle is given, *Parcere subjectis et debellare superbos*); a census of ironworkers; congratulations and rebukes to various representatives with the armies; a proclamation of victory; plans for an expedition to the Isle of Wight; a scaling-down of exorbitant bids for the construction of army caissons. Three deal with matters of police; three are orders to representatives on mission; two lay down principles of government for the guidance of those in public office, including among other things solicitude for the preservation of religious liberty.

The letters are addressed in seven cases to representatives with the armies, seven others are sent to representatives in the departments, three to the minister of war, two to the "constituted authorities," one to an army, one to the Paris sections, one to a national agent (a local official, replacing the old *procureur-syndic* in the districts and communes). The signatures are curious. Five [112] are signed by "the members of the Committee of Public Safety charged with the correspondence." In the first two these are Carnot, Saint-Just and Thuriot; in the next two Prieur de la Marne replaces Thuriot and in the last of the five Prieur yields in turn to Collot d'Herbois. One other letter is signed by Carnot, Saint-Just and Thuriot and one by Carnot, Collot and Saint-Just, though neither refers to the signers as especially charged with correspondence. Seven then may be taken as emanating from this subcommittee, to which Saint-Just seems to have belonged as in the days of the first Committee of Public Safety.[113] But two-thirds of all the letters bear other signatures; such important ones as those "to the constituted authorities" are signed by nine or ten members; others by five or six; some by only two, Saint-Just and Collot or Saint-Just and Lindet. Why the subcommittee was given so small a proportion of its assigned task to carry out, it is impossible to say; there is no apparent relation either to the subject matter of the correspondence or to the addressees.

It is naturally difficult to classify the miscellaneous decrees into compact groups. However, it appears that eighteen of these are questions of appointment. Twelve relate to changes in government buildings, e.g., the spoils of the churches to be moved from the workshops of the national printing office so that the latter may be extended; a great health institution with baths and mineral waters for soldiers and the poor to be established in the Pyrenees; a lighthouse to be built; marbles secured for paving the Pantheon; the wing joining the great and the small Luxembourg turned over to the committee on public instruction; lightning rods to be erected at once on the Meudon château; while two of the twelve encourage the fine arts, one by giving various halls of the Louvre to the Conservatory of the Museum of Art and by otherwise housing the artists then lodged in these rooms, the other by removing from the former Academy of Painting, Sculpture and Architecture the pictures, statues and bronzes on view there, returning them to their creators if still alive, and if not, submitting the objects to a jury to decide which were worthy of a place in the Museum and which should be excluded to be returned to the artist's family. Apparently the Committee had a poor opinion of the Academy's show. Six decrees are in the field of music and the stage (the Opera is requested to study the new work *Brutus,* with view to early production; a large orchestra, instrumental and vocal, is established for popular concerts under the auspices of the committee on public instruction, 50,000 livres being appropriated for a year's expenses; the National Institute of Music is authorized to add 240 stringed instruments and singers for the concert of July 14 and to consult an architect for necessary changes in seating the orchestra and lighting the amphitheater; the play entitled *The Thirteen Year Old Hero* is to be produced by the theater of the rue Favart for its educational value in developing republican virtues among the young; the decree is repealed which authorized the Opera to produce *La Journée du 10 Aout 1792, ou la Chute du Dernier de nos Tyrans,* a drama in four acts mixed with songs and declamation; 12,000 copies of patriotic songs and hymns are to be circulated in the army and navy). It is worthy of note that ten decrees signed by Saint-Just (the eight here mentioned and the two under appropriations) have to do with music and the fine arts. Seven of these were passed in June and July, 1794, when the Terror was at its height and just before the end. This would indicate in part the need of escape from horror and nervous tension into an ideal world of beauty. In this connection it is impossible to avoid reference to the decrees of June 24 and 25, not signed by Saint-Just, establishing an elaborate technique for selecting the artists best fitted to restore damaged paintings in the National Museum. It is, however, clear that music and the stage were largely used for propaganda purposes, as in contemporary Russia. Five decrees encourage foreign trade (the government helps citizens collect foreign drafts under certain circumstances, encourages Maltese trade and proposes a reciprocity agreement with the Bâle tanners). Two deal respectively with the modified flag, the organization of government in the Windward Islands, taxation questions and newspapers (one forbids any journal to use the words "Public Safety" in its title). Decrees are devoted to the following topics among others: transportation for the Committee's agents (six carriages to be always ready in the Tuileries stables); an immediate report from the excise on the quantity of sulphur on hand in trade and in the government stores and how to secure it; the ministry of marine to rescue, if possible, the British radicals, Muir, Palmer and Margarot on their way to exile; no interference with the people of Champs, Chauny district (Saint-Just's native heath) in their quarrel with the ex-curé; financial accounts of a representative's mission; harbor works at Dunkirk; preservation of the Herduis ironworks' water supply from being drained off by neighboring communes; levy of a pound of old rags on every citizen to replenish the diminishing supply of paper; a map for the Committee, showing the roads, rivers and canals of France; measures restoring relatively normal conditions at Commune-Affranchie (Lyons); proper delivery of mail addressed to the former Executive Council; slaughterhouses close to the city hospital and dangerous to the patients' health to be investigated; leave of absence for certain officials (one, his friend Gateau); finally, an enigmatic decree from the joint Committees of Public Safety and General Security, signed on 9 Thermidor, 2 A.M. by Barère, Saint-Just, Collot d'Herbois, Voulland, Louis du Bas-Rhin, Amar and Élie Lacoste summoning the commander of the mounted force to appear before them.

It is impossible to tell how far the signatures to decrees indicate a share in their composition. Certain types of decree would probably be referred for scrutiny to those who had specialized in that general field, though no doubt in many cases and in view of the need for haste, decrees were signed by any who happened to be present.

No one can make such a study of even a relatively small number of the Committee's acts without being impressed by its versatility and prodigious energy, its stout-hearted courage, its quick-fire insistence on immediate action where speed was possible and desirable, coupled with its willingness to wait patiently for results when slow education was the only path of progress. Nor can one fail to note the common sense of most of the decisions and the surprising humanity of many. These men evidently took their duties seriously and tried to govern well. In their effort and its spirit, Saint-Just had his full share.[114]

X

THE GOVERNMENT SHALL BE REVOLUTIONARY

ONSTITUTIONS do not win battles. Although the new charter of liberties took the heart out of the department rebellion as a national affair, though the risings in Normandy and the Gironde were a flash in the pan and Charlotte Corday's knife dealt her own cause a deadly blow, yet the great cities of the Rhone remained defiant that summer of 1793. The Vendée was in flames. July saw Mayence in the East, Valenciennes and Condé in the North capitulate to the Austrians. The border fortresses were in the enemy's hands.

When the delegates of the primary assemblies poured into Paris from all over France to commemorate the first anniversary of August 10 by a great Festival of Unity, at which the result of the nation's referendum on the constitution should be joyfully proclaimed, public excitement ran high. The undercurrent of alarm was overlaid by a powerful wave of patriotism and revolutionary determination. Men saw red; their furious anger at betrayal made it inevitable that blood would flow. Here the Terror in its intensive form began. Here too men began to realize that they could not throw aside the iron weapon of dictatorship then in their hands, while the country remained in peril. The moment for ushering in that idyllic harmony, which they would one day enjoy under the gentle sway of the new constitution, must be regretfully postponed. Danton's friends, it is true, believing in a broad-based republican unity, urged that the Convention had now fulfilled its mandate and should dissolve in favor of a constitutional Legislative Assembly. For the time being they carried the Convention. But Robespierre in a fighting speech at the Jacobins, the evening of August 11, denounced the plan as certain to destroy the republic. In that opinion the provincial delegates generally concurred. This becomes less surprising when one remembers that they were Mountain men, and that the very fact of their living in Girondist territory would make them all the more partisan. Though the Convention did not reverse its decree, this powerful opposition prevented its being carried out and the question remained in abeyance for the next two months.

During August and September a series of drastic measures, of which the most significant were military conscription, the Law of Suspects, establishment of the maximum and of a reorganized Revolutionary Tribunal centralized authority enormously. The military situation mended slowly and by the end of October the worst of the crisis had passed. The fall of Lyons took the heart out of the Girondin revolt; Wattignies checked the Austrian menace and the Vendéans were badly beaten. But before that had taken place, the Committee of Public Safety resolved to intrench itself definitely as long as there was any doubt about the outcome. It seemed clear that such gains as had been made were due to concentration of power in the hands of the government and to the new sources of energy tapped by the Terror. It would be an error to relax too soon.

Late in September, a group of alarmists attacked the government's policy and there was talk of changing the Committee's personnel, but another vigorous speech by Robespierre enabled it to weather the storm and to secure a vote of confidence. In its name, Saint-Just on October 10 read the decisive "Report on the necessity of declaring the government revolutionary until the peace," one of the landmarks in the history of the First Republic. It was a veritable jeremiad. In terse and biting terms the speaker made plain the evils of the existing situation and the drastic remedy which they required.

The core of the trouble he found in the fact that while the laws were revolutionary, those whose duty it was to execute them were not. With equal clarity he set forth the cure, laying bare in a sentence the whole philosophy of terrorism.

It is time to announce a truth which must never in future leave the minds of those who govern: the republic will be established only when the sovereign will shall grip and hold the monarchist minority and rule over it by right of conquest.

What follows develops these two points, the diagnosis and the cure.

The Committee had carefully estimated the causes of their present misfortunes, he said; it found them in the weakness with which decrees were executed, the lack of economy in administration, the instability of public policy and the caprices of passion which sought to twist the government from its fixed path. Punishment must fall not only on traitors, but on the indifferent as well. Had there been no plots, it would be fine to rule by maxims of peace and natural justice, but between the people and its enemies there is nothing in common but the sword. They must be governed by iron who cannot be governed by justice.

Saint-Just then began to give a bill of particulars. The generals were out of sympathy with the nation because they were not the nation's choice; they lacked the respect of their soldiers, which was prejudicial to discipline; almost to a man they were royalist, secretly dreaming of treason. In like manner, the public service was shot through with treachery. Owing to the method of appointment in vogue, whereby six ministers selected their subordinates and these in turn filled the places below them, it was possible for the enemies of France to gain control of the whole administration in three months. It was a waste of energy to make laws if they were not going to be carried out because the republic's enemies were in its very government. Within six months the hospital administration had supplied grain to the Vendéan rebels, he asserted. Thirdly, rich monopolists and crooked contractors were sources of evil; the three billions they had stolen were rotting the republic, recruiting for the enemy, corrupting the generals, seducing the judges. These billions were competing with the state in all its purchases, with the people in the market place, the merchant at his counter. Saint-Just rarely showed a trace of humor. But in his denunciation of those who, supposed to enforce laws against grafting were themselves grafters, a grim smile may have flickered across his face as he drew the classic parallel, "So the consuls, Papius and Poppaeus, both bachelors, made laws against celibacy." Patriotism, he went on glumly enough, had become just a matter of lip service.

In such a situation, and with agriculture and commerce at a standstill, it was impossible to establish the constitution, he argued; it would become the guarantee for attacks on liberty, since it lacked the force to repress them. On the other hand the utmost rapidity of movement was necessary, for the republic had 1,200,000 men to feed, rebels to conquer, harbors to be fortified, ships to be built, the treasury to be filled, Paris provisioned, armies rallied—there must be activity everywhere.

Remembering that just a week later Saint-Just was sent on his famous mission to the Army of the Rhine, his views on the duties of such an office have special interest.

Nor is it unimportant that the representatives of the people to the armies be severely warned of their duties; there they must be fathers and friends to the soldier; they should sleep in the tents; they should be present at military exercises; they should not be on terms of familiarity with the generals, so that the soldier may have more confidence in their justice and impartiality when he approaches them; the soldier should find them day and night ready to hear him; the representatives should eat alone; they should be frugal, remembering that they are answerable for the public safety and that the lasting fall of kings is preferable to a transitory self-indulgence.

Those who make revolutions in the world, those who wish to do good can sleep only in the tomb.

The people's representatives in the camps ought to live there like Hannibal before he reached Capua, and like Mithridates they should know, if I may so say, all the soldiers by name; they must follow up every injustice, every abuse, for great vices have crept into our army discipline: battalions of the army of the Rhine have been seen begging for alms in the markets: a free people is humiliated by such indignities; they are dying of hunger, they who respected the spoils of Belgium!

Every one of these injunctions Saint-Just put into practice during his own missions.

His study of the military problem was not limited to the functions of a representative. He had definite ideas on the theory and practice of warfare. The generals seemed to him mainly imbecile, the officers lax and lazy, not studious of the art of war, debauched, absent at drill and fight, commanding haughtily and hence weakly. The veteran laughed in his sleeve at the stupidity of his commanders—reason enough for defeat. On the side of theory, Saint-Just laid down the rule that each people must have its own style of fighting. Greece had the phalanx, Rome the legion; so the French nation should develop a characteristic method, copying neither its enemies nor the old school of the monarchy. That method was indicated by the impetuous energy, the passion for liberty of the French people contrasted with the slow coldness of its foes; the French military system should be a vigorous offensive [*l'ordre du choc*].

In like manner, he pointed out, the military administration was in sad need of reform. There were not enough cannon, nor horses to pull them; even the fodder of what horses there were was stolen. It was not enough that the government be severe with aristocrats, it must be equally so with those who robbed the soldier and squandered public moneys.

Finally Saint-Just put his finger on a characteristic vice of French bureaucracy. The ministry was a world of paper, he lamented. In Rome and Egypt they thought much and wrote little. Verbose correspondence and wordy orders were a mark of inertia; real government was laconic. Now there was as much red tape as in the old régime; the expense of it was terrific and nothing accomplished. "The demon of writing makes war on us."

He concluded by a rapid summary of the evils to be overcome: aristocracy, avarice, inertia, graft, bad technique. To combat them he proposed in the Committee's name a decree commencing with the famous phrase, "The provisional government of France is revolutionary until the peace," establishing the authority of the Committee of Public Safety and its responsibility to the Convention, arranging for food requisitions, for an armed force to function against counter-revolutionists, for a financial investigation of all who had handled public moneys since the Revolution began and an accounting of their fortune.

The report was ordered printed and the proposed decree was adopted by the Convention. Never had Saint-Just spoken more trenchantly. Making all allowance for the one-sided assumption that all parties but his own were corrupt and incapable, that patriotism was a monopoly of the Mountain and that conditions were as bad as they possibly could be, it is nevertheless true that the evils he depicted were real and called for drastic treatment. The utmost alertness and energy were needed to pull the republic through. These qualities were possessed by the Mountain to a superlative degree and by no member of the Mountain more than by Saint-Just. The sort of government set up in this decree and elaborated by subsequent measures, culminating in that of December 4, 1793 (14 Frimaire, year II), put into their hands just the keen and powerful machinery necessary. If the Constitution of 1793 had been put into operation at this time, it is hard to see what could have prevented foreign armies from marching through the streets of Paris and restoring the Bourbons twenty years before they did.

One other question of policy in time of war brought Saint-Just to his feet again six days later. On this occasion it was not so pivotal a decision, but it had its importance.

It all began with the reading by Barère, October 9, of letters giving news of the armies. One written by a certain Odet from Marseilles reported the hanging of Beauvais-Préau, representative of the people, and of the former mayor of Toulon by the English in that city. Odet's reaction to this war-time atrocity was typical of a psychology that always recurs under similar circumstances. If he could, he would with his own hands tear out the heart of the last Englishman. They respect nothing, these ferocious English.[115] Reprisals were at once resolved upon.

Put in shape by Robespierre and Fabre d'Eglantine, they called for the arrest of all British subjects in France except workmen employed for the past six months and children under twelve in French schools. For the Committee, Barère then proposed to prohibit importation of all British goods. These decrees were immediately adopted. The following day they were reconsidered and fused into a single decree, without changing their essential purport. A petition of protest from English sympathizers with the Revolution, resident in Paris, went unheeded.

A deputy from Verdun, named Pons, suggested on the thirteenth that since the Austrian, Prussian and Dutch satellites were no less barbarous than the English, it was open to question whether they should be allowed different treatment. He demanded that they should be included in this measure or that the Committee should explain the reason for the distinction. The proposition was referred to the Committee.

The government's reply was made by Saint-Just in his "Report on the law against the English," October 16. His argument was briefly as follows. The more people the law seeks to terrify, the fewer it actually succeeds in terrifying. The Committee's original proposal was to prohibit English goods in the interest of French industry. The idea of arresting the English was added from the floor, but the Committee accepted it. The reason for the embargo was because England sent France only finished manufactured articles. This enriched the English and helped them to make war on France, while their trade competition depressed French manufactures and served to depreciate French currency. It would be hurtful to France, however, to extend the embargo to other countries, which sent raw materials, leather, metals, wood, necessary for French industry. As for the arrests, they were directed against the plotters and spies of the English government, not against the English people as such. Their schemes were endless, only recently English corsairs flying the tricolor had seized American vessels to alienate France's last friends. But despite the trickery of Pitt, "a day of revolution among us overthrows his vast projects, as the

traveler's foot destroys the long efforts of a laborious insect."
It was a silly idea to think that this law would make the war
popular in England and hence more dangerous. It was an insult
to the English nation to identify it with London's merchants or
the British court. If that people was worthy of liberty, this
measure would help it to break its chains.

Our Carthage is the London court, not England. . . . Let England
awake; we are its friends to help it free itself from its kings.

The Committee was sorry it could not make exceptions from
arrest even in favor of Englishmen long resident in France.
Who could answer for an Englishman when so many Frenchmen themselves conspired against their country? There was no
reason why the detention of foreigners should deprive them of
anything except the right to correspond with their country and
do harm to us. They should be kindly treated, for this was a
measure of precaution, not of resentment. "The law of detention may well be extended to all foreigners, but not the law
prohibiting all merchandise, for the reason I have developed."

It is interesting to note that the Rousseauist in Saint-Just out-
weighs the terrorist at this point. Foreign women who had married good citizens should certainly be exempt from the decree,
he insisted. "He who does not believe in Nature cannot love his
country." A policy so suspicious that it looks at everything
through fear rather than discernment deceives itself. "Mothers
have no country but that of their children." As for reprisals
against atrocities, they must be of a military nature. The Committee felt that the best reprisal against Austria would be to
place the scaffold's infamy in its family and to order the republic's soldiers to use the bayonet when they charged.

The Convention adopted the brief decree proposed by him
for the Committee.

There was a good deal of customary war-time psychology
about Saint-Just's report which does not stand up under criticism. The gullible acceptance of atrocity-stories, the idea that
Pitt and the English government were peculiarly unfair in their

methods of fighting, the effort to appeal to the English people over the heads of their authorities, the suspicion with which every Englishman was viewed because of his birth—they seem childish enough. But they were not confined to Saint-Just's thinking. So did the Committee think; so did by far the greatest part of France think; so indeed does every nation think of its enemies in war time. Outside of this the report seems well-considered. The light detention of all foreigners at a time when there must have been many spies about does not seem unduly excessive under the circumstances, in view of the large anti-republican element in France itself. The proposed distinction between English trade and that of other countries is clearly motivated. It was the core of the Committee's report; it was conceived from the standpoint of public welfare; it lifts the measure out of the realm of petty malice and war hysteria into the larger dignity of sound policy.

XI
PHILIPPE AND HENRIETTE

MAN'S public words and deeds are less than half his life. The key to them lies concealed in his motives and ambitions, in the intellectual and emotional self he has built up within him. This inner life is conditioned of course by all the influences which surround him and by none more deeply than by his intimate friends and associates. Two figures from the group that pressed closest about him were to play a large part in the next period of Saint-Just's short career. That it was a large part is certain, but just how large is far from clear, for his lips were pressed tightly together in matters that involved his heart. So far as he is concerned the sanctuary remains inviolate; personal letters of his are few and in none is there any word of his best friend or of the woman he loved. Whatever he may have written to either has disappeared. We are comparatively well-informed in regard to the man who played Jonathan to Saint-Just's David, the gentler foil of the more aggressive nature. He was a revolutionary figure of some importance in his own right and we fortunately possess part of his correspondence. The woman, who was his sister, remains a shadow.

Philippe Le Bas came from Robespierre's province. He was two years older than Saint-Just and like him studied law. He was a hard, conscientious worker and his health often suffered in consequence. He seemed to feel responsible for the livelihood of his dozen brothers and sisters and for the happiness of his old father. Though he was received as *avocat au Parlement de Paris* and was presently occupied in an important suit dealing with the affairs of the Prince de Bergues, he gave up these brilliant prospects in the spring of 1790 at his father's request to practice law in his home town, Saint-Pol. "Nothing will hold me back," he wrote; "I can assure you that I will gladly live in a country which I admit has in itself no attraction for me, but which will grow beautiful in my eyes when I know that my presence there is necessary for your happiness." [116] Le Bas was always subordinating himself to somebody or some cause which countered his own desires. The attractive thing about him was that he usually did it with unselfish cheerfulness. The Revolution saved him from provincial obscurity. His appointment to the central administration of the department of Pas-de-Calais in December, 1791, took him to Arras where perhaps he met Robespierre, linked with whom Le Bas and Saint-Just were destined to soar far aloft and to crash when he fell.

When the Convention met, Le Bas went to Paris as a representative of his department. With characteristic modesty he took little part in the debates, though busy enough with committee work and behind the scenes. His letters home give a running commentary on the news of the day. He felt that there was no point in his talking in the presence of so many with greater talent; the important thing was to do well what one had to do, to listen carefully as a foundation for straight thinking and to speak only when one caught sight of some truth which no one else noticed. Personal glory was of no consequence, but only the safety of the republic.[117] He was elected to a number of committees. Prior to the Alsace mission, he spoke but three times and then briefly.[118] Rather surprisingly he defended the September massacres as necessary to insure the success of August 10; though the number of victims was shocking, he agreed, nearly all would have been guillotined anyway. He voted for the king's death without appeal or delay. He approved of Marat. In public affairs he was clearly radical.

As early as February 19, 1793, Le Bas commenced to define his party position more narrowly. Feuillantism and false moderation are no longer the order of the day, he assures his father. A constitution has appeared; he will send it along. Le Bas thinks that it is a stillborn child, although it is the product of those Brissotins who have been running the Convention so

116

long [obviously Condorcet's draft]. One can tell at a glance that it carries democratic principles to extravagance and that nothing is more calculated to make republicanism hated. Perhaps those who made it wanted to make the Jacobins look like Feuillants, he muses. In the light of subsequent events, this first instinctive reaction of Le Bas has peculiar interest. The next letter [119] is undated, but precedes one of April 2. Le Bas says:

Already almost all the sections have accepted the constitution. The rest will follow today.—The departments will without doubt follow so fine an example and will share the patriotic enthusiasm which at this moment animates the Parisians.

This reversal of attitude can only be explained on the supposition that the letter has been wrongly placed and refers to the Mountain constitution of June.

The treason of Dumouriez, the arrest of Marat and the struggle between Girondins and Mountain during April receive comment in this correspondence, though there are unfortunately no letters in the collection for May or June. He fell in line with his party in the expulsion and arrest of the Girondin leaders, though apparently with reluctance. On May 28, for example, when the question before the Convention was "Shall the decree dissolving the Committee of Twelve be repealed, yes or no?" Le Bas was among the 146 who abstained from voting. Saint-Just voted "nay," a straight Mountain vote. Le Bas, though clearly enough a Mountain man, may have hesitated out of chivalry to deprive his opponents of this committee, which was their strongest weapon.

During that spring or early summer, Robespierre introduced his friend to the Duplay family in whose home he lived. From that time on Le Bas joined the domestic group, with whom Robespierre spent as many evenings as he could. Sometimes there was music; Le Bas sang Italian songs very pleasantly, while Buonarroti accompanied on the piano. Sometimes there were readings from Racine; each took a part and no one gave his lines with more spirit than Robespierre or Le Bas.[120] It was not unnatural that as one result of these evenings, Robespierre became engaged to the older Duplay girl, Éléonore, and Le Bas to her sister, Elisabeth. The date for the younger couple's wedding had already been set when the Convention abruptly sent Le Bas on mission to the Army of the North.

For this mission, which took the first three weeks of August, the Convention on August 1, 1793, set apart Prieur de la Marne, Saint-André and Le Bas, instructing them to go at once to the Armies of the North, the Ardennes, the Moselle and the Rhine to advise with the generals on all measures made necessary by present circumstances. These instructions were modified the following day when Couthon, representing the Committee of Public Safety, proposed to send Duquesnoy and Le Bas at once to the Army of the North to correspond thence with the Committee and to take measures required by the republic's interests. This decree was forthwith passed by the Convention. That its instructions were carried out is proved by a proclamation to the army officers of which two versions are extant, one in the hand of Duquesnoy and the other in that of Le Bas and also by references to Duquesnoy as his companion in two of Le Bas's letters.[121] His letters to Elisabeth contain a few details of his activity as representative, which was of the usual type. He and Duquesnoy had just arrested two generals and sent officers before the Revolutionary Tribunal; they did not cease taking every day the measures of prudence and severity called for by the circumstances. They were constantly on the move, inspecting the situation at critical points. But the most vivid impression conveyed by these letters is the agony of separation and his determination to make a speedy end of it.

I hope that my stay in this country will not be long. You must not doubt my eagerness to rejoin you and to put the seal to a union on which hinges the happiness of my life. Be very careful of your health. A thousand greetings to the whole family: tell Robespierre that though I am enraged at him, I am one of his best friends. I embrace you.

In successive letters he complains that any firm deputy with Duquesnoy's help would answer Robespierre's purpose for this mission as well as he and asks her to tell Robespierre this, as well as the fact that his health could not stand this fatiguing life much longer. He writes from Hazebrouck, August 16. She has spoken of the garden and asked if he remembered it.

Could I forget it, my dear Elisabeth? Oh, no! Every spot where I have been able to talk freely with you, to express my tenderness and to hear you say that you loved me, my imagination sees always and finds rest there. When we are in our carriage and my tired colleague stops talking or falls asleep, I think of you; if I sleep too, I still think of you. Every other idea, when public affairs do not occupy me, is an intrusion. Duquesnoy has become dearer to me, since he has questioned me about you and so given me an opportunity to depict my love. My dear Elisabeth, oh you whom I had to abandon at the moment when I thought to unite myself with you forever, you whom I had to leave to undertake a painful and sad journey, when shall I see you again? Now that my presence here is no longer nearly so necessary, will not Couthon have enough regard for his young colleague, will not Robespierre consider that I have done enough, to try to shorten the term of my sacrifice? . . . If in a week at latest I am not recalled, it is certain that I will find some way of going to Paris and once there, they will have to decide to replace me. Everybody in his turn. . . . Do not fail to remember me to citizeness Chalabre, to Calandini, to Robespierre, whom I would hate, if I could hate so good a patriot.

He was too impatient to wait the week he had set himself. He writes Elisabeth from Cassel, August 19, that the letters he has received from her have hastened his decision. Since he has not been recalled, he proposes in concert with Duquesnoy to issue an *arrêté* which will take him to Paris, where he counts on arriving at the end of the week. He bids her make ready for their marriage, since after a brief interval he may have to come back. But at least they would arrange it so that they would no longer need to be so far from each other.

This episode gives us our best insight into the man's character. He was molded of softer clay than Saint-Just. Separation from Elisabeth was so keen a torture to him that he could not stand it long. He did indeed subordinate his wishes to his duty for a while, as he had often done before, but in this case for the first and perhaps for the last time he rebelled in the end and asserted himself even in the face of Robespierre. There was determination and courage in Le Bas, for all his gentleness. If he had not been in the charmed circle of those who ruled, it might have gone hard with him. But he suffered no punishment and he did not have to return to the mission.

Recognition that Le Bas had definitely arrived came in the following month with his election, September 14, to one of the two great committees in whose hands lay France. His colleagues on the Committee of General Security, all Mountain men and of rather second-rate ability, though ferociously terroristic, were Vadier, Panis, Boucher Saint-Sauveur, David, Guffroy, Lavicomterie, Amar, Rühl, Le Bon, Voulland and Moyse Bayle. This list was drawn up by the Committee of Public Safety and elected by the Convention. Saint-Just thus had a hand in his friend's promotion.[122] A poorer choice for such a Committee than Le Bas cannot be imagined, unless he was expected to act as a brake on his more violent associates. However, he seems to have done little work in its ranks, for he was sent to Alsace with Saint-Just in the following month and was his colleague on the later missions to the North. All this took up the rest of the fall, half the winter and a month or more in the spring of the next year. After he returned he was appointed in June, 1794, to the headship of the École de Mars. A month later came Thermidor.

That Le Bas was associated with Saint-Just on mission with the definite purpose of checking his fiery colleague's ardor has been often asserted, but it seems improbable. There is the story, for example, of the cavalryman Deschamps who lost his horse in a battle during which he saved the life of General Meyer. He refused to go to the rear for a remount, not wishing to leave the battle line for a single day and appealed to the representatives. Saint-Just to maintain discipline sent a formal written order upholding the colonel's command. Deschamps in a rage broke out in invectives and tore up the order. Saint-Just, furious, would have him shot on the spot, but Le Bas calmed his colleague with the remark that the soldier's fault was due to an excess of patriotism and should be rewarded rather than punished. Saint-Just yielded; Deschamps won his point and Le Bas, clapping him on the shoulder, declared: "Go, my brave fellow, may the republic count many soldiers like you." [123] The apocryphal nature of this tale seems obvious. Saint-Just's reported *mot* may be an equally apocryphal make-weight. During the lively debates between the generals and the two representatives at Strasbourg, Le Bas became overexcited, whereupon Saint-Just intervened with the remark, "Le Bas, calm yourself, it is the phlegmatic who rule" (*l'empire est au flegmatique*).[124] The fact is that they were dispatched to the two most important fronts when these fronts were seriously threatened and had need of leaders endowed with the utmost courage, energy and intelligence. These men were no doubt selected because they were Robespierre's intimate friends, in whom he reposed absolute confidence.

The letters to Elisabeth during this mission to Alsace touch on public matters, but are still more concerned with their personal affairs. They had been married in August or September and the renewed separation was painful. Le Bas is always hopeful that the mission will soon be finished, though there is no more talk of his being relieved by someone else. He saw clearly that this was no routine assignment for which anyone would do and he repressed his personal impulses accordingly.

In most of his letters there now begins to be mention of Henriette, his sister. While not of remarkable beauty, she was quite pretty and had gained the affection of Saint-Just. A marriage had been arranged to the satisfaction of the two families, but was postponed to a more convenient season. The couple were engaged when Saint-Just left for Alsace.[125]

Elisabeth had become pregnant in the first month of their marriage and Henriette stayed with her as her companion. From Strasbourg, in his first letter (fourth day, second month,

October 25) Le Bas wrote anxiously about his young wife's health and the hardship of their separation, comforting himself with the reflection that Henriette would surely do her utmost to make it less painful, thus gaining a new title to his attachment. Five days later he is all distress because no letters have come. Is she ill? Why does not Henriette write? If she could see his heart, she would groan over his suffering. Two days more and the letters came, one from her and one from Henriette.

. . . You do well to amuse yourself. I thank Henriette for the trouble she takes to keep you occupied and I am not astonished that she does it as much out of kindness for me, as because of the attachment you have inspired in her. You do not tell me if you are established in our new lodgings. . . . I am very well satisfied with Saint-Just; he has talents which I admire and excellent qualities. He sends you his compliments. I do not write separately to Henriette, she will read this letter. Love her as much as she deserves. . . . A thousand greetings to the whole family; embrace them all for me, Robespierre of course with the rest.

Eleven days later (22 Brumaire) he concludes a letter to Elisabeth, "Saint-Just sends you his compliments; he hopes to appease you." Why she needed appeasing, no one can tell.[126] In none of the letters is there any message from Saint-Just to Henriette nor any reference to their relations. On the 6 Frimaire (November 26) Le Bas wrote that he was only waiting for the news of a decisive success in order to leave with Saint-Just, who was equally impatient to see Paris again. Whether he was impatient to see Henriette, Le Bas does not state, which seems strange in view of the intimate nature of the correspondence.

The most charming of all these letters is the one from Saverne on 8 Frimaire.

To my dear wife.
I profit, my dear Elisabeth, of a moment of leisure to talk a little with the one who is dearer to me than life. How many times have I not already longed to see you again! With what displeasure do I

not see the moment of my return to Paris delayed! The region where I am is superb. Nowhere have I seen nature more beautiful, more majestic; there is a chain of lofty mountains, a variety of sites which charm the eyes and the heart. We went this morning, Saint-Just and I, to visit one of the highest mountains, on whose summit is an old ruined fort placed on an immense rock. As we gazed on all the surrounding country, we both fell under its spell [*nous éprouvames tous les deux . . . un sentiment délicieux*]. It is the first day that we have had any relaxation. But as for me, something was lacking: I would have wished to be at your side, to share with you the emotion which I felt, and you are more than a hundred leagues from me! This idea has already saddened me many times to the bottom of my soul and certainly I need all the devotion of which true patriotism is capable to endure so cruel a privation as mine. There is hardly an instant even in the midst of the most serious tasks, that I do not think of you, but one must submit to necessity. The worst is over. Soon I shall be rewarded for so painful a sacrifice. A few days more and I hope to see my Elisabeth for a long time; I hope to increase the pleasure of our reunion by the news of a decisive advantage over our enemies. Saint-Just and I do not cease taking the measures necessary to assure it as quickly as possible; we run about all day long and we exercise the most continuous surveillance. At the moment when he least expects it, such and such a general sees us come and demand an account of his conduct. We are nearing Landau; soon without doubt it will be delivered: that is the end of our mission, everything invites us to hasten it. Saint-Just is almost as eager as I to see Paris again. I have promised him a dinner from your hand. I am delighted that you are not angry at him; he is an excellent man; I love and esteem him more and more every day. The Republic has no more ardent, no more intelligent defender. The most perfect accord, the most constant harmony have reigned between us. What makes him still dearer to me is that he talks to me often about you and consoles me as much as he can. He attaches great value to our friendship, it seems to me, and from time to time he says things to me which flow from a kind heart [*d'un bien bon cœur*].

Adieu, dear friend. I am going to write a few lines to Henriette. I presume that you still love each other well. What a charming trio we will make while we wait for the group to become more numerous! For God's sake take good care of your health. Adieu, my dear wife, receive the assurance of the tender and invariable attachment of your faithful

Le Bas.

P.S. Our courier is still with us; he charges me to send you his compliments. We are very fond of him, he is a brave fellow. A thousand embraces to the family and our common friends.

Soon after, the two representatives had their long-awaited chance to return to Paris, but in a few days they were on the road back again. Elisabeth begged so hard to be taken along that she had her way and Henriette came too. As their carriage jolted along toward the southeast, Saint-Just whiled away the tedium of the journey by reading aloud from Molière, a copy of whose plays was always with him. Years after, when she had become an old lady of eighty, Elisabeth still remembered how she suffered on that journey and how kind and thoughtful Saint-Just was.[127] The two women were installed at headquarters in Saverne, while the men set out for Strasbourg on their way to the front. On leaving, Saint-Just warned them never to interfere in any of the severe punishments which Le Bas and he might find cause to inflict or they would be sent back forthwith to Paris. One morning, however, Elisabeth awoke to find kneeling at the foot of her bed a woman in black with three little children. She implored pardon for her husband. Warning or no warning, Elisabeth could not resist the appeal and when her Philippe returned she interceded with him, receiving only a gentle reprimand and a promise that he would do his best when they reached Paris. So runs the tale, whether it be true or not.[128]

The two representatives returned to Paris early in January, 1794, only to be again dispatched a fortnight later, this time to the Northern Army. During the three weeks of this mission, Elisabeth stayed with her husband's father at Frévent, not far away. Two brief statements suggest that personal relations were as yet unchanged. From Avesnes, Philippe writes to Elisabeth, 13 Pluviôse (February 1), "Saint-Just is well; when we are in difficulties, our good friendship helps us to endure them better." Five days later from Arras, he announces that he expects to reach Frévent in five or six days, which is earlier than he had thought possible. "Prepare all your affairs with Henriette for it may be that we shall return at once to Paris. Saint-Just is well." Yet one cannot escape the curt reference to his friend and the complete absence of any link between his name and Henriette's.

It was not until the end of April that the two men were again sent on mission together, once more to the North. Not long before, however, the family situation had altered definitely for the worse. There are two different versions of the break which now ensued between Saint-Just and Henriette. According to one, he had no more than a platonic affection for her, being really attached to his clandestine mistress, Mme. Thorin. Somewhat inconsistently the writer responsible for this theory goes on to say that Henriette's refusals made Saint-Just desperate and drove him to leave Paris in April, 1794. This unrequited passion, according to Fleury, had a powerful influence on the fate of France, presumably by making him callous to suffering. But Mme. Thorin was not his mistress in Paris. This fact together with inherent improbabilities discredits this version. According to the other account, it was Saint-Just who jilted Henriette and for the most trivial reason. He caught her one day taking snuff, a habit which he could not endure and the engagement was broken.[129] It seems probable from the silence already noticed in Le Bas's letters that the couple were never very ardently attached and if the snuff story is true, it was doubtless merely the pretext for ending a relation which had lost its interest.

The tension between the two men which this break naturally produced is reflected in the remainder of Philippe's correspondence with Elisabeth. From Noyon, he wrote, 13 Floréal (May 2):

We reached here yesterday. Saint-Just and Thuilliers [sic] have left us, the one to visit his mother, the other his wife, who live not far from Noyon. They return this morning and we expect all to go today to Réunion-sur-Oise. . . . We are at present very good friends, Saint-Just and I; there has been no question of anything. We at once acted together as usual. Gateau and Thuilliers [sic] have seemed very much pleased at this good harmony; they augur well of it and we too. . . . Advise Henriette to stop being so sad; but it is possible that a more powerful voice than mine has spoken. So much the better. A thousand greetings to the whole family and to our good brother Robespierre.

This hopefulness, with the apparent suggestion that the quarrel might be patched up, did not last. The next three letters are silent on the subject, though his sister is mentioned in two of them. On 25 Floréal, "a few leagues from Maubeuge," he writes:

My position is not agreeable; domestic griefs mingle with the hardships inseparable from my mission. That undermines my existence. Again, if I were reassured about you! Come, come, I never had need of more courage. May I be the unhappiest of men, provided only the Republic triumphs! . . . A thousand greetings to Henriette. I dare not speak of her to Saint-Just. He is such a strange man! . . . Adieu, my dear Elisabeth, let us hope for better days.

And two days later,

I have no conversation with Saint-Just on the subject of my domestic affections or his. I am alone with my heart. Kiss Henriette for me. Schillichem [his dog] caresses me constantly and I return his affection.

He wrote again on the twenty-eighth,

I received today, my dear friend, a letter from Henriette addressed to Saint-Just and to me. Saint-Just had opened and read it: he handed it to me without saying anything except that it was only for me. It had to do with Désiré [Philippe's brother], of whom I said a couple of words to him another time, which he seemed to hear with much indifference. . . . Henriette tells me that you complain of my silence. Apparently you have not received all my letters, for I have written you almost every other day. It is my only pleasure. There is hardly any one but you to whom I can explain myself; there are so few friends!

His last letter while on this mission is from headquarters at Hantes, dated 3 Prairial (May 22). It concludes:

I am waiting here for your brother and Gateau who should come from Réunion. I hope soon to have occasion to go and see you. My compliments to the family, to Henriette. The person whom you know is always the same. I embrace you.

On this note of sadness the correspondence comes to an end and with it our knowledge of the situation. There are two more glimpses of Henriette. Le Bas, now in Paris, informs his father on 30 Prairial (June 18) that on the preceding day Elisabeth had borne him a son.

I regretted very much that you were not with us. You would surely have shared our joy. Henriette and Désiré are in good health.

It seems likely that within a year Henriette was married. Lanne, a friend of Le Bas, who acted as witness at the official recording of his son's birth, fell victim to the Thermidorians on 17 Floréal, year III, eleven months afterward. In a farewell letter full of messages to his relatives and friends, he wrote "Tell —— [the name is blank in the printed version], tell Henriette, tell their husbands that I loved them until death." [130]

Whether or not Saint-Just and Le Bas found it possible to renew their friendship on the old footing, no one knows. Hamel [131] speaks of the break as "an almost imperceptible cloud" on their affection, but that can hardly be true in view of the citations from the letters. It is also a fact that when, not more than a week after his return from the North, Saint-Just was sent out again on his last mission, he went with different colleagues, Gillet and Guyton.

Seven weeks later and it was over for them both. They stood together at the end, rallying around Robespierre, the fallen leader.

Of the two in their personal relations, it is Le Bas who comes off best. It is he without doubt who, though the weaker, is the more human and lovable. But then it is he who has the more fully revealed his heart. Perhaps if Saint-Just had dropped his mask of stoicism and permitted us to see what he really thought and felt about the people with whom he came in daily contact, we should be less inclined to wonder whether he felt at all. The bare fact that he had a few friends who admired and loved him like Le Bas is perhaps the only evidence that Saint-Just was something beside a power house of revolutionary energy. But however it may have been with him, this chapter should be proof that some at least of the terrorists (for so Le Bas must unquestionably be classed) were naturally gentle and affectionate, even though they embraced a rigorous policy in the belief that by such means only could the republic be saved.

XII

THE MISSION TO ALSACE: ORDER
OUT OF CHAOS

THE Convention soon realized that if the energies of the nation were not to be wasted in jealous bickering and mere futility, if the war was to be won, a regular liaison would have to be made between Paris and the departments. None seemed better fitted for this missionary work than the members of the Convention itself. Their task was therefore a double one; by their authority to bring order out of chaos, smoothly functioning efficiency out of a confusion of tongues, and by their enthusiasm to sink revolutionary propaganda into the minds and the fear of it into the hearts of men. For this function they were armed with very extended powers. Their decrees had the force of law, at least provisionally, and could be set aside only by the Convention. Ten years in irons awaited those local administrators who attempted to suspend one of these decrees. Representatives might and did remove generals and judges, reverse their decisions or direct the fashion in which they should be carried out. One of their chief duties was to weed out undesirable members of the local administrations, seeking the advice of the popular societies for this purpose. The success of these missions depended of course on the personality of the representative. Since nearly half of the Convention was sent sooner or later either to the armies or to the departments, the results must have varied widely. Some were inefficient braggarts, who interfered seriously with military operations; some were sadists who drenched the land with blood. But in the main they were not unpopular; coming in from outside with a more national outlook, they often curbed petty local extremists who fed on village rancors. On the whole they were

129

an immense, perhaps an indispensable factor in the success of the war. Among the most successful missions were those of Jeanbon Saint-André to Brest, the key to the naval operations against the English, of Prieur de la Marne to Brittany where he helped defeat the Vendéan revolt, and those of Saint-Just and of Carnot to the Armies of the Rhine and the North.[132]

Saint-Just's first experience as a missionary of the Convention was in his own department. Things were going badly at the front in March, 1793. By vote of the Convention, March 9, eighty-two representatives were ordered to the departments to stimulate recruiting. They were to go in pairs, each pair covering two departments. Saint-Just's name stood second on the list, perhaps because he was designated for the second group of departments, Aisne and Ardennes.[133] Three days later, Garat, minister of the interior *ad interim,* sent up a letter which was read in the Convention, informing it of riots in the departments of Maine-et-Loire, Haute-Vienne and Aisne, due either to recruiting or the food question. The Convention would agree that the representatives should be sent out at once. Boyer-Fonfrède moved that those designated for the three departments named depart straightway, which was so ordered.

From this it appears that Saint-Just and his colleague, Deville, did not leave Paris before March 12. They were back by March 29. On that day it was announced at the Jacobins that Saint-Just was in from the Ardennes, where he had found all the forts dismantled by the fault of Beurnonville, ex-noble minister of war. A member designated only as C. proposed that the society write to citizen Saint-Just requesting that he present himself before it to attest the truth of these statements. Another moved that the same invitation be extended to Danton. Both propositions were carried.[134] Saint-Just duly appeared at the Jacobins on the thirty-first and confirmed the report of his discoveries. His remarks were brief and to the point.

I announce to the Society that Beurnonville is a traitor. Citizens, I have not found a single worth-while man in the government, I have found good only in the people. The time to unmask Beurnonville has not yet come. The mask should be crushed on his face, not lifted. In the towns which I visited, I found neither arms nor sufficient munitions. Weary of writing to Beurnonville and receiving no answer, I have returned to Paris to present the picture of our situation; if I cannot make myself heard in the Committee of General Defense and make it adopt vigorous measures in conformity with the critical circumstances in which we find ourselves, I shall take up my mission again and shall charge myself with the execution of the measures which the danger of our position demands.[135]

The same day, the Committee of General Defense was informed by a member that Saint-Just, having returned, had measures to propose for the safety of the republic. The Committee resolved that Saint-Just should be heard as soon as he presented himself. This occurred the following day, when he read a proposed decree, since lost, drawn up by him and his colleagues. He set forth the bad condition in which he had found the frontier fortresses. After Saint-Just had spoken, various members expressed their views; of these there is no record. This seems to have been the end of the matter unless it can be traced further in a discussion within the Committee, April 2, on a plan by the Dantonist Fabre relating to the provisioning and defense of fortified places. The plan was adopted with amendments and the Committee resolved that it should be drawn up in appropriate articles and presented to the Convention. It looks as though Saint-Just had stirred up this agitation, but that the Committee, being Dantonist, preferred to give the glory to one of that faction.[136]

Nothing further is known of this mission. A tangible result of it is undoubtedly to be found in the two following documents. At a public session of the departmental council of the Aisne, held in Laon, March 20, an address to the Convention on the subject of recruiting was drawn up and sent to all the departments. It declared that the patriotism of Laon's citizens had triumphed in spite of perfidious instigations. They had the consolation of seeing their ardent youth hastening to the frontiers under the banners of the republic in numbers superior to the quota. A similar letter from the administrators of the department of the Ardennes was read in the Convention, April 3.[137] The mission was an obvious success.

Again on May 8, Saint-Just was included by the Convention in a delegation of ninety-six to go that very day by twos to each Paris section to confer fraternally on the measures already taken and those proposed to raise an army against the Vendéans.[138] Nothing more is known of this affair.

The Committee of Public Safety in its session of July 18 "charges Saint-Just, one of its members, to go promptly to the departments of the Aisne, the Oise and the Somme to carry out there an object of public interest." [139] We are completely in the dark about this second mission to the Aisne or whether it was even carried out. The Committee decided, July 23, to send troops from various forts and camps to reinforce Valenciennes; to replace the denuded garrisons, 10,000 National Guards were to be requisitioned from twelve departments, three of which were the Aisne, the Oise and the Somme.[140] The mission may have had to do with this matter.

It was therefore as a veteran of two and perhaps three missions that Saint-Just was sent to Alsace in the autumn. The military situation was grave in the East as well as in the North and the West. The French had been driven from Germany; Mayence was taken in July. A series of incompetent commanders lost ground in Alsace steadily all through the summer. Oddly enough Napoleon Bonaparte was trying to get a post in the Army of the Rhine and Bouchotte, Beurnonville's successor, wrote on the margin of the petition:

See citizen Buonaparte, his proposition is that of a patriot. If he has ability, make the most of it to advance him.

For some reason the thing fell through. The climax of disaster came when the important Wissembourg lines were captured by the Austrians, October 13. The great success at Wattignies in northern France two days later threw into even darker relief the continual defeats of the two eastern armies, those of the Rhine and the Moselle. The Rhine Army was huddled in

THE MISSION
TO ALSACE

By permission of the
Clarendon Press

Scale of Miles

front of Strasbourg, hard pressed by the victorious Austrians under Wurmser. Back of the Saar in Lorraine, the Army of the Moselle stood at bay before the Duke of Brunswick and his Prussians. Far to the north in the Palatinate the important outpost of Landau still held fast, but isolated as it was and with a garrison rent by factionalism, its fall appeared only a question of time. Alsace seemed lost.

It was at this juncture that on the twenty-sixth day, first month, year II (October 17, 1793) the Committee of Public Safety decreed "that citizens Saint-Just and Le Bas, representatives of the people, betake themselves at once to the Army of the Rhine to investigate the events which have occurred at Wissembourg and at Lauterbourg; they are clothed for this purpose with the necessary authority to take such measures of public safety as they shall judge fitting." Two days later, Barère reported to the Convention that the Wissembourg lines had been forced as a result of treason, whose authors the representatives then at the front hoped to discover; he added that the Committee had sent one of its members, Saint-Just, to the spot and it was hoped that the enemy would soon repent their accidental advantage.[141] For some reason the Convention did not act until October 22, when with dignity,

after having heard the report of the Committee of Public Safety, it decrees that citizens Saint-Just and Le Bas shall proceed to the Army of the Rhine, there to take necessary measures of public safety. They are invested with the unlimited powers possessed by the other representatives of the people.

This confirmation regularized the matter. But they had already gone and they were really the Committee's special agents, superior to other representatives.

Saint-Just appeared, not like a representative, but like a king, like a god. Armed with immense powers over two armies, five departments, he found himself greater still by reason of his lofty and proud nature. In his writings, his words, his slightest acts, in everything appeared the hero, the great man of the future, but not the greatness suitable to republics. . . . A man so superior to others

133

would not have been endured two days in the cities of antiquity. Athens would have crowned him and would have driven him from its walls.

So wrote Michelet. Carnot's son, no friend to Saint-Just, declared that this mission merits the historian's attention as one of the most important and characteristic of the Revolution; low passions and interests played no rôle in it. Saint-Just showed himself the true representative of the terrorist system "in its awful grandeur." He proceeded with extreme severity, but the audacity of the state's enemies was no less extreme and the means they used more odious. Counter-revolution was marching forward with uplifted head; if it were not paralyzed by fear, it might in turn paralyze the Committee's efforts to defend the frontier.[142]

The representatives reached Saverne the very day of the Convention's decree and were in Strasbourg, October 23. The situation which confronted them was appalling. The city seethed with factional strife. Dietrich, the old moderate republican mayor of 1790, was in prison and in two months was to lose his head at Paris. He still had many partisans in Strasbourg. After his fall, the mayoralty had come into the hands of Monet, a radical young lawyer from Savoy, bold, active, a ready talker, willing to work in harmony with the representatives. He had a strong following. A third and equally powerful faction rallied around the still more extreme public prosecutor, Euloge Schneider.[143] There were dark rumors of a great conspiracy to deliver the city into the enemy's hands. The army was discouraged and lacked everything, from discipline down to shoes. There were not enough men, there was not enough money. Before victories could be won, the defeatist atmosphere must be corrected, strict vigilance restored, capable commanders appointed, funds and supplies procured, reinforcements brought up. Then the drums might beat for a forward movement, but not till then.

Saint-Just and Le Bas at once addressed themselves to their task. Of necessity they tackled several of these problems simultaneously. Among the more important were civic and military discipline and the securing of funds and supplies.

The second *arrêté* issued by them dealt with treason. It was published at Saverne, second day, second month (October 23), just before the representatives left for Strasbourg, which they reached some hours later. It established at Saverne a revolutionary commission consisting of five members, to function until the expulsion of the enemy from the Rhine departments. This commission should move about through the district as it saw fit. It was to arrest any in the Haguenau district denounced as agents or partisans of the enemy, to shoot those convicted of these crimes and to send all suspects to Mirecourt under arrest. It must keep the Convention informed of all judicial proceedings, and might requisition the aid of civil and military authorities. The members' pay was designated.

Two days later at Strasbourg, they addressed a letter to the local popular society, informing it of their purpose to establish a commission there to punish "in a prompt and terrible fashion" the faithless agents of the various army administrations. For this purpose they needed six men, revolutionary and incorruptible, and requested the society's zealous aid in their investigations. This letter, like many other of their communications and decrees, was signed by them as "the representatives of the people sent with an extraordinary mandate [*envoyés extraordinairement*] to the Army of the Rhine." The decree instituting this commission was issued on the fifth day of the second month (October 26). Convinced, they said, that bad administration, the impunity of thefts and the contacts of the enemy with bad citizens had been among the causes of the army's defeats, convinced also of the necessity of prompt punishment on the spot, they decreed that faithless agents [*agents prévaricateurs*] of army administrations and agents or partisans of the enemy should be shot in presence of the army; that the army's military tribunal be converted into a special revolutionary commission for the punishment of such crimes with no restrictions on procedure; suspect military chiefs should be re-

135

ferred to the representatives of the people. On 21 Brumaire
(November 11) they decreed that the property of those shot
under the foregoing decree be confiscated to the republic.
Arrests greatly increased under the new court; it is said that
over 20,000 crowded the prisons. On October 28, *cartes de
sûreté* were ordered printed, which the committee of surveillance distributed to every citizen who presented a *certificat de
civisme;* anyone who could not show his card on demand thereafter was imprisoned as suspect.[144]

Suspicion of treasonable contact with the enemy was not
unfounded. Pro-Austrian citizens had already made overtures
to General Wurmser, himself an Alsatian, promising that they
would do their best to expel the French, if Strasbourg might
become a free, imperial city. Wurmser replied that he had no
orders to that effect.[145] These rumors were increased tenfold at
the end of October by the seizure at the French advance posts
of a letter signed by the Marquis de Saint-Hilaire and addressed
to a citizen of Strasbourg. It was to be delivered by a man recognizable by his stammering and spectacles. It declared that
émigrés, disguised as National Guards, would surprise the city
within three days and that honest folk had best don the white
cockade to escape the subsequent massacre. The letter was a
forgery, written by Metz, pastor of Gries, with the Christian
object of destroying a personal enemy, Edelmann, one of the
department administrators, who stammered and wore spectacles. It was, however, believed authentic by Saint-Just and Le
Bas.[146] They issued a decree on the ninth day, second month
(October 30) ordering the committee of surveillance to make
domiciliary visits with armed men that night throughout the
city, taking steps to arrest suspects without disturbing public
tranquillity. On the same day they made a proclamation to the
citizens, reminding them that for several days the arrest of suspects had been in order. The names of all such should be
handed in within the day. To the popular society of the city
they wrote inviting opinions on the patriotism of every member of the departmental administration. Three days after came

another decree, revoking the latter body entirely and ordering the arrest of all but five, three of whom were left in provisional charge; the municipal body was also dismissed and arrested with the exception of Mayor Monet. The popular society was directed to select from its number a provisional committee of twelve to carry on the city's business. A similar fate befell the administration of the district of Strasbourg. The fallen authorities were to be out of town by eight o'clock next morning. On 16 Brumaire (November 7) officers of sections holding office May 31 and all others with Girondin sympathies were likewise ordered under arrest.

The popular society either did not approve of these drastic measures or did not credit the plot; at any rate it requested the reinstatement of the dismissed officials. Saint-Just and Le Bas replied in a long letter, dated 24 Brumaire. They addressed the members of the society as "brothers and friends." They were convinced, they said, that the plot to surrender Alsace was genuine and that the enemy had attempted to gain information and surprise Strasbourg. On their arrival the army seemed in despair; it lacked food, clothing, discipline and leaders. There were no police in the town; the poor groaned under the yoke of the rich, who depreciated the currency and outbid the indigent for foodstuffs. The city gates closed late; the theaters, the houses of ill fame, the streets were full of officers; the fields were covered with vagabond soldiers. While the people were unhappy, the army betrayed and dying in misery, while crime and counter-revolution were marching through the city in triumph, what were the constituted authorities doing? The accounting which they had to make to the French people was terrible; they neglected the supply of grain, carts, firewood; they made bargains for candles at seven francs a pound; the soldiers of liberty rotted in the hospitals; the authorities were so negligent that it was impossible to get evidence of a single act of watchfulness and energy on their part. Meanwhile letters were surprised announcing information in the hands of the enemy and that enemy at the gates! As a result of the recent police measures and taxes on the rich, the writers continued, the indigent were relieved, the army clad, fed and reinforced, aristocracy reduced to silence, gold and paper at par. Why had this not been done before?

People owe one another the truth; we will tell it to you. You are indulgent toward magistrates who have done nothing for the country. Your letter demands their return; you talk to us of their administrative talents, you tell us nothing of their revolutionary virtues, their love of the people, their heroic devotion to liberty. We have had confidence in you; we have requested your members to watch over the safety of the posts, to replace the expelled authorities. We have listened day and night to soldiers and citizens; we have upheld the weak against the strong. We speak to you at this moment in the same spirit. It is not the return of your indifferent magistrates which should occupy you, but the expulsion of an enemy who devours your fields and the discovery of conspirators hidden in every sort of disguise.

They had received word that two millions in gold were in the hands of the old authorities; this must be verified.

Time will perhaps unravel the truth; we examine everything in cold blood and we have won the right to be suspicious. Our duty is to be inflexible in matters of principle. We owe you friendship, we do not owe you weakness. We owe all to the fatherland; we persist in our decree until the danger is over.

This is perhaps the best summary of the representatives' view of their task and how they dealt with it.[147] It may be added that the imprisoned administrators complained on their own account to Bouchotte, who replied, November 23, that Saint-Just and Le Bas were great friends of the popular system, that they enjoyed the confidence of patriots and had taken this rigorous step only because they considered it necessary for public safety.[148] Final echoes of the affair are heard a month later. In their decree of 25 Frimaire (December 15), Saint-Just and Le Bas ordered the directory of the department of the Moselle at Metz to take steps at once that the Strasbourg ex-officials detained there be treated with proper humanity. This decree they signed as "representatives of the people sent with extraordinary mandate to the Armies of the Rhine and the Moselle," the Committee having thus extended their authority six days before.

The only other matter of civic discipline has to do with the famous Schneider case. A former Capuchin monk, preacher at the Stuttgart ducal court and a learned Hellenist, he crossed into Alsace in June, 1791, and became Constitutionalist episcopal vicar. As the Revolution progressed, Schneider's mildly pink liberalism deepened several shades to the most lurid Hébertist crimson. He gave up his orders, ceased even to write commentaries on Anacreon and became public prosecutor of a revolutionary tribunal, a local Fouquier-Tinville. This roving tribunal was established by the representatives Mallarmé, Milhaud and Guyardin, October 20, before Saint-Just's arrival.[149] It is not to be confused with the commission set up by Saint-Just. Like that other German extremist, Anacharsis Cloots, and recalling the somewhat similar examples of such great ecclesiastical secessionists as Melanchthon and Bucer, Schneider exchanged his Christian name for the Greek Euloge. Nodier, who as a small boy quite innocently applied to him for lessons in Greek, describes him as a man of thirty-five, ugly, fat, short and vulgar, with round limbs, round shoulders and round head. The face of this rotund individual was grayish, pock-marked and flecked with red, while his closely cropped black hair presented a curious contrast to his bushy brown eyebrows, beneath which gleamed evil eyes under reddish lashes.[150]

This unpleasant person was licentious, venal and cruel. Whether as charged he illuminated his portable guillotine, whether he requisitioned women and money on pain of death is not proved. There are two versions of his marriage. The less probable is Nodier's, according to whom the beautiful daughter of the aristocratic prisoner Stamm came to Schneider begging mercy for her father; the following day Schneider went to the prison, asked Stamm for the girl's hand and leading both to the window, pointed out the guillotine decked with flowers and ribbons; the daughter fell terrorized at her father's feet, imploring his consent to the marriage, but once married she went to Saint-Just, demanding justice against her husband. Saint-Just, outraged, ordered Schneider's arrest. The less sensational version of Taffin, one of the judges in Schneider's court, is more likely and makes the wooing almost equally abrupt. Schneider, being smitten with the charms of Mlle. Stamm, wrote to her parents:

Fellow-citizens,
Permit your daughter to read the few words which I inclose to her; if you consent to our marriage I promise you on the faith of a republican to make her happy.

Interesting citizeness,
I love you, I am asking your virtuous parents for you; if you give me your hand, I will bring you joy.[151]

We have textual extracts from the proceedings of Schneider's ambulatory court with entries like the following:

Audience of 8 Brumaire. Dorothée Frantz of Ruprechtsau, convicted of having sold two heads of lettuce for twenty sous and of having thus depreciated the value of the *assignats,* condemned to a fine of 3,000 livres, to be imprisoned for six months and to be exposed on the scaffold [*au poteau*] for two hours.[152]

In these undertakings Schneider received strong support from the local Alsatian extremists who were German-speaking and wished to keep Alsace for the Alsatians. He also imported from beyond the Rhine a number of German ex-priests, radicals like himself. There was, however, a rival faction of extremists led by Mayor Monet, whose desire was to Gallicize Alsace and draw closer to the revolutionary movement in the rest of France. Monet brought in from other French cities a contingent of extremists, whom he organized into a society known as the Propagande, some of whose members went about in a sort of uniform consisting of a short, very snug jacket, girt about by a tricolor sash in which were thrust huge pistols with shining handles and from which hung a large hunting knife. On their hair, worn in ringlets to the shoulder, was the liberty cap; their necks were bare; they wore boots of raw leather.[153] The extremists did not all dress like Balkan brigands; their more common garb was a dark cloak with a huge saber trailing on the ground; to make the face as ferocious as the costume, the ultrarevolutionary cultivated a pair of heavy moustaches. Lacoste and Baudot, two representatives already on mission in Alsace at the time of Saint-Just's arrival, and who became hostile to him, were strong supporters of the Propagande. This group and the followers of Schneider had one thing in common; they were both Hébertist and believed in a lavish use of terrorism. For all his loud talk, only some thirty victims were actually guillotined by Schneider, according to surviving records. But fines were inordinately heavy, thousands fled and the fear of Schneider hung like a cloud over the land.

Such was the situation from August to October. When Saint-Just came, an antipathy sprang up between the two from their first meeting. Both were proud and dominating. Saint-Just, handsome, elegant, courteous, successful, was envied and disliked by his ill-favored rival with his coarse clothes and coarser ways.[154] The stoic in Saint-Just could not endure Schneider's loose morals, his instinctive restraint was repelled by his opponent's extravagance in speech and conduct, his financial integrity by the other's corruption. As a deist, he disliked the religious attitude of the extreme party, bordering as it did on atheism, which he had now discarded; as a fervid nationalist in war time, he was suspicious of foreigners and of cosmopolitanism. Yet it was just then that the Hébertists were at the height of their power. On October 5, they put the revolutionary calendar through the Convention; November 10 marked the Festival of Reason and the dechristianizing movement spread rapidly over France during these two months.

For a while the current was flowing so strongly in this direction that Schneider was impregnable and even Saint-Just had to make concessions. Thus Teterel and Baudot (both Hébertist) proposed before the Propagandist Club, November 24, to demolish the tower of Strasbourg Cathedral down to the platform. This notion that church spires should go, being symbols of inequality, was not uncommon at the time. Saint-Just and Le Bas saved the cathedral, though at a price, by their skillful decree of the same day (4 Frimaire) ordering the municipality to destroy within a week all the statues around the Temple of Reason (the cathedral) and to hoist the tricolor on the tower of the temple. Another decree of that date transferred to Paris all the vases of the Strasbourg temples and the patriotic gifts of citizens.

When Saint-Just began issuing severe decrees, Schneider took the opposite tack and tried to appeal to the moderates, but without much success. He made his fatal error when he carted his guillotine in the wake of the finally victorious French armies, so alienating instead of liberating the debatable country. Thirty thousand are said to have sought refuge in the Black Forest and were at once placed on the list of *émigrés*.[155] On 17 Frimaire (December 7) Saint-Just and Le Bas requested Schneider to make a report to the Committee of Public Safety of his activities as "civil commissary," which the now alarmed terrorist accordingly did, justifying his acts as best he might. Nevertheless he had the bravado to drive into Strasbourg in a carriage drawn by six horses; a beautiful young woman sat beside him; twenty-five horsemen with drawn sabers acted as escort. Behind trooped his shouting followers.

This open departure from republican simplicity gave Saint-Just and Le Bas their coveted opportunity, which they were keen enough to see and bold enough to seize. They issued the decree of 23 Frimaire (December 13) declaring that Schneider, prosecutor at the revolutionary tribunal, former priest and born a subject of the emperor, had that day entered Strasbourg with insolent ostentation, drawn by six horses and surrounded by guards with drawn swords; the representatives of the people sent with extraordinary mandate to the Armies of the Rhine and Moselle decreed that the said Schneider should be exposed to public view on the following day from 10 A.M. till 2 P.M. on the scaffold of the guillotine, in order to expiate the insult to the morals of the young republic. He should then be taken, from brigade to brigade, before the Committee of Public Safety. The commander of the fortress was made responsible for the carrying out of this order, which he must report by 3 P.M. of the twenty-fourth.

Nodier was there and tells us about it. He was caught up in a great crowd pressing toward the scaffold in the Place d'Armes. Then he had a glimpse of Schneider held on either side by one of his own black-bloused assistant executioners,

preceded by that pale man whom I had seen in a little *calèche* and followed by two of his hussars of death who pricked him, laughing, with the points of their swords to make him move forward. . . . His little eyes seemed sunk in their sockets. His pallor was frightful and yet he wiped the sweat from his forehead. As he approached the guillotine, the acclamations redoubled either from fury or gayety, for I heard without comprehending them. Soon there was a great silence and I realized that Schneider was mounting the scaffold, but I did not know whether it was to death and that was what none of my neighbors could explain to me for there was not one who spoke French. After that, bursts of applause succeeded one another, interrupted by terrifying pauses. . . . Each time I thought his head was falling and I stood on tiptoe to see the top of the death-machine and to assure myself that the knife was still suspended and I found that I was glad when I saw high in the air that bloody blade whose sight had frightened me on the preceding day.[156]

But Schneider was doomed, as well he realized. On 26 Frimaire, Saint-Just and Le Bas were requesting the committee of surveillance in Strasbourg to nominate a new public prosecutor and three and a half months later, on 12 Germinal (April 1), Schneider was executed in Paris, doomed alike as Hébertist and foreigner.[157]

The Committee's distrust of Schneider's conduct is shown by its sending Garnerin, a special agent, to investigate his arrests. It may be said at this point that of eight known special agents

143

of the Committee, at least four were chosen because of personal relations with Şaint-Just. Lambert was a shepherd in a village near Reims; he met Saint-Just at a relay station and made such an impression through his rustic, sturdy honesty that Saint-Just recommended him to Robespierre. Demaillot had been a teacher of Saint-Just. Garnerin met Gateau and thus entered into relations with Gateau's friend, Saint-Just. Vieille was mayor of Soissons; he states that he became a Committee agent on Saint-Just's invitation. A fifth, Pottofeux, was designated during his trial after Thermidor, as "friend of Robespierre and Saint-Just." [158]

The very day that Schneider stood on the platform before the jeers of the populace, Le Bas and Saint-Just were writing a letter to Robespierre, which is of interest from several points of view. Le Bas informs his correspondent that they had just reached Strasbourg on the twenty-third and had surprised more than one person. (This was perhaps after their brief visit to Paris.) They had found evil to repair and were more than ever convinced that the exercise of power calls for much wisdom. As for the army, they had seen General Pichegru. Things were in fair shape. Landau had not surrendered as had been reported and they hoped it would soon be relieved. They attacked often, a system disconcerting to the enemy. A defensive policy was not in keeping with the army's character. They were sending to the Committee of Public Safety, the public prosecutor at the revolutionary court of Strasbourg. He was a former priest, born subject of the emperor. He would be exposed before departure on the scaffold of the guillotine. This punishment, which he had drawn on himself by his insolent conduct, was also dictated by the necessity of repressing foreigners.

Let us not believe in cosmopolitan charlatans, and let us trust only ourselves. I embrace you with my whole heart.

Saint-Just added this postscript:

Too many laws are made, too few examples: you punish only striking crimes, hypocritical crimes are unpunished. Punish a slight abuse in every party; that is the way to frighten evil persons and to make them see that the government has its eye on everything. Hardly does one turn his back when aristocracy becomes the fashion of the day and does harm under the color of liberty.

Engage the Committee to give much prominence to the punishment of all faults in the government. You will not have done so for a month before you will have cleared up this labyrinth in which counter-revolution and revolution march pell-mell. Direct the society's attention, my friend [*i.e.*, the Jacobins], to strong maxims of public welfare; let it occupy itself with the great measures needed to govern a free state.

I invite you to take measures to find out whether all the factories and workshops of France are active and to favor them, for in a year our troops would be without clothing; the manufacturers are not patriotic, they do not want to work, they must be forced to and no useful establishment must be allowed to fail.

We will do our best here. I embrace you and our common friends.[159]

In this letter, Saint-Just's strong, dominating character stands out in sharp contrast to the chatty, amiable Le Bas. He talks to Robespierre as though he were the master. There was more in this than youthful bravado, for Saint-Just had wit and experience enough to realize that no one could reach the guillotine by any quicker road than by incurring Robespierre's hatred. That statesman was too serious to smile indulgently at the pertness of a handsome boy, too egotistical to listen patiently to advice from an inferior, hardly from an equal. It is clear that he was used to listening to it from Saint-Just, almost clear that he was used to taking it. The letter shows, too, Saint-Just influencing his leader against the ultrarevolutionaries and urging on him that curious notion of a diabolical league between moderates and extremists which was to obsess the Robespierrists in their last days. He was not the first to suggest it, but it is interesting to see how early he threw his weight into this scale.

The rival Hébertist group felt the weight of Saint-Just's disapproval no less than the followers of Schneider. In spite of Monet's personally friendly attitude, Saint-Just disliked his club, the Propagande, and obtained a decree from the Convention ordering its dissolution.[160] This act and the fall of Schneider a week later ended serious opposition. A few Propagandists went about muttering that it would be necessary "to burn the dictators' moustaches."

While civic discipline took much of the representatives' time and thought, army discipline was no less important. A whole series of decrees deal with absence from duty. The general is warned to give only limited permissions to leave camp; surgeon majors are particularly denounced for giving hospital tickets to men who do not need them (7 Brumaire). Generals are to sleep and eat in their tents at the head of their divisions and brigades (9 Brumaire). Every soldier or other person who tries to enter the city hidden in caissons, wagons or otherwise shall be shot that very day (10 Brumaire). "Citizen Texier, captain of chasseurs of the Rhine, met today at 7 P.M. in the streets of Strasbourg by citizen Saint-Just, representative of the people, of whom he asked the way to the Comedy, shall be taken to prison according to established discipline for having left his post which is on the banks of the Rhine" (15 Brumaire).[161]

Some fifteen decrees order the arrest of officers or soldiers, usually for aristocracy, graft or neglect of duty. One (21 Brumaire) arrests for eight days the clothing storekeepers of Strasbourg who insolently hold soldiers in the city after the hour that the gates close; the merchants are to be escorted to work daily and returned to prison at night.

Generals are to inform their troops that complaints are to be sent in writing to the representatives (5 and 7 Brumaire).

The third important category into which the decrees naturally fall is money and supplies. Some concern food. An exact account of the rations is called for at the outset (2 Brumaire). The administrators of eight adjoining departments must within twelve days turn into the military storehouses of Strasbourg the quantities of grain and fodder previously indicated to them, on pain of the revolutionary tribunal (3 Brumaire). Those of the department of the Meurthe fail in this task and are arrested

(22 Brumaire) as are also the municipal authorities of Neu-brisach (16 Brumaire). An *arrêté* of the Council-General of the Department of the Vosges, dated fifth day, second month, year II, 5 P.M., illustrates the effect produced by Saint-Just's decrees. That of the third had just arrived. The Council-General, considering that though by its *arrêtés* of August 22 and 27, September 9, 21, 28, and October 5 and 7 it had taken the most pressing and active measures to speed up the delivery of grain and fodder needed for the army, though it had sent commissioners into all districts to hurry matters, it yet heard with pain that frontier towns threatened with siege were without provisions, decreed as follows. The decree of the representatives should be circulated at once in every village.

As soon as it shall reach the communes, it shall be published at sound of drum and all citizens without distinction, all inhabitants of every age and sex shall be required, *all other labors ceasing,* to devote themselves without relaxation or discontinuance to the threshing of grains and oats, to winnowing and cleaning them, to putting them into sacks, to bundling up the hay and to loading everything into wagons which shall at once be driven to the stores designated by the annexed table, so that deliveries may be effected within the limits fixed by the decree of the representatives of the people.

A new and heavier requisition followed; local officials were instructed to publish at once the quotas of villages and individuals; everyone must hand over immediately all the grain already threshed and not absolutely needed for personal use, which would be credited on his quota; commissioners were appointed to execute this decree; any person who hindered its execution would be denounced at once to the representatives of the people. Tables were appended giving the amount required from each district and the place to which deliveries should be made.[162]

Some of the decrees concerned the supply of horses and carts, of muskets and military equipment. Among the most spectacular were those dealing with clothing. They began with relative mildness. The municipality of Strasbourg was instructed to requisition from the citizens within eight days 5,000 pairs of shoes and 15,000 shirts (10 Brumaire).[163] The military stores were ordered to deliver to the general-in-chief at once 1,000 cloaks for the troops at the front (15 Brumaire). Results not forthcoming, the mayor of Strasbourg was requested to "excite the zeal" of all citizens to furnish shoes, clothing and hats (17 Brumaire). Since this was likewise of no avail, the representatives tried their hand at the citizens' zeal by the terse letter of 25 Brumaire to the municipality.

Ten thousand men are barefoot in the army; you must unshoe all the aristocrats of Strasbourg within the day, and tomorrow by 10 A.M. ten thousand pairs of shoes must be on their way to headquarters.

With this was coupled a proclamation to the inhabitants.

All the cloaks of the citizens of the city of Strasbourg are requisitioned. They must be turned in tomorrow evening to the storehouses of the Republic. The municipality is charged with the execution of the present decree.[164]

In a similar spirit, the muncipality was required to secure from the rich 2,000 beds within twenty-four hours for the soldiers' use, while horses were to be provided for the surgeons (24 Brumaire).

The decree which perhaps caused more commotion than any other was that of 10 Brumaire regarding a forced loan. As usual in war time, the prosperous citizens were profuse in their expressions of loyalty, but had done comparatively little in the face of a great emergency. With elaborate, but sarcastic politeness, the representatives began,

. . . Informed of the good will of the citizens of Lower Rhine for the fatherland, convinced by the advances made to them . . . that the country has no ingrates in these parts, touched by the sensibility with which the well-to-do citizens of Strasbourg have expressed their hate of the enemies of France and their desire to aid in overthrowing them, struck by the army's utter lack of equipment, which the

148

rich of this city have offered to repair, still more touched by the energy of these rich who, suggesting that a loan be levied on opulent persons, have demanded measures of severity against those who may refuse to follow their example;

Wishing at the same time to relieve the people and the army,

they proceeded to levy 9,000,000 livres on the citizens whose names and quotas appeared on an appended list, 2,000,000 to be used for indigent patriots, 1,000,000 on the fortifications, 6,000,000 to go into the army treasury. The sum was due within twenty-four hours. Subsequent decrees show that the loan did not come in promptly and on the seventeenth it was ordered that the wealthiest on the list who had not paid up within twenty-four hours should be exposed for three hours at the guillotine. It is impossible to tell how much was collected. The tax was levied on only 193 persons.[165] One was reported to have handed Saint-Just the key to his house on a plate, asking him to pay his debts, but the Convention, even after Thermidor, treated this tale with hilarity and refused to heed the complaints of the Strasbourgers. A letter from an agent named Berger to the minister of the interior (19 Brumaire) informs him that

they howl, but they pay. . . . The guillotine is in permanence; that is what makes them march; the *assignat* has recovered favor; no one speaks of silver any more except secretly. In a short time, Strasbourg will be no longer recognizable.[166]

Other drastic measures were taken to uphold the maximum. Any attempt to prevent army purchasing agents from requisitioning cattle at this figure was a capital offense (7 Brumaire); anyone convicted of speculation or of having sold at a price above the legal rate should have his house pulled down (3 Nivôse). The latter decree was carried out in at least one case.

A few miscellaneous acts may be added. The women of Strasbourg were invited to abandon German fashions in dress, "since their hearts are French" (25 Brumaire). In every commune or canton a free school in the French language was to be established (9 Nivôse). So much to win the well-disposed. On the other hand agents of the republic were warned that they had no further excuse for neglecting the service. "Make them realize that the lives of rascals are henceforth in danger" (10 Brumaire). All noncombatants were forbidden to walk on the city ramparts under penalty of three months in prison (4 Frimaire). So much to fill the country's secret foes with fear.

The energy and thoroughness of these two young men cannot be contested. A more general estimate of their success must be deferred until some account has been given of the army's progress during this period. Its triumph was the ultimate purpose of their whole mission.

XIII

THE MISSION TO ALSACE: THE
AUSTRIANS EXPELLED

AINT-JUST and his colleague showed their realization that even the revolutionizing of Alsace
was of secondary importance to the military campaign by devoting their first decree to the latter
object. It was issued at Saverne, the junction point of the two
armies; that of the Moselle stretching northwest, that of the
Rhine southeast. The decree gave orders to the authorities of
the Meurthe, the Upper and Lower Rhine to hasten the conscription, for the reinforcement of General Sautter's depleted
battalions (first day, second month). They likewise sent the
Committee of Public Safety an account of the military position, concluding with an appeal for a bold general and for
arms.[167]

Upon their arrival in Strasbourg next day they made a hasty
survey of the situation and on the third launched two proclamations to the troops, made a long report to the Committee,
and to strike an encouraging note sent the Convention a Prussian flag under escort of the officer who captured it. The proclamations are couched in the same terse, confident style with
which Napoleon less than three years later electrified the Army
of Italy.

We arrive and we swear in the army's name that the enemy shall
be vanquished. If there are traitors here and even those indifferent
to the cause of the people, we bring the sword to strike them.
Soldiers, we come to avenge you and to give you chiefs who will lead
you to victory. We are resolved to seek out, to reward, to advance
merit and to pursue all crimes, whoever have committed them.
Courage, brave Army of the Rhine, you will be henceforth happy
and triumphant with liberty.

All chiefs, officers and agents of the government are ordered to satisfy within three days the just complaints of the soldiers. After this interval we shall hear these complaints ourselves and give examples of justice and severity such as the army has not yet seen.

The other proclamation was somewhat longer. It began with good news from other fronts, forbade anyone to leave camp without a signed permit from the general and sought to arouse an attitude of intelligent coöperation with this rigorous policy.

. . . Soldiers of the Army of the Rhine, despise the enemy before you. He has not defeated you. He has tricked you. False deserters have held out their arms to you. You have embraced them. One does not embrace tyrants, one kills them.

Be on your guard then. Love the discipline which brings victory. Exercise yourselves in the manual of arms. Stay in your camps and prepare to win in your turn.

Outside of military operations and discipline, the need of reinforcements and supplies and the punishment of civilian suspects, an endless feud with the representatives already on the ground runs through all the correspondence. A whole cloud of deputies were already in the region; on their arrival at Strasbourg, Saint-Just and Le Bas met Ruamps, Milhaud, Lacoste, Mallarmé and Borie. Besides these, Guyardin and Niou were also in Alsace. But in spite of, or perhaps because of their numbers, they had accomplished little. They were constantly writing to Paris about their revolutionary activity, but the state of affairs in October was eloquent of their failure. It is not surprising that in their first report to the Committee of Public Safety (3 Brumaire) Saint-Just and Le Bas wrote of the five they had met:

Whatever may be the cause of the existing dissatisfaction with most of them, it has become almost impossible for them to accomplish anything and they realize it. Perhaps it would be best to employ them elsewhere and at the end of a certain time to give them an honorable retirement by recalling them to the Convention. Two active representatives are enough for this army.

According to the nature of our mission, we have thought it our duty to act by ourselves.

The report tells further of a conference with General Carlenc on the Wissembourg defeat, which is attributed to lack of discipline, permitting a surprise by the enemy; this defeat was the fault of the leaders. The great need was a truly republican general, believing in victory. Such a one was Pichegru, for whom they had sent. They were doing their best to provision Strasbourg and to overcome abuses; they were convinced that raw recruits must be amalgamated with existing corps; they needed twelve more battalions at Saverne and 2,000 cavalry at Strasbourg, besides more arms; the most difficult task was the relief of Landau; the enemy would try to fortify himself in the gorges [of Saverne] from which he must be dislodged at once. If the Committee displayed all the energy of which it was capable, no second campaign would be needed and Alsace would be saved. A postscript by Saint-Just alone suggests that since they had to be everywhere at once in view of their extraordinary mission, it would be well that in recalling their colleagues, the Committee send at once two representatives to stay at Strasbourg.

Their next report was from Strasbourg on the fifth (October 26). They were asking their colleagues with the Army of the Moselle to send six battalions for the gorges at Saverne, which must be held at all costs. In view of success elsewhere, all energies should now be concentrated on the Rhine; reinforcements must be hastened. Various skirmishes are described. Pichegru had not yet arrived. They had visited all the posts; the army was good and needed only an energetic chief; there was a general outcry against their previous commanders. A postscript bears the welcome tidings: "Pichegru has just come; he is a resolute man, we are going to install him and strike."

The Committee replied on the sixth, approving Saint-Just's operations and announcing reinforcements.

That day three of the representatives to the Army of the Rhine, Mallarmé, Guyardin and Lacoste, stung by the airs of superiority which they felt in their newly arrived colleagues, wrote a long complaint to the Committee. We have had no answer from you to our important dispatches, they declared. The only reply was the decree sending Saint-Just and Le Bas, a decree of which we learned through the public press. Our colleagues have not only failed to show the least desire to join us, but have even expressed themselves explicitly on this point; they wish to isolate themselves from us and dub themselves "extraordinary deputies." We fail to see, either in the text or spirit of the decree, any right to that title. Have you given it to them by some special action? We do not know, but it is none the less true that this title makes a bad impression on the public and seems to cancel our authority or at least weaken it in the general opinion. In their proclamation, the new deputies announce that they are going to make examples which have never been seen hitherto. Evil-disposed folk regard that as directed against us. And so on at great length, concluding with an assertion of willingness to allow Saint-Just and Le Bas to examine their conduct if necessary, but not to assume a position over them which was surely not intended by the Committee nor the Convention.[168]

In reply to the request of Saint-Just and Le Bas and before receipt of the letter from Mallarmé, Guyardin and Lacoste, the Committee on 7 Brumaire (October 28) decreed the recall of Ruamps, Milhaud, Lacoste, Mallarmé, Borie and Niou and that two new deputies be sent to Strasbourg; also that twelve new battalions be sent at once from adjoining departments. On the thirtieth, Carnot in the Committee's name advised Saint-Just and Le Bas to attack the enemy not in front, but on the flanks and rear; the first task was to relieve Landau.

To a request from the Austrians that a parley be arranged, Saint-Just and his colleague sent the ringing answer (11 Brumaire): "The French Republic receives from its enemies and sends them in return naught but lead."

A more aggressive French campaign began to take shape in the next few days. Pichegru received his formal appointment to command the Army of the Rhine on October 27. On the thirtieth, the brilliant young General Hoche was placed over the Army of the Moselle. For the first time, the French troops were acting under leaders of whose republican convictions and military capacity they felt equally assured.

The Committee's plan of campaign, the outline of which seems already familiar to the two representatives, was communicated to them formally by an official set of instructions drawn up by Carnot under date of 12 Brumaire (November 2). It hinged on the formation of a special army corps in the neighborhood of Bouquenom and Saarwerden (some forty miles northwest of Strasbourg across the Vosges). This force would be protected by the mountains from the main body of the enemy, would be in a position to raise the siege of Bitche while defending Phalsbourg and the gorges of Saverne and would then be ready to relieve Landau (fifty odd miles northeast of Saarwerden), thus placing the Austrian army in front of Strasbourg between two fires. Meanwhile the Committee would send to Strasbourg the twelve battalions desired. This plan might have to be modified locally by Saint-Just and Le Bas if necessary; they might even propose an alternative. The Committee was disposed to second them with all its force, but they must bear its limitations in mind.

Your ingenuity must create new resources, your energy must double your strength. Your decrees are perfectly revolutionary; we expect everything from the wisdom and firmness of your measures.

Carnot would come down if they wanted him, though the Committee was reduced to five and overwhelmed with work.

This letter was accompanied by a personal note from Robespierre. He had not forgotten for a moment either the Army of the Rhine or "our two commissioners." He had pressed forward all necessary measures and had reason to believe nothing had been neglected. He commended to them the Committee's well-conceived plan, devised in the same bold spirit as the one that had proved so successful in the case of the Army of the North.

We are counting a great deal on the energy you have communicated to the army and the activity you are displaying. For myself, I have no doubt of success if you apply yourself [169] to the execution of our plan.

These dispatches crossed one of 13 Brumaire from the two representatives to the Committee. They had given an incomplete idea of the position in their letter of the second from Saverne. [An obvious error for the first.] The 100,000 men they were supposed to have at their disposal were scattered all the way from Huningue to Landau, dispersed in garrisons by an act of folly. Hasten your concentration at Bouquenom, they urged; let the new force march on Bitche and Wissembourg, send us our twelve battalions at Saverne, our 2,000 cavalry at Strasbourg. While you take the enemy in the rear at Bitche, we will take him on the flank at Saverne, in front at Strasbourg and as soon as he retreats, we will if you think it desirable throw 7,000 men into the Brisgau by Kehl. This will force the enemy at Huningue to fall back on Kehl, making us stronger in the Upper Rhine. Then we will fall on the enemy like thunder from all sides, relieve our garrisons and get back our 100,000. This, except for the bold Kehl idea, was essentially the Committee's plan. In this letter, the statement occurs: "We have already tried three or four brigade chiefs; one must be shot today, condemned by the military court." [170]

There was to be no doubt of the side taken by the government in the feud between the deputies. The Convention, after having heard the report of the Committee of Public Safety, decreed on 13 Brumaire that Ruamps, Soubrany, Niou, Milhaud, Guyardin, Mallarmé, Borie and Cusset be recalled, while in their place Lémane, Baudot, Ehrmann and Lacoste should be the representatives of the people to the Armies of the Rhine and the Moselle.[171] This action seems to have superseded that of 7 Brumaire. Why Lacoste is not clear; he was destined to be Saint-Just's bitterest opponent. Perhaps it was because he was more capable than his comrades or because it was still important to make concessions to the Hébertists, of which faction he was a member.

156

On the fifteenth, Le Bas, ignorant of the Convention's decree, wrote Robespierre:

Hérault has just announced to us, my dear Robespierre, that he has been sent to the department of Upper Rhine. He proposes a correspondence with us; our surprise is extreme. For the rest, it is not the only thing which seems to us extraordinary. Why are not those replaced who were here when the Wissembourg lines were forced and why leave here representatives forced by the nature of their mission to isolate themselves from their colleagues! I have no time to tell you more but I hope you will soon write us your ideas on this.

To which Saint-Just added a postscript in his queer, owlish way:

Confidence is no longer of value when one shares it with corrupt men; then one does his duty simply for love of country and this sentiment is purer. I embrace you, my friend.[172]

Milhaud, not yet knowing his dismissal, wrote the Committee on the sixteenth in a far more optimistic vein than had been his wont. Hitherto his letters were jeremiads, but the confident energy of the "extraordinary deputies" had apparently been communicated to their colleagues or else these felt the need of bestirring themselves to keep up the new pace. Terror is the order of the day here, he brightly informs his correspondents; the courts are all rivaling one another in severity against egoists and conspirators. All the rich counter-revolutionists are being arrested. "Our colleagues, Saint-Just and Le Bas, have deported all the administrative bodies into the interior and we have arrested and deported the whole staff of the National Guard to Dijon." The army was being electrified; Wurmser's nephew was a prisoner and they were sending him to Paris.

The Committee's letter of the twelfth either was delayed in transmission or seemed not sufficiently explicit, for we find Saint-Just and Le Bas writing impatiently on the sixteenth,

Our last letter will have instructed you as to our views on the Army of the Rhine. You have announced your plan relative to Bouquenom; we have not received it. Count on our activity to execute what you prescribe. We embrace you.

A second communication from the Committee on 17 Brumaire (November 7) supplemented that of the twelfth; together they form the working outline of the government's scheme. This was to make an extraordinary effort on the Rhine; the Army of the North, though victorious, would act on the defensive temporarily. A force of 20,000 would be detached from that army to unite with the corps to be concentrated near Saarwerden and neighboring localities. This force would march first to Bitche, then to Landau, then back to Strasbourg, though these arrangements might be changed. The important point was to assemble a mass of men in a safe place, where it could be used as desired. Great secrecy was enjoined.

The Committee wrote further (24 Brumaire), congratulating Saint-Just and Le Bas on their zeal and skill. Since these two had instructed the Committee that the advance should begin between the twentieth and twenty-fifth the Bouquenom force would have to be cut down to 15,000 new troops plus an equal number detached from the Army of the Rhine. The enemy should be held in check before Strasbourg, and the gorges carefully guarded. The Committee approved the flank movement at Saverne; the Brisgau suggestion seemed a bit bold, but would be excellent if it could be carried out.

Hoche in his young ardor modified the Committee's plan and pointed his men toward a more distant and difficult goal. There would be a strong feint toward Deux-Ponts, seizing the gorges of the Vosges. The Prussians, fearful of a flank attack, would abandon their Saarbrück camp. Hoche would then march on the heights of Kaiserslautern, about sixty miles northeast of the point of departure near Saarwerden and thirty-five northwest of Landau. This would compel the raising of the siege of Landau. Pichegru would coöperate in a secondary sense, holding the Austrians before Strasbourg and sending aid to Hoche.[173]

With the opening of the campaign, Saint-Just and Le Bas made a circuit of the posts, visiting Hoche's army. On leaving Strasbourg, 25 Brumaire, Saint-Just wrote Hoche encouragingly; they would look for him at Landau. Next day he wrote from Saverne to Bouchotte, stating that he had urged Hoche strongly to put himself in harmony with Pichegru.

The latter is determined and knows his business. I have seconded him as well as I could. Discipline and hope fill the army. Everything seems to me wisely combined. . . . You have no idea of the bad spirit we found in Alsace. I have done my best. Suffice it to tell you that silver is at par with paper in Strasbourg, and that they are exchangeable for one another. Yesterday I took 10,000 pairs of shoes from the feet of the Strasbourg idlers.[174] They were turned over this morning to Pichegru who must send them at once to Hoche who needs them.

Lémane, one of the new representatives, in his letter of 26 Brumaire (November 16) to the Committee, gives the impression of being rather bewildered and incompetent, but determined to hitch his wagon to the star of the two officially favored deputies. He wrote that he found his brave colleagues, Saint-Just and Le Bas, performing prodigies. He would perhaps find it not impossible to do something worth while, so long as he had only to follow the path they had traced for him. They had left him surrounded during their absence with counselors whom they had chosen in their wisdom. For all that, he saw their departure with tears in his eyes.

A surprise attack by the Prussians almost carried the fort of Bitche, November 17. Saint Cyr, in his memoirs on the Rhine campaign, says that it is a question which was the more astonishing, the temerity of the Prussians or the negligence of the governor. Afterward, Saint-Just and Le Bas had the commandant arrested.[175] A description of the attack filled most of their report of 1 Frimaire (November 20). The ditches, glacis, walls and stairways were still smeared with the enemy's blood. The Cher battalion by its bravery alone saved the fort. But the republic was victorious along the whole line from the Rhine to

159

Saarbrück; Vantzenau, Brumpt, Bouxwiller and Deux-Ponts had all been captured. The writers did not rest half a day in a single place; they were exercising the most rapid surveillance of the campaign.

Lacoste's reaction to the surprise attack on Bitche was less calm. He came to the ferocious conclusion that the proper procedure was to guillotine a quarter of the inhabitants of this country, preserving only those who took an active part in the Revolution; the rest should be driven out and their property sequestrated (Bouxwiller, 4 Frimaire).

Barère, in the Committee's name, read a report on military operations to the Convention (5 Frimaire). Saint-Just and Le Bas, he announced cheerily, had in a few days revived the hopes of patriots, foiled plots, shot traitors at the head of troops, rallied scattered forces, reawakened public spirit and completely overawed avarice and egoism. Describing the attack on Bitche, Barère, like Falstaff and his men in buckram, makes 10,000 men assail the fort, where Saint-Just's letter reads 6,000; he doubles the number of prisoners.

On the fourth Saint-Just and Le Bas were back in Strasbourg. Their authority extended apparently to army movements even beyond the borders of their mission. A fragment of a letter to the Committee (5 Frimaire) has been preserved in which they suggest that the enemy might attempt something with the forces at his disposal in Luxembourg; the two Armies of the North and the Ardennes should make feints to the right and that promptly. In its decree of the ninth, the Committee ordered these directions sent to the general of the Army of the Ardennes at Sedan, "so that he may take the steps which seem to him best adapted to fulfill the object demanded"; signed by Carnot.

The spirit of the soldiers was kept high not only by rigorous discipline and appeals to patriotism, but by a realization that the two representatives thought of them as men, not as machines. Their decree of 5 Frimaire is an example. After requisitioning all horses and wagons near the camp, they ordered that all precautions must be taken to transport and give medical attention to the wounded. Every surgeon absent from combat or hospital on the day of an attack should be punished with two years in irons. Everyone requisitioned by the general to go with his horses and wagons to the battlefield to gather up the wounded must obey on penalty of six months in prison. With this should be coupled the last decree issued by them in Alsace, dated Strasbourg, 9 Nivôse (December 29), which invited every well-to-do citizen of Strasbourg, Saverne, Haguenau, Landau, Wissembourg and the cantons of Lower Rhine to give hospitality during the winter to a soldier, mutilated during the campaign in the service of his country.

On 7 Frimaire, Saint-Just and Le Bas wrote from Saverne to the Committee, reporting the army's continued success.

Send us the boots which have been promised us for a month. We declare to you that we shall sooner leave all the rich in Alsace without shirts and shoes than have the army lacking them. The French people consists of the patriots; the rest are helots or nothing.[176]

The attack on Kaiserslautern was a failure. The Duke of Brunswick retreated to a strong position and managed to resist the best efforts of Hoche, who waged energetic, but unsuccessful battle from 8 to 10 Frimaire (November 28-30). He did not, however, meet the usual fate of a defeated general. It was recognized that his lack of success was due neither to treason nor incapacity, but rather to an excess of republican zeal. Even Saint-Just and Le Bas, who preferred Pichegru, stood by the downcast soldier and wrote him an encouraging letter from Bitche (12 Frimaire), filled with military counsels. No doubt he valued their support in the highest degree; whether he was equally appreciative of their technical advice, one cannot say. At Kaiserslautern you have assumed a new obligation, they wrote him inspiringly; instead of one victory, you owe us two. The enemy is apparently intrenched up to his teeth; do the same yourself, mounting redoubts and batteries on the heights of Rentel, Saussekil and Anweiller.[177] We are sending intelligent

men to help you in this task; let no difficulty prevent the placing of these batteries. They will help a great deal in the efforts
against Wissembourg and Landau. We advise you, if the enemy
advances against Deux-Ponts, to await him there, but to attack
first; that is the way to keep up the soldiers' courage and confidence. There must be the closest liaison with all the divisions of
the right as far as Brumpt. The whole line must strike at once
and unceasingly. All commanders must be friends; the march on
Landau must be made with the greatest rapidity. So Saint-Just.
Carnot expressed himself with similar gentleness (15 Frimaire).
The Committee still preferred a more direct attack on Landau
rather than a resumption of the Kaiserslautern operations, but
left the question to Hoche's judgment; he had their entire confidence.[178]

The plan of a double attack, in which Hoche with the Army
of the Moselle was to drive back the Prussians, while Pichegru
with the Army of the Rhine advanced more deliberately against
the Austrians, had failed. There was nothing for it but to adopt
the Committee's original project, combining the force of both
armies against one antagonist at a time. Leaving the Prussians,
Hoche came south in December and began a turning operation
against Wurmser's right flank, while Pichegru continued to
hammer the Austrian front. This closer collaboration raised
the question of a unified command and in connection with
this knotty point the bad feeling between Lacoste and Saint-
Just broke out afresh.

The relations between these representatives were surely not
improved by the Committee's decree of 19 Frimaire (December
9) extending the powers of Saint-Just and Le Bas to cover the
Army of the Moselle, with which and with whose general
Lacoste and Baudot had closely identified themselves. The decree continued that Saint-Just and Le Bas should go at once
to the two armies to execute the measures and movements
resolved by the Committee. They were authorized to requisition necessary supplies and all local authorities were compelled
to obey their requisitions. A second decree on the following

day ordered the National Treasury to turn over to them 25,000 livres from the 50,000,000 placed by the Convention at the disposal of the Committee.[179] To make matters worse, on the twenty-first the Committee sent a circular letter to representatives Javogues, Laporte, Hérault, Bassal, Prost, Ehrmann and Lacoste, informing them with the utmost brevity that their mission was concluded and that they were to return at once to the Convention. Such a frank indication of position would have disconcerted a less stout-hearted fellow than Lacoste, but he managed to evade the decree as other deputies had before him, and on one or another pretext to continue his mission, which in fact outlasted that of Saint-Just.

A week later Lacoste's outraged feelings boiled over in a letter of unprecedented length to the Committee. He complained that Alsace had long been sold to the Austrians, as Toulon to the English; there were not four patriots in Strasbourg, three-fourths of the Alsatians were not French and detested the Revolution. On his return to Strasbourg, he found that the infamous penalty inflicted on Schneider had made the aristocrats more insolent than ever, that Lémane was ridiculous, that Saint-Just and Le Bas, back from Paris, persisted in calling themselves extraordinary envoys and in isolating themselves from their colleagues. They insultingly erected themselves into veritable censors. At Saarbrück they did the same with Richaud and Soubrany,[180] at Nancy they were at the gate of Faure without seeing him. The effect was most pernicious; it encouraged the aristocrats against the ordinary deputies, from whom it took away public confidence to such a point that the civil and military authorities refused to obey their decrees unless sanctioned by the extraordinary representatives. Here was a veritable dictatorship and a monstrosity. Thanks to Lacoste and his friends everything was going well until these two came, haughtily manifesting quite different principles. Hence he, Lacoste, desired his own recall. If these methods could deliver Landau, so much the better. The hostile attitude of Saint-Just and Le Bas toward those pure patriots, the Propagandists, was in itself enough to wreck the cause. He had just learned that the extraordinary deputies had renewed the department authorities, appointing a lot of tailors, wigmakers and the like. If the latter were capable, well and good; it was much to be feared that they were not and in any case the action should not have been taken without informing the other deputies. Lacoste's courage in writing such a letter against members of the two great Committees cannot be denied, but it must be remembered that the Extremists had not yet lost their power and one might well feel that the more exaggerated one's sentiments in a leftward direction, the safer one's head. The fact that Soubrany and Milhaud were just at this time sent by the Committee on a fresh mission to the Army of the Pyrenees shows that the Robespierrists were not yet prepared to break with their group.

Baudot made his protest to the Committee in a separate letter (29 Frimaire), inveighing against the exclusiveness of Saint-Just and Le Bas in a similar vein, though more mildly. He also desired his recall. Lémane, for his part, was quite willing to resign if he had to put up with Baudot much longer, so he told the Committee (30 Frimaire). He was disgusted with the retinue surrounding this deputy, "five hussars, fifteen horses, his wife and all the paraphernalia of a public fair," none of the tranquillity necessary to so important a commission, much noise and little work.

Baudot was never made for this country. What a difference between him and Saint-Just and Le Bas!

The generals, though certainly not congenial, were at first less quarrelsome than the deputies. Hoche wrote the Committee (29 Frimaire) that the day after his interview with Pichegru, Saint-Just and Le Bas ordered the two generals to concert measures for the prompt relief of Landau. He was working daily for that object and had moved his headquarters to his extreme right wing.[181] To the deputies of both groups, however, a commander in chief seemed essential, though as was to be expected they did not agree on the proper man for the post. Lacoste and Baudot proposed to the Committee (Oberbronn, 1 Nivôse, December 21) that Pichegru be removed. He had neither activity, daring, nor did he carry conviction; Hoche was the man for the place. They would have taken this step on themselves were it not for the confusion between their powers and those of their colleagues. On the second they wrote from Niederbronn, once more in a rage. The army had just won a great victory over the Austrians, capturing the heights of Reichshofen, which was in some degree due to the representatives' continual prodding.

We were today in Hatry's division, opposite Reichshofen, occupied in surveying all the military operations and in putting our hands to the task. But would you believe that the generals on the opposite wing disdained to inform us of their operations, but rather reported them to Saint-Just and Le Bas, who were at Bitche, eight leagues from the battlefield? That is the result of the difference in powers; it is such that while we spare neither rest nor patience to satisfy the soldier and to give activity to the generals, our mission seems to be subordinate, subjected to the benevolence of chiefs to whom one presumes to report everything. We are in no humor to let the national representation be so degraded. We reply to all the little intrigues by sharing the bread and straw of the soldier, by forcing the generals to do their duty and our colleagues to march with us as equals.

Three days later they had taken the bull by the horns so far as the army command was concerned. Circumstances called for immediate action, they wrote the Committee from Sultz on Christmas Day (5 Nivôse) and they could delay no longer. The two armies, being now united, could no longer be under different chiefs; they had appointed Hoche to the joint command. They had two objects in view, to hasten the Landau enterprise and to fix the confidence of the troops, who were decidedly in favor of Hoche and at least vacillating in regard to Pichegru, a man with no idea of the positions of his army and hardly known by his generals.

Carnot personally favored Hoche, though he esteemed

Pichegru and tactfully wrote Le Bas and Saint-Just that the selection of Hoche might paralyze operations unless it received their approval; the important thing was for all to act in harmony.[182]

Meanwhile Hoche, who had turned the Austrian flank and compelled their retreat, was winning victories at Woerth, at Kibelberg and in the gorges of Dahn and Annweiler, eliciting a congratulatory note from Saint-Just and Le Bas (Niederbronn, 3 Nivôse). The news that their rivals had stolen a march on them in the matter of the command, however, filled them with dismay. They wrote the Committee from Haguenau at midnight of the fifth that they had ordered the two generals to concert at once a plan to relieve Landau, giving Pichegru the command of the expedition. The two generals did confer and the first attack next day was successful. They hoped much from the accord which seemed to exist between the generals. Hoche was ardent and young, Pichegru more mature and experienced; his first orders won a decisive success. Yesterday at Haguenau, Pichegru informed them of the decree of Lacoste and Baudot, giving the supreme command to Hoche, who had accepted it. The situation was delicate; it was requisite to think of the fatherland only, to appease bitterness, cast off discouragement and avoid the results of passion. They would act prudently and were going to see Hoche at once.

Why, when you send your members to oversee the execution of your plans, why when you and we are responsible, do you abandon the country to the imprudent and light exercise of authority? You are not ignorant of the fact that those who have destroyed our decree do not know your views.

Count on our hearts; they are incapable of compromising the public interest through weakness. You know what you have to do.

To this enigmatic and somewhat menacing suggestion, they added their hope that all would go well. Justice should be rendered to Pichegru, who had sent 15,000 of his army to Hoche and had to repair the Wissembourg treason with the remainder. Let the Committee make known its intention as soon as possible. This stroke certainly came from an intrigue to divide and discourage the triumphant armies, the letter concluded.

In spite of these unseemly quarrels, victory in fullest measure rewarded the joint campaign. The Committee learned from Lacoste and Baudot (Ritzeth, 6 Nivôse) that Hoche had captured the heights of the Geisberg. The letter was pitched in a much lower key than before. They had held a conference with Saint-Just and Le Bas, with satisfactory result. Had these deputies or the Committee itself informed them of their plans more promptly, they would not have appointed Hoche. They did so, ignorant that another had been invested with this power. However, the result showed that they were not mistaken in their man. [Apparently they were now convinced that Saint-Just and Le Bas had the backing of the Committee.]

Worried letters from the Committee to the two groups of deputies (7 Nivôse) urged them to come to some agreement and expressed to Lacoste and Baudot its "pain and surprise" that they had removed Pichegru. No definitive action in this whole matter of the command should take place until they had talked with Saint-Just and Le Bas. Again on 9 Nivôse, the Committee reassured Saint-Just and Le Bas that "our principles, our views and our hearts are in accord with yours." The remedy for this misunderstanding or intrigue lay in "the love of country and the wisdom of which you have already given unequivocal proofs." Like them, the Committee esteemed the civic virtue and talents of Pichegru. "Do what love of concord and of country inspire you to do and may the Republic triumph." This was signed by Robespierre, Billaud-Varenne and Barère. Robespierre also wrote a note assuring them of the vigor of his personal support. It seems clear that these letters from the Committee must have been sent prior to their receipt of the report written by Lacoste on the sixth.

The Wissembourg lines were evacuated by the retreating Austrians and on 8 Nivôse a brief dispatch was sent to the Convention from Landau, signed by Baudot, Saint-Just, Lacoste,

Le Bas and Dentzel (a representative who had gone through the siege). The order of the signatures suggests that for the moment all jealousy was swallowed up in the elation of success. The dispatch read: "Glory be rendered to the French Republic!" On the same day the five representatives issued an order directing General Hoche to pursue his military operations until further word came from the Committee.

It was not long that they were to remain a happy family. While Landau was enduring its lengthy siege, two factions developed within the garrison, one headed by the representative Dentzel, the other by Delmas and Laubadère. Each group accused the other of desiring to surrender the fortress and each at various times gained the upper hand and imprisoned the leaders of the opposite faction. When the place was relieved, Lacoste and Baudot arrested Dentzel and his friends, while Saint-Just and Le Bas did likewise for Delmas and his associates. All regained their liberty after 9 Thermidor.[183]

The victory of Landau was the climax of the campaign and also of Saint-Just's mission. Alsace had been cleared of the enemy, all the military and political objectives had been gained and early in January, 1794, the two deputies returned to Paris. By 17 Nivôse (January 6), Saint-Just was once more signing decrees of the Committee of Public Safety.

Hoche continued to win victories, but refused to carry on an extended winter campaign in the Palatinate. For this he was arrested by the Committee, April 11, and remained in prison until after 9 Thermidor. Saint-Just has been represented as vindictively avenging himself in this fashion, but he was only one of those who signed the decree of arrest and had nothing to do with the order to wage war in the Palatinate.

Factional strife continued in Strasbourg after the departure of Saint-Just and Le Bas. The friends of Schneider and those whose wealth had been attacked by Saint-Just broke out so violently that the very names of Le Bas and Saint-Just could not be mentioned in the local popular society without cries of indignation being heard. So Monet, their partisan, was constrained to admit. But after Schneider's execution and the fall of the Hébertists, Saint-Just's friends regained control.[184] The representatives Goujon and Hentz, writing from Strasbourg as late as 4 Thermidor (July 22), still find echoes of the famous mission; "Strasbourg is in a better condition, the measures of Saint-Just and Le Bas have had happy results."

Lacoste continued to make fresh enemies. Complaints of the number of arrests ordered by him were made by the committee on national domains (8 Pluviôse), by Faure, former representative to the Army of the Moselle (21 Pluviôse) and even by Mallarmé, who requested the Committee to warn Lacoste and Baudot that there must be some degree of *ensemble* and regularity in their proceedings. This casts an interesting light on Lacoste's complaint of Saint-Just's exclusiveness and interference with other representatives, for Lacoste was also accused of interference. Indeed the constant recurrence of similar incidents in other parts of France makes one wonder whether jealousy was perhaps not general, even inevitable among deputies on mission, armed with overlapping authority. On 7 Ventôse (February 25), the Committee suppressed the revolutionary tribunal which Lacoste and Baudot were operating in Strasbourg.

After his arrest (13 Prairial, year III) on the charge of tyranny, falsehood and extreme terrorism during his Moselle mission, Lacoste wrote two pamphlets in which he not only defended his humane conduct, but denounced Saint-Just and Le Bas for having established at Strasbourg "a commission of blood, which covered the frontiers with mourning." They had caused the arrest of 20,000 persons. The success of the military campaign had been due to the measures taken by Baudot and himself against the stubborn resistance of Saint-Just and Le Bas. He appended various documents, one of which was a letter he wrote the Convention on 27 Frimaire, year II, demanding the recall of his rivals, and another a letter of Milhaud after their fall, alluding to Saint-Just as "the little dictator" and "the vain triumvir." [185]

Baudot, arrested the day after Lacoste, made a similar defense. Their commission at Strasbourg judged sixty-nine cases, he asserted, of whom sixty-four were acquitted, four condemned to various penalties and but one executed. "Saint-Just and Robespierre were so indignant at the justice of this tribunal, that they addressed to us, in the name of the Committee of Public Safety, a letter full of insults, with the order to suppress it at once and to send the accused to Paris." He had released many imprisoned by Saint-Just, whose régime he went on to describe as far more severe than his own.[186] Much as Baudot disliked Saint-Just, he could not help admiring his young colleague's bravery nor associating himself with it. Years later he told Edgar Quinet,

Saint-Just and I fired the batteries of Wissembourg. People applauded us a great deal for that. Well! we deserved no praise for it. We knew perfectly well that bullets could do nothing against us.

And again in his *Notes historiques* Baudot said regarding Saint-Just,

I too have seen him with the armies and I never saw anything like it. . . . My testimony will hardly be suspect.[187]

A correct view of Saint-Just's attitude toward these men is of importance, affecting as it necessarily does our estimate of his judgment and character. Their statements while in prison cannot be taken at face value, while on the other hand it was easy enough after Thermidor to denounce their fallen rival. Lacoste, it appears, was a drunkard [188] and no one who talked of guillotining a quarter of the inhabitants can have been very well poised. Baudot, according to his own admission in the pamphlet previously quoted, loved gayety and pleasure; he attached himself to the extremist party with its loud talk and exaggerated policies because this was for him the path of least resistance and the one that promised the most satisfaction. What had epicureans such as they in common with the stoicism of Saint-Just and Le Bas?

Shall it be said then that Saint-Just and Le Bas were merely supercilious in regard to their colleagues, filled with self-importance and vanity as the Committee's special representatives and ambitious to reap all the glory of saving Alsace? Or had they some reason to feel the other deputies unworthy of their confidence, perhaps gossipy, perhaps of doubtful ability or loyalty?

Human nature being what it is and politics what they are, the verdict cannot be clear-cut. It is altogether likely that the responsibility placed on Saint-Just went to his head. He was very young, with a clever youth's confidence in his own powers. All his life he had the pride of Lucifer. Exclusiveness was the cardinal error of the Robespierrists; people grew to fear and hate them because of it and it was for this reason that they fell.

On the other hand, most of the other deputies were men of little account. They had a record of consistent failure in Alsace and the situation was too delicate to permit of trifling. Painful as it was to them, this new mission was actually of superior authority, sent especially by the Committee to clarify a confused situation and to bring order out of chaos. It was impossible to be confidential with other leaders, whose acts were under scrutiny and whose judgment was already regarded with suspicion. Lacoste and Baudot, having but recently arrived,[189] might justly feel exempt from this censure and resent the discrimination. Lacoste in particular seems to have been a man of energy and tenacity; many of his decrees and letters show sound sense and a clear head. On the matter of Hoche versus Pichegru, he backed the better man. But on other occasions he spoke the wildest folly. Perhaps he did so when in his cups; there was some defect of habit or of balance here which made it unwise to trust his judgment very far. Again his temperament was as dominating as Saint-Just's own; Alsace was too small at that critical moment to allow two leaders of equal power. Finally, Lacoste and his colleagues made themselves impossible by affiliating with the ultraviolent party and supporting the German

Schneider. The conviction was gaining ground at Paris that the extremists and those foreigners who had announced themselves as pure revolutionists were really linked in a diabolical conspiracy to discredit the cause. Saint-Just could not have struck hands with Lacoste without exposing himself to grave suspicion in the eyes of his own group. Nor was he likely to, being himself one of the most active protagonists of this particular theory.[190]

One other aspect of this mission gives ground for controversy. The most diverse opinions have been formed regarding the extent and quality of Saint-Just's terrorism. It may be fairly assumed that Le Bas followed his lead in most of these matters, occasionally perhaps moderating his friend's ardor. Lacoste's assertion that Saint-Just established a commission of blood has been accepted in some quarters. Lurid tales were told of his Spartan rigorism, such as that of his visiting the troops and being welcomed by a young officer, his childhood friend, who broke discipline by rushing out to greet him without dressing properly; Saint-Just is said to have embraced him with the words: "Heaven be doubly praised, since I have seen you again and since through the person of a man so dear to me, I can give a lesson of discipline and an example of justice, by immolating you to the public safety." He then turned him over to the military commission to be shot.[191] Dismissing such fables, there are the contemporary utterances of those who admired and those who hated him. There is the letter from his friend Gateau to Daubigny, adjunct minister of war, found among Robespierre's papers.

Strasbourg, septidi, 27 brumaire.
It was high time Saint-Just came to this unfortunate army, and that he dealt vigorous axblows to the fanaticism of the Alsatians, to their indolence, to their German stupidity, to the egoism, the cupidity, the perfidy of the rich: otherwise it would have been all up with these fine departments. He has vivified, reanimated, regenerated everything, and to finish this job there is coming to us from all corners a column of revolutionary apostles, solid sansculottes; the holy guillotine is in the most brilliant activity and the

beneficent Terror is producing here in a miraculous way what one could not hope from at least a century through reason and philosophy. What a masterful son of a gun this lad is! [*Quel maître bougre que ce garçon là!*] The collection of his decrees will be without contradiction one of the finest historical monuments of the Revolution.[192]

There is the letter from an officer in the same rough revolutionary style as the preceding.

Well now, Rougiff, three cheers for the French Republic! Five hundred *émigrés* sent to hell at Turckheim by the republicans. Saint-Just and Le Bas are there! You may rest in peace! These hairy rascals [*bougres à poil*] will not come back until they have exterminated those that are left.[193]

There is Guyardin's letter early in November, beginning

Terror is the order of the day; the aristocrat is in consternation and the hidden traitor trembles, seeing himself impotent to harm. . . . Saint-Just and Le Bas rival us in measures which are severe, but indispensably necessary for the public safety.[194]

There is the officer Legrand's opinion that "the more one examines Saint-Just's conduct, the more one is persuaded that the profound Machiavelli was only a child in comparison." [195]

Obviously they had a reputation among their friends for rigorous methods. How this was magnified by their enemies into extreme ferocity may be illustrated by the following supposed interview. On October 31, it is said, Taffin, one of the judges of Schneider's court, went to Saint-Just. As soon as the latter saw him, he burst out, "Well, how many heads?" "But," stammered the judge, "the commission has only been sitting for twice twenty-four hours; it has been trying to raise the value of the *assignats* and hopes that in a short time the national paper . . ."

What? [Saint-Just interrupted furiously.] What is all that song and dance you are giving me? [*que me chantez-vous là?*] Are you there to spend your time about paper? No! but to exterminate the traitors with which the department swarms! So, in office for twice twenty-four hours and you haven't yet bumped off [*fait sauter*] two dozen heads! Go tell the members of your commission that if they don't want to take heads, I will take theirs myself and in short order!

Soon after came Schramm of the military commission. "We have condemned several individuals to imprisonment," he reported; "several others to deportation." "Deportation!" roared Saint-Just; "imprisonment! Is that your job? Shoot! Shoot!" [196]

The entire falsity of this tale is obvious. The authority for it is a member of the Hébertist faction, a bitter enemy of Saint-Just. The coarse colloquialism of the language and the violent temper attributed to Saint-Just were equally foreign to his nature; that he was a man of extreme courtesy, cold, laconic speech and stoical self-restraint is the unanimous testimony of those who knew him, borne out by the evidence of his written words. Instead of regarding the increased value of government paper as of no consequence, his decrees show that the attainment of this end was an important object of his mission and he reported his achievement of it to Bouchotte with pride in his letter of 26 Brumaire.

Another statement of Saint-Just's harshness, far too long to quote, is embodied in an appeal to the Convention by the publisher Treuttel of Strasbourg for reimbursement of the losses suffered by him in connection with the levy of nine millions on the rich.[197] The petition abounds in references to the "pains and sufferings" which this mission caused the citizens, "the barbarities" of "these tyrants," the "crying injustices performed at Strasbourg by the conspirators Saint-Just and Le Bas," etc. Treuttel's business, according to his story, was ruined by an assessment far beyond his ability to pay.

To this it may be remarked that Treuttel's petition is dated 20 Fructidor, which was after Saint-Just's death. It was easy to denounce him then. Treuttel also disingenuously confuses Saint-Just and Schneider in a common accusation; in fact it seems to be Schneider who did him the greater amount of damage. It is entirely possible that this levy of nine millions was a rough and ready calculation which may have gone too far in more than one individual case. Treuttel may have had a real grievance. But a single line that he wrote throws his otherwise unknown personality into relief for an instant like a flash of lightning in a dark night. He appends to his petition a copy of the decree levying nine millions. When he comes to the sentence, "Two millions shall be taken from this tax for the needs of the indigent patriots of Strasbourg," Treuttel introduces a parenthetical comment of his own, "Was this object necessary in a commune where there are no indigent people except lazy ones?" There seems to speak the hard-boiled business man who has no patience with social service and has not been educated up to Community Funds. Saint-Just was not a popularity-seeking politician, like Baudot and Schneider; he was too self-sufficient to care for applause. The fact that Strasbourg was a besieged city is in itself evidence enough that business could not have been going on as usual. In spite of Treuttel's cold indifference, there must have been unemployment and suffering among the poor. In any event, it is clear that the public cause needed funds to provide the army with equipment essential to win the campaign and it is also clear that for all their profuse promises, the rich had not been doing their share. Whatever the justice of specific assessments, the principle of the levy seems warranted by the circumstances.

Even those predisposed against Saint-Just sometimes felt it necessary to admit that there were limits to the man's cruelty. It is said that the Committee of General Security was considering a project of mass drownings when Saint-Just arrived. The suspects were to be loaded into boats on pretext of an enemy attack; the Austrians would shoot at the boats, supposing them loaded with troops; the French would also fire on the boats and sink them as though by accident. "Saint-Just would have none of it; he was no Carrier." [198]

Eulogists have gone to the other extreme. Buchez and Roux asserted that not a drop of blood was shed by Saint-Just and Le Bas during their mission. Michelet said that the guillotine, permanently erected in the public square of Strasbourg, was to terrify traitors; it obtained all the effects of terror without the necessity of shedding blood.[199]

This was apparently not true. Hippolyte Carnot believes that they proceeded with excessive severity, though justifying them because of the real danger from *émigrés*.[200] The most reliable information seems to be that furnished by Chuquet. He quotes a letter written by Saint-Just and Le Bas on December 2 to the revolutionary commission which they had created. "Your procedures languish," their rebuke runs; "you are too slow in hearing the accused and you allow your verdicts to be foreseen; you were appointed to be prompt, just and severe, but remember that death is under the seat of unjust judges as well as under that of the guilty." To this the judges replied that their task was difficult; thirty or forty came up for trial every day who must be fairly heard. "Give us back your confidence or take back your appointments: we shall do better perhaps, with knapsack on back and gun on shoulder." This spirited reply restored the support of the representatives. From 7 Brumaire to 16 Ventôse (October 28, 1793–March 6, 1794) the commission pronounced 660 judgments; 282 persons were acquitted, 62 sentenced to death, 34 to irons, 34 to ordinary imprisonment, 24 to detention until the peace, 36 [officers?] were degraded, 188 [officers and soldiers?] sent to the interior for incorporation into other regiments.[201] The greater part of these cases seem to have been military, but as the mission was established to have jurisdiction especially over bad administration, grafting and intelligence of traitorous citizens with the enemy, it must have included these civil cases as well. In that event, if the figures are to be relied on, we have an exact statistical summary of the Terror in Strasbourg, so far as it was a matter of the courts authorized by Saint-Just. As will be observed, the period covered is something over four months or twice the length of Saint-Just's mission. No doubt the great majority of these executions took place during the mission, as with its end Alsace ceased to be in danger. How many of the victims were shot as opposed to those guillotined there is no way of telling, though the major part were probably officers or soldiers who suffered the former penalty; the *Œuvres* contain no direct orders of execution by either method. In addition, the criminal tribunal of the department, sitting at Strasbourg, Schelestadt and elsewhere pronounced 22 death sentences between August 30, 1793, and February 7, 1794, while Schneider's roving court condemned 32 to death between October 23 and December 13.[202] For these, however, Saint-Just and Le Bas cannot be held responsible.

So far as the numbers executed are concerned, there is little to choose between Schneider's court and Saint-Just's. It would seem a case of the pot calling the kettle black. It is quite impossible to wash the red stains off Saint-Just's hands, either here or at Paris. He believed in the method of terror and he used it. Whether in the long run it did more harm than good is another question. But it certainly worked in Alsace. The only opening for discussion is whether there was any difference other than party label between the Hébertist and the Robespierrist. The clearest distinction seems to be one of general approach. The Hébertists were loud-mouthed fellows, talking vaguely in superlatives, interlarded with oaths and coarse expressions, spreading general uneasiness by the looseness of their denunciations; they reeled about, many of them tipsy, threatening to take off the heads of half the population. The Robespierrists were cold, quiet, restrained and businesslike; nearly as deadly perhaps in fact, but much more certain of what they were doing and why they did it. They were rarely if ever guilty of wholesale slaughter, like the September massacres or the *noyades* of Carrier at Nantes and the *fusillades* of Fouché at Lyons. These were the work of anti-Robespierrist extremists. The Robespierre group had a reason (good or bad) for each of their death sentences. Further, almost all the executions ordered by Saint-Just's commission were directly connected with the discipline, efficiency and proper conduct of the campaign, while Schneider decapitated civilians, sometimes for no worse offense than "singing insulting songs." The latter's court was more strictly speaking a "terrorist" machine than the former, which while also interested in creating a certain psychology, was even more directed toward the elimination of specific abuses. General Dubois admitted that Saint-Just and Le Bas were right in shooting the chief culprits. "That measure," he said, "was absolutely necessary to restore confidence and discipline." Legrand, one of the best-informed and most sagacious men in the army, asked himself whether terrorism if properly and skillfully used could produce the same results as heroism and came to the conclusion that it could, "though it is not to the credit of the human race." [203] It should also be noticed that for every man sent to his death by Saint-Just's court, four were acquitted.

The mission to Alsace was one of the most constructive episodes in Saint-Just's life. So much of his brief span was taken up with denunciation and destruction that it is refreshing to see him occupied with building up a better order. Of course he really did a great deal of that in the Committee of Public Safety, but it is hard to disentangle his work there from that of others. In Alsace it stands out clearly. The Alsatian mission justly deserves its reputation as one of the most successful in the history of the Revolution.

XIV

FIRST MISSION TO THE NORTH: INSPECTION

HILE Saint-Just and his comrade were putting new life into the Alsace campaign, events at Paris had been moving swiftly. The Girondin leaders, Mme. Roland, the ex-Duke of Orléans, Bailly, first mayor of Paris, had all paid the supreme penalty. With these events Saint-Just had obviously nothing to do. Following the principle of cellular subdivision, which holds true of omnipotent political parties no less than of biological organisms, the Mountain, deprived of external opposition, began to disintegrate. During Frimaire the moderate wing, headed by Danton and Desmoulins, started their campaign for clemency. Robespierre tried to steer a middle course between them and the Hébert ultras, being really sympathetic with neither group. In Frimaire he tended to favor the moderates, during Nivôse the extremists. It has been said that his irresolution was painful until Saint-Just came back from the Rhine, full of energy and radiating confidence, for this determined young man was wont to say, "I know where I am going." [204] This is true enough of Saint-Just, but not quite fair to Robespierre. Already the notion that the two wings were both hostile to the republic's best interests and even in some dim way connected in that hostility, had begun to form in his mind. There is no doubt that Saint-Just also held this view, whoever may have first suggested it. At least a week before his return from Alsace, Robespierre read in the Convention (5 Nivôse, December 25) a report which linked together the two evils of moderation and excess. While Saint-Just no doubt strengthened this conviction, there is nothing to indicate the younger man's direct responsibility for the idea.

Meanwhile the northern campaign was at a standstill.

Jourdan felt that his 15,000 effectives were inadequate for an offensive operation; in consequence he was replaced in command of the Army of the North by Pichegru, January 6, 1794.[205] Perhaps it was because they knew and approved of this general, as well as because of their brilliant work in Alsace, that Saint-Just and Le Bas were selected to put life into this dead sector. On 3 Pluviôse (January 22) the Committee of Public Safety decreed that Saint-Just should leave for the Army of the North "with the unlimited powers of representatives of the people to investigate army conditions, to survey in particular the situation of the towns of Lille, Maubeuge and Bouchain and to take such measures as the interest of the Republic requires." Nothing was said about Le Bas. He was, however, included in the Convention's decree of 7 Pluviôse, which was the official mandate. Whether Le Bas received verbal instructions to accompany Saint-Just, whether his name was accidentally omitted from the Committee's decree or whether he went along at Saint-Just's request, afterward regularized by the Convention, is not known. The fact that the two men left immediately after the Committee's decree and at least three days before that of the Convention, illustrates where the real power lay. Bouchotte wrote Saint-Just (4 Pluviôse), "You have left for the North without giving us warning; I am sending you the information I had prepared for you." In view of contradictory reports, he continued, it was hard to know what was going on up there. By the eighth (January 27) Saint-Just, Le Bas and Pichegru had reached Guise. They went straight on to the important city of Lille, which they gained the next day in the midst of a terrible snowstorm, as Le Bas wrote his wife.

Here on the ninth they issued seven decrees, the first two being signed also by Florent-Guyot, a representative already on the ground. The first had to do with the defense of the town and suggests lessons learned at Strasbourg. The city gates and those of the citadel were to be closed between 3 P.M. and 8 A.M. Any officer not in at closing time would be discharged. Foreigners must stay indoors after six. Unauthorized persons found

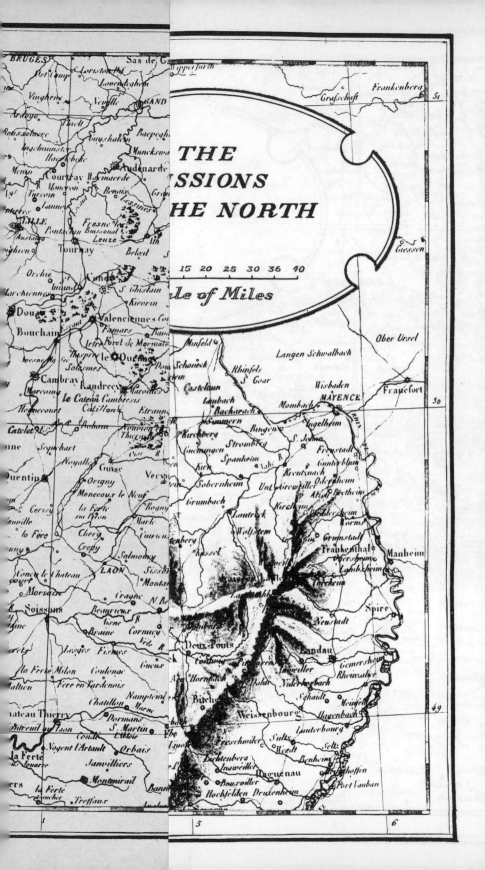

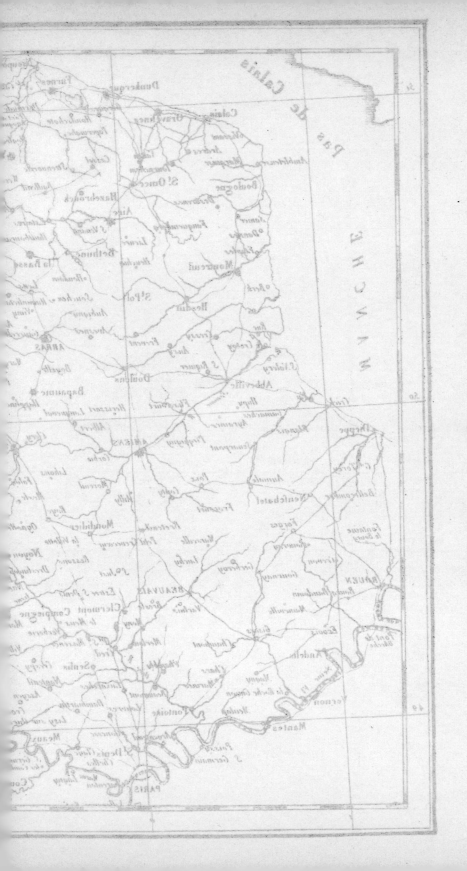

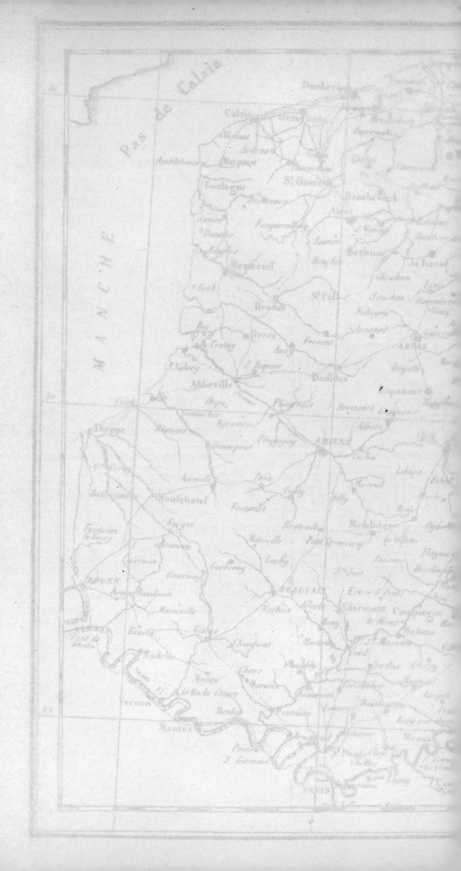

in the fortifications would be imprisoned for six months. Soldiers unattached to the garrison must leave within twenty-four hours. No one might communicate with detained suspects. The criminal court was ordered to raze the house of anyone convicted of speculation and of merchants violating the maximum. The last clause received the approval of Collot d'Herbois in a session of the Jacobins (28 Pluviôse). The discussion turned on the patriotism of the rich at Lille.

Saint-Just and Le Bas have already pronounced that the houses of those who do not execute the laws shall be demolished [said Collot]. There is a lesson which ought to be put in practice everywhere. The representatives of the people should make a commentary on this salutary text.[206]

Another decree of interest for the light it throws on Saint-Just's social ideas requisitions all cattle in seven localities for the army, which has meat for three days only. Cows can be taken only after no more oxen are left. A third of the animals shall be taken from those who have more than four beasts. There shall be no levy on those who have less until this third is used up. Levies shall then be made successively on those who have four, three, two and one. Any attempt to hide cattle shall be met with confiscation. Otherwise the cattle shall be bought at the maximum and evaluated by experts. Complaints shall be referred to the representatives and must not delay purchases. As at Strasbourg, there was a forced loan assessed on the rich, though the decree is missing; it was perhaps levied by predecessors of Saint-Just and Le Bas. Their own dry decree is drastic enough:

The forced loan will be doubled for the rich of Lille who have not paid their quota in ten days. It will be tripled ten days later.

Rigorous as most of their measures were, the representatives tried to temper justice with mercy. They ordered the liberation of the Saint-Pol committee of surveillance (Lille, 10 Pluviôse). The committee would resume its functions, but was cautioned to respect in others the patriotism in whose name it had claimed its freedom. On the other hand the postmaster who had contemptuously called that committee the dregs of the people was himself imprisoned for a month to expiate his insolence. This action indicates once more a policy favorable to the lower classes. One recalls that Saint-Pol was Le Bas's home town; members of the committee were doubtless boyhood friends. A letter of the same date to the Committee of Public Safety carries the news that the enemy had drawn ten men per company from several divisions for service at Trèves. An offensive in the North was therefore desirable.

This first mission in the North was really an inspection. No serious campaign could be undertaken until spring. Meanwhile the new general had an opportunity to study his problem, while the representatives would see that supplies were on hand, correct any glaring evils and report their findings to Paris. The task was entirely different from the long, hard pull required in Alsace. It called for the covering of a wide territory in a brief time. So after two days in Lille, 11 Pluviôse found them at Cambrai, the twelfth and thirteenth at Réunion-sur-Oise (revolutionary name for Guise); a letter on the thirteenth was written at Arques; on the fifteenth and sixteenth they were at Maubeuge. There are also decrees signed by them at Arras and at Réunion-sur-Oise, all on the sixteenth, the last day of the mission.[207]

A considerable letter to the Committee (12 Pluviôse) bears renewed witness to the imperative tone they did not hesitate to use to this all-powerful body. The language is without question Saint-Just's; Le Bas would have written otherwise. The letter complained that the area set aside for the Army of the North, presumably meaning its supply area, was insufficient, since it had been fixed on a basis of 100,000 men and there were now 240,000. The organization of supply trains was without common sense. All the wagons were started from the same point along one road, which was choked with 700 carts; bread and provisions came up late, the cavalry was perishing. Why not establish caissons and food depots at the points where it was desired to station the armies?

Are you going to wait until you are attacked or do you intend to attack? In the latter case prepare the position of the stores, make ready your plans this very evening, place your cavalry, direct the supply trains, in order to facilitate the onslaught of our forces at the opening of the campaign.

Increase the supply area by half, since by incorporation of other forces the army is increased by half and more. That is about the state of affairs. The roads are impassable. We made eight leagues a day by post horses from Douai to Guise. . . .

It would be very wise on your part to become the aggressors, to open the campaign first, and since your army will be very strong you will be able simultaneously to direct one army on Ostend, one on Beaumont, to invest Valenciennes and to attack the forest of Mormale. Let us always be the boldest, we shall also be then the most fortunate. We are about to leave for Maubeuge; we shall write you from there.

The man was a very dynamo of energy.

From Arques Saint-Just and his colleague sent this curt, scathing note to one Prutin, an army commissary.

What is to be thought of the man who, entrusted with the army's needs, has left the division of Arques for four days without provisions? That man is you; we will investigate your conduct within three days and you must expect rigorous punishment if you are guilty.

At Maubeuge, the representatives believed that they had unearthed a plot to deliver the place to the enemy. A number of suspects were arrested and a letter sent to the authorities of Arras requesting them to seize an Englishman named (in Saint-Just's orthography) Faëlding.[208] The promised letter from Maubeuge was largely concerned with the conspiracy and the steps taken to foil it as well as with the unsatisfactory state of the army's food supply. It closed with the adjuration:

Arms are needed. Hasten recruiting. The army will open the campaign in three weeks at latest.

Possibly in consequence of this plot scare, the representatives published a savage decree at Arras; all ex-nobles in the departments of Pas-de-Calais, the North, the Somme, the Aisne, were to be arrested within twenty-four hours and placed under close confinement. Local committees of surveillance were made responsible for execution of the order.

One of the more violent deputies on mission, the ex-priest Le Bon, was operating in this sector. He was cautioned several times by the Committee and ultimately lost Robespierre's personal confidence, but though he recalls Schneider on more than one count, the two were not put in the same category. He always spoke with respect of the work done by Saint-Just. So in a letter to the Committee from Bapaume (19 Pluviôse) after recounting the obstacles placed in his path by counter-revolutionaries, he wrote, "Fortunately for me, Le Bas and Saint-Just keep the department of the North in awe; for in spite of my good intentions I have not been able as yet to make a dent in it." From Arras he wrote brutally a fortnight later (3 Ventôse), finding evidence of the value of Saint-Just's and Le Bas's decree against the nobles in the swarms of weeping country women who came to him seeking the return of their former landlords; it seemed to him indecent that they should want their masters back for a morsel of bread. As late as 8 Floréal (April 27) he was still enforcing this measure. Perhaps having Le Bon's activities in mind, the Committee stated (1 Ventôse) that having been informed that the decree issued by the representatives Saint-Just and Le Bas, relative to the arrest of former nobles in the departments of the North, Pas-de-Calais, the Aisne and the Somme, was being abused by malevolent persons who gave it an arbitrary and vexatious extension to non-noble citizens, the Committee now ordered that the authorities charged with the decree's execution should restrict themselves within its terms and literal sense.[209]

A long printed circular of instructions from the Committee to the national agents, dated Paris, 15 Pluviôse, purports to be signed by ten members including Saint-Just, but this is obviously impossible as he was still on mission. The return of the deputies was not on the twenty-fifth of that month as Vellay incorrectly says (*Œuvres*, II, 185), but on the twenty-fourth at latest, when Saint-Just began signing the Committee's decrees once more. The mission had lasted from January 3 to February 12, counting from Paris to Paris. The two representatives were formally received at the Jacobins on 6 Ventôse (February 24).

Epigrams grew like fungi with little root and with ephemeral substance on this as on all Saint-Just's missions; for example the story that at Guise he complained that not enough arrests were being made and when told that the prisons were full, replied: "The cemeteries, not the prisons, should be gorged with traitors." [210]

Again there is the usual conflict of testimony about Saint-Just's terrorism. Dumont, likewise a terrorist, denounced him before the Convention as having fed the courts with victims, sent without examination to the scaffold. But this was in December, 1794, when the current of opinion was running the other way and Dumont was anxious to save his own skin.[211] On the other hand, the apologists assert that, as before, Saint-Just and Le Bas obtained all the results of terror without bloodshed. They imposed their will by their own dignity.[212] There is no proof of either statement.

However these things may be, there is no doubt of Saint-Just's revolutionary activity nor of its success. Two letters from the war minister (10 and 17 Pluviôse) give him a general survey of the whole military picture and in particular of the bad spirit in the North. New men were appearing with louder voices than the true sans-culottes. Though the enemy was advancing, these men were whispering the notion of peace, exaggerating French successes to give a false sense of security, announcing great captures to hamper requisitions; "if you can clean up all that, you will be doing one more good job." [213]

The victorious campaign of 1794 was the sequel of Saint-Just's first northern mission. That sequel seemed to show that he had done "one more good job."

XV

TREASONS, STRATAGEMS AND SPOILS

OT long after his return, Saint-Just was honored by being elected president of the Convention, though the youngest member of that body. He served as such from 1 to 16 Ventôse (February 19–March 6, 1794).[214] This did not prevent him from taking a most conspicuous part in the stormy events of that well-named month. Four times he mounted the tribune to denounce plots against the state or crookedness among its agents or to propose far-reaching plans for social reconstruction; two of these speeches were delivered during his presidency. Among the Indulgents (Danton's friends) were a considerable number of venal deputies, who had been involved in the scandal of the East India Company, in stock manipulations, fraudulent army contracts and the like. Such were Delaunay d'Angers, Fabre d'Eglantine, Julien of Toulouse, Chabot, Basire and others. Among the Extremists (Hébert's friends) were some rich foreign radicals who had taken a leading part in working for dechristianization, the maximum, and ultraviolence. Such were the Belgian Proly, the Austrian Frey brothers, the Danish Diedrichsen, the Spanish Guzman, the Prussian Cloots, the English Boyd, and the Jew Pereyra. As long ago as October 12, Fabre, knowing that some of his grafting friends were under suspicion, had sought to draw a red herring across his own trail by denouncing the Extremists to the Committees as involved in a stupendous "foreign plot" to discredit the Revolution by overviolence, while revealing its secrets to the enemy. They were all spies and foreign agents, he said, not honest enthusiasts for the cause. He even went so far as to double-cross some of his own associates by connecting them with the other group, as for example Julien of Toulouse and Chabot, who were intimate with Proly, while Chabot had married the sister of the Freys. He likewise identified Hérault-Séchelles with both groups. This denunciation was believed by Robespierre, Saint-Just and their associates and on the strength of it Fabre escaped suspicion for a long time until a forged decree he had signed linked him up with the East India Company scandal and he joined his presumably reproachful accomplices in prison. But though disillusioned about Fabre, the Committees held fast to the substantial truth of the story he had told and continued to believe in a mysterious underground connection between important members of the two extreme parties, seemingly poles apart in policy. The connection lay in the fact that both were selling the country out to its enemies: the Indulgents, by frauds, by advocating clemency to aristocrats and by crying peace where there was no peace; the Extremists, by making the Revolution ridiculous through excess.[215]

As the winter of 1793-94 wore on, the food situation grew steadily worse and with it public restlessness. Food was seized by rioters without formality of payment. Attacks on the Committees came from both sides, but those from the Left were the more ominous. For prudential reasons, if for no other, the government veered steadily toward the Left; the swing in that direction which was already marked in Nivôse was accentuated during the following month. On 17 Pluviôse (February 5), Robespierre made a notable declaration of policy before the Convention, in course of which he went so far as to say that social protection was due only to peaceable citizens and that the only citizens in a republic were the republicans. Royalists and conspirators were only outsiders, or rather enemies. On 3 Ventôse (February 21) Barère presented the elaborate tables of maximal prices, which the Convention had decreed in principle during the previous October. Yet the ground swell mounted steadily and the tempest of public anger beat in torrents upon the plunging ship of state.

The Indulgents none the less retained strength enough in the Convention to put through a decree on the fourth requiring the Committees of Public Safety and General Security to present a report on "incarcerated persons." Saint-Just was appointed by the Committees for this duty. The result was the famous report of 8 Ventôse (February 26), considered by some as the sequel of Robespierre's speech of 17 Pluviôse, the two together marking the definite program of their faction.

The portion of Saint-Just's report which has seemed most significant to recent historians lies almost concealed in a paragraph or two toward the end. The first ten pages were devoted to a justification of the Terror and a denunciation of the Indulgents. He defended a drastic policy on the ground that while one must of course be just, it was more important to be just to the public than to the private interest. This dangerous theory, suggesting the occasional necessity of punishing innocent men for reasons of public policy, has been invoked on various occasions from Pontius Pilate to our own times with little advantage to public welfare. But in practice, Saint-Just had no doubt that those punished by the Tribunal were really guilty. He contrasted the moderation of the existing system with the cruelty of the old régime, asserting that Louis XVI used to hang 15,-000 smugglers a year and break 3,000 on the wheel.

Citizens, by what illusion could one be persuaded that you are inhuman? Your Revolutionary Tribunal has put to death 300 rascals within a year. Has the Spanish Inquisition done no more? And for what a cause, great God! Have the English courts destroyed no one this year? And Bender, who roasted Belgian children! And the German dungeons, where people are buried, nobody mentions them! Does anyone talk of clemency to the kings of Europe? No: do not let them soften you.

Poor Louis XVI is here most foully slandered. He was no butcher and Saint-Just knew it, though it was the fashion of the time to say so. As for Bender, every war seems fated to have its quota of atrocity stories and the Belgian children here play their customary rôle. But there had been plenty of cruelty under the old régime, leaving Louis XVI out of it, and the penal code was barbarous enough all over Europe. Saint-Just, in denouncing the hypocritical holier-than-thou attitude of foreigners, makes an excellent point.

Pity for criminals and traitors was to Saint-Just a clear index of treason. The first of all considerations was the preservation of the republic. From this standpoint justice had nothing in common with "a cruel clemency," but rather with severity. He excoriated the Indulgents as "marching with slow steps," as opportunist and defeatist. Silence was no longer possible concerning the immunity of the great offenders, "who wish to destroy the scaffold because they fear to mount it themselves." Weakness now might result in thirty years of civil war, he predicted. In Saint-Just's mind there was a close connection between the corruption of his opponents and their easy-going policy. Their own vices kept them from being strict with others.

One would think that each one, frightened by his conscience and the inflexibility of the laws, said to himself: We are not virtuous enough to be so terrible; philosophic legislators, take pity on my weakness; I dare not say to you, I am corrupt; I prefer to say to you, you are cruel!

With this neat thrust he pinioned the Chabots and Fabres and cast suspicion on their fellow Indulgents who had not yet been caught.

So far the report had been one of those philippics for which he was noted and in which he excelled. But in the next two paragraphs, he turned abruptly to a constructive social program of such breath-taking comprehensiveness that it probably had a share in his party's fall. It is not too much to say that these two paragraphs, with the action motivated on them, changed the course of history.

Indeed, the course of events leads us perhaps to results which we had not anticipated. Wealth is in the hands of a rather large number of the Revolution's enemies; their needs make the working people dependent on their foes. Do you think that an empire can exist, if civil relations bring about a state of things contrary to the form of government? Those who make revolutions by halves only dig their own graves. The Revolution brings us to recognition of this principle, that he who has shown himself his country's enemy cannot own its land.

We need a few more strokes of genius to save us. Is it then for the gratification of its tyrants that the people spills its blood on the frontiers, and that all families wear mourning for their children? You admit this principle, that he only has rights in our country, who has helped to set it free. Abolish pauperism, which dishonors a free state; the properties of patriots are sacred, but those of conspirators are there for the unfortunate. The unfortunate are the lords of the earth; they have the right to speak as masters to governments which neglect them. These principles are subversive of corrupt governments; they would destroy yours, if you let it be corrupted; do you then crush injustice and crime, if you do not want them to crush you.

Having laid down this truly revolutionary doctrine, the speaker turned to less contentious issues. The way to make democracy unshakable, he asserted with obvious truth, was to get people to take part in public life. The ordinary man sits in the popular societies as a spectator instead of as a judge. It is painful to see him applauding officeholders and so putting himself in second place. It recalled to Saint-Just's mind the society at Strasbourg, when Alsace was being lost; a society made up of job holders, really hostile to the Revolution.

He insisted that to make the republic flourish, the important thing was to punish the guilty and purify the government of aristocrats and financiers. Justice was more redoubtable than mere terror. Terror was a double-edged weapon, which some used to avenge the people and others to establish tyranny; terror filled the prisons but passed like a storm, leaving a frightful calm; "we are always more indulgent after than before terror." Here Saint-Just was attacking the Extremists and suggesting once more the connection between them and the Indulgents.

A revolution had taken place in government, he continued, but it had not penetrated social conditions. Government rested on liberty, social conditions on aristocracy. *"Dare!* This word contains the whole policy of our revolution."

The foreigner sought to rule by fomenting discord in France;

he should have war for war; his partisans must be met with sequestration.

As for you, destroy the rebel party; make liberty hard as steel; avenge the patriot victims of intrigue; let good sense and modesty be the order of the day; let there not be a single unfortunate or poor man in the state; only at this price will you have made a real revolution and a true Republic. Ah! what thanks will you get for the misery of the good and the prosperity of the wicked?

Your committees present to you the following decree:

Art. 1. The Committee of General Security is invested with the power of liberating patriots under arrest. Every person who claims his liberty shall give an account of his conduct since May 1, 1789.

Art. 2. The properties of patriots are inviolable and sacred. Those of persons known as enemies of the Revolution shall be sequestrated for the profit of the Republic; these persons shall be under detention until the peace and then banished for life.

At the end of the speech, the Convention arose with one consent and adopted these proposals amid unanimous applause. It decreed further that the report be printed and sent to the municipalities, popular societies and armies. Danton, the Indulgent leader, no doubt alarmed at the Committee's evident drift toward the Extremists, offered an additional article, proposing that each revolutionary committee send the Committee of General Security a list of its members and their revolutionary activities. This was directed against "false patriots with red caps," by whom he meant the Hébertists. The article was referred to the Committee of Public Safety, where it died. That night at the Jacobins, Collot d'Herbois eulogized the decrees and the report of Saint-Just, "that young and courageous athlete of liberty." The Convention had ordered, Collot said, that it should be printed and distributed to all the popular societies. He could say that they were hungry and thirsty for it. When one heard great principles developed, one felt all their force; Saint-Just's speech belonged in this category; "we spent last night discussing it and we could not tire of hearing it; it contains maxims too fine and too wise for me to refrain from making it my duty to propagate them as far as in me lies." He then quoted various nuggets from the report, concluding that these were the virtues that should be practiced. His remarks were punctuated by applause.[216] Five months later, Collot was Saint-Just's bitter enemy. It may be added that on the twenty-fourth, Tallien reported to the Convention a letter from his colleague Ysabeau on mission at Bordeaux, who had read the speech of 8 Ventôse aloud in the Temple of Reason with great effect.

Some writers have considered the social program of the closing paragraphs the whole point of Saint-Just's speech.[217] It may certainly be said that as the days passed, this bulked larger and larger, that it may well have contributed to the crisis of Thermidor and that had that crisis been safely passed, it would have perhaps become the outstanding characteristic of the French Revolution. Possibly the modern Russian experiment would have been antedated, at least in the matter of proletarian dictatorship, though not of communism. But as one reads the report of 8 Ventôse, one must wonder whether Saint-Just and his friends quite realized at that moment the importance of what they were doing. The scheme is so incidental to the main point of the report, which is the maintenance of Terror despite the wishes of the Indulgents, that it is almost buried in a few paragraphs, though it reappears as a part of one of the decrees. Either its full purpose was consciously understated lest alarm be excited or Saint-Just and Robespierre were starting something bigger than they knew, which gradually grew in potentialities the more they discussed it and thought about it. The latter seems the more reasonable explanation; the main purpose of Saint-Just on 8 Ventôse was to see that Chabot, Basire, Fabre and their ilk stayed behind prison bars until their cases were properly disposed of. It should be said, however, that the second article was not ignored by public comment, as appears from a debate in the Convention on 10 Ventôse, concerning the danger of suspects eluding the law by deeding their property to personal friends.[218]

During this session, reports were received from the front and the air was electric with the war spirit. Certain departments had sent delegates to Paris to study the manufacture of saltpeter, powder and cannon. A representative of these made a patriotic speech to the Convention, congratulating it on its efficient labors. To Saint-Just as the presiding officer fell the lot of making the official reply, which was appropriate in view of his own martial exertions. He spoke as follows:

All French republicans are called on to defend the fatherland, but not all in the same way. You help save liberty by preparing the mine, which in bursting will pulverize the enemies of the French Republic. Citizens, your desires are shared by all the French; no peace until the vanquished tyrants prostrate themselves before our triumphant Republic. Continue to work zealously; the whole nation is watching you and applauds your labors. The Convention invites you to remain at its sitting.[219]

The applauding Convention ordered that the remarks of the delegate and the reply of its president be printed. It is interesting to notice that whatever their original hostility to the war may have been, the Robespierrists were in no wise slackening in their purpose to prosecute it to the bitter end. Usually the pressure of foreign war is a unifying force, ending for the time being all internal factional strife. It was distinctly otherwise in the French Revolution, attesting the depth of internecine hatreds and suspicions. Under such circumstances, the republic's victory is amazing.

Meanwhile the social program sketched in the decrees of the eighth was being matured by the Committee of Public Safety. Progress was made so rapidly that by the thirteenth (March 3), Saint-Just was able to report additional measures to the Convention. He presented for the Committee, he said, a plan for carrying out the decree of the eighth. The best way to strengthen the Revolution was to make it turn to the profit of its supporters and the ruin of its opponents. Let the Convention lead rather than follow the progress of the Revolution, determine its plan and precipitate the results for the benefit of humanity. A great stroke of this kind would shake the thrones;

small measures were pin pricks, not felt by hardened opponents. He summoned his hearers to avenge the people for twelve centuries of crimes committed against their fathers.

Let Europe learn that you will no longer permit one unfortunate or one oppressor on French soil; let this example fructify the earth; let it spread everywhere a love of virtue and happiness. General well-being [*bonheur*] is a new idea in Europe.

I propose to you the following decree:

Art. 1. All the communes of the Republic shall draw up a list of indigent patriots, containing their names, ages, professions, the number and age of their children. The district directories shall turn these lists in to the Committee of Public Safety as quickly as possible.

Art. 2. When the Committee of Public Safety has received these lists, it shall present a report on the method of indemnifying all the unfortunates with the possession of the Revolution's enemies, according to the table which the Committee of General Security has presented and which will be made public.

Art. 3. In consequence, the Committee of General Security shall give precise orders to all committees of surveillance in the Republic, so that within a period fixed for each district according to its distance, these committees shall hand in to it respective reports on the names and conduct of all those imprisoned since May 1, 1789. The same shall be done for all those imprisoned in future.[229]

The decrees were adopted. Danton, alert to the peril of allowing his rivals to run off with all the popular measures, arose at once, gave his hearty assent to the Committee's plan and proposed that the Convention make a start by establishing a colony of wounded veterans near Paris. The plan was referred to the Committee of Public Safety.

The great proposal of Robespierre and Saint-Just was now fully and definitely launched. It consisted frankly in confiscating the possessions of the suspects, as those of the Church and of the *émigrés* had previously been confiscated. But instead of selling these lands or holding them as security for the depreciated *assignats*, they were to be turned over bodily to poor republicans. In this way a complete social revolution would take place, the rich would become poor and the poor prosperous. It was not socialism, for there was no question of government ownership, or communism, since private property was continued, but it partook of their nature inasmuch as the sanctity of original ownership was denied. Property was no longer a natural right, but a social privilege. Saint-Just had traveled far from his original individualism.

It has been pointed out that this socialization of the Revolution went far beyond anything that the Extremists had ever suggested. It affected the property of some three hundred thousand suspects. It would have prolonged the Terror indefinitely. It was not only a humanitarian measure for the equalization of rich and poor; it was a shrewd political maneuver, calculated to build up a strong body of grateful and enthusiastic Robespierrists. That this change would have been permanent if it had been carried out can hardly be doubted. The economic results of revolution almost always resist reaction.

To work out the application of the Ventôse decrees was an involved and difficult task, but the government set resolutely about it. The local committees were often slow to act and filled with prejudice for or against suspects. In some regions, a beginning of sequestration was made even before the sifting of suspects had begun. Saint-Just was especially active in the effort to centralize and speed up the process.[221] But it was two months before much was accomplished and in fact the scheme never really got on its feet.

It was hoped with reason by the Committee that this legislation would satisfy all the social and economic demands of the Hébertists. It was in fact a definite bid for their support and they would have been well advised to fall in line. Unfortunately for both groups, they failed to do so. Hébert had for many weeks been denouncing the greed of merchants and farmers, to which he attributed the food shortage, and had called for a greater use of the guillotine. He and his friends felt that the Indulgents were clogging the Convention's progress and that the Committee was not strong enough to shake off their baneful influence. Talk was heard of a new "holy insurrection" to overthrow the Committee, place the Hébertist General Ronsin in supreme command of the army and make Mayor Pache "grand judge." With 11 Ventôse the crisis began to come to a head. Posters were up calling for a dictatorship. On the fourteenth an important meeting of the Cordeliers took place. This club was the focus of the movement. Incendiary speeches were made by Vincent, Carrier, Momoro and Hébert, calling for an insurrection and the table of the Rights of Man was veiled with crape in token of the eclipse of liberty. The fifteenth was to have been the great day. But Paris did not rise. Only one of the forty-seven sections of the city took any interest in the scheme.

The following day, indignant protests began to rain on the heads of the luckless Extremists. Barère reported a decree in the Convention against seditious pamphlets and plots; in the course of his speech he complained that popular agitation seemed to redouble as soon as the decree proposed by Saint-Just was passed. These men actually chose the moment when the lands of their enemies were being confiscated for their benefit, to stage an insurrection. But if they would only be patient, in a few days the report on Chabot and his associates (the Indulgent corruptionists) would be ready.

At the same time, Saint-Just will make a report on the means of assuring the government and prosperity of the people. The Committee has charged one of its members, Saint-Just, to present to you at the first opportunity ideas on the way definitely to assure the representation, the government and all legitimate authorities against the attacks of conspirators and the intrigues of the foreigner's hirelings.

Barère repeats himself about Saint-Just as though the name itself was a word to conjure with. Barère's projected decree, which was passed by the Convention, directed the public accuser to inform himself concerning the authors and distributors of manuscript pamphlets circulated in the markets, to find out the identity of the conspirators against the public safety and the promoters of alarm in the minds of those bringing food into

Paris, and called on the Committee of Public Safety to make an early report on the means of assuring the government and the well-being of the people and of preserving them from the intrigues of conspirators. It was by authority of this decree that Saint-Just made his speech of 23 Ventôse.

It was natural enough for the Robespierrists to be pained and disconcerted at the failure of their Ventôse decrees to satisfy those who professed to be the especial champions of the poor. But they must have been surprised at the backing they received from one unexpected quarter. The Council-general of the Commune, usually in close sympathy with the Extremists, refused to follow the lead of the Cordeliers. At its session of the sixteenth, the day of Barère's speech in the Convention, the President of the Commune replied in almost the same words to a delegation from the sole insurrectionary section. He was supported by no less a person than Chaumette, Hébert's influential colleague in public office and party allegiance, who deprecated the least outbreak in Paris at the moment they were beginning the spring campaign and at the moment when, "after Saint-Just's excellent and solid report" the Convention had passed one of the most popular existing decrees. He offered some intelligent proposals for the provisioning of Paris, which the Commune unanimously adopted.[222] All of this goes to show that some of the Extremists at least were loyal and sensible and did not deserve to be lumped in the same accusation with the rest.

An effort by Collot and Billaud on the seventeenth to reconcile the factions was only partially successful. Hébert and certain followers were ready for it and the crape was torn off the table of the Rights of Man in the Cordeliers' clubhouse. But Vincent and others stubbornly held their ground. The revolt began to grumble and thunder distantly once more; the wind seemed to have changed and the storm to be coming back; no one could quite tell whether the flashes were those of heat lightning or something more serious.

On the twenty-first, the Committees received what purported

to be a circumstantial account of a very definite impending outbreak, to be accompanied by massacre. They met next day and approved Saint-Just's "Report on the factions of the foreigner." They further ordered the arrest of the Hébertist leaders, to be carried out after this report was delivered in the Convention.

Once more Saint-Just mounted the tribune, cold, erect and self-contained, with the paper in his hand which was to motivate the destruction of another group of republicans. He seemed to glory in invective. There are passages of great eloquence in this speech of 23 Ventôse. Its twenty-three octavo pages fall naturally into these divisions: (1) the famine plot, (2) characteristics of a patriot in contrast with an Extremist, (3) plans of "the foreigner," meaning the nations at war with France, (4) peroration.

Beginning with an exposition of the familiar foreign-plot theory, he developed the idea that the foreigner, alarmed at the decrees depriving the Revolution's enemies of their property, felt the need of moving more rapidly. The new plan was to cause a food shortage and use it to arouse the people against the government. The speaker did not formally accuse the Hébertists of being the agents in this plot, but clearly implied it. He indignantly swept aside Extremist charges against the government.

You the friends of kings, you who made them pale upon their thrones, you who framed the democratic state, you who avenged the people's murder by the tyrant's death and who took the initiative of the liberty of the world?

What friends have you on earth except the people as long as they keep their freedom and the hemlock when they have lost it?

He then described the famine plot in more detail. Here foodstuffs were buried, there arrivals of grain intercepted, elsewhere the citizens embittered by seditious speeches. The prime author of the scheme was the English government. Two days before the session of Parliament the policy had been discussed in the Council (presumably the Cabinet), whose exact words Saint-Just professed to quote. The best English policy, it had been there stated, was to delay military operations and to stir up civil war in France by corrupting the Republic.

At this point he opens the second and longest part of his oration, a definite attack on the Extremists. His term for them is *le parti de l'étranger*. There were Italians, bankers, Neapolitans, Englishmen in Paris, who gave out that they were persecuted at home. These new Sinons introduced themselves into the popular assemblies; they declaimed at first against their own governments; they insinuated themselves into ministerial antechambers; they spied on everything; they slipped into the popular societies; soon they appeared linked up with magistrates who protected them. War must be declared on these Tartufes of patriotism.

To Saint-Just the imitative spirit was the sign manual of crime. Marats cropped up everywhere, he complained; there was one at Nancy, another at Strasbourg. This one called himself the Marat of the Rhine; he was a priest and an Austrian, he was counter-revolutionary.[223] So it was with those who had the modesty to usurp the names of the great men of antiquity; that affectation concealed a sly fellow who had sold his conscience.[224] "Simple good sense, energy of spirit, coldness of intelligence, the fire of a heart ardent and pure, austerity, disinterestedness, that is the patriot's character." The so-called patriots of these latter days blushed for the names of their fathers, calling themselves after heroes whom they imitated in nothing. The hero slew a tyrant, lived modestly and purely; his shameless imitator slew his country, enriched himself, his life was soiled with vice. What was he after? To make men talk of him, that he might gain power and sell himself tomorrow for a higher price. A whole class of such men existed, with haggard air and affected fury.

What! Our government would so far humiliate itself as to become the prey of a scoundrel who has made merchandise of his pen and his conscience, and who varies his colors according to his hopes and dangers, like a reptile crawling in the sun? . . .[225]

Rascals, go to the workshops, go to the ships, go till the soil; bad citizens, whose task imposed by the foreigner is to trouble public peace and to corrupt all hearts, go to the battlefields; vile artisans of calamity, go learn honor among the country's defenders; but no, you will not go: the scaffold awaits you!

The Jacobins had overthrown the king by the generous violence of patriotism; these men sought to overthrow a free government by the violence of corruption and to massacre the Jacobins.

Patriots, reflect! Why not say to those who proposed this crime: "The people is no tyrant. If you would do to the present order of things what the people did to tyranny, you are wicked men who should be unmasked. It is the people which reigns today, it is they whom aristocracy would dethrone."

The popular societies were full of charlatans nowadays; officeholders lobbying for promotion, selfish notoriety-seekers who run about the streets, hoping to hear people say: "Do you see who is talking? Do you see who is passing?" They want the splendor of Persepolis. We offer the quiet happiness of comfort and tranquillity, the luxury of a cabin and a fertile field. The day after a man got a lucrative office, he requisitioned a palace; he had subservient lackeys; his wife grumbled about the times, she could not buy ermine and jewels at a decent price, she complained that one had no end of trouble finding table delicacies. [One can imagine the sarcasm with which Saint-Just must have mimicked the parvenu husband and his fretful spouse.]

The husband has climbed from the pit to the brilliant boxes at the show and while these wretches enjoy themselves, the people cultivate the soil, make shoes for soldiers and the arms which defend these indifferent poltroons. . . . "Were I the minister," says this one; "were I the master," says that one, "all would go better."

They wanted a revolt so that they could eat pheasant. It was not the plain people who complained of the times. They lived in antique fashion on chestnuts, on bread, on vegetables cooked in oil, on fruits and cattle which they raised themselves.

The third part of Saint-Just's speech dealt with the enemy's strategy. The kings of Europe were looking at their watches at this moment, for this was the precise hour they had been led to expect the fall of Paris. If his auditors were satisfied with words, if they did not act and that severely, the plotters, who had bent before the momentary storm of feeling, would return more daring than ever. The foreigner's one desire was to get rid of the example the republic's existence gave the world. His craftiness was well illustrated in the seeming gulf between Indulgents and Extremists, both of whom he supported. It was just a trick to throw dust in people's eyes. The government's secret information indicated that the foreigner would concentrate on creating famine and discord in France. His army would make feints until the Convention was replaced by a regency which he would recognize, proposing peace. But he had failed. The guilty were surrounded and would soon be under arrest. The plan of corruption would be checked by a drastic law. The war would be continued with fury.

Let us enlarge our souls to embrace all the happiness we owe the French people. . . . Let justice and virtue be the order of the day in the French Republic! . . . What! They destined you to languish beneath a regency of tyrants which would have given you back the Bourbons! . . . The ashes of your defenders would have been cast to the winds! Far from you, this picture! It is now only the dream of tyranny; the Republic is once more saved. Take your flight toward glory. To share with us this sublime moment we summon all the secret enemies of tyranny, who in Europe and throughout the world carry Brutus's dagger beneath their cloaks.

The long decree which followed provided among other things for the arrest of the conspirators, the apprehension of those who had fled, a wide extension of the law of treason, a tightening up of governmental authority, the creation of six popular commissions to judge suspects, carrying out the decrees of 8 and 13 Ventôse. This drastic decree was unanimously adopted with loud applause. From every side arose demands that the speech be printed. Legendre (Dantonist) demanded that it be sent to the municipalities, the armies and the popular societies and that public functionaries be designated to read it on *décadi* in the Temple of Reason. This motion was adopted. According to another account, the Convention also ordered it translated into all languages.[226] Next day, the Committee ordered 200,000 copies printed.

On the twenty-third, Saint-Just by request read his speech at the Jacobins. "It is difficult to depict the attention with which Saint-Just's speech was received," ran the account of the session. "He was often interrupted by the most lively and sincere applause." Billaud-Varenne, Hébertist though he was, made a violent address at the Jacobins the following night, praising Saint-Just's report for having "already thrown a great light on the conspiracy planned against liberty, on that conspiracy the more distressing because concocted by men who had assumed the mask of patriotism." [227] The report was read with effect in the sections of Paris and in the departments. Dumont wrote from Amiens that it had "dealt the last blow to our enemies." [228]

It was clearly regarded as one of the young orator's masterpieces. From the critical standpoint, the unfairness of the accusation is none the less apparent. The Hébertists were not traitors, though they were unwise and extravagant, less balanced and able than the Robespierrists. In their exclusive interest in the proletariat, they were forerunners of a class-conscious type that was at least premature, considering the rudimentary development of industry. Saint-Just paints a fine ideal portrait of the true patriot, simple, modest, efficient, which was in deserved contrast to the Extremist type. But there was absolutely no evidence of any artificial interference with the food supply; there were desperate raids on grain carts, but they were the unorganized work of the poor; there was withholding of supplies by the country folk, but that was an automatic consequence of the valueless currency, as Saint-Just well knew.

Nor was the selfish, luxurious, office-seeking character sketched so vividly by him a true picture of all the Hébertists, though it was doubtless a well-known type, probably occurring in all the political groups. It was distinctly not true of Chaumette, who lived simply and chastely and was an ardent social reformer, interested in school and hospital improvement. Nor was it true of Cloots, the eccentric Prussian enthusiast. Least of all was there any actual substance to the "foreign plot," the horrid combination of both wings sold out to Pitt, that gigantic nightmare which obsessed the unhappy Robespierrists and led them as in a Greek tragedy to slay their brothers and then fall on their own swords. The impossibility of any foreign government's buying out two whole political factions is matched by the absurdity that their leaders, who had so deeply damned themselves in royalist eyes by regicide and terrorism, should wish or dare to restore the Bourbon throne.

Not that the Hébertists were the absolutely innocent victims of calumny. In spite of Hébert's denials, there seems to have been a very definite plan for an insurrection on 15 Ventôse (March 5). This was not subsidized by any foreign state nor participated in by the Indulgents. It was not even approved by some of the Extremists (for instance, Chaumette) nor is it likely that all the diabolical details whispered to Saint-Just and swallowed by him were part of the plan. The scheme was to stage another popular *journée,* a great mass movement of the proletariat such as had signalized August 10, May 31 and June 2. Saint-Just's argument that such a violent "putsch" was directed against the people as represented by the Convention and therefore treason could have been urged with equal cogency by the Girondins to condemn the action of the previous June, which he whole-heartedly approved. Who after all were "the people" and where was one to draw the line between legitimate insurrection and a factional uprising? It all depended on whose ox was gored. The Extremists were indeed violent, but so was the whole Mountain by contrast with its predecessors. It was all a matter of degree; who should say what was the proper mean? When Saint-Just denounced parties and urged the citizens to unite against all factions alike, he spoke wisely, but he strangely overlooked the fact that he belonged to a very definite party himself. Moreover Danton had been saying the same thing for months.

The inevitable question of Saint-Just's sincerity arises. He probably thought some of the Extremists guilty of corruption by the foreigner; the bankers affiliated with Chabot would be quite reasonably so regarded. He doubtless believed that because of hostility to the government, all must be destroyed, whether or not their hostility was due to the same motive. If they were permitted to survive, there was formidable danger of their overthrowing Robespierre, whom he firmly considered the best ruler for France. The factor of personal advantage was involved of course, as with other public men in similar crises; there is no reason to suppose it alone controlled his action. He had a definite theory of the government he believed in; this theory he followed through various trying contingencies with great consistency; it is probable that he was doing so now. It was no time, he felt, to be overnice as to whether this or that individual was or was not in the foreign plot or any other plot; the whole lot of them were a menace to the republic and for its sake they must perish.

The last of the four reports made by Saint-Just in this crowded month of Ventôse dealt like the rest with traitorous conduct, conspiracy and corruption, with "treasons, stratagems and spoils." As the speech of the thirteenth was a sort of short appendix to the epoch-making report of the eighth, so that of the twenty-seventh was a brief sequel to the important address of the twenty-third. It was a report in the name of the Committees of Public Safety and General Security on the arrest of Hérault-Séchelles and Simon, which had taken place two days before.

Hérault was one of the unique characters of the Revolution, a man of noble birth, great wealth and elegance, who retained the dress and manners of the old régime to the end. He was skeptical, witty and libertine. He was in turn Feuillant and Girondin and was formerly supposed to have been a follower of Danton.[229] In reality he became a Hébertist in his last period, more from self-interest than principle, conceiving that this group would ultimately win control. Proly, Hébertist banker and reputed son of Kaunitz, became his secretary. Robespierre grew suspicious that Hérault was responsible for leakage in the Committee's papers. After his return in Nivôse from a mission to the Haut-Rhin, the Committee insisted on either his resignation or an investigation of his conduct. The alternative was not pressed at the moment, but Hérault ceased to attend its sessions.[230]

Personal relations between Hérault and Saint-Just had never been cordial. The ironical epicurean, to whom life was a pleasure and a jest, and the serious ascetic to whom it had become a crusade, were spirits as alien as Voltaire and Savonarola or, if one prefers, Torquemada. They were antipathetic on the constitutional committee; Saint-Just had repelled the other's advances in Alsace. There is also the story, told in the *Histoire de la Révolution par deux amis,* that a quarrel arose between them at a dinner, resulting in Hérault's challenging his adversary to a duel. Saint-Just refused on the ground that such conduct was unworthy of two political leaders. Hérault in fury denounced him as a coward and a rogue and threatened to give him "twenty kicks in the belly," not one of which he would dare resist. Saint-Just remained cold and impassive. Saint-Just is then said to have undermined him with his colleagues while Hérault was on mission, his fall being due to Saint-Just's personal vengeance.[231] Whatever the credibility of the incident, the deduction is false; Saint-Just was also on mission at the time Hérault was absent; the latter's credit with the Committee was already gone before he left Paris. Nevertheless it was not without grim satisfaction that the young orator found himself once more the Committee's spokesman on this particular occasion.

Saint-Just told how an *émigré* had been arrested in Hérault's apartment and how Hérault and Simon had forced their way into the prisoner's cell in an effort to coach him for the trial. He recalled how the Committee refused to deliberate in Hérault's presence, because of his contacts with Proly and his seizure of diplomatic papers. Simon was a friend of Schneider's and the bearer of a friendly and counter-revolutionary letter from Hérault to a refractory priest. The Roman senate was honored for the virtue with which it smote Catiline.

A more formal report by Saint-Just was planned for the next day. So Couthon told the Convention on the twenty-eighth. It was never delivered. The case of Hérault was destined to be merged with that of a far greater figure. Until then, Saint-Just had respite.

XVI

THE BREAK WITH DANTON

T WAS inevitable. Danton was an opportunist, or if one prefers, a realist. Robespierre and Saint-Just have always been considered devotees of dogma. The antithesis was not in fact so sharp. In economics, the Robespierrists adopted the maximum which they had originally opposed (Saint-Just's shift from individualism was especially pronounced); in foreign policy, they conducted with fiery determination a war which they had originally disliked; in the question of government, they formulated and then laid aside a radically decentralized constitution in favor of a highly concentrated revolutionary system of Committees. But on certain things, chiefly matters of attitude and conduct, they were adamant. The Revolution must be controlled by true patriots, who were to be recognized by austerity of life, unflagging energy, simplicity of manners, refusal to compromise with internal or external enemies. They also clung with obstinate blindness to the fatal "foreign plot" theory. Danton, on the other hand, was tolerant of human frailty, reveled in the enjoyment of life's good things, believed in negotiating terms with the foreign enemy and desired to bury old feuds and coöperate with old foes for the greater glory of France.

Between the elastic Danton and the rigid Robespierre there could be no more real sympathy than between a Henry IV and a John Calvin. Paris was well worth a Mass to Henry, and for France's safety Danton would sup gladly with the Girondins or the devil; to Robespierre and Saint-Just, Girondins and devils were equivalent and communion with them or with any not of strictest Mountain orthodoxy was playing with hell-fire. It was dangerous and disloyal; it placed those advocating such a policy under grave suspicion as to their genuine patriotism and true allegiance to the Revolution.

Moreover Danton's heresies were not limited to a general preaching of clemency. Slowing up the Terror was dubious enough in itself. But Danton was the recognized head of a faction of crooks. His own venality was suspected, though without the grave reasons that have since been disclosed.[232] Thousands of course believed (and many still believe in spite of all evidence) that he was rather unfortunate in his associates than personally culpable. Robespierre and Saint-Just, suspicious by nature, happened to have pretty good warrant for their suspicions in this case that there was fire behind the smoke. Nor was this the end of it. The foreign plot theory had become an article of Robespierrist faith. Since Danton persisted in defending notorious rascals like Chabot and Basire, since he wished to open the prisons, he was apparently a traitor to the Revolution.

Saint-Just's reports of Ventôse made it perfectly clear that the Committee was if anything more hostile to the Indulgents than to Hébert's party. Almost any politician with his eyes open would have felt that the fall of the Extremists merely cleared the way for a final grapple with the other branch of the conspiracy, as the Robespierrists viewed it. Danton did not see it or would not believe it. A week after Saint-Just's speech against the Hébertists and even before they had mounted the scaffold, Danton left Paris. He spoke in the Convention on 29 Ventôse for the last time. Tired of politics and sick of bloodshed, he took his pretty young wife, Louise, and sought to drown the silly shouting and clamor in the murmuring of the great trees and the fountains of Sèvres. No one could rouse him from his fatal lethargy. To those who warned him that Robespierre was busily employed in preparing his overthrow, he replied in his characteristic Rabelaisian way, "If I thought he even had the notion of it, I would eat out his entrails." To those who counseled flight, he answered wearily, "One doesn't carry one's country off on the soles of one's shoes."

Robespierre was reluctant to take the final steps that broke the Mountain in two. When Camille Desmoulins months before, at Danton's suggestion, started the campaign for clemency in the *Vieux Cordelier,* Robespierre had actually gone over the proofs of the first two numbers of this journal. As late as December 20, Desmoulins was still appealing for the help of his old college comrade in the campaign against terrorism. But as succeeding issues showed that the policies of the two groups were increasingly divergent, Robespierre permitted a mutual friend to warn Camille at the Jacobins that he was grazing the guillotine. The break came on January 7, when Robespierre, defending Camille at the Jacobins as a spoiled child, declared that his writings should be burned. The journalist's overclever reply, "Burning is not answering," snapped the old tie between the men and Robespierre furiously denounced him. With Danton the personal friendship had never been so close. But the political prestige of this man was so great that Robespierre hesitated still longer before launching the attack upon him. According to rumor, it was Billaud and Saint-Just who urged its necessity and finally overcame his scruples. It was not until 9 Germinal (March 30) that the two Committees were summoned on important business. Lavicomterie, of the lesser Committee, relates that many of those present had no idea what was to be brought up. Saint-Just drew papers from his pocket.

What was our surprise to hear the report against Danton and the rest! The report was so seductive! Saint-Just read it with so much spirit! After the reading, we were asked if anyone wished to speak. No! No! [233]

Prieur, on the contrary, would have it that there was distinct opposition in the Committee, Lindet and Carnot being particularly outspoken. Carnot is said to have asserted that there was not a single proof of Danton's treason; they had heard nothing but slanderous suspicions. Of course they could condemn anyone they chose, but the fall of Danton would drag down many others; these splits within the party endangered them all. However, the dissidents supported the majority, the decision once made.[234]

Early in the morning of 11 Germinal (April 1), Danton, Desmoulins, Lacroix (or Delacroix) and Philippeaux were placed under arrest before the matter was brought up in the Convention. This stroke is usually represented as evidence of the Robespierrists' Machiavellian policy. Saint-Just, reading his report in the absence of Danton, already under arrest, with cold cowardice strikes a man whose hands are tied behind his back. But there is evidence that this course was more repugnant to Saint-Just, who was forced into it by the Committees against his will. A Thermidorian pamphlet gives Vadier, who belonged to the Committee of General Security, as authority for the statement that Saint-Just by his obstinacy almost ruined the whole business. He wanted the accused present in Convention when he read his report "and such was his stubbornness that, seeing our formal opposition, he threw his hat into the fire in a rage and left us abruptly." Robespierre was of the same mind, but Vadier pointed out that this course exposed the Committees to the risk of being guillotined themselves.[235] If this is true, the sportsmanship of Saint-Just is worthy of all praise. It is in keeping with his warning to his opponents on 9 Thermidor just before opening his attack, and one is inclined to accept it. He was brave and fair enough to cry "On guard" before he struck.

The Dantonists were in consternation at the news that their chiefs had been cast into prison in this summary fashion. It was serious news indeed, for fallen leaders who entered the republic's jails rarely came forth except in the executioner's cart. A feeble effort in their behalf was made by Legendre as the morning session of 11 Germinal came to order. He demanded that those just arrested be given a hearing in the Convention; "citizens, I believe Danton as pure as myself." Robespierre, whatever his views of the night before, quickly put a quietus on this plan. There were to be no privileges, no idols. Danton had no more rights at the bar than Brissot or

Chabot or Hébert. Before this fierce onslaught, the timid Dantonists quailed; they faltered a few excuses and were silent. The door of the hall swung open; with every eye upon him, Saint-Just made his entrance alone, came down the aisle and mounted the steps to the tribune.[236] Barras remembered how the speech sounded. Phlegmatic, in sententious tone, Saint-Just recited the most singular and monstrous indictment ever dreamed of, holding the manuscript in a hand that remained motionless, "while the other makes but one gesture, inexorable and from which there is no appeal—a gesture like unto the very knife of the guillotine." [237]

One third of this, his most ambitious effort, was devoted to a historical summary of the factions that had cursed the Revolution hitherto, the remainder to a furious invective against Danton and his associates.

The Revolution, he began, is in the people, not in the reputation of a few individuals. There was something terrible and exclusive in the sacred love of country; it immolated private affections to the public interest; it led a Regulus to Carthage, a Marat, victim of his own devotion, to the Pantheon. The Committees, filled with this sentiment, had charged their spokesman to demand justice against the men who so long had betrayed the people's cause, who had conspired with d'Orléans, with Brissot, with Hébert, with Hérault and now with the kings leagued against the republic.

May this be the last example you must give of your inflexibility toward yourselves! May you, having repressed them, behold all factions extinguished and enjoy in peace the fullness of your legitimate power and of the respect which you inspire!

After these stirring introductory appeals and others of like tenor, the speaker launched forth in an extended analysis of partisan corruption since the opening of the Revolution. He depicted the career of the Orléanist party, which failed because it lacked resolution. Its first policy was to destroy the pro-Bourbon nobility, hoping that through Mirabeau's help the throne might be preserved. With Mirabeau's death, intrigue replaced efforts at constitutional revision. The Orléanists then pinned their faith to Brissot, but the revolt of Dumouriez and the execution of d'Orléans ended the second phase of their continuing effort. The faction survived none the less and there could be no peace in the state until their present standard bearers, the Indulgents, were dead.

Let the past teach us! . . . it is with the débris of factions who have escaped the scaffold and who fear the future, that new factions are formed.

There was a Cassandra quality in this pregnant saying, for Saint-Just and his friends fell at the hands of a miscellaneous group of ex-Dantonists and ex-Hébertists.

He went on to show how unreal (from the Robespierrist standpoint) the various party divisions were. Mirabeau and the Lameths, the Lameths and Lafayette, Brissot and d'Orléans, Ronsin and the Freys were only apparently hostile to one another, while working through them all and blending them all into a certain unity were the foreign enemy abroad and a ring of traitorous grafters at home. At the head of this ring was Fabre d'Eglantine, the Cardinal de Retz of the day, who played on human hearts like a musician on his instrument; he was a royalist, a coward, a double-crosser.

Then came the heart of the report, the tremendous denunciation of Danton.

What, when all Europe except us who are blind, is convinced that Lacroix and Danton have stipulated for royalty; what! when the evidence taken on Fabre d'Eglantine, Danton's accomplice, leaves no further doubt of his treason; when the French ambassador in Switzerland informs us of the *émigrés'* consternation at the arrest of Fabre, Danton's friend, our eyes still refuse to open! Danton, you must answer to inevitable, inflexible justice. Let us review your past conduct and show how since the first day, you, an accomplice in every scheme, were always against the party of liberty and that you conspired with Mirabeau, with Dumouriez, with Hébert, with Hérault-Séchelles.

Danton, you served the tyranny; you were opposed to Lafayette, it is true; but Mirabeau, d'Orléans, Dumouriez, were likewise against him. Do you dare deny that you sold yourself to these three men, the most violent conspirators against liberty?

Saint-Just now plunged into a long, intricate review of Danton's career, seeking to substantiate these general statements. Danton with Brissot drew up the Jacobin petition, which was intended to provoke the massacre of the Champ de Mars. Danton supported the Girondin war policy and Brissot's liberticide opinions. Danton retired to Arcis when he saw the storm of August 10 approaching and though he returned to Paris on the ninth, that terrible night found him asleep. As minister he helped enrich Fabre, carried on a feigned war with the Girondins, was friend and supporter of Dumouriez whose attempted insurrection he approved; his hand was in the Belgian treasure chest. He saw the revolution of May 31 with horror. He was suspected of holding conferences with the imprisoned queen.

Bad citizens, you have conspired; false friend, two days ago you spoke evil of Desmoulins, your instrument whom you have destroyed, and attributed shameful vices to him; evil man, you have compared public opinion to a prostitute; you have said that honor was ridiculous, glory and posterity an absurdity: these maxims must have reconciled you with aristocracy, for they were those of Catiline. If Fabre is innocent, if d'Orléans and Dumouriez were innocent, no doubt you are too. I have spoken too much: you will reply before the court of justice.

This was the high point of the report. While there are further references to Danton, his indulgence toward traitors, his responsibility for the last writings of Desmoulins and Philippeaux, his willingness to enthrone the young Capet and his lavish dinners with the English, with Guzman the Spaniard and with the infamous Sainte-Amaranthe, most of the remainder is taken up with Danton's followers.

Desmoulins, lacking in character, full of vanity, began as Danton's dupe and finished as his accomplice. A rhetorician, he attacked the revolutionary government and proposed a committee of clemency for its foes; like Hébert, he attacked the people's representatives to the armies, whom he dubbed proconsuls; he defended the infamous Dillon and opposed the law against the English, for which service he received the thanks of English journals.

Fabre wept when Camille called the Convention the court of Tiberius; the crocodile weeps also. Fabre, who slipped into every group, praised every member of the Committee to his face and spoke ill of all the rest. Accomplice of Chabot, he accused him when he knew himself accused.

Hérault betrayed the Committee's most secret deliberations to foreign governments. "We recall that Hérault was, with disgust, the mute witness of the labors of those who drew up the constitution, of which he adroitly made himself the shameless reporter."

When the country was invaded and prospects at their darkest, Hébert and Danton demanded that the constitution be put into effect, in order that this transition to a weaker form of government might lead the republic from life to the tomb. This was the moment pitched on by Philippeaux, with the aid of Fabre, to attack the government as associated with treason.

Hébert and all those who for the last four years conspired under the veil of patriotism, had been wont to repeat Vergniaud's epigram: "The Revolution is like Saturn: it will devour all its children." No, the Revolution would not devour its children, but its enemies, with whatever impenetrable mask they might be covered. Not one true patriot would perish.

But at the end, Saint-Just seemed less sure. For after a final denunciation of these men, the débris of the Orleanist faction, who must be ruthlessly destroyed, and after an appeal for the subsequent establishment of an idyllic state of gentleness and mutual regard, he concluded:

You may tear from life men who, like us, have dared all for truth; you cannot tear out their hearts nor take away the hospitable tomb, beneath which they find refuge from slavery and from the shame of having permitted evil men to triumph.

This is the proposed decree: The National Convention, having heard the report of its Committees of General Security and Public Safety, decrees the accusation of Camille Desmoulins, Hérault, Danton, Philippeaux, Lacroix, for complicity with d'Orléans and Dumouriez, with Fabre d'Eglantine and the Republic's enemies and for having participated in the conspiracy tending to reëstablish the monarchy, to destroy the national representation and the republican government. In consequence it orders their trial with that of Fabre d'Eglantine.

The decree was adopted unanimously, "in the midst of the most lively applause" as the *Moniteur* has it. No other speeches or comments followed. It was too dangerous a subject for those not in the inner Robespierrist ring to touch.

That night at the Jacobins, with poor Legendre, the embarrassed Dantonist, ironically enough in the chair, Saint-Just was invited to read to the society "an interesting report" which he had presented that morning at the Convention. As on 23 Ventôse, a hurried call for the manuscript had to be sent to the printer. Couthon filled in the interval by giving a summary of Saint-Just's argument and roundly scolding Legendre for his maladroit performance that morning. The unhappy chairman stumbled through his apology once more; he believed in Danton; he deferred to the Tribunal's judgment; he would be the first to denounce anyone who tried to hinder today's decree. The Robespierrists clearly had the situation well in hand. Saint-Just then read his report, enthusiastically received as usual; Robespierre capped it by a further explanation of the foreign-plot theory.

The collaboration between the two was never closer. On other occasions, as in Thermidor, the plan of battle called for a speech by each man, two tremendous assaults delivered in quick succession. But perhaps because this contest with Danton was regarded as the most difficult crisis of all, it was handled with unusual care. Saint-Just, normally jealous enough of his own originality, was content here to be in part the mouthpiece of another. Most of the points which he made in this report were not his own but Robespierre's, whose notes for the speech have been preserved and published.[238] A critical analysis of the notes proves, it is true, that Saint-Just wrote a preliminary version of his report, which he probably read to the Committees and which except for a few lines is now lost. Robespierre's notes were written with the purpose of rectifying and completing this preliminary report. The existing version of Saint-Just's report had the benefit of Robespierre's suggestions, many of which were adopted.[239] It was Robespierre who was responsible (among lesser charges) for the following accusations: Mirabeau's influence over Danton; Danton's deliberate purpose to provoke the massacre of the Champ de Mars; his retirement to Arcis-sur-Aube shortly before August 10; his slumber on the eve of that occasion; his support of Orléans and Dumouriez; his treasonable conduct in Belgium; his collaboration with Brissot; his politico-social gatherings; the falseness of his friendship for Desmoulins whom he accused of private vice; his corruption in rewarding Fabre out of the public funds; his opposition to the expulsion of the Girondins and his treachery toward Hanriot; his contemptuous remark that "public opinion was a harlot." The responsibility for these charges is therefore Robespierre's, though of course Saint-Just accepted them and made them his own. In every case they are rearranged and restated; some of Robespierre's material is omitted, much is added. The organization, the style, the fury of the attack are wholly Saint-Just's.

Such was the case against Danton. Was he guilty of these charges? In some cases, yes; in others, no. He was once an Orleanist, was probably paid by Mirabeau, did sign the Jacobin petition with Brissot, did retire to Arcis before August 10 and slept a part of the night before; he tried for a *rapprochement* with the Girondins; was a friend of Dumouriez and may have tried to save the queen; he was almost certainly willing to take money for political services (like Mirabeau) though he did not always perform them. On the other hand, his support of Orléans, of Mirabeau, of Brissot dated from earlier periods in the Revolution when such conduct was not unorthodox; Robespierre, Saint-Just and all the rest were once monarchists. It is true that Danton was inclined to prolong his support of these men after the more advanced groups had forsaken them, but the policy of revolutionary unity always appealed to him far more than that of revolutionary purity. Dumouriez was his favorite general, but he was in no wise sympathetic with the general's treason; the Brissotins became his bitterest enemies, thanks to Mme. Roland, but it was to Danton's great regret. That he deliberately sought to provoke the massacre of the Champ de Mars is ridiculous; that he was negligent of his duty on the night of August 9 equally so. The vivid journal of Lucile Desmoulins is ample evidence of the contrary. Had it not been for his preliminary labors with the sections and the arrest of Mandat at five o'clock on the morning of August 10, which he brought about, there might still have been a king of France today. There is no valid reason to discount Danton's devotion to the republic and to the Revolution; the charge that he conspired against them, which is the basic charge of this report, cannot be maintained. There is of course no excuse for Danton's venality, but it does not seem to have involved actual treason. He was an easy-going person, fond of the pleasures of life; he felt that in a time of upheaval, there was no need to be too nice about financial details and he might as well get his share; if subsequently he could not render the expected political services, that was not his fault. This attitude is indefensible; it shows a Danton corrupt in money matters, perhaps not altogether honorable in political bargaining, but not a Danton who sold his country for money. Like Mirabeau, he was willing to accept pay from dubious sources for saying what he believed; if it involved saying something else, he would accept the pay and remain silent. Not admirable, but not treasonable. Aside from this, his furious driving power rendered inestimable services to the Revolution and, if he had had luck, his broad-minded policy of conciliation and clemency would have rendered still more.

The real issue was political, not juridical, as in all the great *procès* of the Revolution from that of the king to that of the Robespierrists themselves. The charges of conspiracy and black-hearted crime were made in every one of these cases with monotonous regularity and with as little foundation in one as in another. The fundamental differences between Danton and the Robespierrists were matters of temperament and policy. These differences were threefold. (1) The Robespierrists felt that times were still critical and that clemency would weaken republican energy. Danton himself seemed to be growing torpid and to prefer repose. This judgment of theirs, that Terror should be maintained, was simply a time judgment; they proposed to end it in due season. But they exaggerated their antipathy to what they considered the premature clemency of the Indulgents into an idea that the latter were really defeatist and traitorous. (2) The Robespierrist leaders, who were puritans, disliked luxury and licentiousness and maintained an entirely legitimate and praiseworthy opposition to graft. (3) They cherished an ambition (selfish or unselfish as one chooses) to rule untrammeled and likewise a fear lest Danton follow up the ousting of Hébert by the ousting of Robespierre. The element of self-preservation enters into every one of these great clashes, from that with the Girondins to that with the Thermidorians. It was a question of which side struck first and hardest.

The verdict on Saint-Just's denunciatory reports must be the same in almost every instance. They rarely prove their case from a juridical standpoint. They are generally justified from the political standpoint. In the case of the Dantonists, the justification is the most difficult. Saint-Just was undeniably right that corruption must be rooted out; he was less certainly so that political terrorism must be maintained, at least to the point to which it was subsequently carried.

Desmoulins wrote a brief reply to the report, from his prison cell. Had he but the time, the materials, the paper necessary, how he would confound M. le Chevalier de Saint-Just, he said, how he would convict him of the most atrocious calumny. But Saint-Just wrote at his leisure in a bath, in a boudoir, while he, Desmoulins, had not even a place to rest his inkwell and only a few hours to defend his life. "What else is it but the duel of the Emperor Commodus, who, armed with an excellent blade, forced his enemy to fight with a plain cork-tipped fencing foil." However, it was now proved that those who accused us of conspiracy were themselves conspirators. The Committee had kept silence for five months on Chabot's charges; in the interval, Batz, Benoît and Julien de Toulouse, whom he denounced, had escaped. Desmoulins now in his turn denounced Vadier, Voulland, Amar, David, Collot d'Herbois, the "Tartufe" Barère and others.

There are witnesses that the great republican Saint-Just said once spitefully: "Ah! they want a republic; it will cost them dearly!" . . . I come to what concerns me in this report. In the memory of man there is no example of so atrocious a slander as this document. In the first place, there is no one in the Convention who does not know that M. the former Chevalier Saint-Just vowed me an eternal hatred for a light pleasantry which I permitted myself a month ago in my memoirs. Bourdaloue said: "Molière has put me in his comedy, I will put him in my sermon." As for me, I put M. de Saint-Just in one of my numbers; he puts me in a guillotine-report, in which there is not a word of truth so far as I am concerned. When Saint-Just accuses me of being an accomplice of Danton and Dumouriez, he shows himself up as a patriot of late vintage [*un patriote d'hier*]. Who denounced Dumouriez first and most vigorously? . . . Does not Saint-Just recall my history of the Brissotins? Can vengeance be blinder? [240]

Poor Camille's effort was of course quite hopeless. His denunciations were futile and had no more foundation than those of his adversary, while his charge that Saint-Just was merely avenging a malicious witticism is quite untenable. Desmoulins was too deeply involved in the clemency campaign to escape an attack directed on that policy and all who supported it. His ridiculous juggling with Saint-Just's name deprives him of the dignity to which his unfortunate fate entitled him.

The Dantonists were placed on trial, on 13 Germinal. The trial lasted four days and proved very stormy. Danton fought for his life with all his tremendous forensic power. As he roared forth his sarcasms in that great bull-like voice, the audience was visibly swayed in his behalf and conviction began to seem doubtful. The Robespierrists became exceedingly uneasy. Fouquier wrote anxiously for instructions; the accused were making terrible scenes, was it necessary to summon the witnesses they demanded?

At this juncture, deliverance for the hard-pressed Committees came with suspicious suddenness. One Laflotte, a former minister of the republic to Florence, now a prisoner in the Luxembourg, made a signed statement to the police authorities on the fifteenth that on the preceding evening he had been approached by Arthur Dillon, another prisoner, who told him that the Convention and the people were evidently on the Dantonist side and that there was grave danger that the Committees would assassinate all prisoners; Dillon proposed to resist and had worked up a scheme which Laflotte now promised to divulge to the Committees if they would accord him a personal hearing.[241] The plan, a part of which appears in Laflotte's letter, proved to be a prison revolt, aided by the formation of a friendly mob in the outer court. This mob would be won over by the distribution of a thousand *écus,* provided by Lucile Desmoulins, who was in close touch with Dillon. When they had gained their liberty, the prisoners would massacre the Committees. Armed with this fresh ammunition, Saint-Just hastened once more to the Convention on 15 Germinal and read the "Report on a new conspiracy."

The public accuser of the Revolutionary Tribunal, he said, stated that the revolt of the guilty had made necessary a suspension of the case until the Convention took proper measures.[242] The revolt of the criminals at the very feet of justice was itself proof of their guilt. The conspiracy was now clear. Dillon, who ordered his army to march on Paris, declared that the wife of Desmoulins had made use of money to excite a movement to assassinate the patriots and the Revolutionary Tribunal.

We thank you for believing us placed at the post of honor; like you, we will cover the fatherland with our bodies.

To die is nothing provided the Revolution triumphs; behold the day of glory; behold the day when the Roman senate fought with Catiline; behold the day whereon to consolidate public liberty forever. Your Committees answer for [your safety] with an heroic watchfulness. Who can refuse you his respect in this terrible moment when you struggle for the last time against the faction which was indulgent for your enemies, and today recovers its fury to combat liberty?

The remainder of this brief burst of rhetoric repeated these two points in various forms; the heroism of the Committees, who esteemed honor above life, the guilt of the accused revealed by their revolt. Not even the king nor Custine nor Brissot had enjoyed the frightful privilege of insulting his judges.

The decree proposed by the Committees to meet this new situation read:

The National Convention, having heard the report of its Committees of Public Safety and General Security, decrees that the Revolutionary Tribunal shall continue the proceedings relative to the conspiracy of Lacroix, Danton, Chabot and others; that the president shall make use of all measures given him by law to make his authority and that of the Revolutionary Tribunal respected and to repress every attempt on the part of the accused to trouble public tranquillity and to impede the march of justice;

Decrees further that every one accused of conspiracy who resists or insults national justice shall forthwith lose his right to speak further.

At Billaud-Varenne's suggestion, the Laflotte letter was then read to the Convention, which voted the decrees unanimously and without comment. That it should have done so simply proves how far that body had lost its independence of judgment. Some voted under the influence of war psychology, when all things are credible; the prison revolt, that hoary myth, had served as pretext for the September massacres and was still good for more; timid revolutionists swallowed it as children accept the bugaboo stories of an unscrupulous nursemaid. Some voted at the crack of the Robespierrist whip; they heard their master's voice and feared to disobey. The leaders themselves must have acted and voted tongue in cheek; the Dantonist trial had reached a critical impasse and for the country's sake must be brought to a speedy conclusion.[243]

And so it was. The following day ended the case as well as the lives of Danton and his associates. A week later Lucile Desmoulins, Dillon and Simon paid the supreme penalty for their real or supposed "prison conspiracy." At last the Robespierrists were undisputed masters. For the next three months they had their way without serious opposition.

Even at the height of this titanic struggle, the Committee of Public Safety took time to consider questions of administrative reorganization. A decree reported by Carnot was adopted by the Convention 12 Germinal, the day following Saint-Just's great speech against Danton; it suppressed the Provisional Executive Council and the six ministers composing it, replacing them by twelve commissions. During the discussion of this measure in the Committee, Saint-Just is said to have made a considerable speech attacking the policy of the minister of foreign affairs toward neutral powers. Its main thesis was that the government was spending needlessly large sums of money to purchase the neutrality of states like Turkey, Denmark, Sweden, Switzerland, Genoa and Venice, states whose neutrality was assured through their own self-interest. It concluded that all secret funds for this object be abolished, that further expenditures of this type be limited to sums appropriated by the Committee for a specific purpose and that all diplomatic correspondence with these courts, except that of Turkey, be published.

The supposed speech is a forgery. A searching analysis has substantially proved this, both from internal and external evidence; [244] the document is in reality the product of one d'Antraigues, an agent of the *émigrés*, living in Italy, who made a specialty of turning out revolutionary counterfeits. It was in fact published at the time outside of France and recognized as not genuine by the Italian Greppi, the French diplomats Barthélemy, Bacher and Jacob, the Austrian statesman Thugut and others. Its purpose was to alarm the neutrals as to the sincerity of French friendship.

XVII

SAINT-JUST THE TERRORIST

T IS as terrorist that Saint-Just has lived in history. The solid effort he spent on constitutional and economic reconstruction has vanished from men's memory; so too almost have his social idealism and his romantic picture of a happier France; hardly any but specialists recall the practical common sense, the capacity for instant decision, the driving power and the courage which he showed on his military missions. But those who know the Revolution even superficially can never dissociate Saint-Just from Robespierre nor either from the guillotine. It is as one of the ruling triumvirate in the Committee of Public Safety during those bloodstained months of 1794 that Saint-Just is unforgotten; as the orator whose white-hot epigrams and heaped-up masses of black suspicion sent group after group to their doom. He is a young angel of death, austerely beautiful but pitiless. He is cruel, with a cold, inhuman cruelty, insensible to any pleading. To counter his will or to excite his anger means swift and absolute destruction. In him, Terror is personified.

The portrait is not without elements of truth. To what extent it should be modified, this chapter seeks to discover.

The Terror was a combination of vigorous, arbitrary action and formless, vague suspicion, terrorizing government and people alike. On the one hand it meant drastic decrees issued by a small, highly centralized authority at the expense of a regular constitution and of individual liberty; on the other hand, it meant a state of constant alarm, the government fearing fine-spun webs of conspiracy ensnaring and paralyzing its martial action, the individual trembling in terror of some enemy's denunciation, false, perhaps, but no less deadly. All normal checks and balances were hurried ruthlessly aside, all elements of a people's energy cast into the crucible and out of it was welded a great, sharp sword, which was pressed in haste into the government's hand that the republic's numberless foes might be struck down. But always when not in use, this sword hung like a sword of Damocles over the head of every member of the government and of each individual Frenchman. Saint-Just's report of October 10, 1793, on the necessity of declaring the government revolutionary until the peace, definitely established this régime. He had nothing to do with setting up the Committee of Public Safety nor the Revolutionary Tribunal, with the elaborate law of 14 Frimaire or the terrible decree of 22 Prairial.

The common sense of the average man revolts with horror from this welter of bloodshed. The history of the twentieth century is proof enough, however, that cruelty is not peculiarly a French characteristic. The very fact of the increasing spread of violent forms of government makes vital a far profounder study of their classic prototype than can be attempted here. Most historians agree that the guillotine was a blunder as well as a crime, though a few seek to justify it. That the Terror in the sense of concentrated authority saved France so far as the war was concerned, there is small reason to doubt. But the mass of suspicion and slaughter worked far otherwise. Instead of saving the republic, the guillotine destroyed it. Group after group of really loyal patriots was separated from the main body and annihilated; Feuillants, Girondins, Hébertists, Dantonists, Robespierrists crumbled away in turn until republicanism had lost its flower. Through this process of decimation its strength was gone and there were no leaders left against the day of military usurpation. The republic committed suicide by opening its veins.

The truth of the matter is that there was no logical criterion by which to measure the proper limits of terrorism, if it were to be permitted at all. It is extremely difficult even for posterity to decide which group was really correct in its time-judgment and when the guillotine should have been slowed down. The First Republic would have been more lasting if defeated leaders had been merely deprived of office or, if they obstructed the government's action, sent to prison rather than to death.

Saint-Just's contacts with the Terror were twofold, as member of the Committee of Public Safety and as representative on mission. One thinks first of the decrees he signed and the extent to which they concern themselves with matters of police. One thinks next of the number of times the Committee used him as its mouthpiece to denounce its foes before the Convention. It is said that John Calvin's schoolmates, playing on words, called him "the Accusative" because of his sharp criticisms; the term exactly fits Saint-Just. He had a talent for that sort of thing; the Committee recognized his gifts and his power. One report, delivered on 26 Germinal (April 15, 1794) related specifically to "the general police, justice, commerce, legislation, and the crimes of the factions."

It was motivated by a wave of puritanism. The Dantonist trial had sickened the public with corruption in high places. On 17 Germinal, Couthon announced that the Committee of Public Safety was preparing great measures dealing with the purification of public morals and that four reports on this subject would be successively presented. Saint-Just was in charge of the first, which he delivered on the twenty-sixth.

The keynote of this discourse was sounded in the sentence: "It is not enough, citizens, to have destroyed the factions, we must also repair the evil which they have done the country." The nature of this evil he proceeded to unravel in a good many pages, going back to the early days of the Revolution for his start. He presented it as fundamentally an economic evil. In various ways, he believed, the enemies of liberty had sought continuously to foster famine. A notable instance was the deliberate effort to discredit the *assignats*. The original theory, that *assignats,* being promptly exchanged for national lands, would not be measured against goods, that specie would remain in circulation and that the rapid sale of lands would retire the paper money—all this did not work out. The system of annual installment payments for land, intended to facilitate sales, made it possible for *assignat* holders to use their funds over a period of eleven years for speculation in foodstuffs. They paid 5 per cent to the state and made 100 per cent in speculation. This twelve-year payment system was for the rich; the poor did not buy land. There was so little desire to favor the common people that the Constituent Assembly repealed the decree which had permitted the poor to buy land for five hundred livres, payable over twenty years. Meanwhile the monopolists sent their foodstuffs abroad. Merchants feared to restock, in view of the uncertain condition of trade. So the storehouses grew empty.

Turning from sound economic analysis to the profitless search for scapegoats, Saint-Just blamed the Girondins on one side and Hébert on the other for spreading such distrust of Paris that her commerce was ruined. A Paris business man could secure his merchandise from the seaports only for cash paid in advance. Bills of exchange were no more; people lived like savages without confidence or good faith. Hence the food shortage. The same forces produced the same result politically through federalism, a system invented to tear France apart, that its tatters might later be united again under a master. This plan was still not entirely abandoned, he solemnly asserted; it would be destroyed only by the reappearance of abundance. To secure its return, federalism must be extinguished by a severe police and by the recall of all officials to order; the accomplices of the factions must be sought throughout France; civil confidence must be restored; it must be made clear that the revolutionary government means neither war nor conquest, but the transition from evil to good, from corruption to virtue. [The vicious circle in this reasoning should be noticed; federalism will be destroyed only when abundance reappears, abundance will reappear when federalism is destroyed. The French may be the most logical nation in the world, but in emotional excitement their logic vanishes as quickly as that of any other people. Saint-Just, naturally clear-headed, was swept off his feet by the prevailing hysteria.]

The central portion of the report is taken up with a justification of the government's severity. They had been severe, yes, but judiciously; "it was necessary to avenge our fathers and to bury under its débris that monarchy, immense sepulcher of so many enslaved, unhappy generations," it was necessary to resist crime, destroy plots and punish hypocrisy. Liberty had arisen from the midst of storms even as the world itself came out of chaos and as each human being cries when he is born.

From these reasonings and many more of the same sort, he reached the conclusion:

You must therefore direct your attention to the policing of the state and exercise a very rigid censorship upon the enemies of the Revolution and upon the public authorities. Encourage the judges to render justice bravely, protect them, make them respected too, but if they depart from your decrees punish them severely.

Coming to particulars, he gave a detailed list of reforms to be made. The courts had been careless for the last two years. The time had come to wake up all officeholders; some had protected traitors and scoundrels; the army commissary department must give an accounting along this line; it had called two of its members, Gatteau and Thuillier,[245] men of blood because, being charged by the Committee of Public Safety to hunt out crooks, they denounced a storehouse keeper who had offered them 50,000 *écus* for their silence. The accounting officers must justify their indulgence toward their employes. The departments must account for the lofty air they often assumed toward the poor. The authorities would have to answer for every criminal coalition against public liberty. The justices of the peace must explain why justice had been refused to the rural poor.[246] The army courts must account for the discipline of corps commanders and for their excessive politeness toward men in power.

He finished by a series of revolutionary precepts, whose general purport was an attempt to distinguish between extremism and legitimate terrorism, which he here calls exaltation: "Exaltation is the stubborn resolution to defend the rights of the people and the Convention; exaltation is contempt of wealth, courageous simplicity of habits; exaltation is virtue and not fury." The private lives of the people must not be tormented; patriots must not be wrongly included among the accomplices of conspirators. "Let revolutionists be Romans, not Tartars."

The bill in eighteen articles which Saint-Just then read, was expanded by the Convention into twenty-six, becoming the decree of 27 Germinal. The first five articles provided for the fuller execution of the Ventôse decrees. Those accused of conspiracy should be brought from all points of the republic to the Revolutionary Tribunal of Paris.[247] The popular commissions should be established by 15 Floréal. The Committee of Public Safety was expressly ordered to inspect the doings of public officials. The next eleven articles dealt with former nobles and foreigners, restricting them with certain exceptions from living in Paris, fortified towns or seaports during the war. Most of the remainder was taken up with provisions calculated to keep public officials strictly to their tasks. A drastic article directed that anyone who in future complained of the Revolution, if he had no definite occupation and was neither over sixty nor infirm, should be deported to Guiana. On the constructive side, the Convention was to appoint a commission of three to codify existing laws and another to draw up a body of civil institutions for the conservation of morals and the spirit of liberty. The latter was Saint-Just's pet hobby; the former became Napoleon's.

The speech and the decree are admirable expressions of the Robespierrist ideal, perfectly embodied in Saint-Just himself. It was distinctly classic; Greek in its search for a golden mean in policy, Spartan in its moral asceticism, Roman in its civic severity. Waiving the dubious fairness of their attitude toward other parties, waiving also their absurd historical theory of the

Revolution, the Robespierrists certainly advocated a noble ideal. If only they had been able to make an end of their own Terror and to introduce a normal government, France would have been spared the corruption and ignominy of the Directory.

Saint-Just's official share in terrorism was not limited to his missions and reports. The decree of 27 Germinal extended the police power of the Committee of Public Safety, somewhat at the expense of the Committee of General Security. The sequel of this action was the creation of a bureau of general police within the former Committee with the immediate purpose of controlling governmental agents. It began to operate on 4 Floréal (April 23) and was reorganized by a decree of the Committee of Public Safety on 2 Messidor (June 20), naming Lejeune as bureau chief and dividing the bureau into four sections.[248] Lejeune and his subordinates drew up daily reports, based on denunciations and other material. These reports, each dealing with a specific case, were presented to the member of the Committee of Public Safety in special charge of the bureau, who made brief marginal notes, e.g., "arrest," "remove prisoner to Paris," "investigate," "refer to Carnot." The handwriting of these notes indicates which member of the Committee directed the bureau at a given time. From 4 to 9 Floréal the notes are in the hand of Saint-Just; on the ninth there are also notes by Robespierre and from 10 Floréal to 12 Prairial (May 31) they are all by the party chief. On 13 Prairial both men are functioning, from 14 Prairial to 11 Messidor (June 2-29) Robespierre alone, on the twelfth both again. Robespierre now vanishes. From then until 9 Thermidor (July 27, when the Committee of Public Safety ceased to control the bureau)[249] Saint-Just's notes appear three times (12, 14, 18 Messidor). Other notes on 18 and 24 Messidor are in Couthon's writing. The remaining reports are either without notes or contain merely the annotation "for examination" in the hand of Lejeune.[250] After the fall of the Robespierrists, a further reaction presently set in which forced Barère, Billaud, Collot and other Thermidorians to defend their own conduct during the Revolution. In so doing, they made much of this police bureau as the chief agency of terrorism, asserting that the anti-Robespierrists on the Committee had nothing whatever to do with it. Their statement that Saint-Just was the member of the Committee originally having special oversight of the bureau [251] is proved by the marginal notes to be correct. The same notes prove, however, that he was in sole charge for only five days at the start. After that, he wrote notes on five other days at scattered intervals; on three of the five, Robespierre or Couthon were also writing notes. The fact is that while Saint-Just seems to have been intended for the direction of this bureau, the plan did not work out because he went on mission to the North on 10 Floréal and did not return permanently until 10 Messidor. How completely he had abandoned any active connection with the bureau is shown by his failure to resume control of it in the month that remained before his fall. The statement of the Thermidorians that they had nothing to do with the bureau is decidedly less accurate. The whole question was investigated by the deputy Saladin, who made a famous report to the Convention on the revolutionary conduct of Billaud and his friends.[252] Saladin questioned the sole control of the Robespierrists, particularly in view of the fact that Robespierre was long absent from the Committee and Saint-Just almost continually on mission in the North. He recalled the fact that even when they signed decrees of arrest, their colleagues signed with them. He quoted a speech of Barère's made on 7 Thermidor, identifying himself with the work of the bureau, and finally the *Réponse* of Fouquier-Tinville, in which the public prosecutor stated:

I never had knowledge that the bureau of general police of which Billaud speaks was an establishment distinct and separate from the Committee of Public Safety and I must believe so all the less because on several occasions I saw Lejeune, one of the chief secretaries of this bureau, come to have his work approved in the meeting place of the Committee of Public Safety. . . . Further, all the orders given me in the meeting place of the Committee, as well as all the decrees transmitted to me, were entitled: *"Extract of the registers of the Committee of Public Safety"* *and signed by more or less of the members of that Committee.*

Saladin concluded that these orders of arrest were not, as pretended, the sole work of Robespierre, Couthon and Saint-Just.

Robespierre's own explanation of the bureau was given in his last speech on 8 Thermidor, when he declared:

I was charged momentarily, in the absence of my colleagues, to watch over a bureau of general police recently and feebly organized in connection with the Committee of Public Safety. My short period of control was limited to the responsibility for about thirty decrees.

For years historians have speculated about the question. A recent study of the papers of the bureau gives the correct answer. A report of the bureau, after it had been annotated by the member of the Committee especially in charge, ultimately formed the basis for a Committee decree. The "minutes" or original form of the decrees still exist in considerable quantity among the documents of the Saladin committee. Usually these are written by the member in charge and signed by him, but in many cases are signed also by other members of the Committee. More convincing still, minutes exist in the handwriting of other members of the Committee. For example, there is the decree of 13 Floréal, arresting a general named Santerre (not the famous Santerre); it is in the writing of Carnot and signed by him, Barère, Robespierre and Collot d'Herbois. There are 31 minutes in the writing of one of these other members of the Committee, besides 24 signed by anti-Robespierrists. This out of a total of 121 minutes studied.[253] It seems clear that while the Robespierrists were mainly responsible for the functioning of the bureau, they were not solely responsible. It was just one of the Committee's bureaus, like Carnot's war-bureau, and the ultimate authority rested with the whole Committee.

Saint-Just worked hard to secure the creation of the popular commissions called for by the decree of 23 Ventôse. None were actually brought into being until 24 and 25 Floréal, two months later, when the two commissions provided for Paris were created, though not the four intended for the departments. He was anxious to put the Robespierrist social program into effect as soon as possible; other members of the Committee delayed it as much as they dared.[254] The commissions of the Museum, as the first two were called because they met at the Louvre, did not begin to function until 26 Prairial, a month after their appointment, but they made up for lost time by sending in long lists of Paris suspects for the approval of the police bureau and the Committee of Public Safety. Saint-Just had no personal responsibility for these lists. They were ultimately approved not only by the whole Committee of Public Safety, but also by that of General Security. Further, those named on the lists were not necessarily executed if condemned. The decrees creating these two commissions described their task as "the enumeration of all suspects for deportation."[255]

Quite a different category of cases also resulted in long block lists. These were the so-called prison conspiracies which, though more imaginary than real, alarmed the government from time to time during the spring of 1794. The Museum commissions had nothing to do with these lists. The most important of these "conspiracies" was that of the Luxembourg in Messidor, not to be confused with the Dillon "conspiracy" in Germinal, of which the same prison was the scene. A list of 159 prisoners was drawn up, accused of being Dillon's agents and accomplices and of having expressed regret that they had been unable to assassinate the patriots. Two copies of this list exist, one signed by a police official named Lanne, the other by Saint-Just alone. It reads:

Le Comité de Salut Public arrête que les nommés Latour ancien capitaine de Hussards, Duclos, Feneson cousin Ex-noble, La Roche Dumaine Ex-noble, Dorival ancien Commissaire de Police, Maurin cydevant quartier Maitre [sic] de la Garde de Capet . . . [the names, blocked off in groups of ten, continue to the number of 159] seront conduits au Tribunal révolutionnaire; ordonne qu'ils seront ex-

233

traits sur le champ de la Maison ditte [*sic*] le Luxembourg et conduits à la Conciergerie pour être jugés sous le plus bref délai,—charge la Commission des administrations civiles, police et Tribunaux de l'exécution du présent arrêté, auquel effet elle pourra se consulter avec l'accusateur public près le dit Tribunal.

The decree, which is signed "St. Juste," is not in his writing and bears no date; the document has three signatures at the top of the first page, "Levin et Dumont," the third illegible.[256] This was not Saint-Just's personal enterprise; the whole Committee knew of the list as is proved by the fact that the names were turned over to Fouquier for trial by Pierre, who was secretary of the whole Committee and had nothing to do with the bureau of police. On 5 Thermidor another prison conspiracy furnished a list of 49. This was the Carmes affair, apparently in reality a plan to escape. The list was signed by Saint-Just, Couthon, Carnot, Billaud-Varenne and Collot d'Herbois.[257]

In sum, Saint-Just cannot be exempted from his part of the responsibility for sending long block lists before the tribunal (though he seems to have signed only two), but it is a responsibility which must be shared by every member of the two Committees, Robespierrist and non-Robespierrist alike. The names themselves rarely emanated from the great Committees in the first instance; in the case of the prison conspiracies they were worked out by police officers; in other individual cases they poured in from all France, usually in the form of denunciations from some local committee of surveillance.

Fouquier-Tinville explicitly denied that he held nightly conferences with the leaders on pending cases, asserting that he did not even know where Saint-Just and Couthon lived and was in Robespierre's lodgings only once.[258]

The share of Saint-Just in public executions was active and genuine, though it has been exaggerated and was in no sense unique. Did he do it as a public duty or because he liked it?

There are many stories of his ferocity. He signs a list of

names to be sent before the court without reading it or stopping his conversation. He wants to cut the prisoners' food supply to fifteen sous apiece. He avenges personal enmities by arresting Gellé, Thorin, Lauraguay. He has people arrested for eating chicken or carp (there are two versions) at an inn or a market, when he wished the delicacy himself.[259] Lejeune relates that a man lost his mind and denounced the new order; Saint-Just persuaded the man's mother to let him be taken to Paris for a cure; a fortnight later she read his name in a list of condemned.

Vilate, a protégé of Barère's, told the famous story of how Barère invited Robespierre, Saint-Just and himself to dine at Venua's the day after the trial of the queen, which took place October 17, 1793. Saint-Just was late and Vilate was sent for him; he found him writing at the Committee; at the mention of Robespierre's name, Saint-Just arose and followed his guide. As they walked along, Saint-Just seemed surprised and thoughtful. "Robespierre dine with Barère!" he exclaimed; "he is the only one whom he has forgiven." Vilate found the expression obscure. When they were all seated in a private room, Vilate was asked for details of the queen's trial. He mentioned her dignified reply to Hébert's charge of incest. Robespierre, electrified at her answer, broke his plate with a blow of his fork. "That imbecile Hébert," he cried, "it is not enough that she is really a Messalina, he has to make her into an Agrippina too and to give her this triumph of public interest at her last moment." Silence fell on the group, finally broken by Saint-Just, who reflected in his puritan way, "Morals will gain by this act of national justice." "The guillotine has cut an important knot of European court diplomacy," added Barère. Young Vilate was all agog at his wonderful privilege of hearing these great men discuss public questions in this intimate fashion. This was only a prelude, he writes, of the great political conversation which followed. Robespierre did not conceal his fear of the number of the Revolution's enemies. Barère included in this category all nobles and priests, all lawyers and physicians.

Saint-Just outlined the points of his speech on confiscation of the goods of deportable suspects. Barère, impatient to show his zeal for principles, declared: "The vessel of the Revolution cannot arrive at port except upon a sea reddened with waves of blood." Saint-Just agreed. "That is true," he said. "A nation regenerates itself only upon heaps of corpses," quoting Mirabeau and Raynal in support of his opinion. Robespierre saw two dangers to avoid; on the one hand an excessive effusion of blood which would revolt humanity; on the other an inadequate amount, under the influence of a false sentimentality, prejudicial to the general welfare. Barère concluded that it was necessary to begin with the Constituent Assembly and the chief members of the Legislative; this débris must be swept away. The whole dinner was marked by an air of suspicion; Vilate felt that his presence was a decided obstacle to the freedom of conversation. His feeling at the time of writing was that they were three miserable rhetoricians, rivaling one another in ferocity, who under pretext of regenerating morals were transforming the republic into a vast cemetery.[260]

Contemporary popular opinion is only slightly reflected in verse and caricature. A bit of doggerel represents the executed Dantonists predicting to Charon the fall of their rivals:

> Lorsqu'arrivés au bord du fleuve Phlégéton,
> Camille Desmoulins, d'Églantine et Danton
> Payèrent pour passer cet endroit redoutable;
> Le nautonier Caron, citoyen équitable,
> A ces trois passagers voulut remettre en mains
> L'excédant de la taxe imposée aux humains:
> Garde, lui dit Danton, la somme toute entière;
> Ce sera pour Couthon, Saint-Just et Robespierre.[261]

A caricature represents Satan and his wife disputing over their creative achievements. "I made Mirabeau," the lady boasts. "I did worse, I made Robespierre," her husband rejoins. But the wife wins the argument with the crushing answer, "It is possible to go further; I made Saint-Just." [262] On the other hand, although the Thermidorian period produced a great number of caricatures, Saint-Just rarely figured in them, the extent of his influence being then unrealized.[263]

The tales of sheer brutality told above are mostly refutable. The story of his signing a list without stopping to read it or interrupting his conversation emanated from Trinchard and seems to refer to the list of 159. Trinchard makes several errors in his story, which was told after the fall of Saint-Just when the narrator was trying to save his own head.[264] Barère's statement about the fifteen sous is suspicious because the decree giving each prisoner forty sous is in Saint-Just's own handwriting and is signed by him.[265] There is no truth in the persecution theory as related to his youthful grudges; he had nothing to do with the arrest of Gellé, Thorin and Lauraguay (or Lauraguais). Lejeune's stories are discredited by the fact that he turned violently against his patron's memory when he himself was under arrest and fearful that these past favors would damn him. Even Fleury does not accept them nor the gustatory tales which are obviously doublets and legendary on their face. As for the account of the Barère dinner, this too was written by a man in prison, seeking to curry favor with the new régime; it was modeled on a satirical Thermidorian libel against the Jacobins in which the identical conversation occurs, but no part of which is attributed to Saint-Just.[266]

In point of fact all these and other like denunciations of the Robespierrist trio as monsters in human form are of Thermidorian origin and hence valueless. They are no more trustworthy than would be a group of stories about Jefferson Davis originating in Boston in 1865. The Thermidorians had the added advantage that their opponents were dead and could not answer back. On the other hand, it is equally clear that no criticisms of the Robespierrists in their heyday of power were possible. Only a few bold fellows like Lacoste dared oppose them and even this was before the fall of Danton and Hébert had given "the triumvirate" their brief moment of complete supremacy.

The most vivid personal description of Saint-Just is beyond

all doubt that by Charles Nodier, who, it will be recalled, was in Strasbourg during Saint-Just's mission there. Though only a child, he was ordered under arrest and went to Saint-Just's lodgings in the hope of help. The picture is so remarkable that it is cited in full; it is inserted here because its author seems uncertain whether at heart Saint-Just was cruel or humane.

I went to see Saint-Just, that terrible Saint-Just, whose name I had never heard except in connection with a host of menacing epithets. My heart beat violently and I felt my legs almost giving way when I entered his office. I tried then to overcome my emotion and I found a little courage, that factitious and poorly estimated courage which one affects in default of anything better and which for those who know it is, in reality, only the camouflage of fear. Saint-Just paid no attention to me.

He turned his back to me and was reflected in the mirror of his mantelpiece between two girandoles full of candles, as with meticulous care he adjusted the folds of that wide and large cravat, on which his motionless head was raised as on a monstrance, according to the cynical expression of Camille Desmoulins, and which the imitative instinct of the strange young fops of the day began to make the fashion. I profited by the time this lasted and which seemed very long if I measured it by my impatience and disquiet, to study in the mirror's reflection the countenance of the supreme judge who was to decide my fate; I gave myself up to that examination without fearing that my gaze would be met by his, for I was in the shadow and he looked only at himself. The face of Saint-Just was very far from presenting that gracious combination of delicate features with which we have seen it endowed by the flattering pencil of a lithographer. He was good-looking, none the less, though his ample and somewhat disproportioned chin owed something to the complaisant material with which its many folds half enveloped it. The arch of his eyebrows, instead of rounding in uniform, regular semicircles, rather approached a straight line and their inner angles, which were bushy and severe, blended with one another at the least serious thought one saw passing across his face; his eye was large and habitually thoughtful, his complexion pale and grayish like that of most of the active men of the Revolution, probably the result of laborious vigils and rigorous mental exertions. However (and I only recalled this detail later in turning the pages of physiognomists), his soft and fleshy lips indicated an almost invincible tendency to laziness and voluptuousness. If he had tasted them, as everything that we know of his first youth and everything that remains of his first writings lead us to believe, he had triumphed over them with rare power at the moment when his life became a rôle; and nothing explains better perhaps the incoherence of his philanthropic theories and his revolutionary frenzies. The man who feels obliged to create for himself a new character because of circumstances foreign to his nature, cannot escape falling into falseness; and falseness is the generative principle of all crimes as of all errors.

At the very instant of which I speak, Saint-Just was necessarily preoccupied with something quite different from his cravat. A young man who was seated beside him, at a table lighted by two candles, was hardly able to follow his rapid and almost brutal dictation, in which all sorts of ideas were whipped into instant shape. A fresh sentence had already assailed his ear before a fresh sheet could be placed under his hand and this was repeated more than a score of times while I waited, each of those laconic sentences, in which one would vainly seek a period or a punctuation mark, calling for a special sheet. These sheets then passed by dozens into the workroom of the German translator, who finished them up with equal expedition if possible, when they distributed themselves in two columns under an indefatigable press, which turned over its output, still damp, to the billposters. What Saint-Just was thus improvising, while artistically interlacing the knots of madras with floating ends, was [a series of] irrevocable laws or decisions with no appeal; for such was the actual value of the decrees of a representative of the people on mission in a besieged town: temporary but absolute sovereign, who waved his sword back and forth over the populations, like the reaper over the swaying grain and who owed no accounting for anyone's blood except to God, if he believed in a religion, or to himself, if he had a conscience. I am far from contesting the importance of the services which the rigid severity of Saint-Just might then render to invaded provinces and routed armies; but nothing has ever seemed to me more frightful than the insulting conciseness of those proscriptions in a single line, which sometimes struck down a whole class of citizens at one blow, sudden, unexpected and mortal as a pistol shot fired by an assassin's hand; I think I still hear them echoing in the curt, sonorous, vibrant speech of that handsome young man whom Nature had formed for love and poetry; I cannot recall without trembling the persistent recurrence of that cruel word, Death, which armed them all at the end like the scorpion's dart, and which produced upon me the effect of some horrible rhyming game [*bouts-rimés*] whose monotonous and revolting assonance had been imposed by the executioner.

Meanwhile Saint-Just had reached the end of his toilet and his butchery. He turned completely toward me, the rigid scaffolding on which his head rested permitting no oblique movement. He informed himself as to the reason for my arrest which I knew no better than he, then of my name, my country and my age. At my last answer, he jumped quickly toward me, seized me by the arm and drew me near the light to the place where he had been a moment before. "That is true," he said, "eleven or twelve years at most. He has the look of a little girl. Are your parents *émigrés?*" "No, citizen," I answered, "they are far from it. My father presides over a court and my uncle commands a battalion." Saint-Just's irritation was manifestly making visible progress, but I knew already that the results would not be unfavorable to me. My order of arrest contained nothing in which I was personally involved.

"An order of arrest against a child," cried Saint-Just, violently crumpling up the paper; "an order of arrest, because he is from Franche-Comté and because chance has caused him to lodge in an inn where the Propaganda has observed some suspicious travelers! And it is so that these wretches flatter themselves they will make the Mountain adored! Oh! I will soon bring justice on these outrages, which daily endanger our most precious liberties! An exemplary and terrible justice! They dare threaten me when I do not give them blood! Well, the Propaganda shall have blood; I promise it! I will bathe it in the blood of the new tyrants whom it unchains upon the fatherland!"

In this moment of exaltation, of which my order of arrest was only the remote occasion, but in which he showed in spite of himself a deep and cruel aversion to the extremists, Saint-Just, moved to the highest point, had meanwhile lost almost nothing of his external impassiveness. His hand was clenched on a lifeless scrap of paper, but his face was calm. What I have just written shuddering, he said as coldly as if still giving dictation. How strange! An unalterable thirst for justice, an irresistible love of humanity from time to time dominated that ferocious soul, from which every sentiment of justice and humanity had not departed. Like the rest, alas, he knew how to kill without pity; but while killing, the unfortunate man was no doubt under an illusion: he thought he was being humane and just. Authority is so unfortunate in that all its faults are crimes!

"Be off," continued Saint-Just, addressing me in a tone which he tried to soften. I asked nothing better!

"What are you doing at Strasbourg?" he resumed, calling me back from the door, as I hesitated a moment before bounding over the sill on the run. "I am studying, citizen. I came here a few months ago with the intention of learning Greek." "Greek! It would be more natural, it seems to me, to come here to learn German. And why Greek, since the Spartans left no writings? But who then is the savant who occupies himself with giving Greek lessons at Strasbourg?" "Euloge Schneider, citizen, the elegant translator of Anacreon, one of Germany's first Hellenists." "The Cologne Capuchin!" cried Saint-Just. "Euloge Schneider, the Anacreontic! Go, go," he continued with a smile of bitter irony, "go learn Greek of Euloge Schneider. If I thought you might learn something else from him, I would have you strangled!" [267]

Other contemporaries, like Nodier, shared mixed emotions of admiration and dislike. Levasseur, despite his personal jealousy of Saint-Just when they were both representatives on mission in the North, drew a sharp line between him and his rivals in the following words:

Perhaps we would have worked out of this chaos, perhaps as the younger Robespierre and Saint-Just affirmed, we would have returned to clemency after a few more days of revolutionary rigor, if perfect homogeneity had prevailed within the government; but it was not so. In the Committee of Public Safety at the side of Robespierre and Saint-Just, men inflexible but led by principles and sincerely desiring the republic, though capable of odious and bloody measures to make it triumph; at the side of Couthon, their friend and agent, were Billaud-Varenne and Collot d'Herbois who took part in the revolutionary crisis only for their own interest; who in politics knew only how to shed blood and who could see nothing in the reëstablishment of order but the end of their influence. The elevated views of Saint-Just frightened them, for they realized that there would be no place for them in a regular and liberal government; hence began the hatred which was soon to find powerful sustenance. [268]

The justice of this estimate is borne out by the tone of a letter which Thuillier, inspecting supplies in the Northern

Army, received from Saint-Just under date of September 21, 1793.

> I recommend you, my friend, to acquit your mission according to my heart, that is to say with inflexible justice. Let no rascal get away with anything [*ne passe rien à aucun frippon*]. The Republic is the primary consideration and our tenderness must be entirely for it.
>
> Monnevieux wants to be placed. I invite you to be useful to your compatriots with discernment. I embrace Gateau and yourself.[269]

Valuable evidence is afforded by Saint-Just's marginal notes on the reports of the police bureau. He was strict. When special exemption from the law of 27 Germinal is sought for an old soldier, Saint-Just notes, "The law and country above all else." He was perhaps even stricter than Robespierre. On two reports Saint-Just calls for arrests, while Robespierre's notation on the same cases demands further investigation; in both, Robespierre's authority was superior. But Saint-Just too tried to be fair; his conception of strictness implied justice. The administration of Corbigny having placed seals on the papers of all ex-nobles, but finding nothing suspicious, desires the Committee "to decide on the fate of those who have conducted themselves well." Saint-Just comments, "Ask by what right they punish those who conduct themselves well, after having admitted this to be the case." An imprisoned judge, whose papers are under seal, requests an immediate trial. Saint-Just notes on the margin, "If the innocence of this citizen is proved by his papers, they must be placed at once under the eyes of the Committee, that justice may be done him." A farmer complains of his arrest by the national agent Rollet and incloses his certificate of good civic standing [*civisme*]. Saint-Just orders, "Write to Rollet demanding an account of this arrest, set the laborer at liberty." A woman named Fleury is arrested on the charge of spreading false news. Saint-Just queries, "Who is this Fleury and what false news did this poor woman report?" A widow accuses the local directory of having paid too little for a pig she sold to it. Saint-Just remarks, "Demand an accounting of the directory and remind it that the Committee will do

justice to the people in the smallest details of their interests."
A sergeant asserts that the municipal officials refuse to give his
father, sixty-six years old and infirm, the assistance provided by
law. Saint-Just observes,

Write to this municipality and demand an explanation of its conduct. Write to the volunteer to encourage him and assure him that
justice will be done him.

A national agent makes a report of his success in crushing
Catholic fanaticism. Saint-Just comments, "Write this national
agent that he must limit himself to his legal duties, respect the
decree establishing the liberty of cults and do good without
false zeal." One of Saint-Just's most frequently recurring marginal comments is the single word *"renseignements"*; another is
"s'informer." [270] This painstaking care in the examination of
individual cases, sparing no trouble to get at the facts, suggests
that though like other members of the Committee he signed a
few block lists, he probably did not send masses of people to
death in a spirit of cynical indifference. Those in the prisons
were in most cases survivors of one of the destroyed factions.
Saint-Just's reports against the Girondins, the Hébertists and
the Dantonists show how prone the government was to see the
goblin of conspiracy behind every hedge. These suspicions were
still lively, for the party in power felt none too secure. Absurd
as these fears seem to us when connected with the idea of a
prison plot, the concept of an antigovernment conspiracy was
not entirely without foundation, as witnessed by the success of
9 Thermidor a few weeks later. Explicable as it is, this prison-
plot scare is the least creditable part of Saint-Just's record and
constitutes an exception to his general practice. It may have
been good politics, but it cloaked rank injustice to individuals.
In any case, these lists were not condemnations but transfers to
the Revolutionary Tribunal, where the accused had a chance,
slim as it was.

What then is the verdict? Inevitably a mixed one. Saint-Just
would probably have seemed to us a very unpleasant and alarm-

243

ing young man, in whose company we should have felt distinctly uneasy. There was a certain element of the fanatic about him; everyone who devotes himself so utterly to a rather desperate cause, everyone who so completely lacks a sense of humor and the ability to enjoy himself in relaxation is fanatical. The thing that made Saint-Just seem so terrible to his contemporaries and still terrible to us was his apparent lack of ordinary human qualities and amiable weaknesses. And so they thought of him as the pitiless Executioner, the Spirit of the Guillotine. But that is not a fair portrait. He had no wanton delight in bloodshed as such; though he appeared unhuman, he was not inhumane.

To clarify our thinking, it may be well to sum up the items on the debit and the credit sides separately. From the very beginning, Saint-Just showed an imperious, ambitious nature. He worked hard for local leadership; he suffered acutely at initial failures. He had a thirst for domination. When the whirlwind of Terror was sweeping over France, the only sure way to dominate was to ride the storm. To impress one's personality on others, one must make the mental fashion of the moment one's own and seem to excel one's rivals in it. A masterful leader in those days could not afford to be squeamish; he must himself direct the Terror or run the risk of suffering from it. But all this was instinctive and subconscious in Saint-Just; it would not be fair to accuse him of deliberately assuming a terrorist attitude for personal advantage; he was no hypocrite. It was easy for him to adopt the popular tendency and to lead it, because it accorded so perfectly with his own habits of mind. Saint-Just was (at least on the surface) cold and suspicious; his normal style of public speech was epigrammatic, icy; his manner was impassive, his face expressionless. He saw conspiracies, traitors and corruptionists everywhere; some were real no doubt, but others imaginary. In the art of making out a case in apparent proof of these conspiracies, he was the most successful man in France. This was because at bottom he really believed them himself, though demonstration often lagged behind intuition. Again, he sincerely admired Robespierre and accepted his point of view. This was natural because they were so much alike. Most of the things that are said here of Saint-Just might also be said of Robespierre. Certainly if any man was suspicious, it was Robespierre and Saint-Just followed, when he did not suggest, the master's suspicions. In the fourth place, Saint-Just was always more interested in abstract issues than in concrete personalities. Liberty, the people, the republic moved him far more than the fate of any individual. The letter to Thuillier shows that. Men and women must be sacrificed, must sacrifice themselves if need be for these ideals. Stoic and Roman models furnished his mental pattern. One must be austere and tragic, one must repress every natural instinct and carry a dagger for every tyrant, if one would be a noble successor to Zeno and Brutus. This classicism was not peculiar to Saint-Just, it was in the air of the eighteenth century, but no one was more consistent in it than he. Hence because of natural tendency, personal advantage, conscious conviction and artistic theory (or if one prefers, moral emulation) he was inflexible and rigidly severe. It was easier for him to condemn than to excuse. Finally, if he really did crush down a native tendency to sensualism, the repression may have found vent in ultra-vigor toward others as toward himself. It did not go so far as the sadistic cruelty of a Carrier, but it may have had its share in producing here as so often in history, the monkish ascetic, the unsympathetic puritan.

Not all of these factors listed on the debit side are essentially ignoble. There is nothing more praiseworthy than self-mastery for the sake of a great cause. But they all concur in producing the terrorist and such he unquestionably was.

On the credit side, there must be recalled his dislike of the Extremists. He could not endure the loud-mouthed, coarse *buveur de sang,* who seemed to enjoy establishing new guillotine speed records for sheer love of the game. He always held that the Terror should be kept within reasonable limits. Ultra-violence discredited the Revolution. In his public utterances, he constantly strove to emphasize justice rather than terror. Psychological effects were desirable, but unless the people were convinced that executions were for just cause, the effect was a boomerang. From this standpoint, he made a conscious effort to be fair to individuals and signed many decrees of liberation. His marginal notes on police reports prove that he was not wholly devoid of human pity. He disliked the drastic law of 22 Prairial, even though Robespierre favored it. His social idealism was deep-rooted. He was always interested in the oppressed. This interest bore fruit in concrete legislation like the Ventôse decrees, on behalf of which he labored with unusual zeal. These decrees for the transformation of society could not be carried out except by terrorism.[271] As his *Fragments* show, he hoped that eventually out of all this, a better way of life would be born and that a time would come when gentleness and simplicity would characterize the lives of a happy, pastoral people, ruled rather by moral impulses than by force. Lastly, one must make certain allowances for the uncompromising nature of youth, particularly when endowed with such energy and driving power. His was the zeal of a young reformer, impatient to achieve results at a time when the republic's fate was at stake and every moment counted. If his destiny had been to grow mature in the service of a government which had outlived its birth pangs, if his judgment had developed and his pulse cooled with the years as it would not be unreasonable to expect, his page in history would have been very different. But the record must stand as he wrote it. With all its ghastly blemishes, it is not an entirely unworthy record. In his own view and with all his force, he served the state.

XVIII

AGAIN ON MISSION IN THE NORTH: THE TURNING OF THE TIDE

RANCE is all but impregnable on the south and southeast; readily defensible on the east, but open to attack on the north. From the century before Christ when Caesar had to defeat the Belgae in order to secure Gaul, down to the days when gray-coated thousands of imperial Germans choked all the roads from Liége to Namur and poured over the border after Joffre, this region has been the open road for the invader. The adage that the possessor of Antwerp held a pistol pointed at the head of England might with equal truth have been said of France. If it is a cardinal point of British foreign policy never to leave Belgium in possession of a great, potentially hostile power, it can be no less the permanent policy of Paris. Who knows how many times the armies of the western world have grappled for control of Mons and Cambrai and Valenciennes? Fleurus, where Saint-Just helped turn back the Austrian tide, witnessed the courage of the Duke of Luxembourg a century before and is less than a score of miles from the field of Waterloo. No doubt the eastern border has its importance also. Once in 1792, the Prussians broke through the line of the Vosges from the east and but for Kellermann at Valmy would have reached Paris. France has always been pardonably nervous about the Rhine frontier and it is natural that Saint-Just's first great mission was to Alsace. But in every year of the war, in 1792 and 1793 and 1794, the enemy's camp fires burned in the northern departments, a constant threat to the capital. Dumouriez won Jemappes in 1792 and cleared Belgium, but the Austrians came on again; Jourdan turned them back at Wattignies in 1793, but the relief was momentary. It shows a just sense of the situation's gravity in this northern sector that Saint-Just was sent there not once, but three times.

At the end of April, 1794, there were approximately 130,000 Allied soldiers in this part of France and southern Belgium under the supreme command of the Austrian general, the Prince of Coburg. With 65,000 Austrians, he personally held the center of the Allied line, a salient pushed well toward the south at Le Cateau, Catillon and Landrecies, the latter a weak, but strategically important town, which he had just captured after a siege. It seemed to rank in French psychology with Landau on the eastern front and its fall was correspondingly depressing. Clairfayt with more Austrians and 30,000 English under the Duke of York held the right of the line, which swept northwestward up to Ostend. The left, composed of Austrians and Dutch under the Prince of Orange, over 33,000, were in and about Charleroi.[272] In addition the Austrians had garrisons in a number of French towns, notably Condé, Valenciennes and Le Quesnoy. The main force opposed to them was the Army of the North, which in March, 1794, was 126,000 strong or, including garrisons, 195,000. Pichegru, the commander in chief, had control also of the small Army of the Ardennes, totaling nearly 7,000 or, with garrisons, 33,000.[273] The two sides were not unevenly matched, though the French were somewhat stronger. On the other hand, their armies contained a large proportion of volunteers and recent conscripts, while the Allies were seasoned professionals. The strategy of the Committee of Public Safety, directed by Carnot and accepted by Pichegru, called for a vigorous offensive on both wings in the hope of squeezing out the Austrian center salient. Pichegru himself was in direct charge of the left with the task of capturing Ypres and Tournai and becoming master of the Scheldt. Desjardins, commanding the right wing of the Northern Army, and Charbonnier with his Army of the Ardennes, were to concentrate at Philippeville, cross the Sambre at Thuin and march northwest on Mons. After the first attack, Charleroi instead of Mons became the objective, for this fortress on the east and Ypres on the west formed the pivots of the Allied line. Neither Desjardins nor Charbonnier were very efficient and control of the right was soon intrusted to a council of four, in which they acted jointly with Kléber and Schérer. This wing was to be supported on the east by troops from the Army of the Moselle under Jourdan who were to be moved into the Namur-Liége region.[274]

It was probably under the influence of the alarming news from the center of the line, where the Austrians were on the eve of capturing Landrecies (it fell April 30) that on April 29, 1794 (10 Floréal), the Committee ordered Saint-Just and Le Bas to the North.[275] The two men left Paris that day and reached Noyon on the twelfth, where they separated for a short time, Saint-Just going to the old home at Blérancourt to see his mother. It was to be the last time. On the fourteenth he and Le Bas reached headquarters at Guise, now bearing the revolutionary name, Réunion-sur-Oise. Guise was in the center of the line, some fifteen miles south of Landrecies.

The decrees issued by the representatives during this mission, which lasted from 13 Floréal to 10 Prairial (May 2-29) are almost entirely military. Since Saint-Just was not in a large city like Strasbourg or Lille, the requisitions on the rich which characterized his earlier missions are lacking. There are in all twenty-three decrees, six letters and a proclamation to the troops. Nine of these relate to military appointments and dismissals.[276] Appointments are commonly made in the following form:

The Representatives of the people to the Army of the North because of the good reports made to them regarding the civic virtues and talents of citizen Fusilier, chief of the first battalion of the 56th regiment, appoint him brigadier general, and decree that he shall enjoy the emoluments accompanying this rank.

When the Convention's representatives wished to take any such action, their authority superseded that of the military commanders. Three of the appointments are to the rank of brigadier general, one to adjutant general, one to captain, one to *commissaire-ordonnateur*. A postmaster is rewarded for his patriotism and the exactness of his service by the promise of the first six horses taken from the enemy, to be used for his relays and particularly for the service of the representatives of the people and of the army. So two birds were killed with one stone. A lieutenant colonel is honorably retired after long service and a brigadier general dryly ordered to betake himself to Paris to the War Commission, "the Army of the North having for the moment no need of his services."

Eight decrees have to do with courts, arrests and executions.[277] Military commissions, involving the elimination of jury trial, were set up at Réunion, Maubeuge and Avesnes, the two last being charged in case of siege to shoot anyone who suggested surrender before the place had stood assault. Military discipline was the chief concern of these decrees; only one contains any reference to counter-revolutionaries and there is no mention of a guillotine.[278]

Three other measures are likewise concerned with disciplinary regulations. One, the first they issued (Noyon, 13 Floréal), provided that the local commander should arrest surgeons from military hospitals who left their duties to wander about the town without permission. The second (Réunion, 14 Floréal) was also concerned with keeping up army morale. Every soldier not attached to garrison or staff was forbidden under pain of death to enter headquarters without permission. Two permissions to take complaints to headquarters would be issued to each corps daily; soldiers bearing them must leave town by 5 P.M. It was clear that Saint-Just did not propose to have the corridors of headquarters blocked up by loungers and grumblers. It has been asserted that women were strictly forbidden to enter the camps, that rigorous penalties were inflicted on men with venereal diseases and that officers and soldiers were required under pain of death to send off at once loose women whom they had introduced; a soldier of the thirty-sixth division, having kept his mistress, was shot.[279] Of this type also was the proclamation issued from Cousolre, 27 Floréal. Its swift vigor deserves quotation.

Soldiers,
We recall you to rigorous discipline, which alone can bring you victory and which will spare your blood; abuses have slipped in among you; we have resolved to repress them. Those who instigate the disbanding of the infantry before the enemy cavalry, those who leave the line before combat, during combat or during retreat, will be arrested at once and punished by death.

All cantonments will be patrolled; wandering soldiers will be recognized and arrested; if they take to flight, they will be fired on.

Soldiers, we are bringing you justice; we shall punish those who refuse it to you; we shall share your labors, but whoever is derelict in his duty will be visited by a sudden death.

Despise the enemy before you; an imbecile tyrant hires them; he has only a throne, the spoils of victory—and victory is leading us on.

It was not the army alone which was threatened with the heavy hand of republican justice. An order of 14 Floréal, addressed from Réunion to General Pichegru, motivated by the asserted fact that magistrates of the people had been killed at Landrecies by Austrian troops, in violation of international law, directed him to arrest in reprisal the nobles and former magistrates of Menin, Courtrai and Beaulieu and to send them under guard to Péronne to be held there under responsibility of the commandant.[280]

Date lines of decrees and letters show Saint-Just at Réunion from 14 to 21 Floréal, at Cousolre, about thirty-four miles to the northeast on the twenty-seventh, at Hantes on 3 Prairial, at Thuin (ten miles beyond Cousolre, on the Sambre) the eighth and at Maubeuge on his way home, the tenth. The removal of headquarters to these successive places indicates a military advance, made intelligible by the exchange of letters with Paris.

The day after their departure, Carnot sent the representatives the military laws and maps, "as well as the sabre" which they requested. He wrote again on the thirteenth, minimizing the fall of Landrecies, news of which must have just reached him. He heard that Cambrai was the next Austrian objective; the only danger there was treason, "but we hope that your presence will suffice to foil it." That move might be a feint, concealing a real advance on the Sambre. They should defend this river stubbornly and pursue the general plan of cutting off the enemy salient. A certain strong point at Avesnes should be fortified. "We are going to speak to you of another idea, of which you will make such use as may appear to you proper; we invite you only to weigh it attentively." The idea was the possible recapture of Landrecies, since the enemy had moved his artillery toward Cambrai. They were to tell Pichegru that Jourdan would shortly reinforce him with 25,000 or 30,000 men; if he could begin without them, he should not lose an instant.[281] The letter has several points of interest: the Committee's determined psychology of optimism; the notion of treason at Cambrai (which was to result in the mission of Le Bon); [282] the attempt to direct strategy, even in minor points, from Paris; the discretion given the representatives to modify or discard these instructions. The generals seem to have been considered expert advisers and technicians, whose duty it was to carry out orders given by civilians. One should remember in all fairness that this was not the only war carried on in such fashion; one recalls the military protests at civilian interference from Washington during the Civil War.

The first letter from Saint-Just and Le Bas to the Committee was from Réunion-sur-Oise, 14 Floréal and is in Saint-Just's writing; the letters and decrees of the pair are almost all his composition. They heard the news of Landrecies's fall on their arrival at Réunion; it was due to the extreme disorder in that part of the Army of the North from Maubeuge to Cambrai. The letter amplifies this point and the lack of a plan of movement, suggesting,

The enemy is not in force. We might at the same time advance in Maritime Flanders, invest Valenciennes, Le Quesnoi [sic], Landrecies, and march on Bavay eight miles west of Maubeuge. Answer us at once; do not lose an hour. We shall try to reëstablish order.

This explains the emphasis on army discipline in the decrees of the representatives.

To this Carnot replied the next day. The Committee did not doubt that Landrecies fell because of treason or incapacity. The situation should be investigated and conditions reformed by the representatives. They asked for a plan; there was one already; Pichegru must have informed his division commanders of the center. Detailed operations could not be directed from Paris, depending as they did on the daily movements of the enemy, which could not be foreseen. The general plan was to prevent his progress in the salient and the passage of the Sambre, to force him to raise the siege of attacked towns, to drive him from Cateau, Solesmes and all his posts in succession. Nevertheless, the letter proceeds with detailed suggestions, approving Saint-Just's idea of attacking at Valenciennes and Bavay, but warning him of the dangers involved.

A letter to the Committee from Choudieu and Richard, 17 Floréal, from Lille where they were representatives, reports that Richard and Pichegru had held a long conference with Saint-Just and Le Bas at Réunion-sur-Oise, resulting in confirmation of the previous plan to turn the enemy's right and left flanks, while the center stood on the defensive.

On the nineteenth, Saint-Just and Le Bas sent the Committee a copy of the decrees issued by them up to that time.[283] Next day they wrote Pichegru, rebuking him for not having sent them his plan of operations, of which they learned only indirectly; they felt the plan to be precipitate; hereafter let him warn them in advance before movements were determined.

Courier service between the front and Paris must have been rapid, for Carnot received and answered a copy of this letter the day following. The Committee supposed that the great operation of the passage of the Sambre had been postponed, he said, but the representatives' letter showed it must have taken place the day before. The die was now cast; in case of success, the 25,000 at Guise (Carnot forgets and uses the old name) would become useless and should be employed against the salient or to reinforce Jourdan before Namur.

The right wing did indeed cross the Sambre, 21 Floréal, taking Thuin. Simultaneously the left advanced in Maritime Flanders with great success, defeating Clairfayt at Mouscron, driving him back to Tournai and repelling him from Courtrai. The Austrians were forced to withdraw most of their troops from the salient. For some reason the Committee was not satisfied with this progress and wrote a scathing letter to Choudieu and Richard, 25 Floréal, accusing the army of inertia for not having followed up its successes; they replied expressing their pain and surprise at the Committee's apparent ignorance of the situation, the enemy was in great force and not completely beaten, but they had more victories to report and the general was worthy of confidence.

The right wing, less fortunate, was forced to retreat on the twenty-fourth,[284] retiring behind the Sambre. The Committee received this reverse in silence; was it because the political power of Saint-Just and Le Bas so far outweighed that of Choudieu and Richard? It is possible on the other hand that the situation seemed grave enough to call for a personal explanation. Jacques Duplay, at whose home Robespierre lived, testified at his hearing on 12 Nivôse, year III, that after the fall of Landrecies Saint-Just and Le Bas made a secret trip to Paris to confer with the Committee of Public Safety on plans for the campaign. It has been supposed on the strength of the Committee's register, according to which Saint-Just attended its meeting on 20 Floréal (May 9) that the secret visit was made at this time.[285] But on that date he signed a decree and two letters at Réunion-sur-Oise. The register, which is full of mistakes, is plainly in error here. Since he signed no decrees in the North between 21 and 27 Floréal, his hasty visit to Paris may have been between these dates.

A letter from Le Bas to Robespierre (28 Floréal) mentions a council of war at Cousolre between himself, Saint-Just, Richard, Levasseur, Generals Pichegru, Desjardins, Charbonnier and others. "Things are going fairly well, but they might be better." Saint-Just seems to have been less exclusive than in Alsace.

A second time the right wing crossed the Sambre (1 Prairial, May 20), as described at length together with the engagement of the following day, by Saint-Just and Le Bas writing to the Committee from Hantes on the third. The French were at first successful and Saint-Just writes confidently, adding in post-script,

Read this letter to the Convention. It is necessary that it should be published to encourage the brave folk.

None the less, the army was forced behind the river once more. In a council, Saint-Just insisted on returning to the attack at once; Levasseur vigorously opposed, but Saint-Just carried his point. The army crossed on 3 Prairial and was again driven back. The dogged tenacity and dominating will power of Saint-Just forced them forward again and a fourth crossing was effected on the sixth, only to fail once more. One gets an idea of the desperate fighting for control of the river from the letter of the eighth sent by Saint-Just and Levasseur from Hantes to the Committee. The general note is encouraging, though it is admitted that a part of the army had been driven back across the river and that the enemy had attempted, though vainly, to follow. Munitions are called for and enemy movements indicated. He adds in a postscript,

I have caused 1,600 men to be concentrated at Maubeuge to attack Les Quevettes, 20,000 at Lobbes as an intermediary column and 30,000 are to attack Charleroi this evening. I am writing Jourdan, with whom I correspond every other day; if he takes Dinant, we shall go to Brussels and Mons.

If he speaks by the book, and there is little reason to doubt it, Saint-Just had no small part in directing the movements of this army. His letter to Jourdan of the same date takes on the tone of a commander in chief. He writes to the general of the Army of the Moselle,

I have received your various dispatches. I beg of you to continue to regulate your movements with those of this army; we still have control of the Sambre, today we occupy the camp of La Tombe. We shall try to take Charleroi; you will doubtless take Dinant; then an army corps which we are forming at Maubeuge will march on Mons and another on Brussels.

I embrace my dear colleagues, Gillet and Duquesnoy.

A fifth time the army advanced over the Sambre (10 Prairial) and success seemed in sight; Charleroi was bombarded and almost burned, but once more the French were driven back of the river.[286]

The picture of Saint-Just's refusal to admit failure, the driving power and inspiration which he must have instilled into a discouraged body of men, is magnificent. Years later his jealous colleague, Levasseur, sought to minimize Saint-Just's part in these operations, partly on the ground that Saint-Just could have given no orders without Levasseur's knowledge, partly by the assertion that representatives on mission were not permitted to encroach on the military functions of the generals. The incorrectness of this statement is evident from the letters of Saint-Just and of the Committee.[287]

In the midst of this furious and unremitting struggle, Saint-Just was recalled to Paris. The Committee wrote on 6 Prairial, addressing him only and making no mention of Le Bas, whose presence in the capital was apparently considered unimportant. They told him that liberty was exposed to new dangers; the factions were reawakening more alarmingly than ever. Food riots, more numerous and turbulent than before, though with less excuse; a prison insurrection scheduled for yesterday; intrigues as in the days of Hébert—all these were combined with attempts to assassinate members of the Committee, proving the redoubled audacity of the factions. A fatal aristocratic insurrection was feared. The worst dangers were in Paris. The Committee needed the wisdom and energy of all its members.

Consider whether the Army of the North, which you have powerfully aided in placing on the road to victory, may not get along without your presence for a few days. We shall replace you until your return there, by a patriotic representative.[288]

It was a pathetic appeal for help, leaving the decision with Saint-Just, rather than an imperative recall, but the Committee seemed to have no doubt that he would accede to it, for on the same date it addressed Guyton-Morveau, representative at Maubeuge, informing him that the Committee had "decided to cause our colleague Saint-Just to return here" and charged Guyton to act with Levasseur at Desjardins's headquarters during Saint-Just's absence. They also dispatched a last matter of business to Saint-Just and Le Bas, relative to a denunciation against Barbon, General Ferrand's chief of staff. It seemed to them outweighed by the evidence in his favor. The very interesting admission follows:

Experience is proving to us every day that such denunciations are often dictated either by personal hatreds or by a desire to obtain the places of those one would remove, or finally by a wish to deprive the Republic of those who serve it with zeal and intelligence; we are therefore returning Barbon to his duties, inviting you to watch him and to get all the information you can about him.

Evidently suspicion had its limits and if time had permitted, terrorism might have cured itself.

Le Bas returned to Paris at once; this was the end of the mission for him. Saint-Just delayed a few days more, reluctant to leave the army in the midst of its task, but was back in Paris on 12 Prairial (May 31).

The most important event during his sojourn in Paris was the formation of a new army. It was foreshadowed by a decree of the Committee (20 Prairial, June 8) which provided: (1) that Pichegru, general in chief of the Army of the North, should be in supreme authority over all forces operating against Belgium from the Meuse to the sea; (2) that the Army of the Ardennes, the right wing of the Army of the North and the auxiliary portion of the Army of the Moselle should be under the immediate command of Jourdan, who should act under Pichegru.

257

This important decree was announced to Richard and Choudieu in a letter of like date from Carnot, motivating the Committee's action on the report brought them by Saint-Just and
Le Bas of the misunderstandings between Desjardins and
Charbonnier.[289] Desjardins was retained to act under Jourdan,
Charbonnier recalled to Paris. This was the beginning of the
famous Army of the Sambre-et-Meuse, though the name was not
conferred on it till June 29.[290]

Jourdan, who had reported his movements daily to Saint-
Just and Le Bas,[291] took Dinant, making his junction with the
armies on the northern front, 15 Prairial. The new organization
placed him in command of 96,000 men, whose immediate task
was the capture of Charleroi.[292]

Meanwhile Saint-Just, having reached Paris, wanted to know
what he was expected to do there. Robespierre is said to have
told him that he was sent for to draw up a report on the new
factions threatening the Convention. It is conjectured that
Saint-Just refused to make the report, feeling that his presence
with the army was more important.[293] In any case, after less
than a week in Paris he returned to the front by authority of
the Committee, which announced on 18 Prairial:

The members composing the Committee of Public Safety decree
that their colleague, Saint-Just, shall go without delay to the northern and eastern frontiers to survey the armies of the Republic from
the sea to the Rhine, and to provide for the execution of the decrees of the National Convention and those of the Committee of
Public Safety.

More power was thus lodged in his hands than at any previous
time; he was in some sort supreme over all the armies on the
two important fronts.

Armed with this authority, he went back to camp to begin
the so-called "mission to the northern and eastern frontiers,"
which turned out in reality to be his third mission to the North
or more properly a continuation of the second, which had been
momentarily interrupted. The new mission lasted just half the
length of its predecessor, from 25 Prairial to 8 Messidor (June

13-26).[294] The whole fortnight was taken up with a vigorous siege of Charleroi, which began before Saint-Just arrived. His decrees are hence more military than ever.

Of the score or more of *arrêtés* and letters, he signs fourteen with Gillet and L. B. Guyton, six with Gillet alone and one with Gillet, Guyton and Laurent. Six dealt with supplies; six concerned appointments and removals.[295] Only one (29 Prairial) was devoted solely to an arrest. On the official report that a battalion had fled from the field of combat and considering [most extraordinarily]

that this crime cannot be that of the whole battalion, since bravery and hatred of tyrants exist in the hearts of all the French and that when a troop leaves its post of battle, the cause is in the cowardice of the officers and the negligence they have shown in keeping discipline and forming the soldiers they command for the love of glory, which consists in braving the dangers of war and conquering or dying at the post which the fatherland has entrusted to them,

the battalion chief (lieutenant-colonel) and the captains are placed under arrest. But sentiment lay close to mercilessness in the hearts of these men; witness their decree of 5 Messidor. One Marguerite Bontems, a twenty-two-year-old girl, had been forced by village officials to take her father's wagon and horses sixty leagues to the army; "informed that malignity had caused the commission of this act of injustice to a woman and that the municipal officers of Mesnil-Lahorne have personally exempted themselves from requisitions," the representatives ordered the army *commissaire-ordonnateur* to assess these individuals in the sum of ten thousand livres, to be turned over to the Bontems girl as indemnity for the act of oppression of which she was victim. In general, discipline occupies a very subordinate place in this mission; of revolutionary courts and terrorism there is no hint. Saint-Just must have done his work well in the restoration of order on his previous visit. One savage little *arrêté,* however, provided for order, neither military nor revolutionary. Generals Balland and Desjardins were directed to kill all the brigands in the Chimay country within three days. They were responsible on their lives for carrying out the decree (1 Messidor). Finally, two *arrêtés* were concerned with military movements. General Desjardins was authorized to withdraw two mortars from the fortifications of Givet to complete his siege train against Charleroi (5 Messidor). Gillet and Saint-Just, learning that it was planned to withdraw all the cavalry now operating on the right under Jourdan, for service with Pichegru in an entirely different area, protested against this measure, which was calculated to destroy their cavalry corps.[296]

During this period the new army was furiously attacking Charleroi. Before Saint-Just's return, it had recrossed the Sambre (24 Prairial, June 12) for the sixth time, now under Jourdan. A severe battle on the twenty-eighth with almost equal losses forced it behind the river once more.[297]

Saint-Just, who had arrived by this time, wrote a letter with Gillet and Guyton to Jourdan, evidently designed to spur him on to a further offensive. The Committee's intention, he said, was that the war be pushed with a fury which would exhaust the enemy, inferior in numbers and obliged to make up for that inferiority by painful marches from point to point. Their ordinary strategy being not to resist our first onrush, but to attack us unexpectedly at night, so disguising their weakness, it was for us to attack unceasingly. It would be well to advance every day at dawn. Jourdan's triumphant and rapid march from Arlon led to the hope that offensive combat was according to his taste. The representatives would look after the administration, the obedience of the officers, the supplies; his only task was to win. Let no doubt of himself enter his heart; it should be sensitive only to the republic's glory. Let him maintain the army's enthusiasm by continual successes and by daring. The war of liberty must be waged with fury. He would never have to answer for having pursued the enemy's ruin with ardor, but he would have to answer if he temporized with a foe who was himself temporizing. "It is probable that he will attack you soon; anticipate him, since you have for attack the same military elements you would have for receiving one." The enemy in his despair must not be allowed to abandon one point and to move on another. He must be kept from burning Maubeuge. The best way was to pursue him all along the line of the Sambre.

We are counting on you. It will be with joy that we announce to the Committee of Public Safety new successes at this point. Public opinion is impatient for them.

This stirring admonition (26 Prairial), exaggerating the enemy's "despair" though it did, was both a warning and a stimulus to Jourdan, who realized that his post and probably his head were at stake. For the seventh and last time, the passage of the river was successfully made (30 Prairial, June 18).[298] The actual conduct of the siege of Charleroi was intrusted to an officer named Hatry. It is said that progress was delayed by the inexperience of the artillery, which led the exasperated Saint-Just to give Jourdan an order to arrest Hatry, Bollemont, the artillery commander and Marescot, chief engineer, intending to have them shot, but Jourdan "had the courage to resist." Another story tells of Saint-Just's seeing the preparations to install a battery and asking the captain in charge when it would be finished. "That depends on the number of workers given me," was the answer; "but the work will be carried on without a break." "If tomorrow at six o'clock it is not ready to fire, your head shall fall." It was not ready and Saint-Just was as good as his word. The stories may be true, for Saint-Just was intolerant of failure and success on this front had been long deferred.[299]

Ypres fell, June 18, the very day that Jourdan made his final crossing of the Sambre, and Pichegru pressed forward toward Ghent and Bruges. News of this signal success on the left must have redoubled the efforts of Jourdan and Saint-Just to take Charleroi. In a letter to the Committee from Marchienne-au-Pont, dated 5 Messidor (June 23), Saint-Just, writing with Gillet and Guyton, makes a report of progress. The siege was being pushed with all the activity they could muster; they had been much annoyed by the lack of instruction of many artillerymen, the poor quality of the gun carriages, the difficulty of getting mortars in good condition. Nevertheless, the firing was quite active that day and would be more so the next. Eight new guns had arrived. The French fire was already heavier than that of the defense and the second parallel had been pushed within pistol shot of the glacis. There were daily movements in the open field but no battle of importance, as the enemy kept retreating. Indeed the paucity of their numbers suggested that they were planning a general movement against the left of the Army of the North. To clear up the situation, a body of 36,000 men would march toward Mons next day. Discouragement filled the enemy; many deserters were coming in. The emperor had no influence in the Low Countries. The Austrian army was in misery; the Dutch fought with regret against us [the French]. "Europe is decadent and we are going to flourish." The spirit of the army was exultant; this afternoon the cannoneers serving their guns were shouting: "Long live the Republic! Long live the Convention and the representatives of the people!" In a postscript Saint-Just, writing alone, added that their letter was sent to tranquilize the Committee.

I think I can assure you that we are on the eve of great successes in Belgium. We need a great number of cannon and much ammunition. After Charleroi we shall fall on Namur and Mons. You will do well to await the capture of Charleroi to announce the whole thing to the Convention.[300]

Two days after Saint-Just's letter (7 Messidor, June 25) the town surrendered. Many stories of the actual capitulation were circulated, in all of which Saint-Just figures in one heroic attitude or another. The best authenticated is that told by General Marescot, who was present, in his *Relation du siège de Charleroi*. The commander of the garrison sent an officer to parley about terms. Saint-Just listened coldly and replied that surrender at discretion was all that could be expected. A higher officer came next, with offers of capitulation. "It is not paper that I want, it is the place that I demand of you," was the representative's inexorable answer. "But if the garrison surrenders at discretion, it dishonors itself," the Austrian demurred.

And we! [cried Saint-Just]. We can neither honor nor dishonor you, any more than it is in our power to honor or dishonor the French nation. There is nothing in common between you and us.

When the officer insisted, Saint-Just dismissed him with the cold words,

Yesterday one might have listened to you; today you must surrender at discretion. I have spoken! . . . I have made use of the powers entrusted to me. There is nothing further for me to withdraw. I count on the help of the army and on myself [*sur le concours de l'armée et sur le mien*].

The officer left, but soon returned to announce unconditional surrender. In another more doubtful version, Saint-Just, urged to sign the Austrian proposals, replies, "I left my pen at Paris and brought only my sword," at which the astonished officer exclaims, "M. de Saint-Just is a very great man." [301] The defeated troops were, however, given the honors of war and the officers allowed to keep their swords and baggage.

Saint-Just's own account of the matter, contained in a letter of the three representatives to the Committee, from Charleroi, 7 Messidor, is much more matter-of-fact and modest. After describing a severe, but victorious battle on 28 Prairial, the account of the siege is resumed. "The engineer officer Marescot did himself much honor by the activity with which he pushed his work." This incidentally discredits the tale that Saint-Just wanted Marescot shot. "The artillery reduced the town to ashes." The surrender after a week of intensive bombardment is thus described.

On the sixth, the fire redoubled; on the seventh, he asked to capitulate. He was given a quarter of an hour to surrender after which an assault would be ordered and the garrison put to the sword. He sent us a messenger; we returned the letter without opening it. General Reygnac, commanding the fortress of Charleroi, surrendered at discretion, commending himself to the generosity of the Republic. Jourdan will send you the honorable articles by which you will see that the pride of the house of Austria has passed under the yoke. The captured garrison numbers three thousand men. We have found fifty pieces of artillery. The place is in powder and is no more than a post.

A day too late, Coburg came to the city's relief with 52,000 men, but Jourdan had 75,000 and was flushed with success. On June 26 was fought the great battle of Fleurus, the decisive engagement of the war. It was a terrific struggle lasting fifteen hours, with the French mainly on the defensive. In the end they managed to beat off the enemy, who withdrew.[302] Guyton, Gillet, Laurent and Saint-Just sent a brief dispatch to the Committee from the battlefield (8 Messidor), announcing a "most brilliant victory on the field of Fleurus, already famous for French valor."

This defeat took the heart out of the Austrians, just as Valmy took the heart out of the Prussians in 1792. In both cases, the French disclosed a capacity for resistance hitherto unsuspected. Raw recruits were becoming inured to fire by the summer of 1794 and the Austrians found to their dismay that their inferiority in numbers was no longer compensated by overwhelming superiority in training and experience. And so they began their long retreat, fighting at intervals but always losing. Namur was abandoned. July 10, Ney entered Brussels with some of Pichegru's troops and Jourdan's men reached the same city next day. The lost fortresses, Landrecies, Le Quesnoy, Valenciennes and Condé were all regained during July and August. By the end of September the French had Belgium; the next three months gave them Holland; on January 20, 1795, Pichegru entered Amsterdam. In April of that year, the First Coalition came to an end by the Peace of Bâle between France and Prussia. The English troops embarked for their own land during that month and in a short time, terms were also made with Holland and Spain.

During this mission, Saint-Just's movements may be traced from date lines or other references in decrees and letters. His first two decrees, 25 Prairial (June 13), are dated "at the camp before Charleroi"; two others on the same day "at headquarters, Marchienne-au-Pont," a little over a mile from Charleroi. A letter was dated from this point on the next day, after which he left, perhaps on a tour of inspection. Gillet and Guyton, writing to the Committee on the twenty-sixth, say: "Our colleague, Saint-Just, went today to Vedette-Républicaine," the former Philippeville,[303] about fifteen miles south. On the twenty-seventh Guyton tells the Committee that his colleague, Gillet, has already left for the front and that Saint-Just is about to depart for Kléber's division on the left bank of the Sambre, while he himself is going to the center with Jourdan. The decree of the twenty-ninth shows the three representatives united at Montigny-le-Teigneux and indicates that Kléber has been visited. By 1 Messidor they were back at Marchienne-au-Pont, where Saint-Just remained until the fall of Charleroi.

The Committee passed a decree and sent off a letter to Guyton and Saint-Just, both on 4 Messidor (June 22). The first decreed that an order on the National Treasury for ten thousand livres should be given to citizen Gateau, to be remitted by him to Saint-Just for expenses in connection with his mission. The second inclosed a letter from the council of defense at Sedan relative to an exchange of prisoners, which Guyton and Saint-Just were requested to negotiate; this is the single matter of business relating to the eastern front transacted by Saint-Just on this mission.

His relations with his colleagues varied widely as in Alsace. With some he got along amazingly well, notably with Gillet, which speaks well for him as Gillet was his closest associate. This representative wrote him a number of letters after Saint-Just's final return to Paris, which attest admiration and friendship between the three former coworkers. From Marchienne,

11 Messidor, he sends a batch of military news and renews the old complaint about the weakening of the cavalry. "Don't forget the letter we wrote the Committee to end that measure at once, which may destroy our cavalry irremediably in a very short time. Guyton embraces you. Your colleague and friend, Gillet." To the Committee, Gillet sent a despondent letter, 14 Messidor, regarding the probable necessity of acting thereafter on the defensive. Evidently the importance of Fleurus was not fully appreciated. "Ask Saint-Just. He knows the country. I refer you to him." He set forth his alarms more fully in a private letter of the same date to Saint-Just. "I am unfolding my heart and my anxieties here; do not show this letter to anyone. . . . Adieu, come back soon." Next day another personal letter went to Saint-Just, complaining again of the order to send off cavalry to Pichegru. They were not carrying it out for the moment, until final word came from the Committee; they felt they were saving the republic thereby. Saint-Just was urged to plead the cause before the Committee. "We are a bit forgotten; think of us and rejoin us promptly. Guyton embraces you. Your colleague and friend." The third letter in as many days (16 Messidor) contained another long budget of news and requests for the army. "I invite you with all my heart to rejoin us as soon as possible. I know, however, that you will be very useful to us at Paris in securing supplies for us. Don't forget the cavalry depots." On and on he wrote, asking Saint-Just to get them this and that, ending, "I ask your pardon, dear colleague, for having written so often and such long letters; but when I am proposing to you only measures to overcome our enemies, I have had to count on your patience to decipher me. Adieu; Guyton embraces you." With this communication, the torrent of letters ceases abruptly and entirely. Clearly, Saint-Just was regarded by his friends as a fairy godfather, who could help his old comrades as no one else could. But there is also no mistaking the clear note of friendship throughout. It may be added that the Committee revoked the cavalry order, but only after a violent scene between Saint-Just and Carnot

As late as 1 Thermidor (July 19), the army had hopes of Saint-Just's return. Richard, writing the Committee from Brussels on that date, announces the departure of Guyton.

His going will make a great void, which should be promptly filled. It seems to me indispensable that you send Saint-Just here again and that you charge him with everything which concerns the general administration of this country and with all the great measures that the Republic's interest dictates taking here. This mission is of the highest importance and I think only a member of the Committee of Public Safety can be entrusted with it.

After the Robespierrists had fallen, the tone changed. Dear friend Gillet, now at Waremme (13 Thermidor, July 31), gave the Committee his reactions on hearing the news, which he was hastening to communicate to the army. It would share the indignation of all patriots against the monsters who had sought to destroy liberty at the very moment signal victories were establishing it.

I had the misfortune to have as colleague for a few days the scoundrel Saint-Just, and at the moment when he was conspiring I was asking you to send him back. Could I think him criminal, he who enjoyed the greatest confidence? Would that he had come! He would not have found one perfidious municipality. There is not a soldier in the army who would not have made it a duty to shoot him.

This is hardly honest indignation. There had been too many "conspiracies" by that time to permit any intelligent person to be taken in. Most of them were mare's-nests; even the genuine ones like the proposed Hébertist insurrection and the plot of the Thermidorians were not directed against the republic as such. The former was intended to be and the latter was in fact simply another party *coup d'état* and the good Gillet, like many others, wanted to mount the band wagon as rapidly as possible. It is likely of course that behind his lavish protestations of friendship during the earlier period lay a similar motive. But in any case it is evident that a high value was placed on Saint-Just's services by those who were in a position to know

267

and that, so far as temperament is concerned, he seems to have worked harmoniously with some of them. Le Bon's admiration is another case in point.

On the other hand, there were those who disliked him. Chief of these was Levasseur. He and Saint-Just were constantly at odds on matters of policy.[304] Apparently jealous of the superior authority vested by the Committee in Saint-Just, Levasseur tells one spiteful story after another, designed to show that man for man he was the braver and better of the two. Wakened early May 22 by the sound of cannon, says Levasseur, he ran in search of General Charbonnier; then both ran to the advance posts. The other representatives and generals not arriving, Levasseur ran to find them. He met Saint-Just, Le Bas and Generals Schérer, Kléber and Desjardins, all walking quietly. "What!" Levasseur shouted from a distance, "You come from headquarters, while they're fighting down below?" "Do you think we are afraid?" was Kléber's scornful answer. Levasseur does not give his rejoinder, but Kléber had hit on his thought, though the thought did not refer to the doughty Kléber. When they all reached Thuin, Levasseur asked Saint-Just if he had given orders to advance. "No, but I think there are traitors and they must be sought out." "There is no question of traitors," Levasseur answered impatiently; "hasn't the enemy spies who will have informed him of the separation of ten thousand men from our army and of the movement which has taken place?" Saint-Just had nothing to say. Levasseur goes on to tell how, leaving the generals in council at Thuin, Saint-Just and he climbed a hill to observe the enemy camp. They distinctly saw the enemy firing his cannon.

I said to my colleague: "The representatives of the people ought not to watch a battle from such a distance; let us run into the thick of it." "What do you expect us to do there?" That answer made several officers standing near by smile. I was irritated by it and said to Saint-Just ironically: "I see that the smell of powder disturbs you." I left him at once, putting spurs to my horse. . . .

Next day Saint-Just came to my room; I was busy with my mail and asked him to let me finish my letter. While I wrote, he saw my carbine, picked it up and amused himself examining the hammer; unfortunately it was loaded, it went off, the ball passed near me and pierced my valise, which was on a chair five or six steps off; I rose at once, the gun had fallen out of Saint-Just's hands, he turned pale, staggered and threw himself in my arms.

"Ah! Levasseur, if I had killed you?" "You would have played me a villainous trick; if I must die from a gunshot, let it be at least at the hand of an enemy." Hearing the report, several officers who were near my door hastily entered my room and found Saint-Just in my arms, as pale as death. "Pardon, representative," they said to me, "but the sound of a shot alarmed us and we came in to see what was happening." I told them what had just taken place and thanked them for their kindly interest; they left. Alas! on what hinges a man's life and honor! I might have been killed and Saint-Just would have infallibly been accused of murder by the officers who heard the ironical answer I made him the day before. Fearing, however, that there might be unjust suspicions about the matter, I took pains to walk during the day arm in arm with my colleague. During this walk, I had a conversation with him which deserves to be recorded. As I said to him, "You have therefore suppressed the official defenders at the Revolutionary Tribunal. If your tribunal is composed of angels, you are right; but they are men: *Erudimini vos qui judicatis,*"—he replied, "All the jurors are patriots; in any case, a few executions more and the reign of clemency will become the order of the day." "You are coming to it a little late; a party may perhaps anticipate you and use these methods to overthrow you." "Only a republican like you could speak to me in such a way without seeming to me suspect." If only they [the Robespierrists] had put their pacifying plan in practice, they would have saved much blood; perhaps their power, preserved a while longer, would have been useful to France, on which it weighed so heavily, [instead of] being overthrown at the moment it was about to bear fruit!

Elsewhere, Levasseur describes Saint-Just as "without physical courage and feeble of body to the point of being frightened at the whistling of bullets." He would not credit his leadership in the continued recrossing of the Sambre. "All languished for lack of direction and will power, instead of one's being able to recognize in these events the supposed iron will of Saint-Just." [305] This was all sheer personal jealousy. In politics, he approved and admired Saint-Just. Even in military matters, he really esteemed him. He wrote to him on 13 Prairial from Marchienne: "Your presence, my dear colleague, is very necessary here. Come as soon as possible; it will be a good reinforcement." [306]

It is said that Choudieu also detested Saint-Just, though it does not appear in his letters. He refused at first to go on mission to the Ardennes unless Saint-Just were recalled, until Robespierre intervened, saying, "Can't two republicans like you live together?" Choudieu yielded with bad grace. [307]

As to the difficulty of getting on with Saint-Just, it was probably real. He was distant, imperious, self-reliant. At the same time it should be recalled that such quarrels were frequent among representatives, particularly between pairs of representatives; the two immediate colleagues usually stood together in loyalty to each other.

Levasseur's charges that Saint-Just lacked courage and leadership cannot be maintained. [308] Whether or not he took personal part in battle, he was no coward. The man who stood up in the Convention as spokesman of his party against Girondins and Hébertists and Dantonists, realizing that if anything slipped, he of all others was lost; the man whose relentless energy inspired beaten armies in Alsace and in the North to go forward until those provinces were cleared; the man whose sharp, imperative decrees supplied these armies with what they needed for victory; the man who stood alone in the Committee against a snarling ring of foes during the bitter days of Thermidor and who met his end without word or sign—whatever his faults, and they were many, this man was not a weakling nor afraid.

With the victory of Fleurus, the mission came to an end. Saint-Just left the army that evening and arrived in Paris during the night of 10 Messidor (June 28). It is asserted that he expected to have the honor of reporting to the Convention, but that Barère stole a march on him by listening carefully to Saint-Just's report to the Committee, taking his notes and getting technical details from generals who knew the country. It was then decided to have Barère make the report, while Saint-Just merely announced the victory to the Convention in a few words. He was irritated and refused.[309] However this may be, Barère reported the success in the session of 11 Messidor.

The whole of northern France gave the credit to Saint-Just.[310] It was not far wrong. Charleroi, more than Fleurus, was his work. Jourdan, an able soldier, won the two victories on the field. But if, in the days of the incompetent commanders who preceded him, the army had not been held to its task by Saint-Just's relentless determination, Jourdan would have found no troops before Charleroi when he arrived. Louis XIV's crossing of the Rhine was a gorgeous parade, painted on acres of grandiose canvas. The sevenfold crossing of the Sambre has had no painter, but it was an epic struggle far worthier of memory. For his part in it, Saint-Just deserved well of his country.

XIX

GRANDEUR—AND OUR DUST

O "NIGH is grandeur to our dust" that men have always risen at the bugle call of duty or opportunity and outstripped what they or others would have thought humanly possible. But in quite another and sadder sense the two are related; for close on the heels of splendid achievement often follow failure and oblivion.

Saint-Just returned from the great battlefield of Fleurus on 10 Messidor. Exactly one month later to a day he mounted the guillotine.

The fall of the Robespierrists is a well-known chapter in history. It is unnecessary here to attempt more than a brief summary of its causes and then to tell somewhat more in detail the part played by Saint-Just during the last four weeks of his life. There were at least three underlying causes of the party's fall: (1) a general and growing dislike of the Terror, coupled with a feeling that the army's victories had made it needless, but that it would last as long as the Robespierrists remained in power; (2) the bourgeois dislike of the sans-culotte régime, due in part to the maximum, and more recently to the Ventôse decrees with their menace of a real social revolution; (3) ironically enough, a working-class protest against the new maximum daily wage, decreed 5 Thermidor. In like manner, there were four more immediate causes: (1) personal quarrels within the government, (a) between the two Committees, due to the creation of the police bureau within the Committee of Public Safety,[311] the ignoring of the lesser Committee in framing the law of 22 Prairial and the intrusting of important police reports, such as that against the Dantonists to Saint-Just and other members of the greater Committee; (b) within the Committee of Public Safety, due to jealousy of Robespierre because of his coldness and severity and because of charges of ambition, augmented by his unpopular religious attitude and notably by the Festival of the Supreme Being and the Théot affair, due also to friction between Carnot and Saint-Just, due finally to the close connection between Collot d'Herbois within the Committee and Fouché, the leader of the anti-Robespierrists outside; (2) personal fears of Fouché, Tallien, Barras, Fréron and other recalled representatives that they would be prosecuted for cruelty or corruption while on mission; (3) Robespierre's unfortunate speech of 8 Thermidor, in which he vaguely denounced diverse groups without specifically mentioning names and thus increased rather than diminished the alarm of his opponents; (4) the alliance against Robespierre formed at the last moment between his enemies and the mass of moderate deputies known as the Plain.

When Saint-Just returned, the friction within the Committee was already acute. Robespierre, Couthon and he found themselves arrayed against all the rest, though the absence of some members from Paris and the absorption of others in bureau detail left the leadership of the opposition in the hands of Collot d'Herbois, Billaud-Varenne and Carnot. The addition of the latter to the anti-Robespierrists was at least in part due to quarrels with Saint-Just over military matters. That Carnot resented the active leadership in this field assumed by Saint-Just both in Alsace and the North is highly probable. As far back as Germinal, soon after Danton's death, there was a scene between them in the Committee, during which Carnot accused his opponent of purposing with Robespierre to overthrow all other patriots and to seize the supreme power. Early in Floréal, a still livelier dispute broke out about the powder and saltpeter administration, one of whose agents Carnot had arrested. Saint-Just considered the arrest unjust and was supported by Robespierre. Carnot flung back the charge that the Robespierrists aspired to a dictatorship; this enraged Saint-Just, who cried that the republic was lost if men intrusted with its defense indulged in recriminations of that sort. "It is you," he declared to Carnot, "who are linked with the patriots' enemies; know that a few lines would suffice me to draw up your accusation and to have you guillotined within two days." "I invite you to try it," replied Carnot coldly; "I dare all your rigors against me. I fear neither you nor your friends; you are ridiculous dictators." Saint-Just, more and more exasperated, demanded the expulsion of Carnot from the Committee, to which his adversary is said to have retorted: "You will leave it before me, Saint-Just." Then, turning toward Couthon and Robespierre, "Triumvirs, you will disappear." [312] Other quarrels took place between them, one early in Messidor when Saint-Just, just back from the front, attacked Carnot for not seeking his advice or that of his colleagues before ordering the withdrawal of 18,000 men from the Army of the Sambre-et-Meuse for an unnecessary expedition; Levasseur says this dispute became general and very violent.[313] Saint-Just charged that it almost cost the victory of Charleroi. Saint-Just also opposed an expedition into Holland projected by Carnot and accused him of protecting aristocratic generals, of persecuting those who were patriots and of enveloping his operations in a cloud of secrecy. Barère alleges that on one such occasion, he stood up valiantly for Carnot.

I said to this little dictator, "I am not afraid of you for my part; I have always defended the fatherland openly and without personal interest. Well, it is I who will reply to you at the tribune if you pick on Carnot [si tu t'en prends à Carnot]. You know that I make reports favorably regarded by the Assembly; well, I will attempt one of these reports in favor of Carnot and against you." From that moment, Robespierre and his friend performed against us and especially against me only hostile actions.[314]

As Barère was a notorious trimmer and did not come out against Robespierre until 9 Thermidor, it is extremely unlikely that he said anything of the kind. In view of these strained relations between the two military specialists of the Committee, each of whom was jealous of the other's pretensions, it is not surprising to find from the marginal notes on police-bureau reports that while Robespierre referred seven cases to Carnot

274

during Floréal and Prairial, Saint-Just referred but one.[315]

Another obscure occurrence is credited to Messidor, though some would place it later. There are different stories about what happened at the joint meeting of the two Committees at this time. According to one, Robespierre presented a list of representatives on mission, whose accusation he demanded for corruption in the departments, but the Committees, fearing a crisis, refused. This is unlikely on its face, because the very fact that no one knew just what names Robespierre had in mind was one of the chief grievances against him. Saint-Just is said to have then proposed to the Committees "to have France governed by patriotic deputations, until there should be republican institutions." This peculiar expression is the one reported by the surviving ex-members of the Committee of Public Safety after Thermidor. Toulongeon recalled another even more obscure: "intrust the public safety to an individual destiny." Barère says it all started with Robespierre's proposal of four Revolutionary Tribunals and purports to give Saint-Just's remarks in full, wherein he insisted that the republic was in a state of complete anarchy; the Convention flooded France with laws that were not carried out and often could not be; the representatives on mission usurped all powers, did what they liked with the public moneys and with the armies and exchanged *assignats* for gold. For himself, he saw only one way to save the situation, namely the concentration of power, the unity of governmental measures, the energy attached to those political institutions of which the ancients made such use. His hearers grew impatient and called for a clearer statement of what he had in mind. "Well, I will explain myself," Saint-Just is said to have answered coolly.

There should be a dictatorial power other than that of the two Committees; a man is needed who has enough genius, force, patriotism and generosity to accept this use of public power; especially a man so familiar with the Revolution, its principles, its phases, its action and its different agents that he can answer for the public safety and the preservation of liberty; finally, we need a man who has in his favor the general opinion, the confidence of the people and who is in fact a virtuous and inflexible as well as an incorruptible citizen. I declare that Robespierre is this man; he only can save the state. I demand that he be invested with the dictatorship and that the joint Committees make the proposal to the Convention tomorrow.

According to another, supposed to be an eyewitness, Robespierre was meanwhile walking around the table, puffing out his cheeks and breathing jerkily, evidently under emotional strain. He pretended surprise, exclaiming,

Who inspired you with that proposition, Saint-Just? A dictatorship is necessary to France, I agree with you, but there are many members of the National Convention who deserve to get the vote more than I.

Couthon then seconded Saint-Just's motion, chiding Robespierre for his dangerous modesty. Saint-Just took notes on the opinions expressed by each member.[316] The various accounts agree that the proposal was curtly rejected, to the mortification of its supporters. What is one to make of all this? No faith can be placed in any version of the words actually used, none of the four accounts being in agreement and the most circumstantial (Barère's) being the most suspicious. That something of the sort happened there is little doubt. Prieur and Ruhl, who were present, contented themselves with saying that Saint-Just made a pompous eulogy of Robespierre, following an attack by Amar and Vadier. Hamel thinks that if Saint-Just had proposed a dictatorship, his enemies would have made use of the fact on 9 Thermidor.[317] It may well be that he did not go so far. There was, however, a general idea in the minds of several people that he used some queer expression which pointed that way. This is entirely possible. The obscure language is thoroughly characteristic of Saint-Just, who could be clear or cloudy as suited his purpose. In that case, he may have been putting forth a cautious feeler to test the Committees' reaction. As we shall see in the next chapter, the notion of a dictatorship was not alien to his thinking. It may well be that the growing friction within the Committee, depriving it of that unified will which it once had and which still seemed essential to the republic's safety, suggested a narrower concentration of power. If this could be placed in the right hands by general consent, the victory for Robespierrist policies was won at a stroke. But the scheme failed; henceforth those policies must be fought for at every step of the way. The opponents of the plan were not without warrant in scenting Caesarism, though it finally came from the Right rather than the Left. It was only five years later that an officer of Italian stock, name and speech, made himself master of France. He was just two years younger than Saint-Just.

As a consequence of the discussions in the Committee, from the middle of Messidor on Robespierre ceased to attend its meetings, while retaining his membership. He sought consolation in the more sympathetic atmosphere of the Jacobins, where night after night he poured forth his troubles, his suspicions and his threats. Meanwhile Saint-Just, stouter-hearted than his chief, carried on alone amid the black looks of his fellow Committeemen. He was constant in his attendance and diligent in his labor as the number of decrees he signed bears witness. His courageous sticking to his post had a negative nuisance value; it made his opponents uncomfortable and interfered considerably in the formation of their plans.

So Messidor passed and the fatal month of Thermidor was ushered in. It had barely started when something happened which shows the strain Saint-Just must have been under. On the third of that month (July 21) the Committee of Public Safety ordered the arrest of "the woman Lambert, residing at the house of citizen Lepault, watchmaker, rue Thomas-du-Louvre, no. 259." She was to be taken to the Conciergerie at once, together with the individual living with her. To the decree, which was signed by Collot d'Herbois alone, was appended a note explaining that the arrest was made on demand of Saint-Just, who said that this woman had come to his lodgings "without doubt to assassinate him." [318] What shall be said of this? Two months earlier, one l'Admiral had lain in wait some hours for Robespierre and ultimately fired his pistol at Collot d'Herbois, while a young girl named Cécile Renault was suspected of a similar purpose toward Maximilien. Were the people turning on their leaders and did the woman Lambert really mean to kill Saint-Just? Or was he simply getting jumpy? One does not know.

The two commissions of the Museum, appointed to sift the lists of Paris suspects under the terms of the Ventôse decrees, reported that by 14 Messidor, two weeks after their operations actually began, they had sent in 450 names; they hoped soon to be able to report 200 or 300 decisions per decade. These names sent in by the commissions were for some time not acted upon by the anti-Robespierrist majority of the Committee of Public Safety, whose signatures seem to have been necessary, but on the first three days of Thermidor the lists began to be ratified and sent on to the Revolutionary Tribunal. Better yet, the ratification was not only by the Committee of Public Safety but by the disgruntled and anti-Robespierrist Committee of General Security. To gain this important concession, a further step toward realizing the Robespierrist social policy, Saint-Just agreed that the commissions should report henceforth, not to the police bureau but to the joint Committees of Public Safety and General Security. [319]

For this friendly policy he had a willing ally in Barère. Indeed the latter seems to have taken the initiative by proposing to the joint Committees the decree of 4 Thermidor which at long last organized the four other popular commissions, whose function was to act for the departments as the Museum commissions did for Paris. Robespierre, who had so long absented himself, was especially invited to the joint sitting on the fifth which was planned to end the friction within the Committees; he came. The members sat in uneasy silence until Saint-Just arose and spoke. In the report which he wrote three days later but was never permitted to deliver, he tells us what he said.

Glancing about the room he commented, "You seem to me afflicted: everybody will have to explain himself here frankly and with your permission I will begin." A captured Swiss officer, he continued, had opened their eyes to the fact that Austria was counting heavily on a counter-revolutionary insurrection in France. Saint-Just went on to defend Robespierre against the imputation of tyranny. He declared that since the Republic lacked institutions furnishing guarantees [of individual safety, governmental stability and a just social order], there was a tendency to misrepresent the influence of men who gave wise advice and to consider it in the light of tyranny; that this fell in with the plan of the foreigner according to the very notes on the table before them; that he knew of no tyrant who had not been master of great military credit, of the finances and the government, and that these things were not in the hands of those against whom suspicions were being insinuated. David, with his usual frankness, ranged himself on his side, while Billaud-Varenne declared to Robespierre, "We are your friends; we have always marched together." Even at the moment Saint-Just could not help shuddering, he says, at the man's insincerity.

Other accounts show that Robespierre, who was not entirely won over to the policy of conciliation, burst out with a bitter attack on his opponents. Despite this alarming and probably unexpected interlude, the quarrel was patched up for the moment and it was agreed that Saint-Just should draw up a report on the whole situation, indicating the harmony that now (theoretically at least) prevailed within the government. To seal the truce, Saint-Just signed a decree ordering that certain companies of Paris artillery be sent to the Army of the North, a movement which Carnot desired but which had excited the lively suspicion of the Robespierrists. After this session, Barère of the greater Committee and Voulland of the lesser both expressed their joy that the government's unity was unbroken. Unfortunately Robespierre remained irreconcilable. He seems to have felt that even Saint-Just had deserted him.[320]

The appointment of the four popular commissions was sufficient to complete the alienation of the bourgeoisie from the
Robespierrists. By an unhappy coincidence their staunchest
supporters, the proletariat, were exasperated because on that
very day the Commune set forth a maximum daily wage.[321]
Since the Commune was Robespierrist, this action explains in
large part the lukewarmness of the workers in its support when
the hour of need shortly came.

The truce, such as it was, reached an abrupt end three days
later. Indeed the whisperings and plottings had hardly ceased
during that interval. But with Robespierre's denunciatory
speech before the Convention on 8 Thermidor, the pretense of
friendliness came to an end. That ill-timed utterance, a declaration of war against his foes, was made without previous con-
sultation with Saint-Just and Couthon, who would probably
have prevented it.[322] The gauntlet was thrown down and they
were forced into the fight whether they would or no. This became clear that night at the last meeting which the great Committee was destined to hold.

There are several accounts of this memorable session, which
must have impressed itself deeply on the minds of all connected
with it. The earliest version was given the very next day by
one of the chief actors, though a prejudiced witness, Collot
d'Herbois. Speaking in the Convention on that stormy 9 Thermidor, when everyone's nerves were strung to the highest pitch,
he told how he had reached the Committee the night before,
having run the gauntlet of Robespierre's satellites who threatened him at every turn. (Earlier in the evening he and Billaud
had, in fact, been thrown out of the Jacobins, where Robespierre was reading the speech he had delivered that day at the
Convention.) Saint-Just had arrived at the Committee before
him and was the center of attention as Collot indignantly re-
counted his experience at the Jacobins. As for Saint-Just, "he
was of marble: he announced coldly to the Committee this
report [the one he was commissioned to draw up by the agreement of the fifth], in which he did not hide that several mem-

bers were accused, without, however, his daring to pronounce the decree of accusation against them, for he had that much reticence." Collot insisted that this report was based on groundless statements of Robespierre's spies; one pretended that Collot had said certain things in a café, while the whole world knew that he never set foot in a café; another that he had told Fouché to prepare the decree of accusation against Robespierre, while he had not seen Fouché for two months. We told Saint-Just, Collot continued, that he ought to lay these matters before the Convention if they were true, but that he ought to let the Committee examine the report first. They agreed to send for Fouché, who would have to explain himself in Saint-Just's presence. "We left Saint-Just at 5 A.M., he was to come back at 11 o'clock; he did not keep his word." Fouché was, however, interviewed and confirmed Collot's story.[323]

A month later, at the Convention's session of 13 Fructidor (August 30), further details were added by others present on the occasion. Cambon first remarked that from the anteroom he witnessed a violent altercation between Saint-Just and Collot the night of the eighth. Next Billaud-Varenne brought out that the Committee had felt it essential to arrest the national agent, the mayor, Hanriot and other conspirators [all Robespierrists] and was discussing the matter on the eighth. This admission makes it clear that it was just a question which side should strike first. Barère then gave a vivid account of the famous quarrel, including the statement that at noon on the ninth the Committee received a note in these terms, "You have blighted [flétri] my heart; I am going to open it to the National Convention. Signed, Saint-Just." [324]

But it was in his later reply to Lecointre's accusations that Barère furnished the most complete narrative of the evening. Saint-Just had sent his first eighteen pages to Thuillier. Collot is represented as very violent. Among his remarks to Saint-Just, these are some of the choice bits: "You are a coward and a traitor! You trick us with your hypocritical air! You are only a box of apothegms and you spy on us in the Committee." Élie

Lacoste, a member of the lesser Committee, is supposed to have added: "It is a triumvirate of rascals! It is Robespierre, Couthon and Saint-Just who are plotting against the fatherland!" Barère himself, brave on paper if nowhere else, asserts that he capped the climax by vociferating, "What do you amount to, insolent pigmies, trying to divide the country's spoils between a cripple, a child and a scoundrel! I would not give you a backyard to rule!" Saint-Just made no reply. The infuriated Collot continued the assault:

I know that perhaps you will have us murdered this night; perhaps we shall be struck down tomorrow morning by your plots; but we are determined to die at our posts and perhaps we shall succeed in unmasking you beforehand. You are working out plans against the Committees in our very midst. I am sure that you have in your pockets slanders directed against us; you are a domestic enemy, a conspirator.

According to this narrative Saint-Just turned pale, stammered some sort of answer and emptied a few papers out of one of his pockets; he put them on the table, but nobody wanted to read them. Collot, unconvinced, went on breathing out threatenings and slaughter. Saint-Just might succeed in having them all killed, but the people would certainly tear him to pieces if he did. Collot ranted on for some time with diminishing fury, but Saint-Just recovered his poise and presently took the offensive, accusing his opponent of having talked against Robespierre in a café, a point which he proposed to develop in his report. When the quarrel wore itself out, everybody hoped Saint-Just would go, because the schemes of the anti-Robespierrists must be kept from him of all people. But Barère declares that Saint-Just went on talking all night in an obvious effort to kill time so that his opponents would have no opportunity to formulate their plans. Finally in desperation some of them went into an adjoining room and considered whether it would not be wise to arrest him at once, but decided to wait until they heard his report next day in the Convention. Barère brings out the point that during the general conversation in the Committee, when some of the members referred to the serious political situation and proposed remedies, Saint-Just coolly stopped them, expressed astonishment that he was not in their confidence regarding these supposed dangers, complained that all hearts were closed against him so that he knew nothing of what was going on, that he could not understand this method of improvising thunderbolts every few minutes and implored his colleagues in the name of the republic to return to juster ideas and wiser methods. "Thus," comments Barère, paying his antagonist an unconscious tribute, "the traitor held us in check, paralyzed all our measures and chilled our zeal." At five in the morning Saint-Just left, whereon the Committee betook themselves somewhat belatedly to their plotting. This narrative must no doubt be heavily discounted, particularly in the conversations. However its general outline is plausible, following as it does the earlier and more trustworthy accounts and also because it involuntarily makes Saint-Just stand out in a rather favorable light as one brave man against a pack of furious enemies, which is not at all the effect Barère was aiming after.[325]

What did Saint-Just actually say in this famous report, whose contents so aroused his colleagues' not unnatural curiosity?

He opened this, the last thing he ever wrote, with the questionable statement: "I belong to no faction, I shall fight them all." There was only one cure for them, however, institutions with guarantees definitely fixing the limits of authority. With something more than unconscious prophecy he admitted that this tribune on which he stood might well be the Tarpeian Rock for anyone suggesting that members of government had left the path of wisdom. However the truth was due them if offered with prudence and he could not decently break the engagement he had taken with his conscience to dare everything for the country's safety.

What line had he best take? The Committees had instructed him to report on the causes of the recent commotions in public opinion. "The confidence of the two Committees honored me, but someone this night has blighted my heart and I wish to speak only to you." He uses the phrase of his note to his colleagues and the painful hours are still so vivid to him that he speaks of "this night" as if the agony were still going on, though it was noon when he said these words.

He wished to speak, he said, of certain men who had jealously tried to concentrate power in their own hands by controlling the citizen militia of Paris and by suppressing its magistrates, thus seeking to neutralize the revolutionary government and dominate more easily. These members were among those who had instructed him to report; they thought this would compel him to be conciliatory, if not to take their views outright. He had asked those of whom he proposed speaking to come and hear him. He would tell them without pity just what he thought about them. Then, referring to outsiders who sowed discord in the ranks of the Committee, he exclaimed, "O God, Thou hast been willing that they should seek to alter the harmony of a government that had a certain greatness, whose members have ruled wisely, but have not always been ready to share the glory!"

He denied the slightest intention of flattering Robespierre; "I defend him because he has seemed to me irreproachable and I myself would accuse him if he turned criminal." Billaud and Collot in contrast seemed devoted to purely personal interests. Billaud never spoke except in a passionate way, either against Paris, the Revolutionary Tribunal or the men whose ruin he desired. At other times he closed his eyes and pretended to sleep. In the last few days, his taciturn conduct had yielded to restlessness. Billaud often said with feigned alarm, "We are walking on a volcano"; Saint-Just thought so too, but the volcano was Billaud's dissimulation and desire to dominate. Billaud was bold when he seemed to be getting a hearing, but his last word always came faltering from his lips; he hesitated, became irritated, corrected what he had said the day before; called a man Pisistratus behind his back, but friend to his face; he was silent, pale, with fixed expression, seeking to compose his distorted features. Truth was not of this character.

Having drawn this bitter portrait, Saint-Just returned to the support of his friend, declaring that Robespierre had been led on by those who sought to destroy him, forced to ill-considered measures and to isolate and defend himself, that he might be accused of troubles for which he was not to blame. It was in Robespierre's absence that an absurd military expedition was devised.[326] The army lacked supplies and an agent sent by Saint-Just and his colleagues on mission to point this out was badly received by the Committee, though Prieur did seem to recognize the need. "We had to win; we won." Fleurus helped to open Belgium. Let us be fair to everybody, but not honor the government more than the armies; we ought to praise the victories and forget ourselves. If everyone had been modest and not jealous lest someone else be more talked about than oneself, we should be very peaccable.

Pessimistically he concluded that fame amounted to very little. Let them listen to the ages gone, they would hear nothing now; "those who in future walk among our urns, will not hear more." To do right at whatever price was the task, preferring the title of dead hero to that of living coward. If innocence was to be the plaything of vile intrigues, there was no guarantee of safety in the city. "That is why I ask Providence for a few days more" to turn the attention of the French people to the importance of institutions. Had they existed, what was happening today would be impossible.

When he returned from the army the last time, Saint-Just continued, he recognized only a few faces. The members of the government were scattered on the frontiers and in the bureaus; two or three men ran everything. In this solitude they seemed to have conceived the dangerous notion of gaining more influence; enjoying absolute power, they accused others of pretending to it. He had nothing to complain of personally; they left him alone as a citizen without pretensions who took his own path; they made a mistake, however, when they asked him to make a report in the hope of linking him to ideas he did not share. This he told the Committees flatly, warning them what he proposed to say.

At this point, Saint-Just gives his version of what happened at the session on the fifth, and then mentions a petition which attempted to ridicule religion by asking that swearing be considered blasphemy, punishable with death. Here Saint-Just is magnificent. "Ah! those are not blasphemies: blasphemy is the idea of promenading before God the fasces of Sulla; blasphemy is to frighten members by lists of proscription and to accuse innocence." So they had compelled him not to speak of Providence, sole hope of the lonely man who, surrounded by sophisms, asks of Heaven the courage and wisdom necessary to bring about the triumph of truth.

With this Saint-Just swings into a further defense of Robespierre, who at the session of the day before "did not in fact explain himself very clearly, but his isolation and the bitterness of his soul may be some excuse; he does not understand the matter of his persecution; he knows only his unhappiness." They called him the tyrant of public opinion. What exclusive rights did they have over public opinion, they who held the art of touching souls to be a crime? If Demosthenes was a tyrant, his tyranny saved the liberty of Greece for a long while. After an eloquent apology for the art of which he was a master, Saint-Just reverted to the immediate situation. "The member who spoke at length yesterday from this tribune does not seem to have made it sufficiently clear just whom he was accusing." [So early was Robespierre's fatal mistake recognized.] There was no complaint against the Committees, who were worthy of the Convention's esteem. The whole trouble was that many of the members were away. Couthon was always absent; Prieur de la Marne had been away for eight months; Saint-André was at Port-la-Montagne; Lindet and Prieur de la Côte-d'Or were buried in their bureaus; Saint-Just himself was at the army; the remainder seemed to have profited by their absence. It was of the utmost importance to have a full Committee. Instead of a dozen persons, it had actually been a government of two or three for the last month. Soon the only obstacle to their absolute authority would be the Jacobins, which explained the hatred Billaud and Collot manifested for that society.

Briefly Saint-Just brought his charges to a focus.

There has therefore existed a plan to usurp power by killing some of the members of the Committee and by dispersing the rest throughout the Republic, by destroying the Revolutionary Tribunal, by depriving Paris of its magistrates. Billaud-Varenne and Collot d'Herbois are the authors of this plot.

He offered certain concrete suggestions. Every act of the Committee should be signed by at least six members; [Saint-Just thus abandoned the dictatorship idea if he ever really cherished it, and reverted to extreme democracy]; a study should be made of the wisdom of having Committee members act as ministers, burying themselves in their bureaus, separating themselves from the Convention.

He defended himself for bringing his charges in the Convention without announcing his intention in the Committee, which might have had the deplorable consequence of a sharp quarrel and a widened cleavage.

All previous reports of this nature had ended with a demand for the arrest of the persons attacked. But now, having definitely denounced his opponents, he turned aside from the logical deduction. The members he accused had done their regular work satisfactorily, he said; they had no need to defend themselves on this score except perhaps in the affair of the 18,000 men. His charge was that they used their reputation to forward their ambitions. "They announced the battle of Fleurus and others who said nothing were present at that battle [is there a trace of wounded vanity on Saint-Just's own part here?]; they talked of sieges and others who said nothing had been in the trenches." With all this, however,

I do not conclude against those whom I have named: I desire them to justify themselves and that we may become wiser. I propose the following decree: The National Convention decrees that the institutions, which are to be devised at once, shall contain safeguards of such nature that the government, while losing nothing of its revolutionary elasticity, cannot tend to arbitrariness, favor ambition, oppress or usurp the national representation.

The Convention was asked only to indorse an absolutely impersonal statement; it was not required to go on record in defense of Robespierre or in condemnation of his enemies.

This report must rank among the ablest documents of the French Revolution. Its wisdom far surpassed the denunciatory orations by which Saint-Just overwhelmed Girondins, Hébertists and Dantonists in turn. They were brilliant but destructive; this was definitely constructive. The attack on Billaud and Collot was savage, but it gave the hard-pressed Robespierre a breathing spell without pushing the assault to the extreme point. The other anti-Robespierrists were not even mentioned. The report left a reconciliation possible; more important still, it sought to alter the national fabric in such a way that factional control would henceforth be out of the question.

It was a major calamity for the Robespierrists that the speech was never delivered. If anything could have saved them, this report would have done it. But perhaps matters had gone too far even for that. At all events, Saint-Just never had the opportunity for his master effort.

The events of 9 and 10 Thermidor have been so often described that only a few details personal to Saint-Just need be given here. It has been stated that the plan of the Robespierrists was to steal a march on their opponents by having Saint-Just read his report at the very opening of the session, so that before the other side arrived the decree would have been passed.[327] This is disproved by the fact that Saint-Just sent them a written warning before he began and states in his speech that he had asked them to be present. For some almost childish reason, Robespierre and Saint-Just had decided to dress up for the occasion as if it were a holiday. Perhaps they felt that either victory or death were bound to come and either was worth celebrating. At any rate, Robespierre put on the famous blue coat he had worn at the Festival of the Supreme Being, while Saint-Just appeared in chamois-colored coat, white vest and pearl-gray knee breeches.[328] He wore his high stock, too, and the ample, knotted scarf. The session began with Saint-Just's speech according to plan. He had pronounced scarcely a half-dozen sentences,[329] when he was interrupted by Tallien with a point of order. The speaker had begun, he declared, by saying that he belonged to no faction. "I say the same thing." Tallien then launched the attack his group had planned, being followed by Billaud, who expressed his astonishment that Saint-Just should dare present his report, after violating his promise to read it first to the Committees. Others succeeded in turn, the burden of the attack being made on Robespierre. Saint-Just did not leave the tribune "in spite of the interruption which would have driven any other man from it." He simply came down a few steps, then went up again to continue, but was not able to add a single word; "motionless, impassive, undaunted, he seems to defy everything by his coolness." [330] For a full hour he stood there while the attack stormed on.[331] It reached its goal when one Louchet called for the arrest of Robespierre. The decree passed unanimously. Then Louchet, lest any of the quarry escape, persisted, "We meant to vote the arrest of the two Robespierres, Saint-Just and Couthon." The younger Robespierre had already insisted on sharing his brother's fate and now Le Bas, whom no one had mentioned, did the same. Élie Lacoste formally moved the arrest of the younger Robespierre, which was carried. Next Fréron made the motion for Saint-Just, Le Bas and Couthon. Élie Lacoste seconded the motion. He was the first, he said, to tell the Committee of Public Safety that Couthon, Saint-Just and Robespierre formed a triumvirate, "which had caused Saint-Just to turn pale and become ill." The decree was passed "amid the most lively applause." [332] Collot, who had been presiding, took the floor and demanded as an essential measure that Saint-Just be required to place his report on the desk of the secretaries, which the Convention forthwith voted. In the course of the long speech

Collot made and in which occurs his version of the Committees' session on the eighth, he remarked that the opposition had declared a new May 31 to be necessary. At this Robespierre could not refrain from interjecting: "He has lied." [333] These were his last words in the Convention; they are symbolical of his career and of his failure.

The prisoners were now ordered to the bar and at five in the afternoon (the session began at eleven in the morning) were led away to the Committee of General Security for questioning. From this place General Hanriot vainly sought to free them, but was himself made captive. Then the prisoners were scattered to different jails, Le Bas to the Conciergerie, Saint-Just to the Écossais, the old college behind the Pantheon, where in the Middle Ages young Scotchmen came to study the scholastic method and where later another lost cause, that of the fallen Stuarts, sought a refuge.

As is well known, the municipal leaders caused the prisoners to be released during the evening. A strong cavalry force came to the Écossais and took Saint-Just off in a carriage. At the Hôtel de Ville, the Robespierrists staged their last stand. Levasseur says that Couthon asked, "In whose name shall we speak?" refering to the proclamation they were drawing up; to this Saint-Just made answer, "In the name of the Convention; the Convention is wherever we are." But this is one of the legendary famous sayings that appear more or less anonymously in connection with every important historical happening and that must be fathered on someone. The question has elsewhere been attributed to Robespierre, the answer to Couthon. [334]

The proclamation to the public runs as follows:

PARIS COMMUNE

Citizens   The Ninth Thermidor.

The fatherland is more than ever in danger. Scoundrels dictate laws to the Convention which they oppress. Roberspierre [sic], who caused the consoling principle of the existence of the Supreme Being and the immortality of the soul to be declared; St. Just, that apostle of virtue, who brought treason to an end on the Rhine and in the North, who with Le Bas brought triumph to the arms of the Republic, Couthon, that virtuous citizen who has only the trunk and head of a living man, but who burns with patriotic ardor, Roberspierre [*sic*] the younger who presided over the victories of the army of Italy: who are their enemies? An Amar, a noble with an income of thirty million livres, Dubarran, a viscount, and monsters of that sort; Collot d'Herbois, that partisan of the infamous Danton, a comedian who in the old régime had stolen the money-chest of his troupe; that Bourdon de l'Oise who slandered the Paris Commune endlessly; that Barrere [*sic*] who belonged to all factions in turn and who fixed the wage of day-laborers so as to make them die of hunger. These are the rascals whom the council denounces to you. People, arise! Let us not lose the fruit of August 10 and May 31 and let us hurl all these traitors into the tomb.

The proclamation is signed by Lescot-Fleuriot the mayor and by his secretary.[335]

Other decrees were drawn up, notably one ordering the commanding general of the armed force to direct the people against the conspirators and to deliver the Convention from counter-revolutionaries.[336] If the last part of this order had been carried out, the night would have ended very differently. Outside of this, the issue hinged on the attitude of the sections. The *procès-verbaux* of a number of sectional assemblies have been preserved. They indicate great perplexity of mind. The sections of Observatoire, Faubourg du Nord, Fraternité, Mutius Scaevola, Finistère, Marat and others sent delegates to the city hall to take common action with the Commune. Others, like William Tell, sided with the Convention from the first. During the night they were joined by Poissonière, Vignes, Bondy, Museum, Faubourg Montmartre, Gardes Françaises, Mont Blanc, Contrat Social, Le Pelletier, Quinze Vingts, Cité, Invalides, l'Unité, while Faubourg du Nord, Marat and Mutius Scaevola came over from the other group.[337] This was decisive; the Robespierrists could not win if the people were no longer with them.

When the troops of the Convention burst in at two in the

morning, it was the end; each man met it in his own fashion. The elder Robespierre, seeking to shoot himself, mangled his jaw; his younger brother threw himself from a window and broke his thigh, Couthon fell downstairs and was hurt. Le Bas blew his brains out. Saint-Just faced death as he had faced life, calmly. There is a legend, among others unworthy of repetition, that makes Saint-Just press a pistol to his head as the soldiers entered, then throw it away with the words:

The representatives of the people owe the country, not only the example of their lives, but of their deaths. We have lived in broad daylight! It is in broad daylight that we must die.

There was none of this histrionic play. Saint-Just was a bigger man than that. He and Le Bas had gone into another room, but found it locked and it was then that Philippe shot himself. He and his old friend were alone at the last crisis. The soldiers found Dumas under a table in a state of terror. When asked where the other two deputies were, he pointed to the next room. There the soldiers found Le Bas dead and Saint-Just waiting for them to come. He had a knife upon him, but had not tried to use it; when the soldiers asked if he was armed, he handed it over.[338] Barras went there and found Robespierre in a little room, by the door of which Le Bas lay. Saint-Just was ministering to Robespierre.[339] The leader was removed at once to the rooms of the Committee of Public Safety in the Tuileries; they would take no chances this time. Saint-Just and the lesser lights were locked up in a "low chamber" of the City Hall until day. About nine o'clock they were all brought over— the dead and wounded on stretchers, Saint-Just, Dumas and Payan, with hands tightly bound following on foot, strange mourners in a strange funeral procession. Soldiers held back the pressing crowds with difficulty. The prisoners waited a quarter of an hour at the door of the room where so short a time before they had ruled France; then they were let in and seated in a window embrasure. Quizzical fellows pushed back the inquisitive persons who gathered about to stare at the three, saying, "One side now, let these gentlemen see their king sleeping on a table, just like a man." The anonymous eyewitness who gives us these details pictures Saint-Just's face as very sad and humiliated, his great eyes full of grief. Dumas on the other hand was stolid, Payan tried to brazen it out with an air of bravado, though he was badly frightened. Saint-Just leaned forward to look at Robespierre. Robespierre was indeed lying on a table, his head propped on a box full of moldy bread. He did not move, but he breathed rapidly and his muscles twitched with pain. A fireman and an artilleryman mocked him: "Sire, your majesty suffers." "Well, it seems to me that you have lost your voice, you're not finishing your speech, it was so well begun."

Dumas asked a gendarme for a glass of water. Payan, glancing at Saint-Just, added, "You might bring three." Only enough for two was brought and Saint-Just waited until more came. Now for the first time he spoke and bitterly. For some moments his eyes had rested on the framed copy of the constitution hanging on the wall. Pointing to it with his bound hands, he said in a low voice, half to himself, "After all, that was my work," adding a second later, "And the revolutionary government too." He spoke further, but no one heard what he said except the gendarme who stood nearest and made an ironical answer. Finally they brought the glass of water; Saint-Just drank a little, handing it back with the word, "Thanks."

Élie Lacoste entered shortly after, pointed to the captives and ordered: "Take them to the Conciergerie, they are outlawed." They were at once removed to that prison, which was the death house of the Terror. All but one. Lacoste told a surgeon to dress the wounds of Robespierre and put him in condition to be punished. The horrid details of that crude and painful operation are minutely recorded; when it was over and the bandage which held up his broken jaw was wound over his head and around his forehead, there was fresh opportunity for brutal jesting. One said, "Watch them putting the crown on his majesty"; another, "See him coifed like a nun." Then they put him back on the table with the box under his head. It would do for a pillow they told one another, "until he should go to take his turn at the little window." [340] After a while they must have taken him to the Conciergerie too, for we have the jailer's receipt for his admission and that of Couthon, dated 10 Thermidor.[341]

After the escape the night before, a decree had been passed, outlawing Robespierre and his associates. No trial was therefore necessary; formal identification of the prisoners sufficed. Under the law this was to be done by the Commune, but the Commune was itself outlawed. Fouquier-Tinville, a stickler for formal correctness, was troubled, but the technical difficulty was brushed aside by the Committee of General Security and at three o'clock on the afternoon of the tenth, the Revolutionary Tribunal duly identified its former masters. Number six in the list of those condemned to death was "Antoine Saint-Just, twenty-six years old, without profession before the Revolution, student, ex-deputy to the National Convention." [342] At sundown of that day the carts rolled out, bearing twenty-two of them to the Place de la Révolution. For some time, executions had been on the outskirts of the city; for this, once more the guillotine was reërected in the heart of Paris, in that great square which saw the death of the king and the queen, of the Girondins, of Hébert and of Danton. The French are always logical.

Once more an eyewitness tells us what he saw. Saint-Just was standing in the first cart. His head was erect and beautiful in its pallor. His eyes surveyed the dense throng with composure. His arms were bound behind his back. His neck was bare. The white vest, his holiday garment, in whose buttonhole a red carnation was thrust, was fastened at the top by a single button and fell back discovering his whole breast. There were shouts and hisses as the carts jolted along the rue Saint-Honoré. Saint-Just did not speak.

"The executioner, having shown the people the heads of Robespierre and Couthon, took up by the hair that of Saint-

Just, whose eyes were wide open and had perhaps not yet lost the last flickerings of that mind which had made him an object of fear, while in better times it might have made him so great and so useful." [343]

In some quarters there was undoubted relief at their passing; in others there was regret, for it meant the end of any far-reaching social changes. It did not at once mean the end of the Terror, but as the days wore on it began to receive that interpretation, for the people were sick of violence and the accommodating Thermidorians, hard-boiled terrorists though they were, saw their cue and took it. From then on they did their utmost to identify terrorism with the Robespierrists, both to be wiped out as soon as possible.

As early as 9 Thermidor, the Committees ordered the arrest of Saint-Just's secretary; they did not seem to know his name, but identified him as the one "who accompanied Saint-Just on his mission and who on 9 Thermidor made a great deal of noise at the Jacobins." [344] Four decrees of the eighth, signed by Saint-Just, Barère and Carnot, were redated the tenth and Saint-Just's signature crossed out; they dealt with the establishment of a hospital, quarters for a government commission, a bureau chief's salary, the appointment of hospital surgeons. Saint-Just's last official acts dealt with the relief of pain rather than its infliction. On the same day a proclamation was sent to his old army, the Sambre-et-Meuse, informing it that "infamous tyrants, who had usurped the name of patriots, wished to disorganize victory"; it must have been news to the men whom he had five times led across the Sambre. They were reassured by the information that "the traitors have received the penalty of their crimes; the national representation has delivered France from these modern Catilines." [345]

The campaign of slander began in the Convention with Barère's speech on the tenth, giving pretended details of the "plot." Saint-Just was to have been head of an executive committee (*Comité d'exécution*), Le Bas to have the executive power (*pouvoir exécutif*), the two Robespierres and Couthon

were to be the council; Dumas was to reorganize the Tribunal
in a counter-revolutionary sense. The minor rôle assigned to
Robespierre is striking. In his violent speech two days later,
describing the arrest of the Robespierrists in the City Hall,
Barère asserted that on the bureau of the room where they had
been holding their meeting there was found a new seal, having
as its only mark a fleur-de-lys.[346] On 11 and 18 Thermidor
(July 29 and August 5), arrests ordered by Saint-Just and Le Bas
on mission were canceled and the letter of a national agent in
Alsace requesting the annulment of certain decisions of Saint-
Just's court was read as late as 7 Fructidor (August 24).[347] Thermidorian historical accuracy may be measured by a declaration
of Merlin de Douai, who stated in the name of the committee
on legislation that the first of these arrests had been made on
complaint of "the public accuser, Schneider, that Austrian
priest, that scoundrel, whose head fell by a judgment of the
Revolutionary Tribunal for crimes with which he covered
himself in the court of Saint-Just and Lebas." Barère, speaking
again on the eleventh, informed his hearers that Saint-Just and
Robespierre had taken no part in the constant, daily labors of
the Committee; they considered their colleagues vulgar enough
to attend to these details and so save the country, reserving for
themselves the pretensions and luxury of government; the only
thing that interested them was the police, organized particularly for them and by them. This statement of Barère's was a
deliberate and abominable lie, refuted by a glance at the signatures to the Committee's decrees. He also asserted that Saint-
Just and Robespierre packed the various commissions with
their own creatures. The conspirators had parceled out France
between them;

the one who had the most astuteness and apparent sang-froid went
to look after the command of the Armies of the North and of the
Rhine, already prepared by the intriguers. Saint-Just was the pleni-
potentiary of the North, Couthon and the younger Robespierre
formed the pacific congress of the South; the elder Robespierre
ruled in Paris over heaps of corpses.

The unconscious tribute to Saint-Just's ability and power is interesting. On the fifteenth, Le Bon, now under arrest, was accused among other things of perpetually quoting Saint-Just's saying that the Revolution was like a thunderbolt and one must strike. He defended himself by charging with some point that the Convention had always accepted Saint-Just's reports and couldn't say much.[348]

The climax of the systematic Thermidorian campaign to discredit thoroughly those whom they feared even in their graves was the formidable Courtois report. This deputy had been made chairman of a committee appointed to examine the papers of Robespierre "and his accomplices." The report was made to the Convention on 16 Nivôse and took more than four hours to read.[349] According to the *Moniteur's* account (18 Nivôse, January 7, 1795), Courtois developed the plan of those conspirators "who wished, Saint-Just said, to walk with their feet in blood and tears." A later note alleges that this expression was found on a scrap of paper in Saint-Just's writing. The Courtois report is an absurd jumble, incoherent, rhetorical, full of classical allusions. It contains various references to Saint-Just, but the brunt of the attack is on Robespierre; Le Bon's atrocities are extensively treated and even Collot by this time was under fire. The most extended allusion to Saint-Just occurs early in the report and gives some notion of its character.

A crazy fellow of 26, hardly escaped from the dust of school, all puffed up with his little erudition, had read in a great man's book which he did not understand, that a people grew corrupt through luxury, child of the arts and of commerce; he had read also that another great man, whom he doubtless understood a little less, had formed a nation of heroes within the bounds of a few thousand stadia, and at once our clumsy imitator of antiquity, without examination of localities, customs and populations, applying what was inapplicable, came here to tell us in a conceited tone which would have been comic had it not been atrocious: "It is not the happiness of Persepolis, it is that of Sparta which we have promised you."

Flippant, poorly arranged and unconvincing as it was, the Courtois report met the mood of those who had ordered it and by that very fact gives the measure of the inferior Thermidorian breed which had replaced the sterner generation of '93 and '94. In one respect Courtois was right. Saint-Just was a dreamer as well as a man of action. Of what quality were his dreams?

XX

SAINT-JUST'S DREAMS

T MAY be remembered that when Saint-Just was young, he used to walk up and down the garden of his home in Blérancourt, jotting down his ideas on slips of paper which he later collected and unified. This habit of thinking in aphorisms clung to him all his life. His reports were rarely consecutive arguments, but rather strings of more or less disconnected ideas, many of them suggestive in content and brilliant in expression. The order of the paragraphs might frequently be changed without doing harm to the sense. In this rambling fashion he wrote down his Utopia, his vision of the perfect France that the Revolution was to usher in. It may have been intended as a series of preliminary studies to eventuate in a report. He surely hoped that sooner or later most of the ideas would be translated into legislation. But he never worked them out fully in systematic form. The notes were almost certainly written in 1794. How many people ever saw them in his lifetime, no one can tell. They were first printed by a certain Briot in 1800 and again by Nodier in 1831 under the title *Fragments sur les institutions républicaines.*[350] There are twenty groups of "Fragments," beginning with a loosely connected series of reflections on political and social life, and ending with some very detailed provisions of a legalistic type for the "institutions" which he believed essential to the permanence of the republic.

Indeed the need of institutions is the theme of the whole work. "Institutions are the guarantee of the government of a free people against the corruption of morals and the guarantee of the people and the citizen against the corruption of government" (preamble). Some light is thrown on this rather cryptic statement by the explanation that institutions have as their object to place the citizen and even children in a position to resist injustice legally and with ease, to force magistrates and youth to be virtuous, to give men courage and frugality, to make them just and sensitive, linking them together in harmonious and generous relationships, while subjecting domestic relations and private life as little as possible to the laws of authority; to put union in families, friendship among citizens, the public interest in place of all other interests; to throttle criminal passions, to make nature and innocence the passion of all hearts and to form a fatherland. Institutions are the safeguard of public liberty; they moralize government.

From this and from the concrete illustrations of his thought which are given later, it would seem that Saint-Just used the term "institutions" to mean the gradual formation of moral and civic habits through organized expression. This sometimes takes the form of an austere civic pageantry, sometimes of rules for individual living. At first glance, it seems a rather naïve theory to assume that mental attitudes can be created by external actions, but Saint-Just is psychologically sound on this point. It is not only true that we laugh because we are merry; it is also true that we are merry because we laugh. There is, indeed, an obvious inconsistency in his declaration that domestic relations and private life are to be subjected as little as possible to the laws of authority, while in the same breath he talks of forcing youth to be virtuous and is about to set forth a code, regulating private emotions and conduct on a scale hitherto unheard of. This inconsistency could hardly have escaped him; either he means that they are to be regulated only in so far as may be necessary to secure the results aimed at or (and more likely) he means by "authority" the temporary government of the moment, from whose capricious behests he would safeguard the individual's private life by placing it under the protection of a permanent charter, a fundamental law, viz., the "institutions" herein described. Thus he would make in France not only a new form of government, but a new Heaven and a new Earth. Subsequently (third fragment), he defines institutions in somewhat different terms. While Terror may free us from monarchy and aristocracy, only institutions can deliver us from corruption, he believes. An institution composed of many members and one composed of a single member are both despotic. Here he seems to use this elastic term in the sense of committees to carry out certain social purposes later set forth. Perhaps he conceives of them as in some degree policy-making as distinguished from administrative officials, for in the same paragraph he lays down the rule that institutions should be numerous and composed of few members while administrative positions should be reduced in number and each intrusted to a single individual. One can only guess whether when he wrote these lines, he was leaning away from the committee and toward the principle of dictatorship.

Without institutions (preamble) a republic must rest on the lives of great men, a precarious foundation, for they are but mortal and rarely die in their beds. To prove his point, he cites the examples of Scipio, the Gracchi, Demosthenes, Sidney and Barneveldt.

Striking a personal note, he avows the "touching idea" that the memory of a friend of humanity would be treasured one day, for a man

obliged to isolate himself from the world and from himself, casts his anchor in the future and presses to his heart posterity, blameless for present evils. O God, protector of innocence and truth, since Thou hast led me among perverse men, it was without doubt to unmask them! . . . I implore the tomb as a gift from Providence, that I may no more witness crimes committed with impunity against my country and humanity. . . . I despise the dust of which I am made and which now addresses you; they may persecute and slay that dust but I defy them to take from me that independent life which I have given myself in the ages to come and in the skies.

This melodramatic attitude-striking is disagreeable to us and suggests insincerity, but it was the literary fashion of his day, a form of sentimentality started by Rousseau, whom Saint-Just like most of his contemporaries greatly admired.[351] It was not really natural to his reserved coldness and his style is usually characterized by restraint rather than effusiveness.

The way in which Saint-Just pictured the foundations of society (second fragment), was the way of Rousseau. A distinction was to be made between the natural grouping of human individuals, analogous to the groupings of animals, and political society, which has brought with it new and often undesirable corporate interests. These new interests must needs be supported by force of arms, Saint-Just declared; they are falsely deemed natural interests, for they really spring from a forgetting of nature and natural law. Political society, so far from making an end of the state of war as has been asserted, is actually responsible for causing wars. Indeed, men have gone so far as to treat one another as enemies even within the group, turning the weapon of force (whose only justification is the preservation of collective independence from foreign foes) against the social independence of some within the nation; thus a portion of the people is able to oppress the rest. It is a fallacy that man is naturally brutal and can be governed only by force. Societies so constituted are like associations of pirates, whose only guarantee is the saber; even pirates have some sort of social pact on their ships.

Whatever internal reforms may be possible, he maintained, it is useless to think that states will renounce their political pride and live by the law of nature and justice in international affairs; idle to hope that they will envisage themselves as members of a single family and will drive out the particularistic spirit which makes them enemies and the love of wealth which ruins them. The kind-hearted souls who cherish these illusions do not realize how far we have wandered from right principles. That dream, if it be ever possible, is only for a future which will not come in our time. Hence, without seeking vainly to establish social relations between states, let us limit ourselves to building them between men as individuals. In fact with things as they are, a people which sought to govern itself naturally and renounce arms would soon become the prey of its neighbors; if such a people should renounce luxury and commerce for a simple life, its neighbors would grow rich from its privations, becoming so powerful that they would soon crush it. The example of such an independent society would be too dangerous for the rest. Nevertheless, Saint-Just declares, curiously anticipating our present-day thinking, no nation has a right to make war on its neighbors unless it has a just grievance; but, he sadly adds, if it makes an unjust war (in modern terms, if it is an aggressor state) who can stop it? He then examines in detail the idea that a war of conquest is legitimate if population outruns resources, which idea he rejects on the ground that no such instance has ever been found. Insufficiency of territory does not prove excessive population but a faulty administration. The spirit of conquest is not born of misery, but of avarice and idleness. "I conclude then that men are naturally social and naturally peaceful and that force should never have a pretext for uniting or dividing them."

This really splendid fragment contains both fine idealism and cool realism, however doubtful its sociology. Saint-Just had not changed from the days when in *Organt* he denounced war, though he had since seen much of it and waged it with relentless courage. Perhaps he is a bit disillusioned. The dream of world peace was not for his generation; how could he think otherwise when France was at that moment fighting half of Europe? Yet it was still his dream.

Long laws (third fragment) he considers public calamities; the monarchy was drowned in laws. Too many laws mean public slavery. The mere word "law" does not sanctify despotism; law is often only the will of the one who imposes it. "When human statecraft attaches a chain to the feet of a free man, whom it makes a slave in contempt of nature and citizenship, eternal justice rivets the other end about the tyrant's neck." It would be interesting to know whether in this strong stand for personal liberty, Saint-Just was at last privately revolting against the system of Terror. If he had any leaning toward a dictatorship as suggested above, it is clear that only a benevolent dictator could have satisfied him and only for a passing emergency as under the Roman republic.

He makes the interesting observation that France is more successful in inspiring its sons to sacrifice, particularly of a martial nature, than it is in reforming particular abuses. Only a very few people in the whole country concern themselves with anything outside their own interests and their own households, he laments. Very few take part in the affairs of government. In France the idea "patriot" requires a lively sentiment, quite displeasing to those who take cowardly pleasure in never getting mixed up in anything. Similarly when each community isolates itself, wrapped up in its local interests, you have *de facto* federalism, even though the government be nominally unified. "The day when I become convinced that it is impossible to give the French people gentle, energetic, sensitive civic morals, inexorable for tyranny and for injustice, I shall stab myself." Let us form the *cité* [*i.e.,* build up public opinion]; it is astonishing that this idea has not been yet the order of the day. [Saint-Just's remark suggests that France was an unenlightened mass, governed by a small minority of *exaltés,* like Russia in the early days of Bolshevism. He sets forth the Jeffersonian principle that the task of government is not so much to make people happy as to keep them from being unhappy.] If not oppressed, the individual will be able to find his own felicity. A people which has grown used to the idea that it owes its happiness to its governors, will not long retain it. As long as you see anyone in the antechambers of magistrates, the government is worthless.

But though Saint-Just sticks stubbornly to his master Rousseau's doctrines of human nature's essential nobility and the duty of self-reliance, his brief experience of men and politics as they are had been completely discouraging. It is in this mood that he writes in italics,

It is all very well to be rigorous in principles when one is destroying a bad government, but it is rare that if one is faced with the task of governing in his turn, he does not soon reject these same principles and substitute his own will for them.

There is even deeper dejection in the famous sentence,

The Revolution has grown cold; all its principles are weakened; there remain only red caps worn by intriguers. The exercise of terror has made crime *blasé,* as strong liquors made the palace *blasé.*

One of the greatest terrorists is thus forced to admit the ultimate failure of long-continued terror. Just as the men in the trenches became hardened to the sound of shells, so the guillotine grew finally so much a part of the daily scene that the tough-minded portion of the community ceased to fear it and became indifferent as though drugged or drunken. In Saint-Just's figure, they resembled the drunken courtiers of the old régime, grown cynical and hardened to a people's suffering. The admission is significant. Yet he cannot altogether bring himself to discard the weapon. With double inconsistency he proposes when the moment is ripe to use it to set up a sort of French New Deal, quite contrary to the teaching of his theoretical Jeffersonianism. "Without doubt," he writes, "the time has not yet come to do good." This enigmatic expression, *faire le bien,* at first glance seems to mean to usher in the reign of clemency, but it apparently means more than that, for Saint-Just goes on to say that the individual good done so far is only a palliative. We must wait for a general evil so great that public opinion will support measures necessary to *faire le bien.* "What produces the general good is always terrible or seems bizarre when begun too soon." From this it appears that by the general evil, Saint-Just meant widespread financial distress which would warrant the forcible introduction of semi-Socialistic measures, as foreshadowed by the laws of Ventôse. When that came, the need of terror would be at an end, he doubtless implied, though it would be required in the transition period. "The Revolution must stop when it has perfected public happiness and liberty through the laws."

But when would that perfect society be achieved? He gives his whole case away in the fragment's concluding lines.

They speak of the height of the Revolution: who will fix that height? It is mobile. There have been free peoples who fell from yet greater heights.

That was the fatal weakness of the system of terror. Brissot would have it stop at one point, Danton at another. Was it logical to condemn them as traitorous weaklings when Saint-Just himself wanted to stop, but could not tell how or when to do it?

The last of the fragments devoted to his general philosophy of government is taken up with economic matters, notably with a new attack on inflation. He sets up a simple economic ideal: "It is necessary that everyone work and respect himself." This is the path to abundance and public virtue.

He continues, if we keep on issuing as much money as in the past, people will feel rich enough to stop working, then culture and manufactures will perish. When Rome lost the taste for work and lived on tribute, it lost its liberty. We are already beginning to see citizens who work only one day out of three. Public amusements formerly existed for the nobility and the court; they are still kept up as luxuriously as ever, patronized obviously by those who used to work. Europe has hoped that because of the slight attention we have given this matter, the Revolution would perish. Our victories have frightened Europe less than would a wise fiscal plan. In future, counterfeiting must be made very difficult, the system of taxation simplified and proportioned to the profits of citizens, harshness removed from the collection of taxes. Asserting that up to that time, the whole subject had been looked at "through a prism," Saint-Just next attempts to sketch the progress of economic errors and their effect on public morals.

In 1789 only a small amount of specie was on hand, either because of court conspiracy or by the fault of rich individuals, purposing to emigrate, he declares. Banks shipped commercial paper and securities abroad. A revolution took place in the economic as in the political field; it was no less striking, but attracted less attention. Money was tight, foodstuffs were hoarded. Suspicion and avarice almost broke up society for a moment; no one saw money. Curiously enough, when paper money replaced the vanished metals, the same qualities of human nature produced a directly contrary result. Everybody, fearing to keep the new money and to be surprised by its sudden cancellation, hastened to put it in circulation. Commerce suddenly took on prodigious activity, through haste to convert funds into goods. But this activity was unsound, being based only on suspicion and loss of credit; as we ceased to import goods and exchange turned against us, the immense and daily increasing quantity of paper money measured itself only against the goods on hand. These commodities were hoarded or exported for immense profits or consumed; they became rare, while money depreciated constantly. Meanwhile everyone, having much paper, worked all the less and morals were enervated by idleness. The enormous expenses of a universal war forced still further inflation of the currency. By the sale of national lands and by tributes some thirty millions a month came in, but three or four hundred millions were issued during the same period. The state, which sold the land, was not rich enough to buy its products. It was the foreigner who had brought us to this pass and it was a foreigner, the Baron de Batz, who suggested to us the first idea of the taxes on food,[352] a veritable famine project. Europe counted on famine to excite popular fury, on that to destroy the Convention and on that to dismember France. Taxed foodstuffs do not circulate.

To establish liberty, Saint-Just went on, a possible uprising of the poor must be guarded against; the way to do this is to give everyone some land. Great estates mean poor people. A man isn't made for wage slavery, nor for hospitals or hospices; all that is hideous. Every man should be independent, with a decent wife and with healthy, robust children; there should be neither rich nor poor. The comfort of the whole people should be assured. Opulence is an infamy; the more thousands of livres' income a man has, the less he wants to be bothered with having children. The *assignats* should be withdrawn from circulation, a tax laid on all those who have been managing affairs and the national lands distributed among the poor. Eight months ago anyone who said these things would have had to drink hemlock, but we have grown wise through the experience of misfortune.

Saint-Just's criticism of the policy of inflation is straightforward and sound. Whether his constructive program of land distribution would have solved the problem is another matter. But it is clear that the Robespierrists were headed toward a type of radicalism hitherto unknown on such a scale. Had they lasted a few months longer, the Bolshevik experiment of a proletarian dictatorship would have been anticipated, though curiously enough by a precisely opposite method, the solution being sought in a vast extension of individual ownership.

He has eight concrete suggestions. Make counterfeiting impossible; assess grain requisitions equitably without numerous agents; collect all requisitions throughout France on a single day; make state expenses proportionate to the amount of money in circulation necessary for private business; prevent everyone from hoarding wealth to live in idleness; forbid money being transferred abroad; know exactly the total profits made in a year; give all Frenchmen the means of obtaining the prime necessities of life, depending only on the laws and without interdependence in the social order.

This concludes the first group of fragments, whose object was to expound in a general way some of Saint-Just's political philosophy. The remainder are taken up with detailed propositions for the control of French society, couched in the form of hypothetical laws.

Fragment six, which leads off the second group, is entitled "Certain Civil and Moral Institutions," and has two sections, "On Education" and "Concerning the Affections." The former has become famous as the exposition of Saint-Just's Spartan system of training. It is based on Rousseau in the emphasis on simplicity and naturalness, in the stress laid on moral elements, particularly in the earlier years, and in the definite setting apart of certain periods in the child's life for the accomplishment of specific objectives. This clear notion of objectives in education links both Rousseau and Saint-Just with modern pedagogical thought. Saint-Just differs widely from his master, however, in the emphasis on authority as opposed to the laissez-faire theory of *Émile,* in the regimentation of the children and the almost Prussian subordination of the individual to the uses of the state, in the rigor of discipline and in a different theory of the purposes to be sought in given periods.

Children belong to their mother, says Saint-Just, for the first five years, provided she has nursed them; they belong to the republic thereafter. A mother who has not nursed her own child has ceased to be a mother; she and her husband must appear before the magistrate to repeat their contract or their union has no further civil effect. Between the ages of five and sixteen, boys live and are taught in common at the nation's expense. Their discipline must be strict. They are trained to a love of silence and contempt for rhetoricians; when they speak, they are taught to be laconic; declamations are forbidden and they are accustomed to the simple truth. The only games are those "of pride and interest" [apparently he means contests of emulation]; they need only exercises. Schools for boys from five to ten years old are in the country, one in each section and one in each canton. Here they are taught to read, write and swim. They can neither be struck nor caressed; they are taught what is right and are left to nature. He who strikes a child is banished. Children are dressed in linen at all seasons; their beds are of matting, they sleep eight hours. They eat in common, their diet being restricted to roots, fruit, vegetables, dairy products, bread and water. Instructors of children during these ages must be at least sixty years old; they are elected by the people from a picked group. There is also to be one school for children from ten to sixteen in each section and one in each canton. During this period, education is on a military and agricultural basis. The boys are formed into companies of sixty, six companies constituting a battalion. The instructors appoint a chief each month from among those who are the best behaved. The boys of a district form a legion. They camp annually in the chief town on the Festival of Youth and perform infantry exercises. They learn cavalry maneuvers also and all sorts of military drill. In addition they are taught languages. At harvest time they are distributed among the farmers. From sixteen to twenty-one they enter the arts and choose a profession, in either agriculture, manufacturing or the marine. All children wear the same costume up to sixteen; from then until twenty-one they are dressed as workmen; from twenty-one to twenty-five as soldiers, unless they are magistrates. They cannot wear the workman's dress until they are able to swim across a river, the test being held publicly on the Festival of Youth. Between twenty-one and twenty-five, citizens not in public office must join the national militia. Instructors of boys up to sixteen are chosen by the district directory subject to the confirmation of the general commission of arts, appointed by the government; teachers are selected from among the farmers, manufacturers, artisans and business men. Youths are required to remain under instruction until they are twenty-one, on pain of being deprived of citizenship for the rest of their lives. In every district there is to be a special commission of the arts [*i.e.*, vocational, as indicated above], to be consulted by teachers and to give public lessons. Schools are endowed with a part of the national domains. More tentatively, Saint-Just suggests the formation of groups of young people for discussion, presided over by a magistrate who would choose the subjects to be treated and direct the proceedings; he deems this a type of instruction peculiarly suited to the French.

Only three lines are devoted to girls, whose education was apparently a matter of no importance. They were to be brought up in the home of their mothers. On fête days, a virgin over ten years old must not appear in public unless accompanied by one of her parents or her guardian. It is singular that Saint-Just, so modern in many respects, should here be so oriental.[353]

Upon reading his educational program, no one can remain in doubt that the ideal of the young reformer was Sparta rather than Athens. The cultural value of the plan is negligible. Everything is subordinated to the building of character and citizenship. Its emphasis on vocational training is evident. But there is a healthy common sense running through many of the provisions and the general spirit, though hard, is not without nobility.

Saint-Just may have felt that so stern a training would produce a cold and unfeeling generation if it were not counteracted in other directions. At any rate, the second section of this fragment, in which he deals with the affections, swings to the opposite extreme of Rousseauism and inculcates sentiment to the point of sentimentality. Every man aged twenty-one is required to declare in the temple the names of his friends; this declaration must be repeated every year during Ventôse. If a man quits his friend, he must explain his motives before the people at the request of any citizen, on pain of banishment. Friends cannot write down their mutual contracts nor can they go to law with one another. They stand side by side in battle. Those who have been united through life are buried in the same tomb. The people elect a child's guardians from among his father's friends. If a man commits a crime, his friends are banished. A man's grave is dug by his friends, who join the children in scattering flowers upon it. He who says he does not believe in friendship or who has no friends is banished, as is also a man convicted of ingratitude.

There is no denying the absurdity of this, viewed as matter for legislation. Here Saint-Just is visionary; the only rational explanation is that in his attitude of personal asceticism and his eagerness to build up a solidly moral and healthy-minded community, he has reacted so far from sexual love that he finds it necessary to soften his scheme by providing certain substi-

311

tutes. Unfortunately, as in all such unnatural combinations, the result seems both unhealthy and ridiculous.

His views on sex are expressed only in relation to the family (seventh fragment). Here his legal training is manifest. Although Saint-Just seems to have swung away from his youthful preoccupation with sex as a matter of personal pleasure, a certain loophole is left by a very radical and modern doctrine of marriage, laid down in his opening sentences. The man and woman who love each other, he says, are husband and wife. If they have no children, they may keep their engagement secret; if the wife becomes pregnant, they are required to declare before a magistrate that they are married. This plan would seem to outdo companionate marriage. The rest of the section takes equally advanced ground. No one, says Saint-Just, can interfere with the inclination of his child, whatever his fortune. Community of goods exists only between husband and wife; what they bring and acquire enters into the community. They are united not by contract, but by tenderness; the marriage agreement states only that their property is in common, with no stipulations. If they separate, half of their common property belongs to them and this they divide equally. The other half belongs to the children; if there are no children, it goes to the public domain. A couple must give three months' notice of divorce, in the temple. The public officials immediately appoint guardians for the children. The common property must be duly divided before the divorce. Every engagement made separately by husband and wife is void. Debts are paid out of the portion of the divorced couple; if one of them dies, debts are paid in common by the children and the survivor. A married couple who have had no children in the first seven years of their union and have adopted none, are separated by law and must leave each other. From the foregoing, it is clear that Saint-Just has no interest in the sacredness or indissoluble character of marriage as such; its importance lies in its value to society through the production of children, whose interests are carefully safeguarded. It thus forms a logical pendant to the fragment on education, the corner stone of his plan for the foundation of a strong and healthy nation.

Elaborate arrangements are made for guardianship and adoption. If one parent dies, the survivor becomes guardian of the children, but upon remarriage loses the guardianship. Adoption is established to safeguard poor children and the honor of virgins. Males cannot be adopted after the age of five nor females after their marriage. Those who adopt make a public and inalienable declaration of the sum of money set aside for the child [*dot*], which may not exceed ten thousand livres. A boy's *dot* is only used to rear him until he is five, since he belongs to the country at that age and is brought up at its expense; his *dot* is administered until he is twenty-one, when it passes into his full ownership. That of a girl is administered until her marriage; at twenty-one she likewise receives its full possession. No one can adopt before the age of twenty-one, not even a married couple one of whom is under that age. A couple can adopt only if both are agreed.

The lawyer continues to speak in provisions on inheritance, contracts and penal institutions. Inheritance takes place exclusively between direct relatives, viz., grandparents, father and mother, children, brother and sister. The republic is the beneficiary of those who die without direct heirs. Children inherit from their parents on equal terms. Husband and wife do not inherit from each other; they inherit, share and share alike, from their children if the latter in turn are childless; if husband and wife are separated, they do not inherit from their children. Other rules of less interest follow, the section concluding with the important provision, "No one can disinherit nor make a will."

As for contracts, they are regulated only by the intentions of the parties involved. No one can make a contract before the age of twenty-one nor without the presence of his friends. Only two people can be bound by a single contract. Disputes are settled before the friends of the parties, acting as arbitrators; he who loses his suit is deprived of citizenship for a year. Unwritten obligations are void. "The law does not make the right; the right makes the law."

A few crimes of violence only are considered. He who strikes another is punished with three months' imprisonment; if blood flows, he is banished. He who strikes a woman is banished. Anyone who has seen another struck and has not arrested the culprit is himself imprisoned for a year. Intoxication is to be punished; he who speaks or commits a wrong while in liquor is banished. Murderers must wear black all their lives and are executed if they remove this dress. Saint-Just is below his best thought here and on the subject of contracts.

In another group of proposals the dreamer seems to have given free rein to his fantasy. The sober legislator is silent; the poet speaks. They begin with the tenth fragment, "Certain Moral Institutions Concerning Festivals." Once more the spirit of Rousseau breathes in the opening lines:

The French people recognizes the Supreme Being and the immortality of the soul. The first day of every month is dedicated to the Eternal.

All cults are permitted and protected on equal terms, but any contract or legal document influenced by considerations of cult is void. Public temples are open to all cults. Outdoor rites are forbidden; those taking place indoors may not be disturbed. No priest of any cult may appear in public with his regalia on pain of banishment. Incense is to burn day and night in the public temples and is to be tended constantly by old men over sixty. The temples may never be closed. The French people dedicates its fortune and its children to the Eternal. "The immortal souls of those who have died for their country, of those who have been good citizens, who have cherished their fathers and mothers and never abandoned them, are in the bosom of the Eternal." The hymn to the Eternal is to be sung each morning by the people in the temples; this ceremony takes place at the opening of every public festival. General laws are proclaimed solemnly in the temples. [Saint-Just had become a

believer in God.] [354] There follows a table of fêtes, one for the
first day of each month, beginning with Germinal, which is the
festival of the Divinity, nature and the people. The first of
Floréal is the festival of the Divinity, love and marriage. In
similar fashion the Divinity is recognized each succeeding
month, coupled with one of the following: victory, adoption,
youth, happiness, old age, the immortal soul, wisdom, the
fatherland, labor and friends. Every year on the first of Floréal,
the people of each commune are to elect a rich, virtuous and
well-formed young man between twenty-one and thirty, who
will choose and wed a poor virgin, in recognition of human
equality. Somewhat abruptly the fragment takes up the subject of eloquence, for which prizes are to be offered by lyceums;
they are to be awarded to laconic utterance, to him who has
voiced a sublime thought in the moment of peril or who by a
wise harangue has saved the country, rallied the troops or recalled the folk to moral conduct. The poetry prize is given only
for the ode and the epic.

Fanciful as all this seems, it will be recalled that such a list
of festivals was actually put into effect by Robespierre's famous
decree of 18 Floréal, establishing the religion of the Supreme
Being. Saint-Just's list may have been a variant composed in
connection with this event, though at that time he was with
the troops in the North.

Having discussed childhood, youth and marriage, Saint-
Just proceeds logically to take up the subject of old age, with
which he combines various regulations dealing with temple
meetings and censorship (eleventh fragment). Men who have
lived blameless lives are to be invested with a white sash at
sixty, the ceremony to take place in the temple on the festival
of old age, provided no one arises to accuse them. Respect for
age is to be a veritable cult; those who wear the white sash
can suffer no heavier penalty than exile; they have the duty
of passing judgment in the temples on the private lives of
officeholders and of young men under twenty-one. The oldest
citizen of a commune is required to appear in the temple every

ten days, there to express his opinion of the conduct of office-holders. Public meetings are also held in the temples for the citizens to declare the use they have made of their incomes and to announce the names of their friends. On these occasions the oldest presides; long declamations are forbidden, the bare facts are to be precisely stated. He who strikes or insults any-one in a temple suffers death. Those who do not belong to the sovereign people must retire from the temple before a vote. There is no written record of what takes place in the temple. Officeholders accused by the old men may not speak; their written defense is decently read by one of their friends; with-out discussion, the people decide whether or not the matter is grave enough for the criminal courts. Officials convicted of leading evil lives are banished. Everything which tends to make manners savage or soft is censurable in the temples, but no one may be censured by name except as previously provided. Women may not be censured. A person censured illegally may cause the banishment of the offender.

In spite of these safeguards, the general effect of the institu-tions here provided is obviously calculated to keep the private lives of certain classes of citizens under perpetual scrutiny.

The twelfth fragment concerns funerals. They are to be sol-emn and accompanied by a magistrate; the rites of different cults are to be respected. Each family receives a small field for a burying ground. "Cemeteries are smiling landscapes; the tombs are covered with flowers planted every year by children." Children without reproach may place the pictures of their parents above the door of the house. Like old age, respect for the dead is a cult; martyrs for liberty are to be regarded as tutelary geniuses of the people; it is to be believed that im-mortality awaits those who imitate them. He who outrages a tomb is banished.

Was it because he had seen and perforce inflicted so much suffering that Saint-Just sought to soften the horror of death?

This class of fragments concludes with the thirteenth, de-scribing "certain rural and sumptuary institutions." Every landholder who does not follow a trade, is not a magistrate and is more than twenty-five must cultivate the soil until he is fifty. He is also required on penalty of loss of citizenship to raise four sheep annually for every acre of land he owns. Idleness is punished, industry protected. The republic honors the arts and genius. It invites the citizens to practice good morals and to dedicate their wealth to the public good and the relief of poverty, without ostentation. Every citizen must make an annual accounting in the temples of the use of his fortune. No one can be disturbed in the enjoyment of his wealth, unless it is turned to the detriment of a third party. Domestic service is abolished; anyone who works for a citizen belongs to the family and dines with it. No one may eat meat on the third, sixth and ninth days of the decade. Children eat no meat until they have finished their sixteenth year. The use of gold and silver is forbidden except for coins.

So he emphasizes the bucolic simplicity of his ideal state. But Sparta stood not only for self-restraint in private life, it meant also stern integrity and military hardihood in public affairs. To these the concluding fragments are dedicated.

Saint-Just the administrator found himself interested in government ethics; Saint-Just the soldier, in army ethics. Virtue, modesty, discipline, he insists, are the essential qualities of a public official, bravery and self-restraint those of a soldier. French garrisons can receive no other terms than return to the fatherland and must die rather than surrender as prisoners. No soldier may return to his birthplace if he has left the ranks in combat, has lost his weapon, has deserted, has infringed discipline, has complained of fatigue. A father who embraces his son after the latter has shown cowardice, may not wear the sash of old age. A soldier, next to whom another soldier has been struck down with the cold steel, is dishonored if he returns from the fight without the weapon of him who smote his brother. A commanding general, wounded in battle by sword or bayonet, is demoted unless he has received his wound rallying a broken troop [why?]. A soldier who insults or disobeys his superior, an officer who insults or strikes his subordinate, receive alike the death penalty. A soldier who steals or commits violence on French territory is discharged from the army; if on enemy territory, he is punished with death. No one can leave the army until the end of a war. Women are forbidden to enter camps on pain of death. A wounded soldier may wear a gold star over his wound; if he is mutilated or wounded in the face, he wears it over his heart. The names of victories and accompanying acts of courage are inscribed in the Pantheon; there also books are placed containing the names of those who helped in the Revolution and suffered or died for it. There is to be no eulogy of generals until the end of the war. A standing army of 800,000 is maintained in time of peace, with frequent change of garrisons to keep the troops from losing discipline.

With his admiration for Draconian severity, he heartily approves the institution of censorship. "In every revolution, a dictator is needed to save the state by force, or censors to save it by virtue." This was Marat's theory; here at least Saint-Just espouses it openly. Stressing now the second alternative, he queries why magistrates should be chosen merely to exercise authority; why not also to serve as examples of virtue? The strictest censorship should be exercised on government employes, but never on the people, he maintains. To this end a censor of public officials is established in every district and army until the peace. They take cognizance of conspiracy, graft, oppression of citizens, failure to carry out government measures, besides having surveillance of discipline, officers, generals and the administration. They have nothing to do with military operations nor ethics, nor can they order arrests or perform judicial functions. They may not speak in public. Modesty, austerity and inflexibility are their virtues. Those whom they denounce are prosecuted in court by the public accusers. Censors who wink at an official's guilt receive punishment. Deputies are not subject to censorship, except by the people. All this of course was in time of war; the old men (page 315) sufficed in time of peace.

318

A short fragment on police regulations in war time provides
for the exclusion of foreigners belonging to hostile nations
from employment and from cities. Reformation of laws is suspended to avoid enemy intrigues and conspiracies. The country
is declared in danger; the legislative body must name a committee of public safety, composed of nine of its members, to
have surveillance over the executive council. Evidently Saint-
Just had not yet lost confidence in the value of the machinery
with which he was familiar, in spite of his leanings toward a
dictatorship.

The remaining fragments gather up various odds and ends.
There should be a declaration containing the principles of
social liberty, thinks Saint-Just, as the Declaration of Rights
set forth those of political liberty. Every citizen in private life
has the right to accuse before the courts any official guilty of
arbitrary conduct toward him; the latter, if convicted, is banished, and executed if he returns. A court, refusing to hear such
a complaint, is punished. The ultimate guarantee of liberty is
of course revolution.

Insurrection is the exclusive right of the people and of the citizen.
Every foreigner, every man clothed with public authority, is outlawed if he proposes it and must be put to death on the spot as a
usurper of sovereignty and as interested in fomenting troubles for
the purpose of doing evil or of advancing himself. Insurrections
taking place under a despotism are always salutary. Those which
break out in a free state are sometimes dangerous for liberty itself,
because the revolt of crime usurps its sublime pretexts and its
sacred name. Revolts in free states leave long and painful wounds
which bleed a whole century.

Thus while sanctioning the sacred right of revolution which
he did not dare to refuse, Saint-Just throws all his weight
against its use in the ideal state of his dreams. It would be
unfair to say that the "outs" having become the "ins" sought
merely to perpetuate their power. He felt rather that the people
had won its freedom and thus had everything to lose and nothing to gain by further tumult.

319

One wonders whether it could have been to avoid causes of conflict with other nations or merely to restrict the growth of great fortunes that Saint-Just forbade the ownership of lands, banks or vessels abroad. In case of a naval war, merchant ships must be armed. No treaty can alienate rights of commerce and colonies. The state will buy Negroes on the African coasts for transportation to the colonies, where they become free at once and are each equipped with three acres and necessary tools.

Last of all he deals with the public domain. It is defined as consisting of taxes, estates reverting to the republic and the public lands. There is to be a single tax; every citizen, twenty-one years old, must pay annually a tenth of his income and a fifteenth of the product of his industry. The table of payments is printed and posted up every year. The public domain is used for social welfare and to help the people bear the weight of taxation in hard times. Only those who are virtuous, courageous and humane as well as poor have a right to its benefits. Certain eligible groups are specifically mentioned: mutilated soldiers, old veterans, those who have supported their parents, those who have adopted children, those who have more than four children from a single marriage, old couples who have not separated, orphans, abandoned children, great men, those who have sacrificed themselves for friendship, those who have lost their flocks, those who have suffered loss by fire, those whose goods have been destroyed by war or weather. In addition, the public domain subsidizes the education of children, makes advances to young couples and to those who have no land.

It seems difficult for anyone who has studied the *Fragments sur les institutions républicaines* to deny the idealism of its author. Fanatic or not, he had vision, that rare gift which differentiates a statesman from a routine politician, and he had endless ingenuity. The Revolution produced no more fertile mind. But a statesman must also have wisdom, balance, a sense of proportion. These solid qualities Saint-Just's dreams lack. How far his public career also lacked them will be considered in the final chapter. Perhaps the *Fragments* are no more impractical than most other Utopias. No one has ever tried to reproduce the systems of Plato or More, of Bellamy or Wells, and perhaps their authors would have been the last to attempt it. But Saint-Just seems to have definitely intended to convert some, if not all, of his scheme into law. There are indeed many sound and sensible ideas in it, practical as well as progressive, just as there are many shrewd observations on human nature. Unfortunately these lie side by side with quixotic fancies. Saint-Just's thinking was "spotty"; one never can be sure that any given proposition will be rational without giving it careful study. At times his feet were solidly on the rock; at times he soared into cloudland. If so, it was a cloudland full of noble images as well as poetic caprices.

Political scientist and economist as he was (and he had very definite ideas in both fields), one feels that at heart Saint-Just was most of all a moralist. The success of his political and economic combinations rested in his own thinking on certain patterns of human behavior. If through precept, training and force (if necessary), habits of simplicity, industry, devotion to the state, care for the poor and weak, respect for the experience of age could be inculcated in the lives of a whole nation, the possibilities of a reconstructed society were unlimited. One is reminded of how in like manner, Tocqueville felt that the strength of the young America he described lay less in its Constitution than in the way democracy and integrity permeated the habits of the people. For Tocqueville and for Saint-Just, the *mœurs* were the key to the whole situation.

A few scattered notes of relatively little importance were found among Saint-Just's effects on 9 Thermidor.[355] A procedure is outlined for cases of mob violence: a flag is to be unfurled in the public square as a signal that the people are to deliberate; at once peace must prevail, he who troubles it is to be arrested by the people and turned over to the authorities; the result of the popular deliberation is to be transmitted to the authorities and by them to the legislative body. A note laments the decline of constructive capacity in the Jacobins.

Another says tersely, "Get the laws on education carried out; that is the secret." He demands that priests take up some useful occupation. He insists on the importance of straight thinking in judging one's fellow men. He maintains that the Right (the Girondins) wanted the king's death and only made a pretense of defending him. He stresses the need of calmness in the face of public danger. As though to deny before posterity any idea that he was a communist, he underlines the admonition, "Do not permit the dividing up of property, but the dividing up of rents." It was only large estates, not private property as such, that Saint-Just opposed. Then follows the sixteenth fragment, on censors, somewhat elaborated. Finally come three short letters, addressed to unknown persons; one calls for certain papers wanted in connection with a report, two others seek to speed up the purchase of supplies.

It is in the *Fragments* that the authentic Saint-Just reveals himself. He always maintained that society might be regenerated by a modern Lycurgus, a lawgiver wise enough to establish institutions which would mold human nature into nobler forms. A dream perhaps, and not without unreality, but a great dream none the less.

XXI
SAINT-JUST'S ACHIEVEMENT

HE record of Saint-Just's career is now before us; how shall we assay the man who did, spoke and wrote these things? What was he in himself first and of what significance was his work?

A pivotal point of character confronts us at the outset. His early life was tarnished, as we have seen, by sexual irregularities (of which the Thorin affair and *Organt* are the proof, but probably not the sum) and by one financial scandal, the theft of his mother's silver. Even had all this continued to his dying day, he would have been no worse than Mirabeau and his political services might have been considered apart from these things. But Saint-Just professed a complete reform and drew no small part of his later influence from his alleged puritanism. If, as his enemies assert, this reform was a pretense and his debauchery continued, then he was a hypocrite, and while this would not vitiate the soundness of his political or economic ideas, it would decidedly weaken his reputation as a moralist. Yet this last field was that most congenial to him and to ruin him here is to destroy the very essence of his work.

The charge that Saint-Just was a Lothario to the end rests on three specific allegations. One was the continuance of the Thorin intrigue after his removal to Paris. This we have examined and discredited in an earlier chapter. Another was the Sainte-Amaranthe affair. This lady was the widow of a member of the king's bodyguard and her republicanism was made more pungent and fascinating to many by her royalist past. Her pretty daughter, Émilie, was married to de Sartines, son of the former lieutenant of police, but carried on a lively intrigue with an opera singer named Elleviou. Madame kept a fashionable gambling place in Paris and another in the country at

Sucy-en-Brie. They were crowded by men of all parties. Mirabeau, Pétion, Sieyès, Chapelier, Buzot, Louvet and Vergniaud are said to have frequented them; Desmoulins was there at least twice; later, Proly, Hérault, Danton, Desfieux and Batz were among the patrons. The supposed link between Madame and Saint-Just was forged by a passage in the so-called *Mémoires de Senart,* which reads as follows:

The cruel and ferocious Saint-Just had brought about the arrest of la Sainte-Amaranthe from resentment at not having been able to enjoy her and from fear or suspicion that some other at that moment was being preferred to him. She was in prison, she had dared to complain of the revolting despotism of this monster; Saint-Just demanded her head, declaring her to be an accomplice in that conspiracy, to which she was an absolute stranger [the so-called Foreign Plot]. Saint-Just insisted on it and they sacrificed her to him without proof, without any evidence for the suspicion.[356]

The story gains some plausibility from the fact that a police note was found among Saint-Just's papers stating that the Sainte-Amaranthe woman was under surveillance as suspected of complicity in a royalist plot, all of whose threads were held and of which her house was the center. However, the note is anonymous and not in his hand. The facts are that she was arrested on 12 Germinal by order of the revolutionary committee of the Halle au Blé; was transferred to another prison a fortnight later by order of the Committee of General Security and two months after, when Saint-Just was with the army, she was sent before the Tribunal through the report on the Batz conspiracy which was written by Élie Lacoste, a Thermidorian and unfriendly to Saint-Just. The whole tale is vitiated by the unreliability of its source, the Memoirs of Senart.[357] Mme. de Sainte-Amaranthe was forty-two; to carry greater conviction, Fleury makes Saint-Just desire the daughter. This is absolutely concocted, with no basis even in Senart.

The third allegation is still more wild and partisan. It is a blanket statement by Thermidorian writers that all the Robespierrist leaders were perpetually engaged in "orgies." The silly slander is never told twice in the same way. Barras, in a speech before the Convention on 27 Thermidor, referred to Robespierre's "numerous concubines," continuing his remarks about the fallen leaders in this vein:

These satyrs had country seats in almost all the communes about Paris, where they abandoned themselves to all kinds of excesses. It appears that Robespierre had reserved Monceau for himself; Bagatelle was for Couthon; Saint-Just had Raincy. When these sultans were in these enchanted spots, entrance to them was strictly forbidden; woe to the citizen who did not respect these sovereign orders. Arrested at once as a suspect, he would be included the next day by Fouquier among the number of prison conspirators. This also explains why Couthon, in the name of the Committee of Public Safety, had caused the preservation of all these places, which were famous only as the theater of the debauches of their former masters, while they destroyed Marly, masterpiece of art and Nature, admired by all foreigners.[358]

But all who know the Directory are aware of Barras's own reputation for lack of veracity and character. In spite of his bragging about proofs, the only document he produced to support his assertions was the receipt for a box at the Opéra Comique, rented by Hanriot.

A variant of this charge is the statement in a Thermidorian libel that Robespierre owned the

charming house of the former Princess of Chimasi. There were concocted the plots which were to destroy liberty. There, with Hanriot, Saint-Just and several other accomplices, the ruin of the people was prepared amid the noisiest orgies. There, after banquets for which everything in the neighborhood was requisitioned, the tyrant would roll on the grass, feigning to be seized with convulsive movements, and in presence of the court which surrounded him, take the part of an *illuminé* after the manner of Mahomet to impose on the imbeciles and gain more credit in the eyes of the scoundrels. Sometimes the triumvirate met at Issi, sometimes at Mousseaux; there were concerted the massacre of priests and the triumph of tyranny. Couthon also owned a country house at Mousseaux, it is said. He often went there in the evenings. He had horses so that he might ride in the garden; he had a special kind of saddle made for him, because of his paralysis. Saint-Just requisitioned fine horses for his morning rides in the Bois de Boulogne. He took one the evening on which he was arrested.[359]

The tales of orgies contradict one another, are unsubstantiated and are not taken seriously by any competent historian. There was indeed no limit to the vengeful spleen of the Thermidorians, one of whom had the effrontery to assert that Saint-Just had sent to the guillotine a young girl whose favors he had vainly solicited, and had then caused her skin to be tanned and made into a pair of breeches which he wore constantly. The handsome youth was not always cast in the ungrateful rôle of an unsuccessful suitor. An incoherent letter which poor Théroigne de Méricourt did actually write him on 8 Thermidor from her madhouse prison, the Salpétrière, demanding money, liberty and a political alliance was taken as evidence of some supposed relation, though there is not a line in the letter to suggest it. There was an ex-actress, who for years called herself Mme. de Saint-Just after his death, but who never ventured to do so before.[360]

The case against Saint-Just collapses on examination; it is flimsy and incoherent. There was simply a stupid and savage effort to blacken the fallen Robespierrists by enveloping them all in the same vague and baseless charge of habitual immorality. Levasseur, the colleague on mission who questioned Saint-Just's physical courage, had nothing to say against his morals; his was "a cruel virtue," Levasseur wrote in his memoirs, "but who would dare soil it by contempt? Who, looking at Saint-Just with terror, would dare say, 'I do not esteem him'?" [361] It may be fairly conceded that in the three years of his active public life in Paris, Saint-Just was too absorbed in the enormous pressure of his work and too eager for the success of his cause to have time or interest for the sins of the flesh.

He was always reserved, carefully dressed, punctilious in manner, courteous and cold. There was nothing easy, natural or open about him, none of the expansiveness of a Danton. Everything that he said and did was measured and calculated.

He was prudent and sure of himself, not generous or self-forgetting. He liked to cultivate an air of mystery; it was part of his power. He was so young and handsome, so fascinating and strange that a sort of legend had grown about him; whenever he entered the Convention, "his appearance caused a singular sensation, people stood up in the galleries, saying, 'There he is.' " [362] He was ambitious and haughty; it was hard for him to endure opposition; he took himself very seriously. There was a feeling of theater about him, both in what he did and said. Sometimes he posed as a Spartan, sometimes as a Roman; sometimes as the charming person, who combined the grace and refinement of the old régime with the most advanced political opinions. He was not peculiar in this; Hérault and Robespierre both affected the same combination and practically everybody in the Convention thought of himself as a Roman. So perhaps we are unfair to Saint-Just, attributing to him as a trait of character what was almost a mannerism of the time. But pose or fashion, Saint-Just certainly adopted it and became one of its most extreme exponents.

This theatricality was a marked feature of his literary style. Barère says that he had read a great deal of Tacitus and of Montesquieu; Barante also feels that he sought to imitate Montesquieu. At any rate, he was almost always concise and epigrammatic, preferring to string out a series of polished literary gems rather than to develop a progressive, orderly argument. Sometimes he is clear as crystal, sometimes powerful and trenchant, sometimes oracular, almost always effective. There is no question that he ranked as one of the great speakers of the Convention and deservedly so. In speech and action, he was daring and aggressive.

With these characteristics, one would suppose him self-centered, unlovable; one would not expect him to have any friends. He certainly was not widely popular, but he had a few friends who adored him, as well as others who betrayed him. Perhaps it is not mere chance that in the main those who knew him first, loved him most. He may have grown more moral, but

327

he also grew more cruel after he had been caught up by the whirlwind of the Terror and been forced not only to ride the storm, but to direct it. His great-nephews cherished their parents' memory of him as a silent, gentle youth. "He spoke little," they told Vellay; "he was very good." [363] Of the Blérancourt boys who grew up with him, three were given government posts after he came to power. They were Gateau and Thuillier, who were passionately devoted to him and Vilain-Daubigny who (true to his name) turned crook and ingrate. Through their strong friend's agency the two former were given important duties in connection with the commissary department of the army. [364] It was a field in which there was much corruption and on which the success of the war and of the Revolution greatly depended; the government felt the need of manning it with individuals who were energetic and absolutely trustworthy; Saint-Just took no chances, but picked two whom he had known all his life. They were in Alsace for some time, both before and after Saint-Just's mission there and Gateau was probably with the army in the North in Prairial and Messidor. The seal used by Gateau and Thuillier in Alsace represents a guillotine, flanked by the words, *Subsistances Militaires;* beneath is the inscription, *Guerre Aux Frippon* [sic]. [365] This device is sometimes cited to show Saint-Just's bloodthirstiness, but it was the seal of the commissary administration. Saint-Just when on mission used another seal, representing the republic as a standing female figure, leaning on a pike surmounted by a liberty cap, while the other hand rests on the fasces and ax; the legend read *Représentans* [sic] *du Peuple Français.* [366] Thuillier, who began his career as clerk of M. Gellé and then as secretary of the Blérancourt municipality, concluded it as Saint-Just's secretary and intimate friend. [367] He and Gateau were arrested in Thermidor after their patron's fall and Thuillier was brought before two members of the Committees for examination. He replied courageously, so Gateau tells us, "You have vainly sought to flatter or threaten me; neither fear nor hope will change my heart, and I will not betray friendship or truth, but I shall live to avenge them." He died, however, in prison. Gateau, tired of waiting, finally wrote the authorities, demanding the cause of his arrest. He received in answer a paper containing only these words: "Friend of the conspirator Saint-Just." This filled him with indignation; he resolved to write down for posterity his estimate of the man, "whose innocence I will defend and whom I will avow for my friend, even though everyone on earth abandoned him." This he did in the year III, being finally released from prison in Vendémiaire, year IV. The estimate appeared as *Note extrait des papiers du citoyen* ——, published at the head of the first edition of the *Fragments sur les institutions républicaines*. It is of great importance as the only existing analysis of its subject's character by one who knew him from childhood. The estimate, though not the entire note, is as follows:

I was *the friend of the conspirator Saint-Just*. There then was my indictment, my death warrant and the glorious title through which I deserved a place on your scaffolds. Yes, I was the friend of Saint-Just. But Saint-Just was not a conspirator; if he had been, he would still be in power and you would exist no more. Ah! His crime, if he committed one, was his failure to form a sacred conspiracy against those who plotted liberty's ruin.

O my friend! At the moment when misfortune has crushed you, I have agreed to preserve my life only that I may one day plead the interests of your glory and destroy the slanders which are like the wounds of maddened vultures on your corpse. I remember Blossius of Cumes, who before the Roman Senate proudly confessed his friendship for Tiberius Gracchus, whom the Roman Senate had just assassinated. . . .

Dear Saint-Just, if I escape the proscriptions which cover my country with blood, I will one day unroll your entire life before the eyes of France and of posterity, who will gaze with new emotion on the tomb of a young republican, immolated by faction.

I will force even those who have misunderstood you to admiration and your slanderers and assassins to contempt.

I will recount your courage in struggling against abuses even before the time it could be thought permissible to be virtuous with impunity. I will follow you from the end of childhood, in those deep meditations which absorbed you completely on the science of

government and the rights of peoples, and in those sublime out-
bursts of horror at tyranny which devoured your soul and kindled
it with more than human enthusiasm. I will tell of your zeal in defending the oppressed and unfortunate, when in the severest seasons you made painful journeys on foot to lavish for them your
efforts, your eloquence, your fortune and your life. I will describe
your austere morality and will reveal the secrets of your private
conduct, leaving it to history to make known your public conduct
and your actions in the government, your speeches as legislator and
your immortal missions to our armies.

O day of Fleurus! You must blend your laurels, which nothing
can wither, with the funeral cypress that shades my friend's tomb.
And you, Pichegru, Jourdan, companions of his exploits and his
glory, you will do him justice. You are warriors, you should be
frank. Good faith has always been the virtue of heroes. You will
tell what the fatherland owes his virtues and his courage. You will
not betray the truth, you will not serve envy, for one day you
would be victims of the crime whose accomplices you had become.
You will tell what he did against traitors and how he exercised the
national authority with needful severity; how he gave an example
of frugality and courage to the troops, of activity and prudence to
the generals, of humanity and equality to all those who approached
him.

Tyrant toward his own passions, he had subdued them all that
he might know only love of country. He was gentle by nature,
generous, sensitive, humane, grateful. Women, children, old men,
the weak, the soldiers had his respect and affection; and his heart
beat so strongly with such feelings that he was always made tender
at the sight of these objects, so interesting in themselves.

How often have I seen him shed tears over the violence of the
revolutionary government and the prolongation of a frightful
régime, which he looked forward to tempering by gentle, beneficent
and republican institutions! But he felt that *it was necessary to
loosen, not to break the bowstrings.* He wished to regenerate the
public morals and to restore all hearts to virtue and nature.

He was deeply moved by the corruption of men and wished to
destroy its germ by a severe education and by strong institutions.
"Today," he said to me, "one cannot propose a rigorous and salutary law, that intrigue, crime and fury do not lay hands on it and
make it into an instrument of death, according to caprice and
passion."

I witnessed his indignation at reading the law of 22 Prairial, in the headquarters garden of Marchiennes, by the bridge before Charleroy. But I must say he spoke only with enthusiasm of the talents and austerity of Robespierre, for whom he cherished a sort of cult.

He sighed for the end of the Revolution, that he might give himself up to his ordinary meditations, contemplate nature and enjoy the repose of private life in a rural home, with a person whom Heaven seemed to have destined for his companion and whose mind and heart he would have delighted to mold, far from the venomous meddling of city folk.

It is an atrocious slander to suppose him evil. Neither vengeance nor hate ever entered his soul. I appeal to you, citizens of Blérancourt, under whose eyes his genius and his virtues grew. There are among you those whose political opinions have been corrupted by intrigues, habits and passions, and who have outraged, slandered, persecuted Saint-Just, because he walked a road contrary to that on which you entered.

Nevertheless, after he became member of the government, when you found yourselves led before the Revolutionary Tribunal for unpatriotic acts or words, you did not hesitate to invoke his witness and by his efforts you returned to your homes and enjoyed the embraces of your kin who never hoped to see you again. "They have been my enemies," he said, speaking of you; "I owe them all my zeal and help, provided public interest or inflexible honesty do not require the sacrifice of their liberty or lives." And he succeeded in saving you.

Pliant and sociable in private matters, so he was sometimes irascible, severe and inexorable when the country was involved. Then he became a lion, listening no longer, breaking down all barriers, trampling all considerations under foot and his austerity imparted fear to his friends and gave him a somber, ferocious air with manners despotic and terrible, forcing him afterward to reflect on the immense dangers involved in the exercise of absolute power, when it is entrusted to men whose heads are not as well organized as their hearts are pure.

Such was the man who, hardly twenty-seven, was cut down by a Revolution to which he had consecrated his existence and who has left long regrets to his country and to friendship.[368]

Granted that this eulogy is overenthusiastic, there is no doubt that it was sincere. Saint-Just had fallen, it was the fashion to execrate him as a monster, Gateau was in prison and in danger of his life. He had nothing to gain, everything to lose by such a panegyric. Whatever our final verdict on Saint-Just, no man could be wholly bad who had a friend like that.

Daubigny was made second assistant to the war minister Bouchotte, thanks to Robespierre and Saint-Just. Charges of theft from the royal storehouse were made against him, but dismissed by the courts. They were revived in the Convention by Bourdon de l'Oise and Billaud-Varenne. Robespierre strongly defended him and was backed by Saint-Just, who said:

I join my testimony with pleasure to that of Robespierre and declare that I have always known Daubigny as a good man. He is from my country. I have seen him sell his goods to provide subsistence for his mother, whom he has taken care of for fifteen years. In a word, I know no better friend, no more ardent patriot, no worthier citizen than Daubigny.

The little speech was applauded and Daubigny's nomination confirmed. This was September 30, 1793. Saint-Just's judgment was mistaken, for Daubigny became afterward involved in fraudulent army contracts. To save himself he denounced Saint-Just after 9 Thermidor.[369]

Another false friend of the early days was Augustin Lejeune, a native of Soissons. According to his own story, he knew Saint-Just only by sight when they met one evening at a Laon inn. The date is not given, but it must have been early in the Revolution. Being from the same locality they entered into conversation, during which Saint-Just greatly impressed Lejeune by the simplicity of his ideals and his eloquent exposition of them. His ambition was limited, he said, to a life in the country; all he desired was a wife, children to satisfy his heart, study to occupy his leisure, his extra income to be devoted to his good neighbors if they were poor. Later on, this modesty and generosity were replaced by austerity, ambition and a savage gayety in terrorism, says Lejeune. When the Laon conversation was once recalled to him, Saint-Just tossed it off with airy insolence. "Other times, other language," he said; "when one must model oneself on the enemy of the Tarquins, one no longer reads the Idylls of Gesner." Lejeune believed that his interlocutor had been sincere at Laon, but that he had completely changed. However, some of the earlier and better traits cropped out from time to time, so that the man was a curious mixture of good and bad, sometimes shedding tears at the misfortune f others, sometimes cruel and hard-hearted. One day you would think well of him, Lejeune ruminates, the next you would have to hate him. There is a ring of plausibility in this comment.

Through Saint-Just's influence [370] Lejeune received in March, 1794, the post of bureau chief in the general police, that special service which functioned under the control of the Committee of Public Safety. As such, he said, he organized the bureaus, while Saint-Just determined their functions, giving the proper orders to have denunciations referred to this department. To the police authorities Saint-Just recommended brevity; offenders could be classified as moderates or aristocrats or counter-revolutionaries. The bureau chief relates various anecdotes of his powerful friend's capricious conduct in police questions. Once, the daughter of a chevalier of the order of St. Louis succeeded in obtaining from Saint-Just a continuance of her father's pension and overwhelmed him with her gratitude. After she had left, Saint-Just remarked to Lejeune:

I cannot see her without tenderness. What innocence, what courage in her trouble! How she loves her father!

His eyes were moist as he spoke. Lejeune seized the opportunity to request the restoration of a Soissons official to his post in the war department, the loss of which had reduced him to poverty. Saint-Just promised, but on the following day refused it with angry suspicion; "I have noticed several times that you interested yourself in royalists," he flung at his subordinate. Apparently a young man's natural instinct to help a pretty girl or a sentimentalist's emotion at the sight of filial piety were responsible for this favoritism. It may have been so, but one recalls the other story of how he caused his affectionate friend to be shot in Alsace as an example of discipline. In one case, he is represented as sentimentally weak, in the other as inhumanly stern; the two cancel each other. Their common object is to show that he was not rationally just, but they do so by diametrically opposite exaggerations. Lejeune recalls Saint-Just's fondness for epigrams. To a rich capitalist requesting a hearing on a plan to establish a cotton factory, he replied: "It is not cotton that we need, but iron." When Lejeune asked that the famous violinist Rhodes be exempted from military service, Saint-Just, though very fond of music, answered, "Tell this new Zyrtaeus that we too have our Messenians to fight." Lejeune sponsors the story that Saint-Just turned a stupid general into a courier and an intelligent courier into a general. This stock yarn is told of various historical characters and Lejeune's repetition of it tends to discredit the authenticity of his other information. His general picture is of himself as asking liberty for innocent prisoners and Saint-Just as uniformly refusing; once it was in these words, "The moment of revolution in which we are at this time, is too stormy for us to occupy ourselves with distributive justice; before thinking of the cause of individuals, we must think of the cause of the State." That Lejeune often occupied the rôle he attributes to himself is highly improbable. He was accused in the year III as an agent of the Terror and wrote these things to get himself out of trouble. In the spirit of the time, he denounced Robespierre and Saint-Just as "two anthropophagi," clamoring for long lists of victims. The extremity of his fear vitiates his trustworthiness. A study of the police bureau's papers proves his lack of veracity. At the same time it must be said that the last remark ascribed to Saint-Just is in keeping with the philosophy of the Mountain; even Danton said that the Revolution was like nature, careless of the individual, mindful of the species. Under the pressure of circumstances, the governing party developed a *Realpolitik* worthy of any Bismarck. To this

Saint-Just was no exception, but the political creed of a whole group must not be attributed to him as a trait of personal character.

So much for the early friends of Saint-Just; two speak well of him and two speak ill. But the verdict of all four was rendered at a time when to speak well of him was to court danger to oneself, while at least one of those who spoke ill was a crook and the other a liar.

He made other friends later, of course. They were not numerous, but they were devoted. Of Le Bas, who was closest to him, we have spoken at length. Of his relation to Robespierre, we shall speak presently. The other member of the ruling coterie was Couthon, the cripple. From him we have a single letter addressed to Saint-Just; there are none to Robespierre. It is dated Ville-Affranchie (the republican name for Lyons), October 20, year II and begins:

You have not written me a line, my friend, since we parted; I am vexed with you, since you promised me that whenever we were absent from each other, you would give me news of yourself. Hérault has been kinder than you, I have had two letters from him. You know, my dear friend, that to console myself for the troubles which crush me, I need evidences of the interest of those whom I esteem; tell me then that you exist, that you are well, that you do not forget me and I will be content.[371]

It is illuminating and a little astonishing from the standpoint of revolutionary psychology to find one who was regarded as a murderous terrorist and who was engaged at the moment in a punitive mission, writing like an affectionate schoolgirl.

Even members of the Committee who disliked him, esteemed him. Carnot considered him as very superior to Robespierre and said that he made himself of great value [précieux] in his missions to the armies by prompt and energetic decision, but that his arrogance passed all bounds. Prieur of the Côte d'Or had much the same opinion.[372] Collot spoke of him habitually as the young, vigorous athlete of the Revolution.

One more contemporary record comes through Sainte-Beuve,

335

to whom it was personally narrated by the individual in question, a certain M. Biot, in 1860. He described in great detail how when very ill after the battle of Hondschoote, he was brought to his home in Paris by an unknown young man, a single word from whom proved an open sesame to every barrier. At the journey's end, Biot found that his benefactor was Saint-Just.[373] But though Sainte-Beuve inclines to accept the story, it becomes impossible from the simple fact that the battle of Hondschoote was in September, 1793, while Saint-Just's first mission to the North fell in January, 1794. In 1860, M. Biot must have been eighty-five and the old gentleman's recollections of his youth appear to have been decidedly blurred.

During the Thermidorian period, and with less heat during the half century that followed, Saint-Just was regarded as a bloodthirsty fanatic. His old enemy in Alsace, Baudot, is quoted as saying:

It is not impossible that with much subtlety one should attempt to rehabilitate the memory of Robespierre. The thing is impossible for Saint-Just; his name will remain that of an exterminator [and again], an adolescent Montesquieu with the cruelty of a mature Nero.[374]

At Fouquier-Tinville's trial, Daubigny called Saint-Just "the Ahriman of the Convention." A typical Thermidorian pamphlet contains this diatribe:

Vive la République! The tyrants are no more: Robespierre, Couthon and Saint-Just can no longer put you in chains. They have expiated their crimes and their parricidal heads have just fallen on the scaffold. . . .

Robespierre, tormented by a passion to rule, unable or not daring to seize the reins of government alone, had left no stone unturned during the last four months to divide the members of the Committee of Public Safety among themselves and to embroil them with the Committee of General Security. For this he had associated with himself two of his worthy colleagues, *Couthon,* whose hypocritical gentleness concealed the cruelty and ferocity of his soul, and *St. Just,* a man with a cold exterior, but haughty, dissimulating, ambitious and capable of the greatest crimes. These monsters had for some time been renewing the most horrible proscriptions of the *Mariuses* and *Sillas*.[375]

Another in the form of a satire describes a session of the club organized by the deceased members of the Mountain in the infernal regions. The hall is lighted by lamps set in forty-five skulls of farmers general, spreading a glow redder than a virgin's blood. In the center at the back on a red-hot tripod lounges Robespierre, holding his jaw with one hand, while the other traces with a dagger the vast plan of a universal cemetery. On the left, one sees Lubin weeping, Hanriot gnashing his teeth, Payan picking his, Lavalette taking snuff and Coffinhal reading Audouin's *Journal universel*. On the right, Fleuriot is biting his nails, Chaumette reciting a rosary, Hébert heating his ovens, Dumas in a huff, Sijas unmuzzling a tiger, Couthon meditating a crime, Saint-Just writing a report, and the mob in the background.[376]

Mignet, writing his history under the Restoration, called Saint-Just a well-combed monster.[377] But with the mid-century revolutions and notably with 1848, he was once more glorified. Buchez and Roux spoke of "the ferocious chastity of that young man." [378] Buonarroti's papers, full of the social enthusiasm of his own revolution, contain this eulogy of him:

Proud enemy of kings and grandees, generous friend of the People, he defended Robespierre, whose plans he had shared and in whose sufferings he now had part. Saint-Just had said: the miserable are the powers of the earth, . . . there should be neither rich nor poor, . . . he had it decreed that the possessions of the Revolution's enemies should be given to the People.[379]

Michelet, writing of his death, said, "France will never console herself for the loss of such a hope; he was great with a greatness that was his own; he owed nothing to fortune and he alone would have been strong enough to make the sword tremble before the law." [380] Lamartine, not only poet, historian and statesman, but also the orator of 1848, spoke admiringly of his fellow craftsman as "mute as an oracle and sententious as an axiom, . . . one would say a dream of the Draconian republic." [381]

With the reaction, the pendulum swung back and in later years he has been more or less definitely pigeonholed as a fanatic. Rémy de Gourmont called him a panther, Thiers, "a fanatic, austere and cold, who at the age of twenty, meditated on an ideal society where should reign absolute equality, simplicity, austerity and an indestructible force." [382] Taine denounced him in unmeasured terms as thief, libertine and poseur, a sick madman, a Caligula with soul of steel.[383] It is hardly necessary to repeat the opinions of his two chief biographers; Hamel praised him quite as extravagantly as Fleury condemned. Yet the latter, while calling him "a great culprit" and regarding him with dislike, admitted that Saint-Just would not tolerate theft or corruption in public life, that he was very able, having an instinct for government and a talent for command, together with furious energy, clear-sightedness, self-confidence and daring.[384] For Cuvillier-Fleury on the other hand, he was vacillating and fragile before he became perverse, a rhetorician playing at being tribune, an artist at phrase-making.[385] With even greater hostility, Sainte-Beuve assailed him as "that atrocious and theatrical young man, to whom one is embarrassed, when one surveys his short and sinister career, to apply a single time the humane word of pity." [386]

When, after the passage of nearly a century and a half, one attempts a reappraisal of this man's character in terms of his deeds and his words, one is faced at the outset with a curious contrast in his public utterances. On matters of general public policy, he is clear and statesmanlike; his reasoning is usually sound and convincing. On the contrary, it is almost never so in his denunciation of "plots," though here some of his greatest eloquence is found. It would seem that he was either a cool-headed Machiavellian, not believing a word he said or that he had very poor political judgment and in so far was an untrustworthy leader. In fact his judgment of men was not particularly reliable; witness his mistakes in regard to Daubigny, Pichegru and Hoche. He took violent prejudices. The fury of his philippics was not wholly calculated; it sprang in part at least from deep emotion. Fanatical emotion, no doubt. But no public man can be estimated apart from the age in which he lived. Recall the Middle Ages, when heretics were burned at the stake, or the witchcraft craze of the seventeenth century or the war madness of recent days. Saint-Just was not unusual in having his judgment warped under pressure of great public emotion and strain; few escape it. There was good reason for the hysterical cry "we are betrayed," in 1793 and 1794, when so large a part of the nation hated the government and of real "traitors" to it there were not a few. No ruling group were ever subjected to a more terrific strain than was the Mountain, when all of Europe and half of France were leagued against it. No wonder every man was "suspect," whose loyalty was not clear. The only way out was to adopt the ruthless maxim, *Salus reipublicae suprema lex,* and this the Mountain deliberately did. If an individual or a party stood in the way of winning the desperate fight, it must be destroyed without mercy. In his great philippics, Saint-Just was partly moved by the unreasoning hysteria of his times, partly by the deliberate purpose to crush those whom he and his friends regarded as groups who for one reason or another had become dangerous to the Revolution. It is not necessary to suppose that he believed every detail of the charges brought against them, but he was certainly convinced of the major premise, that they stood in the path of progress and must be removed. This opinion was not always warranted and it is here that the charge of fanaticism lies. But it is the time that was fanatical, not the man only; he was swept up into the current of war madness, as millions of others have been before and since his day. Why should he be stigmatized for lack of calmness at a time when none were calm?

In truth, for all his cold exterior, the basic quality of Saint-Just was intense life, fire and energy, not a red, raging fire like

339

Danton's, but a still, white heat of perhaps even higher temperature. The periods of listlessness and relaxation in Danton find no parallel in Saint-Just. This ultimate characteristic shows early in the wild oats that he sowed (the silver, Mme. Thorin, *Organt*), in his passionate outburst at his restricted sphere of action, in the vigor of his local political leadership. When the Revolution came, he stifled the passions natural to him and compressed his energy into a single, narrow torrent of sheer force like a canalized river or a harnessed Niagara, pouring it with tremendous power into those deadly, epigrammatic speeches, those acts of furious terrorism, that volcanic leadership of the armies. His ideal France was of like tenor, rigorous, Spartan. The family and friendship were to be the outlets of loving-kindness; on other matters he preached a bracing hardness. Life was to be a perpetual training table for athletic patriots. With weakness and corruption, with softness or idleness, with self-seeking or luxury, he had no patience. Ruthless efficiency was his watchword. Perhaps he was intolerant, narrow-minded and a little young in this enthusiasm, but his cardinal sin was not bloodthirstiness; it lay rather in his cold pride and self-sufficiency. He had a sense of superiority that irritated his associates and their opposition in turn angered him. There was no personal generosity or humbleness in him. One thinks of young William Pitt, with his "I am sure that I can save the country and I am sure that no one else can." It was the fault of ardent youth; if Saint-Just had lived, time might have mellowed him. Together with this went the tendency to pose; he dramatized himself in his successive rôles of Lycurgus, Demosthenes or Leonidas. The attitudes he struck in some of his speeches are displeasing to the reader today and unquestionably irritated many of his hearers. I think that he realized this defect and struggled against it; witness his constant praise of modesty as an essential characteristic of the true statesman. Ambitious he was without doubt, desiring to dominate, but there is no more reason to see in this the keynote of his life than there is in the case of any other powerful leader.

Barère rightly sees audacity as one of his prime qualities, saying of him, "It is he who first said that the secret of the Revolution was in the word 'dare,' and he dared." [387] Freely granting his numerous defects, Saint-Just had a strong and not ignoble character.

Such was the man; what of his work?

He made his mark in three different theaters, on the floor of the Convention, at the front with the armies, around the table of the Committee of Public Safety. Without traversing again ground already covered, it should be recalled that in the Convention Saint-Just won approval for constructive ideas and gained fame for destructive reports. He made himself a sort of specialist in three distinct fields: (1) in political science, where his ideas on constitutional reform found expression in public speeches, in the Constitution of 1793 and particularly in his preliminary project for it, in his writings, *L'Esprit de la Révolution* and the *Fragments;* (2) in economics, setting forth on more than one occasion sound ideas in the field of finance, especially regarding currency inflation, and later veering from his original individualism to more doubtful but important projects of a semisocialistic character (the Ventôse decrees); (3) in military reorganization, of which his speeches and his *Notes militaires* as well as his work on mission, show him to have been an attentive student. Having won his spurs by his striking utterances in connection with the king's trial, he became the spearhead of his party in the great drives against the Girondins, the Hébertists and the Dantonists. The decision to overthrow these groups was of course a party and not an individual decision, but Saint-Just was in each case put forward to give the *coup de grâce.* It is clear that they regarded him as their best speaker for this type of work. To what extent the necessary votes were secured by the report or whether the doomed factions would have fallen anyway no one can tell. Of the deadly power of these philippics there can be no doubt. They made on his hearers, who listened to them with a certain shuddering fascination, an impression of inevitable doom, dealt in cold, hard, bright, swift blows. As Barère put it, Saint Just's reports "spoke like an ax." [388]

As representative to the army of the Rhine, he performed herculean labors, stemmed the tide of defeatism, filled the dispirited troops with new courage and helped organize an offensive that swept the enemy clean out of Alsace and saved the eastern frontier. With equal efficiency he operated in the North, driving the baffled French forces back again and again to their task, showing a dogged tenacity that refused to admit defeat, until at last defeat became victory. He was responsible for taking the pivotal town of Charleroi and was present at the decisive battle of Fleurus. Twice his colleagues doubled the area of his authority; such was their judgment of his worth.

Nor were his labors in the Committee the least important of his services to the Revolution; perhaps they were the most important, though they are the hardest to trace. Enough has already been said in the chapter on this subject to banish any notion that the Committee can be divided into "workers" and "politicians," with the Robespierrists in the latter category. The decrees which bear Saint-Just's signature witness to his constructive energy in building up the organism of the republic. Had not the break with Danton occurred, laments one enthusiastic pro-Jacobin, the republic's triumph would have been assured; Danton would have been its force, Robespierre its soul and brain, Saint-Just its organizing power.[389] However that may be, there is no denying the administrative efficiency of Saint-Just. Unhappily the tale cannot stop there. For in addition to these fruitful labors, one of Saint-Just's chief occupations in the Committee as well as outside it was terrorism. Folk feared him as a man of blood; there is no question that he was far more widely feared than loved. To most of his contemporaries he seemed hard and cold and terrible and one side of him was just that. But it is only fair to remember that he was not simply wicked, not wantonly cruel and that so far from his idealism being progressively crushed out, it is precisely in the one great uncompleted work of his later days, the *Frag-*

ments, that the half-built towers of his dream castle for a happier time to come stand revealed.

One more side of Saint-Just remains for discussion. He was not only a constructive worker and terrorist, he was a politician. The main lines of his political faith are familiar because they were those of his party: centralization of government in the hands of a few men at Paris, a machinery capable of instant action, the safety of the state the supreme consideration. In his responsibility for all this, how far was he merely the mouthpiece of Robespierre, how far was he original, determining policies? In short, just what was the relation between him and Robespierre? The point is essential but the problem difficult.

The initial relations between the two are perfectly clear. One need only recall the letter of August 19, 1790: "I do not know you, but you are a great man." Saint-Just was the humble disciple adoring his master from afar. He was still a country boy, writing from Blérancourt to a man who had already made his reputation and whose character and principles seemed to him admirable. In the youth's eyes, his hero was "not only the deputy of a province, you are that of humanity and of the Republic." Beneath the trivial rustic petition for aid in saving the markets of Blérancourt, one senses the trembling eagerness of the boy to call himself to a powerful leader's notice, through whom might come an opportunity for action on the national stage. What attention, if any, Robespierre paid this letter is not known. Two summers later Saint-Just was still in his own eyes "Brutus, languishing forgotten far from Rome." But that fall he was elected to the Convention. Here he at once attached himself to the banner which had attracted him from afar. For his part, Robespierre no doubt saw possibilities in the eager youth and welcomed his support. One writer (not always trustworthy) has phrased the situation rather well: "Robespierre was doubtless appreciative of that enthusiastic adoration; he loved to surround himself with young fanatics; his sententious gravity, the rhetorical and logical language which he used even in familiar intercourse had a great appeal to passionate imaginations; he became from that time on [the time of the 1790 letter] a sort of patron of Saint-Just and his influence contributed to elect him to the Convention." [390] There is no proof of the last two statements; the remainder helps to explain the subsequent relationship. Other qualities in Robespierre that powerfully influenced Saint-Just were his radicalism, his apparently pure patriotism and his moral incorruptibility. One wonders how far Saint-Just's cold reserve and ascetic morals were due to his deliberate modeling himself upon the master's pattern. Lejeune, Saint-Just's faithless friend, credits the latter's entrance into the Committee of Public Safety to Robespierre, who saw in him "a young athlete, very muscular, very supple, whom he might launch into the arena when he chose." Again, there is no evidence for this. Lejeune believes further that Robespierre was more prone to terrorism than Saint-Just, who stifled his natural instincts in harmony with his leader's policy.[391]

Saint-Just grew rapidly in that hothouse forcing bed. The success of his reports gave him a sense of power. He began to stand on his own feet. Still, and to the end, a devoted adherent of Robespierre, the distance between them grew less unequal. The younger man began to give advice, the older to lean on his support. A few contemporary evidences of this newer relation still survive. On Robespierre's side there are three or four, on Saint-Just's only one. The latter, the most striking of all, is chronologically first. It is that extraordinary letter of 24 Frimaire from Strasbourg, in which Saint-Just summons Robespierre to greater zeal in punishing crime and reads him a lesson on supplying the troops properly. Fleury considers it a fragment of a lost correspondence. From Robespierre there is a letter to Saint-Just and Le Bas, written on 9 Nivôse, the day after the deliverance of Landau. He writes:

Friends, I have feared in the midst of our successes and on the eve of a decisive victory, the evil consequences of a misunderstanding or of a miserable intrigue. Your principles and your virtues have reassured me. I have seconded them so far as in me lay. The letter which the Committee of Public Safety is addressing you at the same time as mine will tell you the rest. I embrace you with all my soul.[392]

There is also a letter from Robespierre addressed to Le Bas as well as Saint-Just and bearing date of 15 Floréal, when the two had just begun their second mission to the North. It runs:

My friends, the committee has taken all the measures dependent on it at this moment to second your zeal. It charges me to write you to explain the motives of certain of its dispositions. It has thought that the principal cause of the late reverse was the lack of skilled generals; it will send you such patriotic and instructed soldiers as it may discover. . . . For the rest, it relies on your energy and your wisdom. Greetings and friendship.[393]

This is not the tone of a superior, but of a colleague. Most striking of all is the Committee's panic-stricken letter to Saint-Just on 6 Prairial, telling him of the political danger they were in and begging him to return and help them. The letter was written by Robespierre and had five signatures. Saint-Just returned as will be recalled, looked the situation over, decided that the army had greater need of him and went back to the front with increased authority. Almost the colleague has become the master.

That stage was never reached. The time was too short. Six weeks later both were dead. But for the last half of those six weeks, Robespierre, now disliked by the majority of the Committee, withdrew from its sessions, while the sickly Couthon was irregular in his attendance. Alone of his faction and surrounded by enemies, Saint-Just boldly and unflinchingly carried on. During those bitter days, Robespierrism in the Committee of Public Safety was Saint-Just.

So far as I am aware, there are only two estimates of the comparative ability of these men made by those who knew them both. One was Barère, their daily associate in the Committee. "After the month of March, 1794," he wrote, "Robespierre seemed to me to change his conduct; Saint-Just contributed to it without doubt, but this guide was too young."

Again, "We do not conceal the belief that Saint Just, cut on a more dictatorial model, would have finished by overthrowing Robespierre and putting himself in his place." And once more, "Saint-Just was deeper and more capable of revolutionizing than Robespierre." [394]

The estimate of Levasseur is still more analytical.

Saint-Just was linked with Robespierre in the Convention by a friendship which was not extinguished until their death and which an astonishing unity of doctrine, a common character of cold exaltation and of energetic tenacity made unalterable. He presented, in his views on the Constitution, the counterpart of those of his friend. One had spoken of liberty, the other demanded force; one had held to theories, the other descended to their application. . . . Robespierre has always been considered the head of the revolutionary government. As for me, who have seen the events of that epoch at first hand, I would almost dare affirm that Saint-Just had a larger part in them than Robespierre himself. Although one of the youngest members of the Convention, Saint-Just was perhaps the one who joined to the most exalted enthusiasm, to a prompt and sure gift of rapid penetration, the most stubborn will power and the most eminent skill in organization. With profound convictions, exalted to the point of fanaticism, he had the coldest exterior, because his enthusiasm was the result of mathematical certainty. One could never make him vary his opinion; one could never make him flinch from his resolutions; considering solely the goal he wished to reach, he gave little heed to the kind of measures he would have to employ; the surest seemed to him always the best. To found the republic he had dreamed for a long time, he would have given his head, but also a hundred thousand other heads beside his own. Intimately linked with Robespierre, he had become necessary to him and he would perhaps have made himself still more feared by Robespierre had he not wished his love. They were never seen divided in opinion and if it chanced that the personal ideas of one had to bend before those of the other, it is certain that Saint-Just never yielded. Robespierre had a little of that vanity which springs from egotism; Saint-Just was full of the pride born of well-established convictions; without physical courage and feeble of body to the point of fearing the whistling of bullets, he had that reflective courage which will await a certain death rather than sacrifice an idea.[395]

There may also be a reflection of Carnot's opinion in his son's estimate of the two. Speaking of Saint-Just's loyalty to Robespierre, he said: "That admiration was not exhausted even when he had surpassed him, at least as a man of action." [396]

Of later writers it is hardly necessary to speak, for theirs is an opinion like any other, but many have felt Saint-Just's superiority and some believe that in the end, but for Thermidor, the two would have inevitably clashed and the younger man would have emerged master of France.[397] Indeed it has been said that Robespierre realized this and was jealous of him to the point of fear.[398] In support of this, it is told on Barère's authority that one day Robespierre, speaking of him familiarly to the Committee as of an intimate friend, said, "Saint-Just is taciturn and an observer, but I have noticed that in physique he has a strong resemblance to Charles IX." [399] But other than this slight jest there is no proof of jealousy on the older man's part. Rather he intrusted his life to his friend's keeping, for the great undelivered speech of 9 Thermidor that was to have saved the party was written by Saint-Just. When afterward Robespierre's papers were seized in his lodgings, his only recorded estimate of his disciple was found. It is in four words. "Great talents.—Pure.—Devoted." [400] There is the record of a great friendship.

Weighing the evidence, no one can truly say that Saint-Just was merely Robespierre's echo. His personality was too strong, his mind too independent for that. The two thought along the same lines; the part played by each in the determination of party policy cannot be unraveled. It is probably going too far to regard the younger as the actual leader, whatever he might have become had he lived. But it is likely that with every month his share of the joint product increased, his voice in the deliberations grew stronger.

The irony of history placed this man, whose early impulses were kindly, in a period where his life, all told, was probably a bane rather than a blessing to his fellows. As legislator, as orator, as the inspirer of the national defense at critical moments, he served his country well. He was one of the strong men thrown up by a great cataclysm. Because of circumstances partly beyond his control, he will always be remembered in terms of mass slaughter. For this, if he willfully prolonged it a single moment, no condemnation can be too strong. It is a tragic thing that his place in the human record rests close by the guillotine. It is a source of lasting regret to those who can see the noble promise of his life that he could not have been spared to inaugurate the better things he foreshadowed, or that he could not have seen the way to throw his great influence toward clemency earlier. For like another great dreamer, he was cut off before all the promise of his rich spirit bore fruition. In his youth and in his beauty, in his radical view of society and his passion for freedom, in the poetry of his fancy and the pathos of his early death, Saint-Just was the Shelley of the French Revolution.

APPENDIX 1

THE THEFT OF THE SILVER

Saint-Just's last letter from the prison, one of his two earliest surviving compositions, is given here in full. It is clear evidence of his remorse for his fault.

Paris, ce 27 mars 1787.

Monsieur,

Voici, à ce qu'il me semble, le terme des peines que vous avez bien voulu prendre pour moi, mais je ne me crois pas encore au terme des miennes. Voici la réponse de Rigaux telle que je l'attendais, mais la satisfaction qu'elle me cause est bien contrebalancée par ce que me mande ma sœur. Maman, selon toute apparence, ne va que de mal en pis. Il est triste pour moi de ne pouvoir me dissimuler que je suis pour quelque chose dans sa maladie, par le chagrin que je lui ai causé; mais il n'est pas possible de revenir sur le passé. Le seul remède en mon pouvoir, est l'avenir. Puisse-t-elle avoir le temps d'en faire l'épreuve. Je ne sais point quel est son état; mais j'ai tout lieu de croire que l'on m'en dit encore moins qu'il y en a, au reste, j'espère le connaître bientôt par moi-même. Triste espoir qui me fait craindre ma liberté et avec d'autant plus de raison, que ma sœur me l'annonce d'une manière bien indifférente. Je ne sais si je dois attribuer à son trouble la liberté qu'elle prend de vous prier de m'emmener avec vous. Quant à moi, je suis si confus des peines que je vous ai données, que je n'ose plus rien vous demander, hors d'état de vous prouver ma reconnaissance autrement que par des paroles que j'estime fort vaines. Je ne saurais que vous répéter encore maladroitement peut-être, mais avec vérité, avec quels sentiments,

J'ai l'honneur d'être, Monsieur, votre très humble, très obéissant serviteur

De Saint-Just.

Rigaux, referred to above, was brother-in-law of Descharmes, the Soissons *procureur*.

The episode of the theft was unknown to either Fleury or Hamel. More important, Vellay, the specialist on Saint-Just, discredits the whole story. In an article on "La correspondance de Saint-Just," *Mercure de France,* March 1, 1906, he explains his reason for beginning with 1790 by declaring that the letters published by Bégis are known only through copies and that the imprisonment story is extremely suspicious, full of contradictions and obscurities and cannot be blindly accepted. (Cf. also Vellay, "Autour d'une édition de Saint-Just," *Annales révolutionnaires,* I, 511). It is true that in his pamphlet Bégis makes a number of errors regarding the family, placing Nampcel in the Aisne, while it is actually in the Oise; calling the elder sister Gille-Marie-Anne and making her the wife of Adrien Bayard, who in reality married her younger sister; calling the latter the wife of Jean-Michel-Nicaise de Lassières, who does not appear in any other account; declaring that after his schooling at Soissons, Louis went to the collège Louis-le-Grand at Paris, at the partial expense of the city of Soissons and that he there met Robespierre, Desmoulins and Fabre d'Eglantine, for all of which there is no evidence. But whatever doubt attaches to Bégis's accuracy, the substantial truth of the story appears from the fact that the originals of the two d'Evry letters of the year II are in the Archives Nationales (F ^{7} 4620; Police Général; Comité de Sûreté Générale; dossier Brunet); there are a number of verbal differences from Bégis's version, but they do not change the sense. The carelessness of Bégis appears once more in his incorrect citation of carton F ^{7} 4595 as containing the d'Evry papers.

A number of these letters taken from the original documents have been included in Charles Vatel's *Charlotte de Corday et les Girondins* (Paris, 1864-72), cxli-clvi. M. Vatel, an advocate at the Paris Court of Appeals, though unfriendly to Saint-Just, comments that the theft was not a criminal offense according to French law, since the son of the family is presumptive heir and in this case had still further claim on the objects involved, in view of his father's death. In his opinion Saint-Just's offense lay rather in his nocturnal flight, the selling of the objects and the shock to his mother; it was a grave fault rather than a crime and should have kept Saint-Just humble in later years and from attacking the character of others.

Bégis asserts that Saint-Just was profoundly humiliated by this imprisonment and that he avenged himself cruelly on all concerned. There is no proof of this. De Crosne was indeed arrested and executed under the Terror, but the head of the police was too conspicuous an official to escape. D'Evry too was arrested, 5 Ventôse, year II. After 9 Thermidor he addressed a petition for his release to the Committee of General Security, in which he refers to "the hatred vowed him by the rascal Saint-Just for having exposed to the eyes of the Lieutenant of Police at that time, his atrocious conduct to his mother, whom he had maltreated by his language, by his threats, and had finished by carrying off her most precious possessions." To this hatred he attributed his detention. The petition being without result, he wrote another to the president of the Convention, 22 Thermidor, detailing once more the escapade of "Saint-Just, aussi mauvais fils que mauvais citoyen" and repeating, "the hatred which Saint-Just had vowed for me makes me regard him as the author of my arrest." But it must be remembered that there was no surer road to safety after 9 Thermidor than by blackening the memories of the Robespierre group and representing oneself as their victim and enemy. D'Evry may have really believed this to be true in his own case or to save his neck he may have raked up the old tale. Of course the Committee, made up of Saint-Just's enemies, swallowed it greedily. There is no independent proof that Saint-Just held a grudge against D'Evry when the latter was imprisoned.

APPENDIX 2

SAINT-JUST'S SHARE IN THE CONSTITUTION

Hamel gives a list of ten points in respect to which he finds Saint-Just's handiwork in the constitution. All but one of these break down under examination. The relevant texts for this comparison are the Condorcet plan of February 15, 1793 (*Arch. parl.*, LVIII, 601, 602), the Declaration of Rights proposed by Robespierre, April 24, 1793 (*ibid.*, LXIII, 197-200), the Saint-Just plan of the same date (*ibid.*, LXIII, 204-5), the Mountain committee's report, which we shall designate as the Hérault Séchelles draft, of June 10 (*ibid.*, LXVI, 259, 260) and the revised Declaration of Rights, reported by Hérault, June 24 (*ibid.*, LXVII, 106, 107).

Hamel's ten points are the invocation of the Supreme Being, the right of insurrection, fraternity, Article I (textually the same as Saint-Just's Article II), the fact that neither the constitution nor Saint-Just's project require popular sanction for ordinary decrees, the Executive Council of twenty-four, justice by arbitrators, liberty of religious cults, guarantees of morality and property, the chapter on foreign relations.

The first three points and in part the eighth and ninth refer to the Declaration of Rights. By way of preliminary it may be said that the thirty articles of Hérault's project are essentially similar to Condorcet's thirty-three, which they resemble far more than Robespierre's thirty-eight or Saint-Just's five. The Mountain Declaration was without doubt based on the Girondin. The Supreme Being is mentioned in none of the drafts but Robespierre's, who would have the Declaration proclaimed "in the face of the universe and under the eyes of the Immortal Legislator." The final revision, called for by the Convention and presented by Hérault June 24, contains a preamble with the phrase: "In consequence, it proclaims in the presence of the Supreme Being the following declaration of the rights of man and the citizen." This insertion may show Robespierre's influence, but there is no reason to ascribe it to Saint-Just.

SAINT-JUST AND THE CONSTITUTION

The right of insurrection laid down in Hérault's Article 29 as "the holiest of duties" when legal means of resisting oppression fail is not found in Condorcet (though his Article 32 provides that the method of resistance to acts of oppression must be regulated by the constitution); it is apparently taken from Robespierre's Article 29, where it is likewise designated "the holiest of rights and the most indispensable of duties." The parallel is even closer in Article 35 of the final revision. It does not appear in the Saint-Just plan.

Fraternity as such is not found in any of the drafts except as fraternity between peoples in Robespierre's Articles 35-38, which begin "The men of all lands are brothers."

Any reference to one or another of these points in the *Fragments* is, as has been stated, beside the mark.

Hérault's Article I of the constitution proper is indeed textually the same as Saint-Just's Article II. It is, however, also identical with Condorcet's Article I, from which it is obviously taken. The unity and indivisibility of the French Republic was an axiom of French political theory.

The distinction between laws and decrees is similar in Hérault (Chap. X) and in Condorcet (Title VII, Sect. II). The referendum provided by Hérault's draft (Chap. XI) relates to laws only; in Condorcet's (Title VIII) it seems at first sight to be on either laws or decrees. The indiscriminate use of these expressions is apparently a case of loose terminology, for Condorcet seems to restrict use of the referendum to constitutional and general legislation, that is, to laws rather than to decrees. Saint-Just, though he does not make this distinction in terminology, does so in principle; for him "incidental acts of legislation" do not require sanction by the people (Chap. XIV, Article 1); in his provisions for a referendum, he uses the terms decree (Chap. XIV, Articles 3, 4, 8) and law (Articles 5, 15) synonymously. The plan of Hérault is thus no nearer that of Saint-Just than that of Condorcet. Hamel is wrong in saying that Saint-Just distinguishes laws from decrees. It might be added that Condorcet requires the action of only one department to force reconsideration by the Assembly and of two for a referendum, while Hérault demands the initiative of a tenth of the primary assemblies in one-half of the departments plus one, and Saint-Just that of a majority of the communes in the nation. Obviously the two latter are much more conservative, Saint-Just most of all. The Mountain, desiring to increase the power of the Assembly, had no real interest in the referendum. While it is likely that he had a share in laying down the principles followed by the Hérault project here, the use of the department as a basis of computation is contrary to Saint-Just's policy of minimizing the importance of that unit, and the two plans are too unlike to suggest direct borrowing.

The Executive Council called for by Hérault's draft (Chap. XIII) is made up of twenty-four members, elected by the National Assembly from nominations made by the department electoral assemblies. Saint-Just's Council consists of a member for each department, elected directly by the departmental assembly (Chaps. VIII, IX). Hamel's point of comparison is accordingly false, though there is important influence here, as shown on p. 69 above. Condorcet's plan (Title V) is totally different.

The use of arbitrators in civil justice is provided for in Hérault's Chap. XVII, Articles 5, 6, as well as by Saint-Just (Part II, Chap. I). But the language of two sections inserted in the final revision (Articles 86, 87) is so similar to Condorcet's Title X, Sect. II, Article 1 as to leave no doubt of the parentage.

There is no direct reference to cults in Hérault's project. The nearest approach to it is Article 6 of the Declaration of Rights, providing that "every man is free to manifest his thought and opinions." This is identical with Condorcet's Article 4, which is followed by an Article 6, reading "every citizen is free in the exercise of his cult." The final statement of the matter in the revised Declaration of Rights reads in part: "The right to express one's thoughts and opinions, . . . the free pursuit of religion cannot be forbidden" (Article 7). The "free exercise of worship" was also inserted in the Guaranty of Rights at the end of the constitution (Article 122). There is a whole history behind these clauses. Aulard believes Danton responsible for their ultimate inclusion (*Histoire politique,* p. 304). In any case, it was not Saint-Just so far as we know; his draft is silent in this respect.

As for guarantees of property, while found in Hérault (Articles 1, 17-20, which are identical with Condorcet's Articles 1, 18-21) as well as in the completed constitution (Articles 2, 16-19, 122), the subject is not mentioned by Saint-Just. His references to morality have no analogue in Hérault.

The section on foreign relations is quite a different story.

Hérault's Chap. XXV (reproduced as Articles 118-21 in the final document) derives clearly from Saint-Just's Chap. IX. Condorcet's cumbrous Title XIII differs totally.

Thus of Hamel's ten points, only the last is unqualifiedly correct.

APPENDIX 3
CLASSIFICATION OF THE COMMITTEE'S DECREES

These decrees, unclassified except chronologically, are to be found in Vellay's edition of the *Œuvres*, Vol. II, and scattered through Aulard's *Recueil*. The former contains one decree (August 16, 1793) and five letters (August 16, 17 [2], 24, October 1) not in the *Recueil*, besides a decree (March 3) which in the *Recueil* is signed by Carnot alone and a letter (March 20) of which the *Recueil* gives only a brief analysis. On the other hand, Vellay lacks nineteen decrees (August 5, February 3, 15 [2], 18, 25, 27 [3], March 4, 6, 27, April 1 [2], 16 [2], July 14, 21, 24, 1794) mentioned in the *Recueil*, besides a letter of February 3; Saint-Just could not have signed the decree or letter of that date, since he was at Maubeuge. Of these decrees, only two are given in full; the remainder are brief analyses. The two in full are the decree of August 5, relative to military preparations at Perpignan and that of July 24, sending citizen Frerson after counterfeiters of *assignats*. The latter, signed by Saint-Just only, is curiously paralleled by another decree of the same date, signed by other Committee members, designating citizen Frerson for quite different duties.

The distribution of decrees and letters by date and subject matter is as follows:

1793	Police	Military	Appropriations	Subsistence	Correspondence	Miscellaneous	Total
July	2	0	0	0	0	0	2
Aug.	4	9	1	7	5	1	27
Sept.	3	3	0	1	2	0	9
Oct.	3	9	3	1	4	3	23
Nov.	0	0	0	0	0	0	0
Dec.	0	0	0	0	0	0	0
1794							
Jan.	3	8	0	5	3	9	28
Feb.	10	23	8	4	4	13	62
March	24	21	3	6	2	11	67
April	10	15	5	6	0	19	55
May	0	1	0	0	0	0	1
June	5	6	1	0	1	3	16
July	68	11	9	0	1	15	104
Total	132	106	30	30	22	74	394

APPENDIX 4

THE SAVERNE LETTER OF FIRST BRUMAIRE

Saverne 1 Jour

L'ennemi est à *Bouxviller*; Il a 8000 hommes depuis là jusqu'à *Uttwiller* Il a un gros d'armée à *Reishoffen* où est l'un de ses quartiers generaux. Le general de brigade Sautter qui comande [commande] ici a mis un bataillon dans le poste avantageux de *Lichtemberg* autant à la *petite pierre*. Il y a 5 ou 6 bataillons depuis la *petite pierre* jusqu'à *Saverne*. Ce poste plein de gorges est une autre cote de Biesme [?], mais malgardée comme vous le verrez vu les forces de l'ennemi à *Bouxviller* et à *Reishoffen*. Il vous faut douze bataillons ici. Nous avons ordonné aux authorités du haut et bas Rhin et de la Meurthe de remplir sous 15me les cadres de cette division. Mais hates partout la fabrication des armes et des poudres.

L'ennemi a interet d'ocuper [d'occuper] les gorges de Saverne et Phalsbourg afin de serrer le gros de l'armée qui est actuellement sous les murs de Strasbourg à Schiltigeim.

Il y a eu vendredi une affaire à *Brumpt* ou l'on a très du monde à l'ennemi, mais comme tous les avantages sont dus au soldat et qu'aucûn chef n'est en etat d'en profitter on a reculé encore.

L'ennemi occupe Wissembourg, Lautherbourg, Hagueneau; il vient à une lieue de Saverne. Nous vous avons donné ce detail pour que vous voyez de vous même la situation des affaires.

Nous partons pour Strasbourg. Le plus pressant besoin de l'armée est un chef hardi et qui sache enflammer les troupes. Nous nous informerons de tous ceux qui sont sur la liste de Bouchotte. Des armes, des armes! Envoyez nous en de Caen; faittes desarmer les villes dangereuses. Adieu.

    Le Bas.   St. Juste.

No attempt has been made to reproduce above all of the letter's eccentricities in capitalizing and punctuation. These are obviously due to Saint-Just who held the pen as the handwriting shows; how completely he dominated the mission slips out unconsciously in a phrase which he managed to catch and change before the letter was sent ("je vous ai" corrected to "nous vous avons" in the paragraph before the last). The final sentence is an allusion to the Girondin insurrection, of which Caen was one of the centers. Some of the posts referred to may be identified with Buchsweiler, Ottweiler, Reichshofen, Lichtenberg, Pfalzburg; Brumpt is perhaps Brumath (Brumach). There seems to be no place in the region bear-

357

ing the name Biesme. "Une autre cote de Biesme" may perhaps mean "another hill of Biesme," as we should say "another pass of Thermopylae," referring to a well-known stronghold in some other sector. No such stronghold is known, but the name Biesmes occurs in connection with a river of northern France which traverses the forest of the Argonne and may well have been strongly fortified.

The letter, which has never been published and is here reproduced in facsimile is in the Bibliothèque Nationale, Dépt. des Manuscrits, Nouvelles Acquisitions Françaises, no. 312. An analysis of it exists in Arch. Nat. AF ᴵᴵ 247, pl. 2110, no. 20. This is reproduced, though inaccurately, in Aulard, *Recueil,* VII, 594. Where the manuscript analysis reads "Wissembourg, Lauterbourg et Haguenau," Aulard's transcript has "Haguenau, Wissembourg et Lauterbourg;" where the analysis reads "demande," he prints "Ils demandent;" for "joint," he has "Ils joignent." This sort of thing is unfortunately characteristic of the *Recueil.* It is singular also that the brigadier general's name, which is clearly Sautter in the MS. of the complete letter and proved to be such by other records, is spelled Saulter not only in the Arch. Nat. analysis, but also in the list of generals of the Army of the Rhine found in the *Almanach national* for the year II. Cf. the analysis in *Œuvres,* II, 128 n. Neither Aulard nor Vellay know of the existence of the complete letter.

NOTES

1. Though Louis Jean took the surname "de Saint-Just de Richebourg," it has been proved by the genealogist de Chabre that the family was not noble. For a discussion of this point and an account of the family ancestry, see Dommanget, "La Famille de Saint-Just," *Annales révolutionnaires*, VI, 518; anon., "Notes et glanes," *Ann. rév.*, VI, 411-13.
2. The baptismal record of her son gives her name as Jeanne-Marie. Everywhere else she is called Marie-Anne (e.g., Dommanget, *Ann. rév.*, VI, 519; "Notes et glanes," p. 412; Fleury, *Études révolutionnaires; Saint-Just et la Terreur*, I, 13, by whom, however, her surname is erroneously stated to be Robinet; Patoux, *Saint-Just et Madame Thorin*, p. 9).
3. Fleury (I, 13) and Sainte-Beuve following him (*Causeries de lundi*, V, 335) wrongly date the birth in 1769.
4. His mother speaks of him in 1809 as "Louis de Saint-Just, mon fils." Vellay, "Une Lettre de la mère de Saint-Just," *Ann. rév.*, I, 116.
5. Patoux, p. 11; Suin, "Travail sur les archives de Blérancourt," *Bulletin de la société . . . historique . . . de Soissons*, 1852, p. 186; Vellay, "Les Premières luttes politiques de Saint-Just," *Revue de Paris*, Oct. 15, 1906, p. 819. Fleury with his 1770 or 1771 and Hamel with his 1773 for the date of removal to Blérancourt are both wrong.
6. Dommanget, p. 520; Vellay, "Premières Luttes," p. 821.
7. Fleury, I, 17-21.
8. Vellay, "Premières Luttes," p. 822.
9. In 1793 it had less than a thousand inhabitants (Mühlenbeck, *Euloge Schneider, 1793*, p. 194). Two centuries ago the Duke of Gesvres and his duchess founded a hospice for orphans there and in 1700 the village was the birthplace of Lecat, the greatest surgeon of the eighteenth century (Suin, p. 186).
10. Vellay, "Premières Luttes," pp. 819-20.
11. The Chevalier Armand Jérome Joseph Brunet d'Evry was an officer in the Gardes françaises, proprietor of an important domain at Nampcel and a sort of patron of the family. This relation between the owners of Evry and the Saint-Justs had existed for three generations.
12. The whole cycle of letters is printed from the police archives by Bégis in *Curiosités révolutionnaires. Saint-Just, . . . son emprisonnement sous Louis XVI en exécution d'une lettre de cachet*. See Appendix I.
13. Laurent, "Les Relations de Saint-Just à Reims," *Ann. rév.*, 1923, no. 1, p. 29; *ibid.*, "La Faculté de droit de Reims et les hommes de la Révolution," *Annales historiques de la Révolution française*, July-Aug., 1929, pp. 350-51.
14. Fleury states (I, 22) that the list of complaints was so long that the boy was sent by his mother to the "couvent des Picpus de Vailly" on the banks of the Aisne. But this is an obvious doublet of the Picpus prison in Paris of which Fleury was ignorant. The register of the Vailly house lacks Saint-Just's name and the only source of the statement is current rumor. Besides, Saint-Just was otherwise occupied in 1790.
15. Patoux, p. 15.
16. Fleury, I, 27; II, 6; Patoux, p. 17.

17. Vellay, ed., *Œuvres complètes de Saint-Just*, II, 62.
18. Patoux, p. 22.
19. Fleury, I, 150; II, 280.
20. Patoux, p. 25.
21. Vellay, "Premières Luttes," p. 823.
22. Vellay, *Ann. rév.*, I, 362. The publisher was Demonville (Vellay, "Lettres inédites de Saint-Just," *Revue historique de la Révolution française*, Oct.-Dec., 1910).
23. Cf. the notice of the poem in Grimm's *Literary Correspondence* for June, 1789, cited in Claretie, *Camille Desmoulins and His Wife*, p. 257 n., "*Organt* (first attributed to M. de la Dixmerie, the friend of the famous Chevalier d'Arc, the author of *Lutin*, of the *Sibylle gauloise*, of *Toni et Clairette*) seems to be the work of a young man who has read *La Pucelle* too much and not enough; too much, for every moment we find reminiscences or awkward imitations of the French Ariosto; not enough, because he rarely catches his wit, his elegance, or his genius."
24. Fleury, I, 26; Sainte-Beuve, V, 337, 338; Cuvillier-Fleury, *Portraits politiques et révolutionnaires*, II, 285; Barante, *Histoire de la Convention nationale*, II, 91; Taine, *La Révolution*, I, 303. Contrast Hamel, *Saint-Just*, p. 24.
25. Vellay's idea that the poem is a capital document for the history of the invasion of communal lands by the *seigneurs* seems far-fetched (*Ann. rév.*, I, 506).
26.   "Sa face lourde, et faite pour l'égide,
        S'enluminait d'un gros rire stupide. . . .
        Notre Empereur, courant sur sa chimère,
        Ouvre les yeux et dit: Que faut-il faire? . . .
        Une *Sottise* à ses regards aimable,
        Mais en effet furie épouvantable;
        Un fiel amer de ses lèvres coulait;
        Son œil rempli d'une candeur farouche,
        De l'Empereur la faiblesse irritait.
        En rougissant, elle trame un forfait."
27. Barère, IV, 406 (Barère is wrong about the date, length and subject of the poem); Vellay, "Les Poursuites contre *Organt*," *Revue bleue*, Aug. 10, 1907.
28. Vellay, ed., "Arlequin Diogène," *Revue bleue*, July 27, 1907. Here the playlet is printed in full. Vellay did not discover a mediocre "Épigramme sur le comédien Dubois qui a joué dans Pierre le Cruel"; Saint-Just's autograph original still exists. *Ann. hist. de la Rév. fr.*, May-June, 1934, 260.
29. Hamel, *Saint-Just*, p. 43. This could hardly have been the occasion of the flight mentioned by Barère as the announcement of the poem would necessarily precede its prosecution. Sainte-Beuve asserts that he came often to Paris, meeting Desmoulins and other revolutionary youths (*Causeries*, V, 339).
30. Suin, p. 193. This study is one of the chief sources for the present chapter. Suin found the register of the municipality of Blérancourt a mine of information concerning the early political life of Saint-Just. Fleury was unable to use these archives, which were being put in order; he was told by the mayor that they contained nothing on Saint-Just and had to limit himself to oral tradition (Suin, p. 195 n.). The other authority is Vellay's article, "Saint-Just en 1790," *Revue hist. de la Rév. fr.*, April-June, 1911. This is not based on Suin's work, of which Vellay seems to be ignorant; he does

NOTES

not refer to it here nor in his bibliography of Saint-Just, published in the same journal, July-Sept., Oct.-Dec., 1910. Beside the register, the principal sources are Saint-Just's letters and other documents, published in Vellay's edition of the *Œuvres complètes de Saint-Just,* hereafter cited as *Œuvres.* When not otherwise indicated, the text of Saint-Just's speeches and other writings used in this book is that of the *Œuvres.*

31. Fleury states (I, 103) that the letter is dated May, 1790. No date appears in the *Œuvres,* I, 220.

32. Thérèse's father?

33. The Comte de Lauraguais was an opponent of Saint-Just's election (Fleury, I, 103). Fleury feels that Saint-Just's action had sinister significance in view of the future; Hamel regards it as a just rebuke to the pride of the nobility. In fact it was merely a display of adolescent bravado. The young villager, in high spirits at his recently manifested importance, invades the count's flower-beds and is a little aghast at his own temerity.

34. The letter was addressed originally to "Monsieur Decaisne, royal notary at Blérancourt." This was no doubt his brother-in-law, for his sister Louise married Emmanuel Decaisne, "notaire-royal au bailliage de Coucy-le-Château," resident at Blérancourt (Dommanget, p. 520; Vellay, ed., "Lettres inédites," p. 3). On second thought, Saint-Just apparently decided to leave the family out of it and sent his orders to Thuillier instead. Because or in spite of his letter, Saint-Just was made president of the electoral assembly in October.

35. *Adresse de la communauté de Blérancourt, près Noyon* (Paris, 1790; *Moniteur,* May 20; Hamel, *Saint-Just,* pp. 64, 65; Suin, pp. 193, 194. The decree of April 13 is wrongly dated April 16 in *Arch. parl.,* XV, 577. Both Hamel and Suin used the municipal register. The decree of April 13 was that proposed by La Rochefoucauld (*Arch. parl.,* XII, 716).

36. Fleury, I, 107. Fleury thought there must be some mistake about the mayor's remarks in view of the family's recent arrival in the region. The biographer did not know the family history adequately nor was he familiar with the municipal archives (Patoux, p. 12).

37. This letter, as Vellay observes (*Œuvres,* I, 224) was found among Robespierre's papers after 9 Thermidor and published for the first time in the report of Courtois. The address sent by the same mail has disappeared. Blérancourt had a sheep market on the first Wednesday of every month, which commonly assembled from 20,000 to 30,000 head of sheep. It was thus an important economic interest. Whether due to Saint-Just's intervention or not, the market was not transferred to Coucy (Vellay, "Saint-Just en 1790," p. 386). It is not known whether his personal offer was accepted (Hamel, *Saint-Just,* p. 68), but it probably was not. It remains none the less generous.

38. Suin, p. 196; Vellay, "Saint-Just en 1790," p. 382; Suin had been unable to find the record of Saint-Just's election.

39. "Saint-Just en 1790," p. 383. Vellay surmises that similar relations were entered into with other communes and that as Saint-Just is later given the title, *commandant d'honneur des gardes nationales du canton,* he may have taken part in the formation of most or all of them. So far no record of this has been found. Whether it was adroit self-advancement or zeal for the public good or both, it resulted in his ever-widening local importance.

40. Suin, p. 198.

NOTES

41. Suin, pp. 199-201. Suin suspects that Saint-Just wrote Decaisne's speech, which is in poetic style and dwells at length on the bust of Mirabeau.
42. Again Gellé, the perpetual enemy. At least they were on formal speaking terms. Vellay (*Œuvres*, I, 225) motivates the choice of Saint-Just on his title of *licencié ès lois*. The documents in the case show shrewd sense and knowledge of the law. Cf. Vellay, "Saint-Just en 1790," pp. 386-88; Suin, p. 199.
43. It was for a time wrongly attributed to one Louis Léon de Saint-Juste, marquis de Fontevieille, the confusion arising from the fact that Saint-Just's baptismal name Louis Antoine was disliked in the family and Louis Léon substituted. Fleury, I, p. 109; Hamel, *Saint-Just*, p. 70.
44. Cf. in Part 5 his criticism of the idea that the popular will is always right. "As a general rule every will, even the sovereign, inclined toward perversity, is null; Rousseau did not say everything when he characterized the will as incommunicable, imprescriptible, eternal. It must also be just and reasonable. It is no less criminal for the sovereign to be tyrannized over by itself than by others." This would be dangerous doctrine in the coming days of Terror when public safety was the supreme law.
45. According to Barère (IV, 407), the volume was well received by the enlightened members of the Assembly and the edition exhausted in a few days.
46. Vellay, ed., "Lettres inédites de Saint-Just."
47. Fleury, I, 144-46.
48. Vellay, ed., "La Correspondance de Saint-Just," *Mercure de France*, LX, 60.
49. *Œuvres*, I, 346, 347; Hamel, *Saint-Just*, pp. 54-56. Adrien Bayard was Hamel's grandfather. Unfortunately the numerous letters written to Bayard by Saint-Just and preserved in the Hamel family were lost in a fire a few years before Hamel wrote his biography.
50. Vellay, ed., "Correspondance," p. 60.
51. Fleury, I, 150, 151. Lamartine (*Histoire des Girondins*, III, 94, 95) gives a vivid account of an interview between Robespierre and Saint-Just on the night when the September massacres began. They returned to Saint-Just's lodgings that evening (Sept. 2) wearied with preparations for the massacre. Saint-Just, the more callous, went to bed and slept while Robespierre paced the floor all night. Unfortunately for the truth of this gruesome tale, Saint-Just was then at Soissons. A few days after his election, he presided over a meeting of volunteers for the army. The altar of the fatherland was erected in the cathedral of Soissons; Saint-Just spoke a few words, greeted by great enthusiasm according to a contemporary record (Fleury, I, 157).
52. *Œuvres*, I, 351.
53. Vellay, ed., "Correspondance," pp. 60, 61. After this date the personal correspondence becomes very rare; public affairs absorbed all his energy (*ibid.*, p. 63).
54. Fleury, I, 152-57; *Œuvres*, II, 403.
55. Laurent, *Ann. hist. de la Rév. fr.*, I, 379. Laurent disproves the claim of one Hentz to this distinction.
56. List of addresses of members of Convention in *Almanach national*, year II, 101.
57. So he is remembered by Paganel, a contemporary; Nodier, also a contemporary, says his eyes were large and thoughtful.
58. Desmoulins, *Letter to Dillon*, cited by Fleury, I, 308, and by Matton in his

sketch of Desmoulins prefaced to the latter's *Œuvres* (1838 ed.). Hamel thinks this is too witty to be true *(Saint-Just,* p. 274).

59. On this matter of Saint-Just's appearance and dress, cf. P. P., *Revue hist. de la Rév. fr.,* IV, 328 (citing M. P. Paganel's *Essai historique et critique sur la Révolution française,* Paris, 1810); Fleury, I, 308, 309; Hamel, *Saint-Just,* pp. 43, 277, 278. The recollections of Nodier will be referred to more fully in Chap. XVII. Other pastels were made of Saint-Just. One hanging in the Musée Carnavalet, represents him with small, round, gold earrings. There is also a famous medallion by David d'Angers, reproduced on the cover of Vellay's edition of Saint-Just's *Œuvres* and facing p. 324 of this book. David likewise made a marble bust and he was perhaps painted by Prud'hon (Laurent, "Un Portrait de Saint-Just," *Revue hist. de la Rév. fr.,* XV, 176). Prud'hon's alleged portrait is reproduced in Maurice, B., and others, *Le Livre rouge,* p. 255. It bears the artist's signature and the date 1793. The face of Saint-Just is strikingly stern and mature.

60. Fleury's account of his early participation in nightly meetings at Robespierre's and his share in the abolition of monarchy are unfounded (Fleury, I, 158-62; Hamel, *Saint-Just,* p. 105). Cf. *Œuvres,* I, 352.

61. For the debate in the Convention, see *Arch. parl.,* LII. For Saint-Just's speech, *Œuvres,* I, 353-61.

62. Vellay notes that the curious spelling indicates that the name was still unfamiliar *(Œuvres,* I, 353). Aulard points out that it seems to show that the last two letters of the name were not pronounced *(Société des Jacobins,* IV, 417 n.).

63. The Sunday after (Oct. 28) Robespierre made an anti-Girondin address. Some wag proposed that Roland, the Girondin minister, be asked for a grant from the government fund for patriotic publications to circularize it and Saint-Just was laughingly appointed on a committee to wait on the minister for this purpose (Aulard, *Société des Jacobins,* IV, 438). Subsequent references to Saint-Just at the Jacobins may be found in this work under the appropriate date.

64. *Œuvres,* I, 365-72; *Arch. parl.,* LIII, 390-92. The speech is also obtainable in the *Moniteur* for Nov. 14, whose account is defective, omitting clauses, sentences and even paragraphs. The two first mentioned versions are identical. *Arch. parl.* cites as its authority the printed copy in the "Bibliothèque de la Chambre des Députés; Collection Portiez (de l'Oise), tome 27, no. 7." This collection is its source for most of Saint-Just's speeches; hence the version in *Arch. parl.* is commonly far more trustworthy than that in the *Moniteur,* which is often only an abridgment or paraphrase, not taken from the printed speech.

65. *Œuvres,* I, 364. Even Brissot's *Le Patriote* praised the speech. Here, despite youthful exaggerations, were luminous details, foreshadowing "a talent, which may bring France honor" (Hamel, *Saint-Just,* pp. 117, 118). Barère, his future colleague on the great Committee, spoke of it as a speech remarkable for its energetic conciseness *(Mémoires,* IV, 407).

66. *Arch. parl.,* LIII, 73-78. Beside the dozen or so speeches reported in Vol. LIII, Vol. LIV contains a hundred others on the subject, printed but not delivered.

67. The course of the trial, Dec. 11-27, inclusive, is to be found in *Arch. parl.,* LV.

68. To be found in *Arch. parl.,* LVI; the subsequent votes are in Vol. LVII. During this week (Jan. 1, 1793), Saint-Just, presiding over the Jacobins,

NOTES

called attention to Robespierre's speech of Dec. 28, reminding them that the secretariat would receive subscriptions toward printing the argument. He was a thorough party man.

69. See *Arch. parl.*, LIII, LIV under the appropriate dates.

70. Vellay states that on this day a deputation from the General Council of the Commune appeared at the Convention and set forth the miserable plight of the people in consequence of food monopolists; it demanded that the proper authorities be given the right to tax articles of prime necessity. This furnished the occasion for Saint-Just's speech (*Œuvres*, I, 373). Mathiez makes the Commune demand a fixed tariff of prices (*Rév. fr.*, II, 147). No deputation is mentioned in *Arch. parl.* nor in the *Moniteur*, where Saint-Just's speech appears in the general debate on the projected decree of Nov. 3.

71. Saint-Just refers to paper money as *le signe*.

72. One of them (Serre) who spoke Dec. 2, said he was going to oppose the views of every previous speaker except Lequinio and Saint-Just. Another, Creuzé-Latouche, who on Dec. 8 finally swung the Convention to the side of freedom, referred twice to Saint-Just's clear-sightedness in questions of finance and prices. Cf. Brissot's *Le Patriote*, Nov. 30, which said that "Saint-Just treats the question fundamentally and in all its political and moral aspects; he displays cleverness, warmth and philosophy, and honors his talent by defending free trade" (Hamel, *Saint-Just*, p. 133). Mathiez believes that of all the speakers, Saint-Just penetrated most deeply into the causes of the economic crisis and that the speech of Nov. 29 established at once his reputation as a statesman (*La Vie chère et le mouvement social sous la Terreur*, p. 107). On the respective attitudes of the two parties, see Mathiez, "Girondins et Montagnards" in the book similarly entitled.

73. *Arch. parl.*, VIII, 453, 456, 463, 475-80.

74. Saint-Just's speech is cited here as usual from the version in the *Œuvres*, ordinarily the most correct and coinciding with that in *Arch. parl.* However in this case *Arch. parl.* (LVIII, 480) inserts a passage lacking in the *Œuvres*, which throws considerable light on the situation. After "disadvantageously," Saint-Just continues, "This writing had for title: 'Republican petition of the 48 sections of Paris, for the food supply.' Among other passages one read this: 'When the people know that in the popular assemblies, the orators who harangue and pour forth the finest speeches and the best advice sup well every day' and further along: 'Of this number is the citizen Saint-Just, lift high the odious mask with which he covers himself.' Seeing this, I was in the *Salle des conférences*," etc., as in the *Œuvres*. Cf. Kerr, *Reign of Terror*, p. 41, citing Jaurès, *Convention*, p. 1022, where this passage is referred to as appearing on placards distributed by the delegates of the sections.

75. Fleury's account of this affair is inaccurate and absurd. He attempts to show that it was a sort of insurrection, instigated by Saint-Just (I, 254-58). He is refuted at every point by Hamel (*Saint-Just*, pp. 147-52).

76. *Arch. parl.*, LXX, 589, 590. Vellay has overlooked this report in his edition of the *Œuvres*.

77. On the maximum, see Mathiez, *La Vie chère et le mouvement social sous la Terreur* and the illuminating review of this book by Lefebvre in *Annales d'histoire économique et sociale*, I, 141-45.

78. Kerr, p. 339.

79. It has been shown by Six in the *Revue d'histoire moderne*, Jan.-Feb., 1929,

that the decree of 1781 applied only to those directly entering the army as captains or colonels by purchase, while it was still possible for a private to work up through the ranks to a commission. The middle class were therefore more offended by the regulation than the peasants. On the general subject of military administration, cf. Chuquet, *Guerres de la Révolution*, I, 24-89; Phipps, *Armies of the First French Republic;* Wilkinson, *The French Army before Napoleon.*

80. This had already been attempted on a small scale by Custine, Kellermann, Lafayette and other generals, but had never been made a matter of general regulation; cf. Chuquet, I, 76. The report of Dubois-Crancé (who divides with Carnot the credit for creating the victorious Revolutionary army) is in *Arch. parl.*, LVIII, 358-69. For the ensuing debate, see pp. 451-63, 484, 485, 631.

81. *Œuvres*, I, 412-16. The date of his speech is here erroneously given as the twelfth. In the version of *Arch. parl.* (LVIII, 457, 458) there are a few verbal differences and an additional paragraph.

82. Mathiez, *Révolution française*, II, 182.

83. *Œuvres*, II, 32-45. It was first published in Barère's *Mémoires* (IV, 406 ff.). At the end of the manuscript was a note reading, "No member of the society may fill a public office except by election of the people." Barère conjectures that Saint-Just meant to secure the passage of a decree in this sense, delivering him from the importunities of place hunters among the Jacobins.

84. Aulard, *Histoire politique de la Révolution française,* pp. 280-82; Aulard, *Jacobins,* V, 32.

85. Stern, Alfred, "Condorcet und der girondistische Verfassungsentwurf von 1793," *Historische Zeitschrift,* CXLI, 3.

86. *Moniteur,* VIII, 625; this version is obviously more accurate and complete than that in *Arch. parl.*, LXV, 191, 192.

87. *Arch. parl.*, LXV, 580, 610; Aulard, *Recueil des actes du comité de salut public,* IV, 381 (hereafter referred to as Aulard, *Recueil*). See on this whole subject, Mathiez, "La Constitution de 1793," *Ann. hist. de la Rév. fr.,* V, 497-521; also in *Girondins et Montagnards.*

88. Aulard, *Histoire politique,* p. 297.

89. Aulard, *Recueil,* IV, 492, 498; *Arch. parl.*, LXVI, 257-64. Barère's account of his prominence in this work (*Mémoires,* II, 109) is sheer moonshine; he was not even a member of the committee nor did he make the report as he states on Aug. 15 or any other date. This is an excellent example of the untrustworthiness of memoirs.

90. To call Saint-Just the soul of the constitution, which is animated by his inspiration throughout, is an exaggeration; Hamel, *Saint-Just,* pp. 170, 210, 212-18. Even Fleury credits Saint-Just with a large share in the result and believes that Robespierre in his Declaration of Rights plagiarized the ideas expressed by Saint-Just in his *Fragments sur les institutions républicaines* (Fleury, I, 195, 260-65). But the *Fragments* were probably composed after the spring of 1793 and were not published until years later. See Appendix II.

91. Aulard, *Histoire politique,* p. 308. It is not surprising that Condorcet and the proscribed Girondin deputies thought poorly of the work. Beside the sharp criticism expressed by Condorcet in his essay "Aux citoyens français sur la nouvelle constitution" (Condorcet, *Œuvres,* XII, 653-75) there appeared for example an *Examen critique de la constitution,* the anonymous

work of the Girondin Salle, who, like Saint-Just, lodged in the Hôtel des États-Unis. He wrote also a bitter letter to "M. le chevalier de Saint-Just" from Caen, July 11, which Courtois found among the latter's papers after 9 Thermidor. In it he denounced "the little M. de Saint-Just" and his committee's "constitutional rhapsody," which he stigmatized as "the veritable constitution of the Parisian Empire, a perfidious hodge-podge, a crime of national lèse-sovereignty, which should be quickly punished" (Vatel, *Charlotte de Corday et les Girondins*, I, xcv, xcvi).

92. Cf. Mathiez, *Révolution française*, II, 2, 3; Kerr, p. 16; Nussbaum, *Commercial Policy in the French Revolution*.

93. The story is told on the strength of the *Mémoires de Garat*, cited by Hamel, *Saint-Just*, p. 220. It is true that the revolutionary committee made such an offer over the signatures of Langier, Loys and Dunouy, in a letter read to the Convention June 2. Barbaroux and Lanjuinais rejected the proposal. *Arch. parl.*, LXV, 708.

94. A later reference in the speech shows that Morande was meant, though Saint-Just is a little inaccurate. Morande was a notorious blackmailer, who had finally become editor of a monarchist paper and Brissot's bitter enemy. He escaped death in the September massacres and a story went the rounds that Brissot expressed regret at the oversight.

95. At this point, *Arch. parl.* cites from the *Mercure universel* of July 9 the following incident. Saint-Just did not have the complete list of deputies charged with treason. After mentioning three or four names, he used the expression "et coetera," which was greeted by vigorous "murmurs" from the Right. Saint-Just retorted that only those representatives who had taken flight were involved, whereupon a member of the Right shouted, "Refer the whole business to Marat."

96. Both statements are to be found in the *Mémoires de Brissot*.

97. Vatel, I, xcix-cviii.

98. Aulard, *Histoire politique*, p. 334.

99. Aulard, *Recueil*, IV, 568. For the remaining sessions of the first Committee, see Vols. IV, V at the appropriate dates.

100. Cf. Mathiez, "Le Premier comité de salut public et la guerre," *Revue historique*, July-Aug., 1928; Chuquet, XI, 15. For a more favorable verdict on the first Committee, see Bourne, "The Organization of the First Committee of Public Safety," *American Historical Association Annual Report*, 1894, pp. 247-72.

101. Aulard, *Jacobins*, V, 291-92.

102. Aulard, *Histoire politique*, p. 335.

103. Barère, I, 14.

104. *Ibid.*, II, 347 n.

105. A colorful but exaggerated picture of Barère ("courageous defender of the strongest"), of Billaud ("gloomy, silent, with hesitating and twitching glance, walking as though he were trying to keep under cover") and of the violent, quick-tempered Collot ("his spirit as changeable as his parts on the stage and in the tribune") is given by their contemporary, Vilate (*Continuation des causes secrètes de la révolution du 9 au 10 thermidor*, pp. 13, 14). For a more balanced estimate, cf. Kerr, pp. 206, 207.

106. Aulard, "Convention," *Grande encyclopédie*; Hamel, *Saint-Just*, p. 240.

107. Aulard, *Histoire politique*, p. 338 ff. The classification of functions is nearer the mark here than in the preceding reference. Since the *Histoire politique*

NOTES

appeared eleven years after the article previously cited, Aulard may have abandoned his first position.

108. Madelin, *French Revolution*, pp. 356, 357; Hamel, *Saint-Just*, p. 363.
109. Saint-Just, for example, signs decrees on Sept. 29, 30, 1793, Jan. 10, 11, 13, 14, 17, 1794, though listed as absent on all these occasions. He is marked present May 9, though he was then on mission to the Army of the North. Between Feb. 6 and 10 he is reported as present daily, yet signs none of the 95 decrees registered during that period; Robespierre, reported continually absent, signs decrees on each of these days.
110. Aulard, *Recueil*, XI, 290, 291; XIV, 608.
111. See Appendix III.
112. Those of Aug. 17[2], Sept. 17[2] and Feb. 24.
113. Neither Aulard nor Hamel have discovered this assignment. The *Recueil* prints a letter dated Feb. 3, containing instructions to national agents. There are nine signatures, including Saint-Just's; a postscript is signed by Billaud-Varenne and Barère as "the members charged with correspondence." This letter, in printed form, is in the Bibliothèque Nationale; the original has disappeared. At the time Saint-Just was on mission in the North; we have three decrees signed by him at Maubeuge that very day. It is quite clear that while the letter may be genuine, his signature must have been added by others for the sake of completeness. I have not included this among the twenty-two letters referred to.
114. Fleury's effort to pivot the Committee on Saint-Just alone and ascribe all its power to him, is going far beyond the evidence (I, 285).
115. *Arch. parl.*, LXXVI, 281, 285. A "movement of horror" swept over the Convention at the account of this atrocity. On Dec. 27 a member of the Committee announced that the representative was not dead at all and on Jan. 14 the supposedly defunct Beauvais, safe and sound, wrote a letter from Marseille to the Convention. But as usual, truth never caught up with the lie; the poisoning of public feeling with hate against a nation was done.
116. The whole of this affectionate and self-effacing letter is to be found in Buchez et Roux, *Histoire parlementaire*, XXXV, 318 (hereafter referred to as *Hist. parl.*). A considerable body of correspondence, chiefly addressed to his father and his wife and secured after Thermidor from the family, is contained in this volume, pp. 317-65. The letters cited in this chapter are to be sought there.
117. Letter to his father, Oct. 3, 1792.
118. For these assignments and speeches, see *Arch. parl.*, LII, LXVII, under following dates: Dec. 6, 1792, Jan. 6, 15, May 8, June 19, 26, 1793.
119. *Hist. parl.*, XXXV, 335.
120. *Ibid.*, XXXV, 341 n. The authorities for these details are presumably the widow and son of Le Bas with whom Buchez and Roux were in contact.
121. Mathiez is in error when he refers only to the first decree and speaks of Saint-André, Prieur and Le Bas as in conference with the generals of the Moselle and Rhine Armies at Bitche, Aug. 8 and 9. At that time Le Bas was in Cassel, northwest of Lille, as shown by his letters from that place, Aug. 6 and 9. Mathiez also speaks of Le Bas as member of the Committee of General Security at this time, though he was not elected until his return (*Arch. parl.*, LXX, 107, 133; *Hist. parl.*, XXXV, 339, 340 n., 341-43; Mathiez, *Révolution française*, III, 53).
122. The fluctuations in membership of this Committee are told by Aulard,

Histoire politique, pp. 327-29. Indirect reference to another committee assignment is given by the Convention's decree of Sept. 19 that Vinet and Monuel be chosen to the committee of six on the *émigrés* in place of Lebas [*sic*], whose name was often so spelled, and Lebon, who as members of the Committee of General Security, would be no longer able to carry out the duties for which they had been selected on Sept. 12 (*Arch. parl.*, LXXIV, 407, 408). There is no other reference to this appointment.

123. *Hist. parl.*, XXXV, 347 n.

124. Barère, IV, 409.

125. Hamel, *Saint-Just*, p. 284.

126. Hamel supposes (*Saint-Just*, p. 304) it was because Le Bas was designated for this mission at the express request of Saint-Just, who was thus responsible for the separation from Elisabeth.

127. *Ibid.*, p. 323.

128. *Hist. parl.*, XXXV, 354.

129. Fleury, II, 6, 10, 71; Hamel, *Saint-Just*, p. 285. Cf. *Hist. parl.*, XXXV, 358, where the two are said to have quarrelled over the most futile matter, Saint-Just taking it seriously as might a boy of twenty-four [*sic*]. Saint-Just visited his wrath on poor Le Bas, who suffered keenly from his coldness. It should be recalled that Hamel and also Buchez and Roux had their information from Mme. Le Bas.

130. *Hist. parl.*, XXXV, 362 n. Le Bas's son became tutor of the future Napoleon III from 1820 to 1827.

131. Hamel, *Saint-Just*, p. 285.

132. Aulard, *Histoire politique*, p. 344.

133. *Arch. parl.*, LX, 9, 25. Hamel makes no mention of this mission. Fleury (I, 259) was unable to discover whether Saint-Just was sent by the Convention or the Jacobin Club. He makes the singular error of describing it as a mission to Belgium (p. 258).

134. Aulard, *Jacobins*, V, 109.

135. *Œuvres*, I, 417. Vellay takes his report from the *Journal des débats et de la correspondance de la Société des Jacobins, April* 2. According to the account in Aulard, *Jacobins*, V, 117, this vigorous speech (here summarized in two lines) called forth no comment from the club, being perhaps overshadowed by the more exciting business of Danton's report on his dealings with Dumouriez, followed by a dramatic scene in which Marat, brandishing a dagger, demanded that Danton take with him the oath to die for liberty. It may be added that Beurnonville was replaced by Bouchotte, a member of the Mountain, April 4.

136. Aulard, *Recueil*, II, 591; III, 2, 31.

137. *Arch. parl.*, LX, 470; LXI, 114.

138. *Ibid.*, LXIV, 315, 337, 338. It will be remembered that Le Bas was also one of the ninety-six.

139. Aulard, *Recueil*, V, 290. This time Fleury passes the mission in silence; Hamel knows of it (*Saint-Just*, p. 241), but only that it was short. Vellay thinks that Saint-Just did not go at all, as the Committee's *procès-verbaux* continue to mention his presence during the succeeding days and as Collot d'Herbois, Isoré, Lequinio and Lejeune were sent to the Oise and the Aisne, Aug. 1. (*Œuvres*, II, 46). It is a fact that the register of the Committee mentions his attendance on July 19, 22, 23, 26, 27, 29, but this is not conclusive as the inaccuracy of this record has been already demonstrated. That he was in Paris by July 29 is certain; on this day he signed

for the first time a decree of the second Committee of Public Safety. This very fact suggests that he had been out of town, since he was elected to the Committee, July 10.

140. Aulard, *Recueil*, V, 345. Unless otherwise indicated the decrees, letters and other proceedings of the Committee of Public Safety as well as those of representatives other than Saint-Just are to be found in the *Recueil* under the appropriate dates. Those of Saint-Just when on mission are cited from the *Œuvres*. I have collated them with the original manuscripts, which are for the most part in the Archives Nationales, those relative to the Alsatian mission being in Arch. Nat., AF ɪɪ 135, pl. 1045; 247, pl. 2110, 2111; 249, pl. 2121, 2122; those issued during the missions to the North being in AF ɪɪ 85, pl. 625; 235, pl. 2017, 2018.

141. *Arch. parl.*, LXXVII, 29, 30. This version is from the Convention's *procès-verbal;* a variant account from the *Mercure universel* makes Barère say that "Saint-Just and another representative of the people have left with unlimited powers."

142. Michelet, *Histoire de la Révolution française*, VII, 16, 17; Carnot, H., *Mémoires sur Carnot*, I, 452. Wallon, *Représentants du peuple*, IV, chs. XXIX-XXXII gives a detailed, though unfriendly, account of this mission.

143. Reuss, *L'Alsace pendant la Révolution française*, II, 8, 372, 376, 378. Monet was originally allied with Schneider (Wallon, *op. cit.*, IV, 300) but went over later to Saint-Just.

144. Fleury, II, 15. There is no decree ordering this in the *Œuvres*. Hamel (*Saint-Just*, p. 299) holds that the number of those arrested has been exaggerated by enemies of the Revolution and that many were released by the committee of surveillance with approval of the representatives.

145. Chuquet, IX, 32, 33.

146. Cf. the conflicting views in Fleury, II, 30-32; Hamel, *Saint-Just*, pp. 305-10; Mühlenbeck, pp. 150-76.

147. Chuquet cites this letter and quotes from it the following: "You may be right about a few of them, but a great danger exists and we do not know where to strike; well, a blind man who hunts for a pin in a handful of dust, seizes the handful of dust" (*Guerres*, IX, 33). This sentence is not in the *Œuvres* and is not in tone with the rest of the letter. Fleury (II, 65) gives this legendary *mot* a different setting. Saint-Just was in bed when Monet came in with a request for clemency in behalf of certain persons under arrest; Saint-Just, raising himself on his elbow, eyed Monet coldly and uttered the classic reply.

148. Chuquet, XI, 43.

149. Wallon, *Représentants*, IV, 319-21, 323.

150. Nodier, *Souvenirs de la Révolution et de l'Empire*, I, 12. The most recent discussion of this man, together with a survey of previous accounts, is to be found in Jaquel, "Euloge Schneider et l'historiographie allemande," *Ann. hist. de la Rév. fr.*, Sept.-Oct., 1931, 399-417. His career (notably his editorship of the journal *Argos*) is further studied by Jaquel in "Euloge Schneider en Alsace," *ibid.*, Jan., April, July, 1932, Jan., 1933.

151. Hamel, *Saint-Just*, p. 329.

152. Fleury, II, 55. A number of cases are given here; e.g., a candy merchant is fined 100,000 livres and sentenced to the scaffold for four hours and to prison until the peace for having sold sugar candy beyond the proper price. Others may be found in Wallon, *Représentants*, IV, 340-47.

153. Nodier, I, 18. Nodier, being a romanticist rather than an historian, is not

always to be trusted even though he was an eyewitness of these events. He erroneously identifies Monet as a friend of Schneider and the Propagande as Schneider's supporters (I, 16). Fleury falls into the same error (II, 48, 51). For the correct view of their relations, see Hamel, *Saint-Just*, p. 324; Hamel, "Euloge Schneider," *Rév. fr.*, XXXIV, pt. 1, p. 429; Chuquet, IX, 34; Reuss, II, 378; Mühlenbeck, pp. 373-75.

154. Mühlenbeck, p. 186 n.
155. Fleury, II, 54.
156. Nodier, I, 26. Thirty years later, General Donzelot told Philippe Le Bas, the son, how much he had esteemed his father and Saint-Just when he was a young officer in Strasbourg. He would never forget, he said, the services they rendered, particularly their just punishment of Schneider, whom he could still see on the scaffold with the inscription over his head, "For having dishonored the Revolution" (Hamel, *Saint-Just*, p. 332).
157. Wallon, *Représentants*, IV, 348-53, 379.
158. Ording, *Bureau de police*, 140-46.
159. *Papiers inédits*, II, 259; *Œuvres*, II, 161.
160. Chuquet, IX, 34, citing the decree of Dec. 6, sect. III, art. 17, "every congress or central club established by the representatives of the people, under any name whatsoever, is dissolved."
161. Only two decrees of this type were necessary for the whole month of Frimaire, so distinctly had discipline improved. This vigorous discipline was admired in the army, with whom the new representatives were much more popular than the old (Hanotaux, *Histoire de la nation française*, VIII, pt. 2, p. 59).
162. Archives nationales, AF II 249, pl. 2121, no. 30.
163. The original of this decree (Arch. nat., AF II 249, pl. 2121, no. 49) is signed "St. Just, Le Bas." It may be noted that his usual signature was St. Juste or St. Just, rarely if ever Saint-Just.
164. After Thermidor, the citizens complained to the Convention that though they obeyed the decree to the extent of 6,879 suits of clothes, 4,767 pairs of stockings, 16,921 pairs of shoes and 863 of boots, 1,351 cloaks, 20,518 shirts, etc., these articles remained in the storehouses, rotting and eaten by rats, the purpose being merely to despoil the inhabitants (Fleury, II, 44). Chuquet declares this false; before Saint-Just's arrival the army lacked these things, after he came it was clothed and shod (*Guerres*, IX, 37 n.).
165. The list is given in *Arch. parl.*, LXVIII, 274. The two highest names are those of "Dietrich, *père,* 300,000" and "Zolickoffer, *banquier,* 300,000."
166. Fleury, II, 22, 23, 38; Hamel, *Saint-Just*, p. 303. Fleury, though hostile to Saint-Just, admits that no suspicion of grafting rests on him.
167. See Appendix IV.
168. Cf. the letters of Milhaud and Guyardin from Strasbourg (4 Brumaire) and of Mallarmé and Lacoste from Lunéville (7 Brumaire).
169. The letter was addressed to "Mon ami" and was probably, Aulard conjectures, to Saint-Just.
170. Fleury, II, 82-84, lists a number of military executions and asserts that more than a dozen generals were shot in the Hanheim redoubt.
171. Ehrmann soon fell ill and took little active part in this mission.
172. *Hist. parl.*, XXXV, 350.
173. For this plan and the subsequent advance on Kaiserslautern, see Wallon, *Représentants*, IV, 186-90; Chuquet, IX, Chap. IV. The best account of the campaign in English and one of the best in any language is in Phipps,

NOTES

Armies of the First French Republic; the Armées de la Moselle, du Rhin, de Sambre-et-Meuse, de Rhin-et-Moselle (cited hereafter as Phipps, II), Chap. IV. Phipps, *Armies of the First French Republic; the Armée du Nord* will be cited as Phipps, I. Cf. Dumolin, *Précis,* I, 186-210.

174. The editor, Vellay ("Lettres inédites," p. 7) comments that the personal pronoun shows that these energetic measures were due to Saint-Just's own initiative. Approving marginal notes in Bouchotte's hand accompany the letter.

175. Chuquet, IX, 19.

176. Vellay, ed., "Lettres inédites," p. 10.

177. Vellay wrongly reads Auweiller (*Œuvres,* II, 153).

178. Wallon, *Représentants,* IV, 189.

179. Note also the letter of 26 Frimaire (Aulard, *Recueil,* IX, 442) relative to grain shipments from Dijon and the arrest of that city's commissioners; Saint-Just and Le Bas are to set matters right.

180. Cf. the indignant complaint of Richaud and Soubrany to the Convention from Deux-Ponts (3 Frimaire).

181. Wallon, *Représentants,* IV, 195.

182. Carnot, H., I, 453, 456. Phipps, though elsewhere his judgment of Piche-gru's ability is very severe (I, 284), believes that in this campaign he did his work satisfactorily, if in less spectacular fashion than Hoche and that he had good reason to expect the supreme command; Hoche, though a fine soldier, was aggressive and tactless; relations between the two became increasingly bitter (II, 100-19). General Mangin obviously prefers Hoche (Hanotaux, VIII, pt. 2, pp. 58, 63). Cf. Dumolin, I, 202, 203, 205.

183. Chuquet, IX, 218. It is impossible to enter into the merits of this Landau controversy, which is extremely complicated and in which Saint-Just was only indirectly concerned. An entire pamphlet literature sprang up in regard to it, which is noticed in the Bibliography. For the glowing panegyric on the success of the campaign, read by Barère in the Convention, 12 Nivôse, see *Arch. parl.,* LXXXII, 554. This is the last volume of *Arch. parl.,* covering the lifetime of Saint-Just. Unless otherwise indicated, the *Moniteur* is the source used for subsequent proceedings of the Convention.

184. Fleury, II, 112; Wallon, *Représentants,* IV, 379.

185. Lacoste, *Aperçu des moyens de défense du représentant du peuple; Suite de l'aperçu.*

186. Baudot, . . . *à ses collègues, composant la Convention nationale.*

187. Monin, "Histoire extraordinaire des papiers Baudot," *Ann. rév.,* II, 200.

188. Mühlenbeck, p. 374. Legrand, an officer in the Army of the Rhine, described Lacoste thus: "As debauched as Saint-Just was austere, as intemperate as Saint-Just was sober, as wordy as the other was laconic, as choleric as the other showed himself phlegmatic; his vanity was only puerile; his manners were ignoble" (Chuquet, IX, 40).

189. Lacoste and Guyardin were orginally sent into this area by a decree of July 25, directing them to go to the departments of the Haute-Marne, the Meuse, the Moselle, the Meurthe, the Bas-Rhin, the Haut-Rhin and the Vosges to renew the garrisons in the two divisions of the Moselle and the Rhine (Wallon, *Représentants,* IV, 314 n., citing *Moniteur,* July 27). It has already been noticed that Saint-Just and Le Bas found them in Alsace on their arrival. They were thus in a sense identified with past failures and the soldiers so regarded them. However, Lacoste's mission with Baudot to

NOTES

the Armies of the Moselle and Rhine definitely began on 13 Brumaire (Nov. 3).

190. Cf. also Chuquet's discussion (IX, 166-72); Saint-Just and Le Bas were simple, sober, enemies of display, did not frequent popular societies nor public places, used few words but went straight to the point, though practising terrorism were not extreme, had prodigious influence over the troops, whose discipline they restored; Lacoste and Baudot were constantly addressing the clubs with sounding declamations, lived tumultuously and with display, were jealous of the respect shown their rivals by the army; they felt hated and despised. In a word, though Chuquet does not say it, they were victims of an aggrieved ego and an inferiority complex.

191. Fleury, II, 15, 85. This story is also told of Frederick the Great (Hamel, *Saint-Just*, p. 293).

192. Fleury, II, 45. Hamel with reason interprets the holy guillotine's activity as referring to the period when Schneider was *procureur* (*Saint-Just*, p. 348). This seems justified by Gateau's obvious reference to the Propagande, which club was later dissolved by Saint-Just. It is hardly fair to hold him responsible for these early excesses, which he checked as soon as he felt politically strong enough in the department. Gateau did not know that Saint-Just secretly disapproved some things which he was obliged for a while to tolerate.

193. Fleury, II, 85. Probably Rougiff equals Rougyff, a newspaper owned by the deputy Guffroy.

194. *Ibid.*, II, 39.

195. Chuquet, IX, 34.

196. Mühlenbeck, p. 175. He gives Wolff and Cotta as his authorities for these interviews (presumably Wolff's *Wichtigste Epoche* and Cotta's *Euloge Schneider in Frankreich*, which he cites elsewhere). J. D. Wolff sat with Taffin, Nestlin and Clavel as the four judges of Schneider's court. Cotta was a member of the local committee of surveillance. Both men were partisans of Schneider.

197. Reprinted in the pamphlet, *Tyrannie exercée à Strasbourg par Saint-Just et Lebas. Réclamation de J. G. Treuttel, libraire et imprimeur à Strasbourg, une de leurs victimes.*

198. Fleury, II, 47.

199. *Hist. parl.*, XXXI, 27; XXXV, 347; Michelet, VII, 17; Hamel, *Saint-Just*, p. 300. Fleury denies this, but his refutation consists in a list of Schneider's executions. He does not give any executions directly ordered by Saint-Just, though holding him responsible for Monet's terrorism after Schneider's fall (*Études*, II, 59). Hamel is on surer ground in his refutation of Barante's calumnies (*Saint-Just*, pp. 353-61) than in his attempt to whitewash Saint-Just of all bloodshed.

200. The exaggerated statement of their leniency is interpreted by Carnot's son in the sense that the condemnations pronounced were for crimes envisaged by law and condemned by public opinion (Carnot, H., I, 452).

201. Chuquet, IX, 41. He wrongly states the total as 670. These figures are taken from the *Mémoires* of Legrand, officer in the Army of the Rhine, found by Chuquet in the Archives de la guerre. The letter is not in the *Œuvres*.

202. Wallon, *Représentants*, IV, 443. Jaquel states that "the repressive and terrorist measures of the Revolutionary Tribunal [the exact court referred to is

NOTES

not clear] diminished in extent and vigor after the departure of Schneider" (*Ann. hist. de la Rév. fr.*, Sept., 1931, p. 415).

203. Chuquet, IX, 46, 47.

204. Fleury, II, 117.

205. Wallon, *Représentants*, IV, 206-8. For the mission of Saint-Just and Le Bas, cf. *ibid.*, IV, 210-14 and for other missions in these departments, V, 52-151.

206. Aulard, *Jacobins*, V, 655.

207. This itinerary is based on the fact that the *Œuvres* contain decrees from each of these places on the dates here given. There is clearly an error for the sixteenth at any rate, since Arras is sixty-five miles west of Maubeuge as the crow flies and Réunion-sur-Oise fifty miles southeast of Arras. Even if they went from Maubeuge to Réunion (something better than fifty miles to the southwest) and thence to Arras, they would have covered over a hundred miles in one day. At such speed it is difficult to see how they had time to inspect anything but the scenery. Cf. the statement about roads in the letter of the twelfth. It should be stated that a few of the less important decrees are not mentioned in the text.

208. The letter as printed in the *Œuvres* (II, 195) does not agree exactly with the original. The manuscript (Arch. nat., AF II 131, pl. 1008, no. 3) reads "Dessains" instead of "Dessault" and contains an additional sentence: "Nous comptons que vous répondrez à la confiance que nous avons mise dans votre patriotisme et votre intelligence, dans cette occasion importante." Aulard's *Recueil* is equally inaccurate; the analysis found in X, 686, dubs the unfortunate Englishman Paelding. Was his name really Fielding?

209. Though Le Bon acted under general orders from Saint-Just at Cambrai, their connection was not close; Le Bon complained (18 Floréal) that Saint-Just did not answer his letters. The only letter from the Committee to Le Bon in Saint-Just's writing relates to a supply of bad bread. There are three letters applauding Le Bon's revolutionary activity and urging him to use the torch and sword; they are signed respectively by Barère, Carnot and Billaud, by Billaud and Carnot, by Collot and Barère. Aulard, *Recueil*, X, 757; XI, 266, 316; XIII, 101, 465 n., 583; XIV, 224 n.; *Papiers inédits*, I, 148; Wallon, *Représentants*, V, 84-151; Hamel, *Saint-Just*, pp. 554-57; Kerr, pp. 373-82; Mathiez, "Robespierre et Joseph Le Bon," *Ann. hist. de la Rév. fr.*, I, 1-13; Ording, pp. 124-31. After Thermidor, the anti-Robespierrist members of the Committee tried to shake off responsibility for Le Bon ("Réponse de Barère, Billaud-Varenne . . . ," *Rév. fr.*, XXXIV, pt. 1, 263-66). On the other hand, the growing Robespierrist suspicion of him appears in the letter of one Buissart, 13 Messidor (*Papiers inédits*, I, 250).

210. Wallon, *Représentants*, IV, 211. Cf. Fleury, II, 247. He found this anecdote in the register of the deliberations of the club at Guise. On the strength of this, Hamel accepts it (*Saint-Just*, p. 497), but for the second mission.

211. Fleury, II, 127.

212. Hamel, *Saint-Just*, p. 369.

213. Fleury, II, 132.

214. He presides "or rather he is enthroned," comments Fleury (II, 137); "for this man was never a republican; he is a despot, an autocrat. In creating him, Providence forgot to put him in a suitable environment, where probably he would have been useful." However that may be, there is nothing to indicate that Saint-Just's manner of presiding differed from that of any-one else.

NOTES

215. See the excellent discussion in Mathiez, *Révolution française*, III, Chaps. VIII-XI, incl., and in his special studies assembled in *Études robespierristes*.
216. Aulard, *Jacobins*, V, 664-66. The editor erroneously states in a note that the decree followed a long report in which Saint-Just "attacked without naming them, Hébert and his friends." The speech against Hébert was not delivered until 23 Ventôse.
217. Mathiez, "Les Décrets de ventôse," *Ann. hist. de la Rév. fr.*, V, 193-219, also in *Girondins et Montagnards*, 109-38; cf. his *Révolution française*, 146-49.
218. Another possible theory is that the social policy of 8 Ventôse, while deliberate and important in the eyes of the Robespierrists, was a defensive measure against threatened social revolution on the part of the Hébertists (Walter, "Le Problème de la dictature jacobine," *Ann. hist. de la Rév. fr.*, Nov., 1931, 520-23). Cf. Lefebvre's *Questions agraires au temps de la Terreur*, pp. 46, 57, 58. He considers the Ventôse measures inadequate, since they did nothing for the more prosperous peasants whom it was important to attach to the cause of the republic; he holds further that if it were not for Saint-Just's *Fragments sur les institutions républicaines* there would be nothing to separate the Robespierrists from the rest of the Mountain or to indicate that the Ventôse decrees meant to them anything more than a political maneuver.
219. *Moniteur*, 12 Ventôse. The reply is not printed in the *Œuvres*.
220. *Œuvres*, II, 247. In the *Moniteur's* version (14 Ventôse) there is an Art. IV: "The Committee of General Security shall add an instruction to the present decree to facilitate its execution." By this is apparently meant a series of directions to local authorities.
221. Mathiez, *Girondins et Montagnards*, pp. 126, 127.
222. *Moniteur*, 19 Ventôse.
223. Schneider.
224. Saint-Just was thinking of Anacharsis Cloots and Anaxagoras Chaumette, but had he forgotten the Mucius Scaevola gesture of his own youth? His present manner was unquestionably simpler and more dignified, but was it necessary to accuse the others of anything worse than childish theatricality and poor taste?
225. Hébert, editor of *Père Duchesne*.
226. *Moniteur*, 24 Ventôse; *Journal des débats et des décrets*, no. 540, Ventôse, year II, p. 298.
227. Aulard, *Jacobins*, V, 682, 683.
228. *Journal des débats et des décrets*, no. 543, p. 344; Aulard, *Recueil*, XI, 717; XII, 291.
229. Mathiez, "Hérault de Séchelles était-il dantoniste?" in *Études robespierristes*, 2d series, pp. 222-60.
230. Mathiez, "Le Comité de salut public et le complot de l'étranger," *Ann. hist. de la Rév. fr.*, III, 322; Kerr, 321, 322.
231. Fleury, II, 161.
232. See the essays of Mathiez, notably "La Fortune de Danton" and "Les Comptes de Danton" in *Études robespierristes*, 1st series. Even Madelin in his much more friendly *Danton* accepts the general thesis of Mathiez as fairly proved, though he seeks to weaken its damning force. The views of Mathiez are well summarized in his essay on Danton, published in *Girondins et Montagnards*. This savage attack, though convincing on the score

of venality, is less satisfactory on that of treason, in regard to which the question is one of hypothesis rather than proof and the facts are capable of another interpretation. A more recent and balanced judgment is given by G. Lefebvre in his article "Sur Danton," *Ann. hist. de la Rév. fr.,* Sept.-Oct., Nov.-Dec., 1932.

233. Madelin, *Danton,* p. 285.

234. Carnot, H., p. 375.

235. Vellay, "Saint-Just et le procès des dantonistes," *Ann. rév.,* I, 101. The pamphlet referred to is *P. A. Taschereau-Fargues à Maximilien Robespierre aux enfers,* Paris, year III, which would certainly not be inclined to favor Saint-Just.

236. *Moniteur,* 12 Germinal. This dramatic little scene must have been carefully prepared by the Committees to impress the Convention. According to Barras (*Memoirs,* Eng. trans., I, 180), the Committee of Public Safety entered in a body, Saint-Just bringing up the rear. He too had a distinct recollection that there was something unusual about that moment. But since we know that Robespierre and Barère were already present, having made replies to Legendre, the *Moniteur's* contemporary version must be preferred, which states simply: "Saint-Just, reporter of the Committee of Public Safety, enters the hall and ascends to the tribune." In a coup d'état, everything depends on creating the right psychology.

237. Barras, *Memoirs,* I, 180.

238. *Projet rédigé par Robespierre du rapport fait à la Convention nationale par Saint-Just contre Fabre d'Eglantine, Danton, Philippeaux, Lacroix et Camille Desmoulins,* especially pp. 5-21. Published in 1841 by a Paris bookseller named France, who believed that Robespierre dictated Saint-Just's report.

239. Mathiez, "Les Notes de Robespierre contre les dantonistes; essai d'édition critique," *Robespierre terroriste,* pp. 79-118.

240. "Fragment d'une note de Camille Desmoulins, sur le rapport de Saint-Just. Trouvée dans les papiers de Robespierre," *Papiers inédits,* I, 290-94.

241. *Moniteur,* 16 Germinal. Cf. *ibid.,* 20 Germinal.

242. This assertion was entirely false. Fouquier had indeed described the action of the prisoners in alarmist language, but the point of his letter was whether their witnesses must be heard. They had not "revolted," because they could not; they were not "guilty," until convicted by the court. Saint-Just, like other popular orators, was not above producing his effects by a misleading use of phrases.

243. Madelin (*Danton,* p. 307) suggests that the Committees forged the Laflotte letter. Whether this be true or not (the letter's opportuneness is at least suspicious), it is difficult to believe that they could have taken the plot seriously, unless they were in considerable doubt of their own hold on public opinion in the city. To mold that opinion as desired by the government, the Committee of Public Safety voted on 17 Germinal that Saint-Just's report of the eleventh be printed in an edition of two hundred thousand copies (Aulard, *Recueil,* XII, 421).

244. Mathiez, "Un Faux rapport de Saint-Just," *Études robespierristes,* 2d series, 178-96. It is mistakenly included in the *Œuvres,* II, 333-50.

245. Saint-Just's boyhood friends, who owed their positions to his influence. Gatteau is more correctly spelled Gateau.

246. The civil service was in fact full of corruption. Since most of the population were illiterate, the officeholders were drawn from the bourgeoisie.

But the bourgeoisie was unsympathetic toward the maximum and other social legislation, which it sabotaged. Furthermore the sale of public lands, the food question, army contracts, etc., gave opportunities for speculation and plunder. Hence many unscrupulous adventurers were attracted to an administrative career. The public service was full of ambitious young intellectuals and greedy bohemians, full of appetites and falling avidly on the spoils of office (Ording, pp. 14-18, 119).

247. This closing up of local courts was a further measure of centralization, designed to check local prejudices in favor of or hostile to the accused. It was aimed against the extremes of indulgence and excessive terrorism. By special exception, a few local courts remained (Kerr, p. 393).

248. Ording, pp. 37, 38.

249. *Ibid.*, p. 46.

250. *Ibid.*, p. 42.

251. "Réponse de Barère . . . ," *Rév. fr.*, XXXIV, pt. 1, p. 257.

252. Arch. nat., AD xviii ª, 62. The report is dated 12 Ventôse, year III. Cf. *Hist. parl.* XXXVI, 11, and Hamel, *Saint-Just*, p. 544. Saladin was one of the seventy-three Girondins saved by Robespierre; his report was a condemnation of those under investigation.

253. Ording, pp. 43, 90, 92, 100.

254. Mathiez, *Girondins et Montagnards*, 130-36; *Révolution française*, III, 200.

255. Aulard, *Recueil*, XIII, 483, 513. The decree of 24 Floréal was signed by Voulland, Billaud-Varenne, Robespierre, Barère, Prieur, Couthon, Amar, Élie Lacoste, Louis, Du Barran, Jagot, Carnot and Vadier; that of the twenty-fifth by Élie Lacoste, Robespierre, Couthon, Du Barran and Vadier.

256. Arch. nat., F 7 4435, pl. 3.

257. Ording, pp. 160-66. Hamel (*Saint-Just*, pp. 558-61) confuses the prison-plot lists with those of the Museum commissions. The lists of 154 and 157 referred to by various historians are variants of the list of 159 as will appear by a comparison of texts; Aulard erroneously speaks of them as different lists. Cf. *Recueil*, XIV, 741; *Œuvres*, II, 451, no. 27; the language of the decree above from the MS. original in Arch. nat., F 7 4435, pl. 3; Wallon, *Histoire du tribunal révolutionnaire*, IV, 415-17.

258. *Hist. parl.*, XXXIV, 239, 245, 271. Cf. Mathiez, "Fouquier-Tinville et Robespierre," *Autour de Robespierre*, 137-43.

259. Fleury, II, 277-82. Gellé is here misspelled Gelée. The accusation dealing with the fifteen sous is also found in "Réponse de Barère . . . ," *Rév. fr.*, XXXIV, pt. 1, pp. 68 n., 74.

260. Vilate, *Causes secrètes de la révolutior du 9 au 10 thermidor*, pp. 12-14.

261. Fleury, II, 193.

262. Taylor, *Revolutionary Types*, 121. This author speaks of Saint-Just as "the idol for a brief space of the capricious Parisian populace," whose memory for more than fifty years after his death was so detested that his family hardly dared admit the relationship, but who in 1848 was apotheosized.

263. Fleury, II, 392.

264. Ording, p. 165.

265. Hamel, *Saint-Just*, p. 553.

266. *Ibid.*, pp. 268-72. Hamel's destructive analysis pulverizes the story on grounds of internal evidence also; if Robespierre and Saint-Just had wished to find out about the queen's trial, they would have questioned the president of the Tribunal or the public prosecutor, not an obscure agent like Vilate; they had no social relations with Barère who in his *Mémoires*

speaks of but one dinner with Robespierre, long after the queen's death, Saint-Just not being present (*Mémoires,* II, 201).

267. Nodier, *Souvenirs,* I, 40-44.
268. Levasseur, *Mémoires,* III, 78.
269. Vellay, ed., "Une Lettre de Saint-Just," *Revue hist. de la Rév. fr.,* I, 101-02.
270. Ording, pp. 47, 48, 69, 82-84.
271. Mathiez holds that the Robespierrists were not continuing the Terror without fixed goal, but with the clear purpose of enforcing the Ventôse decrees. The law of 22 Prairial was essential to this object, he believes, and scouts the idea that Saint-Just disapproved it (*Girondins et Montagnards,* pp. 131, 132, 137, 163). Even if this theory is true, the price of indefinitely continued slaughter was too great for the compensating social advantage; the Robespierrists might have confiscated property without bloodshed. That Saint-Just opposed the law is distinctly stated by an eyewitness, Gateau, whom Mathiez ignores for no apparent reason. Ording believes that the law was especially the work of Robespierre and Couthon, but that the remaining members of the Committee had advance knowledge of it (*Bureau de police,* pp. 175-80).
272. Phipps, II, 152. Chuquet's great work stops short of this campaign. Estimates of strength vary widely and no accurate statement is possible. Phipps, I, 250, gives the Allies 106,000 to 128,000 in Oct., 1793; Jomini made them 163,000. Dumolin (I, 225 n.) gives 100,000.
273. Phipps, I, 284. The uncertainty of these figures is further indicated by the fact that in his table of army strength in 1794, he gives the Army of the North alone as 245,822 with the Army of the Ardennes as an additional 37,630 (Phipps, I, 3). This is certainly mere paper strength. On the other hand, he elsewhere more reasonably estimates their effective number in April, 1794, as 150,000 including the Army of the Ardennes (II, 145). Dumolin says 204,200 (I, 225).
274. Phipps, II, 145-47. Cf. Dumolin, I, 221-50, for the whole campaign.
275. Aulard prints a letter from the Committee to Saint-Just, representative to the Army of the North, under the singular date of 2 Floréal [April 21] (*Recueil,* XII, 727). They send him a letter from a Paris Jacobin, who learned from a volunteer of the Vosges battalion that malcontents were discouraging the troops. Saint-Just is invited to verify the fact and to take necessary measures. The Committee's letter is not signed. This would suggest another intermediate mission to the North. But there is no record of his appointment to any such mission and he was apparently in Paris on 2 Floréal, having signed decrees of the Committee on that day as well as on the third, fourth, sixth and eighth. It is true that decrees also bear his signature on the tenth, eleventh and twelfth, though he certainly left Paris on the tenth. Fleury believed that some of his colleagues signed for him on these three days; Hamel (*Saint-Just,* p. 495) that he signed these documents before departure, leaving the date blank. They are few and not important. The same reasoning might be followed for the decrees of the preceding week. But it is unlikely that he would have signed so many in this way. Further, if he was in the North on the second, the elaborate appointment of the tenth, with its appropriation of 10,000 livres for expenses, would be meaningless. We have no *arrêtés* signed by him in the North prior to the thirteenth. It seems inevitable that Aulard or his copyist erred in the date; perhaps it should have been the twelfth.

276. Réunion-sur-Oise, 14, 15, 16, 19 Floréal. The decrees of the mission are to be found in *Œuvres*, II, 403-21.
277. Réunion-sur-Oise, 14, 15, 20, 21, Cousolre, 27 Floréal, Maubeuge, 10 Prairial.
278. Fleury, II, 247. It is true that some of the decrees issued by the representatives have been lost, e.g., the one referred to in Aulard, *Recueil*, XIII, 607.
279. Hamel, *Saint-Just*, p. 499.
280. These men were released by the Committee (21 Prairial), following a letter from Choudieu at Lille (15 Prairial), stating that the Landrecies magistrates had been found alive and well. The Committee tried to be fair.
281. Aulard, *Recueil*, XIII, 214. The "petite Clyse" referred to in this letter is a misreading by Aulard for "Elpe," or as it is properly spelled, Helpe, a tributary of the Sambre.
282. Carnot's letter must have reached Saint-Just at least by the fifteenth. Le Bon says that he began his work at Cambrai on the seventeenth by order of Saint-Just and Le Bas and that he corresponded with them daily (Aulard, *Recueil*, XIII, 444). It seems clear that his appointment to ferret out treason here resulted from Carnot's suggestion, which throws an interesting light on the later effort of this statesman to disclaim all contact with terrorism and make the Robespierrist trio the scapegoats for the whole business.
283. *Ibid.*, XIII, 375. This letter is not given in the *Œuvres*, perhaps because it is preserved only in the form of an analysis, in the original (Arch. nat., AF II 235, pl. 2017, no. 73) as well as in the *Recueil*. Comparison of the two and of the separate decrees, all of which are in the *Œuvres*, reveals many inaccuracies in the *Recueil*, which wrongly reads "Flager" for "Mayer," "Jadet" for "Radet," "banlieue" for "Baulieu" (thus the original, which the *Œuvres* changes to the real spelling, Beaulieu), "Daupont" for "Daupoul." The names are unimportant, but the point is of interest as showing the need of checking up on the *Recueil*. This work is indispensable; it is unfortunate that its accuracy cannot always be relied on.
284. Levasseur to Committee; Thuin, 27 Floréal (*ibid.*, XIII, 557). Saint-Just and Le Bas witnessed the retreat, he wrote, and they would write further regarding it. [We have no report from them.] Desjardins lost his head on the verge of taking Charleroi, where the enemy's numbers were inferior.
285. Mathiez, *Autour de Robespierre*, p. 176; Ording, p. 42.
286. Fleury, II, 250-54. On this occasion, Fleury states, Saint-Just as always made proof of boldness and courage; in visiting the advance posts, he was almost captured at Merbes-le-Château. Now on the tenth, Saint-Just with Guyton and Laurent was writing a decree at Maubeuge, ordering an investigation into the retreat of the fifth. He might conceivably have been in action ten miles away on the same day, but it is improbable that he would then have been interested in past failures. The actual number of Sambre crossings is not at all clear. Fleury speaks of each of the five crossings mentioned above, following in part two sources, *Victoires et conquêtes*, which declares "the stubborn Saint-Just, prodigal of the soldiers' blood, caused the passage of the Sambre to be begun again five different times up to May 29 and always with the same result" (Fleury, II, 258) and the *Manuel des braves*, which also definitely states, "five times the Sambre was crossed, but five times the victorious Austrians drove us to the other bank" (Fleury, II, 260). Mathiez says also that the Army of the

NOTES

Ardennes, "rallied by Saint-Just," crossed and recrossed the river five times prior to Jourdan's arrival (*Révolution française*, III, 188). On the other hand, Phipps, the military specialist, asserts that the army made three crossings between May 11 and June 3, each time being repulsed with considerable loss (Phipps, II, 147).

287. Levasseur, II, 246, 255; III, 226-31.

288. This letter was written by Robespierre and signed by him, Prieur, Carnot, Billaud-Varenne and Barère. It is not in the *Recueil*, nor mentioned by Vellay, but it is to be found in *Papiers inédits* (II, 5), is reproduced in entirety by Fleury (II, 267) and in part by Hamel (*Saint-Just*, p. 512).

289. Aulard, *Recueil*, XIV, 212, 216. Hamel is mistaken in stating that the decree creating the new army was issued by Saint-Just and his colleagues at the Army of the North before his departure from the front (*Saint-Just*, p. 513). According to Levasseur, none of the representatives but himself and Guyton desired the creation of so great an army under a single general, Saint-Just specifically declaring that the Committee would have none of it, for it would be "giving a soldier power very dangerous for liberty" (*Mémoires*, II, 253). However, the Committee's action, taken in Saint-Just's presence and after his report of the situation, indicates that Levasseur's account is open to question.

290. *Moniteur*, 12 Messidor. The Convention, having listened to Barère's report of Fleurus in its session of the eleventh, decreed that "the Armies of the North, the Ardennes and the Moselle, now united, shall henceforth bear the name, the Army of the Sambre-et-Meuse. They continue to deserve well of the fatherland." Phipps, relying on two different secondary authorities, gives two different dates for the conferring of this name, June 13 and June 27, both of which are incorrect (II, 150, 172). The name is never used in decrees or letters during Saint-Just's mission.

291. Cf. his letter of 8 Prairial (Fleury, II, 261).

292. Phipps, II, 153.

293. Hamel, *Saint-Just*, p. 513, basing his statement on the *Mémoire des anciens membres des comités*, p. 102, n. 5. Cf., "Réponse de Barère . . . ," *Rév. fr.*, XXXIV, pt. 1, 67 n.

294. I take the dates of his *arrêtés* as marking the limits of his actual mission. He may of course have reached the front before the twenty-fifth and been active behind the scenes. On the other hand, he may not have left Paris immediately after the decree of the eighteenth. Committee decrees are signed by him, dated as late as the twenty-first.

295. 25 Prairial, 1, 3, 4, 5 Messidor.

296. Aulard, *Recueil*, XIV, 502. This letter, of which there is only an analysis, is not in the *Œuvres*. The original (Arch. nat., AF II 235, pl. 2018, no. 51) refers to the signatories as representatives to the "Army of the North, of the Moselle and of the Ardennes," further proving that at that date, 6 Messidor (June 24), the new designation, Army of the Sambre-et-Meuse, was not yet known. Cf. Mathiez, *Autour de Robespierre*, 157, 158.

297. Phipps, II, 153.

298. *Ibid.*, II, 154. Phipps calls it the fifth time, Dumolin (I, 242) the sixth.

299. Phipps, II, 156, 157. He refers for the statement about Hatry and the rest to Musset-Pathay's *Relation des principaux sièges faits ou soutenus en Europe par les armées françaises depuis 1792*, published in 1806; for the story about the captain to the same work and to Soult's *Mémoires*, though Phipps admits some doubt about this story. It may be remarked that a

military historian of the imperial period would certainly be prejudiced against Saint-Just, while Soult added to this prejudice the fact that (according to Phipps) his name with those of Lefebvre and Jourdan were on Saint-Just's list for accusation. For whatever they are worth, they may be set against the charge of Saint-Just's inexplicable inertia; he was no longer the Saint-Just of earlier missions; he was not in his element (Fleury, II, 300, 302). But Fleury seems ignorant of most of the *arrêtés* issued by Saint-Just during this mission, which was probably the reason for the charge. They indicate that he was as active as ever.

300. Phipps, who calls Saint-Just "as foolish as he was bloodthirsty" (II, 157), blames the Mons diversion severely, asserting that it fortunately failed of execution because Carnot was wise enough to order the plan kept a secret from Jourdan until Charleroi had fallen. Phipps further declares that Jourdan refused to send off this great body without a written order from Saint-Just, which the latter would not give. This may be so. On the other hand, the postscript suggests that Saint-Just did not intend the Mons expedition to take place until after the fall of Charleroi. These were likewise the long-standing orders of the commander-in-chief, Pichegru, who wrote to Jourdan, 15 Prairial (June 3): "You must, I think, second with all your forces the attack on Charleroi, contenting yourself with masking Namur by a corps. . . . This place taken, I think it interesting to sweep the left bank of the Sambre as far as the highway from Maubeuge to Mons, in order to disengage the first of these places from the daily insults to which it is exposed;—thence, all forces toward Mons" (Wallon, *Représentants*, IV, 246 n.).

301. *Hist. parl.*, XXXV, 356; Levasseur, *Mémoires*, II, 11; Fleury, II, 302; Hamel, *Saint-Just*, p. 529; Phipps, II, 158. Phipps wrongly dates the surrender; *Hist. parl.* misplaces the incident.

302. The battle is described in detail by Phipps, II, 159-64.

303. Aulard, *Recueil*, XIV, 320. Duquesnoy, Le Bas's old companion, writing from Vedette-Républicaine, 5 Messidor, informs the Committee that he has been sick for eighteen days. "Our colleague Saint-Just had the kindness to come to see me; I will perhaps have that satisfaction again tomorrow or in a few days" (*ibid.*, XIV, 478). Saint-Just may have run down to Philippeville just to call on the sick representative; he did not have time to go again in Messidor.

304. Fleury's theory that the antagonism arose from an unfortunate incident that wounded Levasseur's vanity at their first meeting is unfounded. He says that Pichegru wanted to introduce Levasseur to Saint-Just, whereat Levasseur haughtily replied, "It seems to me that you should rather present the general to me," addressing Saint-Just (II, 251). This is obviously mixed as Hamel shows (*Saint-Just*, p. 506). The point was rather that one of Levasseur's colleagues accompanying Pichegru introduced Levasseur to the general instead of vice versa, thus offending the representative. The maladroit colleague is not named. Levasseur continues with the statement that Pichegru, who was on a visit of inspection, spent the day, returning to his army in the evening. After he had left, the generals held a council of war. "Saint-Just and Le Bas were there; it was the first time I saw these deputies at the army" (*Mémoires*, II, 237, 238).

305. Levasseur, II, 240-43, 325; III, 230.

306. Hamel, *Saint-Just*, p. 508. The letter is of more value than subsequent memoirs.

307. Fleury, II, 264.
308. Phipps (II, 156) does indeed cite Marescot as calling Saint-Just "that cowardly proconsul, who never showed himself in the trenches," but he quotes this from a secondary authority writing in 1806. On the other hand Fleury, though he dislikes Saint-Just, cannot stomach these charges and disproves them at length (*Études*, II, 258-62), showing how all other writers, even hostile ones, unite in protest against these assertions and in stressing Saint-Just's fanaticism and callousness to bloodshed. Even Marescot is summoned as witness for the defense, testifying to Saint-Just's determination to recross the Sambre at once after a defeat. One may refer also to Carnot's opinion that what made Saint-Just and a handful of other deputies so valuable as representatives to the armies was "the electric spark which they knew so well how to communicate" (Carnot, H., I, 396).
309. Fleury, II, 306. According to Barère's story, Saint-Just took part in the battle, but on his return to Paris obstinately refused to make the report (*Mémoires*, IV, 409). His colleagues on the Committee represent Robespierre as vainly trying to get Saint-Just to come back during the last part of the mission and his ultimate return as due to Robespierre's solicitations ("Réponse de Barère . . . ," *Rév. fr.*, XXXIV, pt. 1, 67 n.).
310. Fleury, II, 305.
311. The Committee of Public Safety had since July 28, 1793, the right to issue decrees of arrest. The police bureau established under this general power had as special duty that of surveillance over officeholders. It did not, however, confine itself to this group, though its other arrests concerned only obscure persons. On the other hand the Committee of General Security encroached on the field of administrative surveillance and arrested officeholders. The police functions of the two Committees overlapped and were never clearly defined. Presumably the Committee of Public Safety would never have entered the field at all, if it had trusted the personnel of the lesser Committee. However, the latter retained control of the great majority of police cases at all times (Ording, Chap. VI).
312. Carnot, H., I, 536. Like all other memoirs, these cannot be regarded as absolutely trustworthy transcriptions of what actually happened. Carnot naturally comes off best in every encounter. The authority for this and most of the other conversations recorded in these memoirs is Prieur de la Marne. An almost identical account of this episode is given in the post-Thermidorian "Réponse de Barère . . . ," *Rév. fr.*, XXXIV, pt. 1, 77-79 n. It seems hardly likely that predictions of this sort should be made early in Floréal. See also Mathiez, *Autour de Robespierre*, 157-59, 165, 167; Ording, p. 22.
313. *Œuvres*, II, 483; Mathiez, *Révolution française*, III, 206.
314. Barère, II, 205-07.
315. Ording, p. 84.
316. "Réponse de Barère . . . ," *Rév. fr.*, XXXIV, pt. 1, 74; Carnot, H., I, 542, 543 (Carnot's son misquotes the *députations patriotiques* of the "Réponse" as *réputations patriotiques*); Toulongeon, *Histoire de France*, IV, 371; Barère, II, 213-16. Mathiez, who can make nothing out of the *députations*, suggests that Saint-Just was really emphasizing the republican institutions, whose establishment he wished to hasten, but this does not explain the enigmatic phrase (*Girondins et Montagnards*, p. 163).
317. Hamel, *Saint-Just*, p. 575. The same writer in his later *Histoire de Robespierre* (III, 694) discredits the whole episode even more strongly.

NOTES

318. Aulard, *Recueil*, XV, 327. Bégis (*Curiosités révolutionnaires. Saint-Just* . . . , *son emprisonnement,* pp. 47-50) asserts that the Lambert woman was his (Bégis's) cousin; that the object of her visit was to bring certain complaints of her fellow citizens against the conduct of Thuillier and Gateau on the Aisne; that she had a lively altercation with Saint-Just on the matter; that he accused her of intending to assassinate him; that she was released on 14 Nivôse, year III (Jan. 3, 1795).

319. It is asserted that Saint-Just began his conciliatory efforts at the end of Messidor, offering to share direction of the police bureau with Billaud-Varenne if the lists were approved, but Billaud refused. This cannot be true, since Saint-Just was no longer in charge of the bureau.

320. Mathiez, *Ann. hist. de la Rév. fr.,* V, 211-17; *ibid.,* "Les Séances des 4 et 5 thermidor an II," *Girondins et Montagnards,* 139-70; Ording, pp. 170-73.

321. Mathiez, *Révolution française,* III, 221.

322. *Ibid.,* III, 215.

323. *Journal des débats et des décrets,* no. 677, pp. 179-80; *Moniteur,* 12 Thermidor.

324. *Moniteur,* 16 Fructidor.

325. "Réponse de Barère . . . ," *Rév. fr.,* XXXIV, pt. 1, 158-60. Fleury, who cites much of this account, though inaccurately, adds the detail that after Saint-Just had emptied his pockets, Collot, still believing that the report was hidden in his clothing, threw himself on Saint-Just, tried to search him and shook him with rage. Finally they were separated and Collot was forced to sit on the table at some distance from his adversary, who was white with anger (*Études,* II, 342). What is Fleury's authority for all this? It is not Barère. Two other contemporary versions of this affair exist, not differing materially from the rest (Carnot, H., I, 545-47; Toulongeon, IV, 376, 377). In the former, Saint-Just's note reads, "Injustice has closed [*fermé* instead of *flétri*] my heart; I am going to open it completely to the National Convention."

326. Saint-Just here repeats the charge about the 18,000, previously mentioned.

327. Fleury, II, 346.

328. *Faits recueillis aux derniers instants de Robespierre et de sa faction,* p. 7 n.

329. The account of the session as contained in the *Moniteur* for 11 Thermidor paraphrases Saint-Just's few remarks; according to it he got a little way past his reference to the Tarpeian Rock.

330. Barras, I, 218.

331. According to Levasseur, who was there, Saint-Just remained leaning against the tribune, "contemplating the Convention with a cold smile of disdain." Fleury, II, 349, 355.

332. *Moniteur,* 11 Thermidor. There seems to have been no relationship between Élie and J. B. Lacoste, but the name was fatal to Saint-Just.

333. *Moniteur,* 12 Thermidor; *Journal des débats,* no. 677, p. 177.

334. Levasseur, III, 153; Fleury, II, 361, 363; Mathiez, *Autour de Robespierre,* pp. 198, 201, 226, 227.

335. Arch. nat., F 7 4433 (pl. 1, no. 13).

336. *Ibid.,* pl. 2, no. 6.

337. Arch. nat., F 7 4432 (pl. 4, piece 14); cf. F 7 4433 (pl. 1, nos. 44-77).

338. Fleury, II, 367.

339. Barras, I, 227.

340. *Faits recueillis,* pp. 1-10.

341. Arch. nat., AF II 47 (pl. 363, no. 49).

NOTES

342. Wallon, *Histoire du tribunal révolutionnaire*, V, 252.
343. Fleury, II, 377.
344. Arch. nat., AF ii 47 (pl. 363, no. 18).
345. Aulard, *Recueil*, XV, 486.
346. *Moniteur*, 12 Thermidor.
347. *Ibid.*, 14, 19 Thermidor, 9 Fructidor.
348. *Ibid.*, 16 Thermidor.
349. The *Moniteur* published it in installments, which appear in the issues of 30 Pluviôse (Feb. 18, 1795), 1, 2, 4 to 12 Ventôse inclusive (Feb. 19, 20, 22 to March 2).
350. Also in *Œuvres*, II, 492-535. Mathiez links them with the Ventôse decrees, "of which they are the crown" (*Ann. hist. de la Rév. fr.*, Nov.-Dec., 1930, p. 579). He recalls Couthon's motion of 3 Floréal, adopted by the Convention, which provided that a member of the Committee whom Couthon did not name, "but who could only be Saint-Just," should be entrusted with drawing up a code of social institutions (*Girondins et Montagnards*, p. 129).
351. On the close relation between the ideas of the two, see Kritschewsky, *Rousseau und Saint-Just*. The kinship is found alike in political, social and religious conceptions.
352. Ording believes that when Saint-Just refers here to *les taxes*, he means the system of the maximum which restricted the profits of commerce in grain. Having made this experiment, Saint-Just reverts to his original belief in the soundness of free trade (*Bureau de police*, p. 181).
353. In another version, Saint-Just prefaces this fragment with the words: "It is necessary, in a Revolution where perversity and virtue play such large rôles, to state all principles and definitions clearly." This sentence also occurs, referring to boys, "They never return to the homes of their parents before the age of twenty-one. The discipline of childhood is rigorous." In other respects, the versions do not differ essentially. (Stéfane-Pol, *De Robespierre à Fouché; notes de police*, Chap. V).
354. Cf. Vellay, "Saint-Just et Mably," *Ann. rév.*, I, 345, where Saint-Just's interest in Mably's assertion of the importance of religious ideas in any social organization is considered as playing a part in Robespierre's plan for a Festival of the Supreme Being.
355. *Œuvres*, II, 536-40.
356. Senart, *Mémoires*, pp. 102, 103.
357. Challamel, *Les Clubs contre-révolutionnaires*, p. 563; Hamel, *Saint-Just*, pp. 470-89; Ording, pp. 105-08.
358. *Moniteur*, 29 Thermidor.
359. Le Blanc, J., *Vies secrettes [sic] et politiques de Couthon, Saint-Just, Robespierre jeunes [sic], complices du tyran Robespierre, et assassins de la République*, pp. 29, 30. Other Thermidorian writers speak of orgies at Auteuil, Passy, Vanvres, Clichy, etc. (see the list in Fleury, II, 207-19).
360. Hamel, *Saint-Just*, pp. 470, 476-77.
361. Quoted by Fleury, II, 9.
362. Hamel (*Saint-Just*, p. 488), who picked up this detail from the son of a member of the Convention.
363. Vellay, ed., "Correspondance de Saint Just," p. 67.
364. Cf. Bégis, *Curiosités révolutionnaires. Saint-Just et les bureaux de la police*, p. 37; Vellay, "Un Ami de Saint-Just: Gateau," pp. 64-79; Vellay, ed., "Correspondance de Saint-Just," p. 66.

365. Bégis, *Curiosités révolutionnaires. Saint-Just . . . , son emprisonnement,* p. 46.
366. Arch. nat., AF II 47 (pl. 368, no. 58). This seal was seized in Saint-Just's lodgings.
367. Suin, pp. 192, 193; Vellay, *Ann. rév.,* I, 64; Mühlenbeck, p. 194.
368. *Œuvres,* Introduction, I, vii-xiv.
369. *Arch. parl.,* LXXV, 372-77; Mühlenbeck, p. 195; Herlaut, "La Vie politique de Villain d'Aubigny," *Ann. hist. de la Rév. fr.,* Jan., 1934. Recall Saint-Just's letter to Daubigny of July 20, 1792 (pp. 31-32, above). Babeuf, who admired the Robespierrists, was furious at Daubigny's lies. Cf. his journal, *Le Tribun du peuple* for Feb. 24, 1796, quoted in Mathiez, *Autour de Robespierre,* 251-54.
370. Bégis, *Curiosités révolutionnaires. Saint-Just et les bureaux de la police,* p. 38; Fleury, II, 207. The latter goes so far as to call Lejeune "the creature of Saint-Just," who was his "protector" and again alludes to him as "the first person of that hideous trinity which finished with Fouquier-Tinville, with Saint-Just in the middle." This combination of names is valueless; the bureau of police was only briefly under Saint-Just's control and Fouquier was far from being a devoted Robespierrist. On Lejeune's untrustworthiness as a source, see Ording, pp. 38, 39.
371. *Papiers inédits,* p. 361; Aulard, *Recueil,* VII, 529.
372. Carnot, H., I, 523.
373. Sainte-Beuve, V, 357 n.
374. Mühlenbeck, p. 117.
375. Roux, *Relation de l'événement des 8, 9 et 10 thermidor,* p. 4.
376. *Le club infernal,* p. 4.
377. Lenéru, *Saint-Just,* p. 20.
378. Fleury, II, 9.
379. Mathiez, "Rousseau, Robespierre, Saint-Just et Couthon jugés par Buonarroti," *Ann. rév.,* V, 93.
380. Michelet, VII, 520.
381. Cited by Lenéru, p. 20.
382. Cited by Fleury, II, 9.
383. Taine, *La Révolution,* V, 302-06, 348-50.
384. Fleury, II, 246, 379-81. The analysis is surprisingly discriminating; Fleury feels that Saint-Just died too young for a definitive judgment.
385. Cuvillier-Fleury, II, 285, 286.
386. Sainte-Beuve, V, 357.
387. Barère, IV, 408.
388. *Ibid.,* IV, 409. One reason why Saint-Just was assigned these tasks rather than a member of the Committee of General Security was because there was bad feeling between the two Committees (Ording, p. 20). Needless to say, it did not make relations better. It is possible that Barère, who considered himself a sort of semiofficial spokesman for the Committee of Public Safety, also resented the selection of Saint-Just by that Committee for so many important reports. Recall the incident of Barère's report of the battle of Fleurus.
389. Hamel, *Saint-Just,* p. 443.
390. Barante, *Histoire de la Convention nationale,* II, 91, 92.
391. Bégis, *Curiosités révolutionnaires. Saint-Just et les bureaux de la police,* pp. 29-31.

NOTES

392. Robespierre, *Correspondance de Maximilien et Augustin Robespierre*, p. 236. Cf. p. 167 above.
393. *Ibid.*, p. 282. Jacques Duplay, son of the man in whose house Robespierre lived, being questioned on the witness stand after Thermidor as to the frequency of Saint-Just's correspondence with Robespierre during his absences from Paris, replied: "I only know that Saint-Just and Le Bas during their missions wrote often to the Committee of Public Safety, but I have no knowledge that they wrote directly to Robespierre" (Mathiez, *Autour de Robespierre*, p. 176). At the same hearing, Duplay gave this bit of testimony to the close collaboration between Saint-Just and Robespierre. Being asked whether Saint-Just and Le Bas came to dine with Robespierre, he stated: "Le Bas dined there often, having married one of my sisters. Saint-Just rarely dined there, but he came often to Robespierre's rooms and mounted to his office without speaking to anyone" (*ibid.*, p. 175). On the other hand, there are stories of quarrels between the two men. An English spy sent his government twenty-eight bulletins from Sept., 1793, to June, 1794, purporting to give inside information about what went on in the Committee of Public Safety. According to him, Saint-Just and Robespierre had violent quarrels over certain prisoners; in most of the cases Saint-Just stood out for the more drastic policy. These reports are commonly regarded as forgeries. There are also the statements of Demaillot, an agent of the Committee, that Saint-Just favored Prost and Robespierre Lejeune in a bitter controversy between these lesser figures. Demaillot says that Saint-Just talked to him "with his well-known frankness" about "the present weakness and indolence of Robespierre." "With his famous sardonic laugh, he said to me: 'Good! Ronsin, Vincent and so many others, useful for a while, perished through ambition; the same fate will befall those who try to imitate them.'" It is scarcely credible that Saint-Just spoke of Robespierre in these terms and they are further discredited because Demaillot wrote them down in prison after 9 Thermidor. Ording rejects the whole story and the idea of any conflicts between Saint-Just and Robespierre; Mathiez on the contrary admits that differences of opinion sometimes existed between them and that the Lejeune-Prost episode was probably one (Ording, pp. 87-89; Mathiez, "L'Histoire secrète du comité de salut public," *Études robespierristes*, II, 144-58). If the latter view be correct, it may explain Lejeune's *volte-face* regarding Saint-Just.
394. Fleury, I, 266 n.
395. Levasseur, I, 203; II, 324.
396. Carnot, H., I, 527.
397. Saint-Just "compared to Robespierre, was a colossus;" only his youth kept him in second place; he had everything his friend lacked, enthusiasm that laughed at difficulties, rapid grasp and prompt conception, belief in his ideas once they were fixed, physical courage and moral force, contempt of the men whom the other feared; power in synthesis and brevity where the other was verbose and diffuse, absolute will-power, everything which makes men strong and dangerous (Fleury, I, 105, 106, 260-65; II, 114); he would have become Robespierre's dangerous rival, for he satisfied better the ideal of the coming time, having in his nature something of the soldier as well as of the Jacobin (Michelet, V, 104; VII, 152); he was Robespierre's pacemaker and leader (Jacquemaire, *Mme. Roland*, p. 288); in the two years of his public life, he had the most absolute power ever attained by any man at his age; when he was in the tribune, the Revolution held a *lit de*

justice; he seemed to incarnate the whole force and destiny of the Revolution, which came to an end when he disappeared (Lenéru, pp. 27-29).

398. Mühlenbeck, p. 117; Béraud, *Twelve Portraits of the French Revolution,* p. 89.

399. Barère, II, 168.

400. Fleury, I, 162. Fleury does not indicate his authority; it must be admitted that he may have had a confused recollection of what Robespierre wrote regarding Saint-Just's brother-in-law, "energetic patriot, pure, enlightened" (*Papiers trouvés,* II, 11). In any case, Robespierre certainly held an equally high opinion of Saint-Just himself.

BIBLIOGRAPHY

I. SOURCES

1. MANUSCRIPTS

Archives Nationales

AD xviii ᵃ, 62. Saladin report.

AF II 47, pl. 363. Jailor's receipt for Robespierre and Couthon. Committee's order of arrest of Saint-Just's secretary, 10 Thermidor.

AF II 47, pl. 368. Saint-Just's seal.

AF II 85, pl. 625. Northern missions.

AF II 131, pl. 1008. Northern missions.

AF II 235, pl. 2017, 2018. Northern missions.

AF II 135, pl. 1045. Alsatian mission.

AF II 247, pl. 2110, 2111. Alsatian mission.

AF II 249, pl. 2121, 2122. Alsatian mission.

C 277 (d 2: 734). Alsatian mission.

F 7 4436 A, pl. 4. Papers found at the lodgings of Robespierre "and the other conspirators."

F 7 4432, pl. 4. *Procès-verbaux* of sectional assemblies, 9 Thermidor.

F 7 4433, pl. 1. *Procès-verbaux* of sectional assemblies, 9 Thermidor.

F 7 4433, pl. 1, 2. Papers of Paris Commune, 9 Thermidor.

F 7 4435, pl. 3. Lists of persons accused in prison plots; other police papers.

F 7 4620. Two letters of Chevalier d'Evry.

W 434 (d 2: 975). Order of Convention outlawing Robespierre and all those who violated arrest, 9 Thermidor.

BB 3 30, *liasse* III. Convention's decree of 16 Ventôse, year III, annulling Saint-Just's and Le Bas's decree of 3 Ventôse, year II.

Bibliothèque Nationale—Département des Manuscrits

Nouvelles Acquisitions Françaises, no. 312. Collection Labédoyère; Autographes et Documents Historiques, Vol. VI. Letter of Saint-Just and Le Bas from Saverne, 1 Brumaire, year II.

2. CONTEMPORARY PRINTED MATERIALS; SUBSEQUENTLY PUBLISHED LETTERS, DEBATES AND SPEECHES OF PERIOD; MEMOIRS

Almanach national. Paris, year II.

Archives parlementaires de 1787 à 1860; Recueil complet des débats législatifs et politiques des Chambres françaises. J. Mavidal and E. Laurent, eds. 1st series, 1787-99. 82 vols. Paris, 1867-1913. Vols. LII-LXXXII cover period from Sept. 22, 1792 to Jan. 4, 1794.

Aulard, F. A., ed. *Recueil des actes du comité de salut public avec la correspondance officielle des représentants en mission et le registre du conseil exécutif provisoire*. 26 vols. Paris, 1889-1923. Vols. I-XV cover period from Aug. 10, 1792, to Aug. 9, 1794.

BIBLIOGRAPHY

Aulard, F. A., ed. *La Société des Jacobins.* 6 vols. Paris, 1889-97.

Barère, B. *Mémoires de B. Barère.* H. Carnot and David (d'Angers), eds. 4 vols. Paris, 1842-44.

Barras, Paul F. J. N. *Memoirs.* G. Duruy, ed., C. E. Roche, trans. 4 vols. New York, 1895-96.

Baudot. *M. A. Baudot, représentant du peuple, décrété d'arrestation le 14 prairial, à ses collègues, composant la Convention nationale.* Dated, "De ma retraite, le 30 prairial, an 3 de la république." Pamphlet.

Bégis, Alfred. *Curiosités révolutionnaires. Saint-Just, membre du comité de salut public de la Convention nationale; 1767-1794; son emprisonnement sous Louis XVI en exécution d'une lettre de cachet; documents inédits.* Paris, 1892.

—— *Curiosités révolutionnaires. Saint-Just et les bureaux de la police générale au comité de salut public en 1794; notice historique par Augustin Lejeune, chef des bureaux; documents inédits.* Paris, 1896. Two reprints from "Annuaire de la société des amis des livres," of which society Bégis was secretary. Anti-Saint-Just. Second contains Lejeune's defence of his conduct during the Terror, written in the year III.

Brissot, J. P. *Mémoires de Brissot publiés par son fils avec des notes . . . par M. F. de Montrol.* 4 vols. Paris, 1832. Vol. IV contains the "Réponse au rapport de Saint-Just" and the "Projet de défense devant le tribunal révolutionnaire en réponse au rapport d'Amar."

Buchez, P. J. B., and Roux, P. C. *Histoire parlementaire de la Révolution française ou Journal des Assemblées nationales depuis 1789 jusqu'en 1815.* 40 vols. in 20. Paris, 1834-38. Vol. XXXV contains Le Bas's letters.

Carnot, Hippolyte. *Mémoires sur Carnot par son fils.* 2 vols. Paris, 1893. Recollections of and concerning Lazare N. M. Carnot. First published, 1861-64. Vol. I covers period.

Carnot, Lazare N. M. *Correspondance générale de Carnot.* E. Charavay and P. Mautouchet, eds. 4 vols. Paris, 1892-97. Vols. III and IV cover the period from Aug., 1793 to March, 1795. They contain military correspondence, including letters from the Committee and from Bouchotte, minister of war, to Saint-Just on mission in Alsace and the North.

Condorcet, M. J. de. *Œuvres.* A. Condorcet O'Connor and M. F. Arago, eds. 12 vols. Paris, 1847.

Faits recueillis aux derniers instants de Robespierre et de sa faction, du 9 au 10 thermidor. Paris, year II. Anonymous pamphlet by eyewitness.

Journal des débats et des décrets. Paris, year II. Especially nos. 540, 543, 677.

Lacoste, J. B. *Aperçu des moyens de défense du représentant du peuple J. B. Lacoste, décrété d'arrestation le 13 prairial, l'an 3 de la république française, une et indivisible.* Pamphlet. N.d.

—— *Suite de l'aperçu* [title-page continues as above]. Pamphlet. N.d.

Landau pamphlets. Laudier, ci-devant premier aide-du-camp du général Laubadère, commandant à Landau. *La pure vérité sur tous les événemens* [sic] *qui ont eu lieu dans la forteresse de Landau.* 1793.

—— *Liberté, égalité. Journal des événemens* [sic] *les plus remarquables, qui ont eu lieu pendant le blocus de Landau . . . par le sans-culotte Blanchard, souslieut. au 22e régt. de cavalerie.* Dated, "maison d'arret [sic] de l'Abbaye, ce 16 ventôse, l'an IIe de la République française, une et indivisible."

—— *Mémoire du citoyen Laubadère . . . , commandant en chef à Landau, sur la conspiration de cette place.* N.d.

—— *Mémoire pour les habitans de Landau.* Signed by the mayor and members

388

of the municipal commission and the secretary of the commune of Landau. N.d.

Landau pamphlets. *Mémoire du citoyen Treich, général de brigade, sur la conspiration de Landau.* N.d.

—— *Précis historique du blocus de Landau.* By an eyewitness, probably General Serviez. Gertruydemberg, 1802.

—— *Rapport des citoyens J. B. Lacoste et M. A. Beaudot [sic] . . . sur la conspiration de Landau.* Landau, 17 Nivôse, year II.

—— *Réfutation faite par les habitans de Landau . . . des faussetés qui composent le mémoire de Treich.* Paris, n.d.

Landrecies pamphlet. *Mémoire historique des évènemens [sic] qui ont précédé, accompagné et suivi le siège de Landrecy par les tyrans coalisés.* Signed by 22 members of the municipal council, including the mayor. Dated Valenciennes, 13 Nivôse, year III. The signatures attest a republican miracle described in a decree by the representatives J. B. Lacoste and Roger Ducos; they award 400 livres to Madeleine Bouche, a soldier's wife, who has brought forth a daughter "portant sous le sein gauche le bonnet de la Liberté, en couleur et en relief." This is taken as a sign not only of the mother's patriotism, but that "la Nature aime à marquer de son sceau le règne de l'indépendance" and is contrasted with the miracles "inventés par l'imposture sacerdotale." The pamphlet is of interest as throwing light on the personality of Lacoste and on the psychology of the times.

Lauraguais, Brancas de. *Recueil de pièces relatives au gouvernement révolutionnaire et au despotisme de ses comités avant le 9 thermidor.* 26 Pluviôse, year III. Contains a letter of Thuillier to Lauraguais's daughter, addressed "citoyenne, sœur et amie," with comment by Lauraguais that his daughter permitted these attentions for her father's sake; a letter from Thuillier to Chollet, *agent-national* of the Chauny district; a decree of the Committee of Public Safety, signed by Saint-Just and seven others (Carnot signs before Saint-Just) arresting Lauraguais; an order of Chollet, sending him to the Revolutionary Tribunal, and other documents.

Le Blanc, J. *Vies secrettes [sic] et politiques de Couthon, Saint-Just, Robespierre jeunes [sic], complices du tyran Robespierre, et assassins de la République.* Paris, year II. Thermidorian pamphlet.

Levasseur, René. *Mémoires de R. Levasseur (de la Sarthe), ex-Conventionnel.* Achille Roche, ed. 4 vols. Paris, 1829-31.

Moniteur, Le. Gazette nationale ou Moniteur universel. Paris, H. Agasse. Vol. VII, July 1-Dec. 31, 1792; Vol. VIII, Jan. 1-June 30, 1793; Vol. IX, July 1, 1793-Feb. 18, 1794; Vol. X, Feb. 19-Sept. 21, 1794.

Nodier, Charles. *Souvenirs de la Révolution et de l'Empire.* 2 vols. Paris, 1850. Originally published, 1831. Especially Vol. I, containing chapters on "Euloge Schneider," "Saint-Just en mission," "Pichegru" and "Les Institutions républicaines de Saint-Just."

Papiers inédits trouvés chez Robespierre, Saint-Just, Payan, etc., supprimés ou omis par Courtois. 3 vols. Paris, 1828.

Pilpay. *Le club infernal.* N.d. Three Thermidorian pamphlets bound in one.

Projet rédigé par Robespierre, du rapport fait à la Convention nationale par Saint-Just, contre Fabre d'Eglantine, Danton, Philippeaux, Lacroix et Camille Desmoulins; manuscrit inédit, publié sur les autographes avec des notes, des rapprochemens [sic] et un fac-simile; suivi d'une lettre de Mademoiselle de Robespierre. France, ed. Paris, 1841. Pamphlet.

"Réponse de Barère, Billaud-Varenne, Collot d'Herbois et Vadier aux imputa-

BIBLIOGRAPHY

tions de Laurent Le Cointre," reprinted in *La Révolution française,* XXXIV, part 1 (Jan.-June, 1898).

Reuss, Rodolphe. *L'Alsace pendant la Révolution française.* 2 vols. Paris, 1881, 1894. Vol. II contains documents of period from 1790 to 1793.

Robespierre. *Correspondance de Maximilien et Augustin Robespierre.* Georges Michon, ed. Paris, 1926.

Roux, député de la Haute-Marne. *Relation de l'événement des 8, 9 et 10 thermidor, sur la conspiration des triumvirs, Robespierre, Couthon et St.-Just [sic].* Dated Paris, 11 Thermidor, year II. Pamphlet.

Saint-Just. "Arlequin Diogène." Reprinted with introduction by C. Vellay in *La Revue politique et littéraire; Revue bleue,* July, 1907.

—— "Épigramme sur le comédien Dubois qui a joué dans Pierre le Cruel." *Annales historiques de la Révolution française,* May-June, 1934.

—— "La Correspondance de Saint-Just." C. Vellay, ed. *Mercure de France,* LX (1906).

—— "Lettres inédites de Saint-Just, 1791-1794." C. Vellay, ed. *Revue historique de la Révolution française,* Oct.-Dec., 1910.

—— "Three Letters of Saint-Just." G. Bruun, ed. *Journal of Modern History,* June, 1934.

—— "Une Lettre inédite de Saint-Just." C. Vellay, ed. *Revue historique de la Révolution française,* IV (1913). Letter probably written in 1790 or 1791.

—— "Une Lettre de Saint-Just à Thuillier." C. Vellay, ed. *Revue historique de la Révolution française,* I (1910).

—— *Œuvres de Saint-Just, représentant du peuple à la Convention nationale.* Paris, Prévot, 1834.

—— *Œuvres complètes de Saint-Just, avec une introduction et des notes.* Charles Vellay, ed. 2 vols. Paris, 1908.

Saint-Just, Marie Anne Robinot. "Une Lettre de la mère de Saint-Just." C. Vellay, ed. *Annales révolutionnaires,* I.

Salle, J. B. "Letter to Saint-Just." Printed in Vatel, *Charlotte de Corday et les Girondins,* I. Letter dated Caen, July 11, 1793.

Senart. *Révélations puisées dans les cartons des comités de salut public et du sureté [sic] générale; ou mémoires (inédits) de Senart, agent du gouvernement révolutionnaire, publiés par Alexis Dumesnil.* Paris, 1824.

Tyrannie exercée à Strasbourg par Saint-Just et Lebas. Réclamation de J. G. Treuttel, libraire et imprimeur à Strasbourg, une de leurs victimes. Versailles, n.d. Pamphlet.

Vilate, Joachim (Gracchus). *Causes secrètes de la révolution du 9 au 10 thermidor, par Vilate, ex-juré au tribunal révolutionnaire de Paris, détenu à la Force.* Paris, year III.

—— *Continuation des causes secrètes,* etc. Paris, year III. Two Thermidorian pamphlets, bound in one. To be found also in Berville, I. A., and Barrière, F. J., *Collection des mémoires relatifs à la Révolution française* (56 vols. in 57, Paris, 1821-27), Vol. XVII.

II. SECONDARY WORKS

The student who desires to orient himself in the whole field before consulting the specialized material given below will find excellent recent surveys of the French Revolution by Crane Brinton (1934), Leo Gershoy (1933), L. R. Gottschalk (1929) and Charles D. Hazen (1932, 2 vols.).

BIBLIOGRAPHY

Aulard, F. A. "Convention." *La Grande Encyclopédie*. Paris, 1898.
—— *Histoire politique de la Révolution française*. Paris, 1909. Friendly to Danton.
Barante, Pierre, baron de. *Histoire de la Convention nationale*. 6 vols. Paris, 1851-53.
Béraud, Henri. *Twelve Portraits of the French Revolution*. Madeleine Boyd, trans. Boston, 1928.
Bourne, Henry E. "The Organization of the First Committee of Public Safety." *American Historical Association Annual Report*, 1894.
Bruun, Geoffrey. *Saint-Just, Apostle of the Terror*. Boston, 1932. Good, brief study.
—— "Deux lettres de Chabot à Saint-Just concernant la conspiration de l'étranger." *Annales historiques de la Révolution française*, X (May-June, 1933).
Caron, Pierre. *Manuel pratique pour l'étude de la Révolution française*. Paris, 1912.
Challamel, A. *Les Clubs contre-révolutionnaires*. Paris, 1895.
Chuquet, Arthur. *Les Guerres de la Révolution*. 11 vols. Paris, n.d. 4th ed. Especially Vol. IX, *Hoche et la lutte pour l'Alsace, 1793-1794* (1893) and Vol. XI, *Hondschoote*.
Claretie, Jules. *Camille Desmoulins and His Wife; Passages from the History of the Dantonists*. Mrs. Cashel Hoey, trans. London, 1876.
Cuvillier-Fleury. *Portraits politiques et révolutionnaires*. 2 vols. in 1. Paris, 1852. Essay entitled "Le Poème de Saint-Just" in Vol. II; Part 1 gives account of Saint-Just's youth, chiefly based on E. Fleury; Part 2 deals with *Organt*. Very hostile.
Dommanget, Maurice. "La Famille de Saint-Just." *Annales révolutionnaires*, VI (1913).
Dumolin, Maurice. *Précis d'histoire militaire: Révolution et Empire*. 3 vols. and atlas. Paris, 1906-13. Vol. I, published first in 1901, deals with the Revolution. Author, a former artillery officer, published work for use in the École de Guerre. Has high opinion of Saint-Just's energy and efficiency on mission. Atlas valuable, especially *croquis* no. 22 for Alsatian campaign, nos. 26 and 29 for operations in the North.
Fleury, Édouard. *Études révolutionnaires; Saint-Just et la Terreur*. 2 vols. Paris, 1852. The most detailed biography. In general hostile and prejudiced, but with some effort at impartial judgment. Not always trustworthy; too much reliance on rumor and imagination.
Gjellerup, Karl. *Saint-Just; Historisk Sorgespil i Fem Handlinger*. Copenhagen, 1886. Drama in five acts. Scene, Paris, 1794.
Hamel, L. Ernest. *Histoire de Robespierre*. 3 vols. Paris, 1865-67.
—— *Histoire de Saint-Just, député à la Convention nationale*. Paris, 1859. Official biography; author had the family papers at his disposal. Very uncritical, strongly prejudiced in favor of Saint-Just. Though Hamel is able to refute some of Fleury's statements, he is also often open to correction.
—— "Euloge Schneider." *La Révolution française*, XXXIV, Part 1 (Jan.-June, 1898). Hostile to Schneider.
Hanotaux, Gabriel, ed. *Histoire de la nation française*. 15 vols. Paris, 1920-29. Tome VIII, *Histoire militaire et navale*, Vol. 2, Part 1, General Mangin, *De la Constituante au directoire*.
Hartmann, Erich. *Das blaue Buch und sein Verfasser*. Strassburg, 1911. Discussion of the *Livre bleu* by Ulrich, a collection of documents published in 1795, relating in part to the Strasbourg Revolutionary Tribunal. Latter are violently

against the Tribunal; though authentic, they are deceiving both in content and arrangement.

Herlaut, Colonel. "La Vie politique de Villain d'Aubigny." *Annales historiques de la Révolution française,* Jan., 1934.

Jacquemaire, Mme. Madeleine (Clemenceau). *The Life of Madame Roland.* Laurence Vail, trans. London, 1930.

Jaquel, Roger. "Euloge Schneider et l'historiographie allemande." *Annales historiques de la Révolution française,* Sept.-Oct., 1931. Best discussion of subject. Excellent section on "L'Œuvre de Mühlenbeck."

—— "Euloge Schneider en Alsace." *Annales historiques de la Révolution française,* Jan., April, July, 1932; Jan., 1933; May, 1935.

Jomini, Antoine Henri, baron de. *Histoire critique et militaire des guerres de la Révolution. Atlas.* Paris, 1820-24.

Kerr, Wilfred B. *The Reign of Terror.* Toronto, 1927.

Kritschewsky, S. B. *J. J. Rousseau und Saint-Just; ein Beitrag zur Entwicklungsgeschichte der sozialpolitischen Ideen der Montagnards.* Berne, 1895.

Lamartine, Alphonse de. *Œuvres complètes.* 40 vols. Paris, 1860-63. Vols. IX-XV, *Histoire des Girondins.* Uncritical.

Laurent, Gustave. "La Faculté de droit de Reims et les hommes de la Révolution." *Annales historiques de la Révolution française,* VI (1929).

—— "Le Plus jeune député de la Convention—Saint-Just ou Hentz?" *Annales historiques de la Révolution française,* I (1924).

—— "Un Portrait de Saint-Just." *Revue historique de la Révolution française,* XV (1923).

—— "Les Relations de Saint-Just à Reims: le berger d'Etoges, Étienne Lambert, ami de Saint-Just." *Annales révolutionnaires,* XV (1923).

Lefebvre, Georges. *Annales d'histoire économique et sociale,* I, 141-45. Able review of Mathiez, A., *La Vie Chère et le mouvement social sous la Terreur.*

—— *Questions agraires au temps de la Terreur.* Strasbourg, 1932.

—— "Sur Danton." *Annales historiques de la Révolution française,* IX (1932). Most balanced estimate of Danton's character.

Lenéru, Marie. *Saint-Just.* Paris, 1922. Character sketch.

Madelin, Louis. *Danton.* Paris, 1914.

—— *The French Revolution.* English trans. New York, 1916.

Mathiez, Albert. *Autour de Robespierre.* Paris, 1926. This, like all the books by Mathiez here mentioned, except his general history of the Revolution, is a collection of essays, highly critical, amply documented, very suggestive, marking a new era in the study of the period. Strongly Robespierrist, not always unprejudiced.

—— "La Constitution de 1793." *Annales historiques de la Révolution française,* V (1928).

—— "Les Décrêts de ventôse." *Annales historiques de la Révolution française,* V.

—— *Études robespierristes,* 1st series: *La Corruption parlementaire sous la Terreur.* Paris, 1927. First published, 1917.

—— *Études robespierristes,* 2d series: *La Conspiration de l'étranger.* Paris, 1918.

—— "Études sur la Terreur; le comité de salut public et le complot de l'étranger." *Annales historiques de la Révolution française,* III (1926).

—— *Girondins et Montagnards.* Paris, 1930.

—— "Le Premier comité de salut public et la guerre." *Revue historique,* July-Aug., 1928.

—— *La Réaction thermidorienne.* Paris, 1929. Continuation of his general history of the Revolution. Early chapters valuable for account of reaction against former members of Committee of Public Safety.

Mathiez, Albert. *La Révolution française.* 3 vols. Paris, 1925-27.

―― "Robespierre et Joseph Le Bon." *Annales historiques de la Révolution française,* I (1924).

―― *Robespierre terroriste.* Paris, 1921.

―― "Rousseau, Robespierre, Saint-Just et Couthon jugés par Buonarroti." *Annales révolutionnaires,* V (1912).

―― "La Terreur instrument de la politique sociale des Robespierristes; les décrêts de ventôse sur le séquestre des biens des suspects et leur application." *Annales historiques de la Révolution française,* V (1928).

―― *La Vie chère et le mouvement social sous la Terreur.* Paris, 1927.

Maurice, B., and others. *Le Livre rouge; histoire de l'échafaud en France.* Paris, 1863.

Michelet, Jules. *Histoire de la Révolution française.* 7 vols. Paris, 1847-53.

Monin, H. "Histoire extraordinaire des papiers Baudot et de leur publication." *Annales révolutionnaires,* II (1909).

Mühlenbeck, Eugène. *Euloge Schneider, 1793.* Strasbourg. 1896. Hostile to Saint-Just.

"Notes et glanes." *Annales révolutionnaires,* VI (1913), 411-13. Anonymous. Notes on Saint-Just's family.

Nussbaum, Frederick L. *Commercial Policy in the French Revolution; a Study of the Career of G. J. A. Ducher.* Washington, 1923.

Ording, Arne. *Le Bureau de police du comité de salut public: Étude sur la Terreur.* Oslo, 1930. Able monograph.

Patoux, L. Abel. *Saint-Just et Mme. Thorin; origines de la famille de Saint-Just.* Saint-Quentin, 1878. Pamphlet, containing two brief essays based on author's investigations at Blérancourt.

Phipps, Ramsay Weston. *The Armies of the First French Republic and the Rise of the Marshals of Napoleon I.* I, *The Armée du Nord.* Oxford, 1926. II, *The Armées de la Moselle, du Rhin, de Sambre-et-Meuse, de Rhin-et-Moselle.* Oxford, 1929. Posthumous work of an English colonel. Able technical discussion; hostile to representatives on mission.

P. P. [Paul Portevin?] Note in *Revue historique de la Révolution française,* IV (1913), 328.

Sainte-Beuve, C. A. *Causeries de lundi.* 15 vols. Paris, Garnier, 3d ed., n.d. [1869-76]. Vol. V contains sketch entitled "Études sur Saint-Just par M. Édouard Fleury." Date of sketch, Jan. 26, 1852. Accepts authority of Fleury; hostile to Saint-Just.

Schnerb, Robert. "Les Lois de ventôse et leur application dans le département de Puy-de-Dôme." *Annales historiques de la Révolution française,* Sept.-Oct., 1934.

Six, G. "Fallait-il quatre quartiers de noblesse pour être officier à la fin de l'ancien régime?" *Revue d'histoire moderne,* Jan.-Feb., 1929.

Stéfane-Pol. *De Robespierre à Fouché; notes de police.* Paris, n.d. [1906]. Chap. V on "Saint-Just et ses principes en matière d'éducation."

Stern, Alfred. "Condorcet und der Girondistische Verfassungsentwurf von 1793." *Historische Zeitschrift,* CXLI. 3.

Suin. "Travail sur les archives de Blérancourt et notes biographiques sur Lecat et Saint-Just." *Bulletin de la société archéologique, historique et scientifique de Soissons,* 1852.

Taine, Hippolyte. *La Révolution.* 6 vols. Paris, 1922. Constitutes a part of his

BIBLIOGRAPHY

Origines de la France contemporaine in 11 vols., Vol. V of the Révolution being Vol. VII of the *Origines*. Originally published, 1878-85. Hostile to Saint-Just.

Taylor, Ida A. *Revolutionary Types*. London, 1904.

Toulongeon, F. Emmanuel. *Histoire de France, depuis la Révolution de 1789; écrite d'après les mémoires et manuscrits contemporains, recueillis dans les dépots civils et militaires*. 7 vols. Paris, 1801-10. Especially Vol. IV.

Vatel, Charles. *Charlotte de Corday et les Girondins*. 3 vols. Paris, 1864-72. Vol. I.

Vellay, Charles. *Annales révolutionnaires*, I (1908), 362. Notice of his own edition of the *Œuvres de Saint-Just*. Contains items on various early works of Saint-Just.

—— "Autour d'une édition de Saint-Just." *Annales révolutionnaires*, I.

—— "Essai d'une bibliographie de Saint-Just." *Revue historique de la Révolution française*, I (1910).

—— "Complément à la bibliographie de Saint-Just." *Revue historique de la Révolution française*, II (1911).

—— "Les Poursuites contre Organt." *Revue politique et littéraire; Revue bleue*, 5th series, Vol. VIII (1907).

—— "Les Premières luttes politiques de Saint-Just." *Revue de Paris*, Vol. XIII, Tome 5 (1906).

—— "Saint-Just en 1790." *Revue historique de la Révolution française*, II.

—— "Saint-Just et Mably." *Annales révolutionnaires*, I (1908).

—— "Saint-Just et le procès des dantonistes." *Annales révolutionnaires*, I.

—— "Un Ami de Saint-Just: Gateau." *Annales révolutionnaires*, I.

—— ed. Various works and letters of Saint-Just. See under Saint-Just.

Vidal, Gaston. *Saint-Just*. Paris, 1923. Emphasis on oratory. Uncritical.

Wallon, Henri. *Histoire du tribunal révolutionnaire de Paris, avec le journal de ses actes*. 6 vols. Paris, 1880-82.

—— *Les Représentants du peuple en mission et la justice révolutionnaire dans les départements en l'an II (1793-1794)*. 5 vols. Paris, 1889-90. Vols. IV and V.

Walter, Gérard. "Le Problème de la dictature jacobine." *Annales historiques de la Révolution française*, VIII (1931). Review of Staroselski's Russian work bearing that title.

Wilkinson, Spenser. *The French Army before Napoleon*. Oxford, 1915.

INDEX

A

Aisne, department of the, 5, 21, 32, 130-32, 184
Amar, André, 87, 105, 120, 219, 276, 291
America, predictions regarding, 26, 72
Anthoine, François Paul Nicolas, 66
Antraigues (Emmanuel Henri de Launay, Comte d') forgery, 222-23
Arlequin Diogène, see Saint-Just, Louis Antoine
Army, *see* Saint-Just, Louis Antoine
Army of the Sambre-et-Meuse, formation of, 257-58, 379
Arras, 116, 124, 182-84
Artois, Charles Philippe, Comte d', 7, 13
Assembly, Legislative, 24, 29-30
Assembly, National Constituent, 16, 19-20, 22-23, 58
Assignats, 27, 47, 49-52, 55-57, 60, 149, 159, 173-74, 194, 202, 226-27, 275, 308
Attichy, 3
Avesnes, 124, 250

B

Barbaroux, Charles Jean Marie, 41, 65, 87, 366
Barère de Vieuzac, Bertrand: Alsatian campaign, panegyric on, 371; characteristics, 274, 291, 366; Committee of Public Safety, activity in, 93-95, 105, 111-12, 167, 367; conciliatory policy, 274, 278-79; Constitution of 1793, relation to, 65-66, 75-77, 365; Desmoulins, denounced by, 219; *Esprit de la Révolution,* on, 362; Fleurus, report on, 270-71, 381; Hébertists, against, 196-97; king's trial, 41; maximum, tables of, 187; military theory, 62; *Notes militaires,* on, 365; *Organt,* on, 360; police bu-

reau, 230-32; Saint-Just, on, 160, 196, 235, 237, 274-76, 281-83, 295-96, 327, 342, 345-47; Saint-Just, relations with, 376-77, 379, 384; terrorism, 235-36, 376
Barnave, Antoine Pierre Joseph Marie, 31
Barras, Paul François Jean Nicolas, Vicomte de, 211, 273, 292, 325
Basire, Claude, 186, 192, 208
Bastille, 15, 26, 39, 61
Batz, Jean, Baron de, 219, 307, 324
Baudot, Marc Antoine, 141, 156, 162, 164-71, 175, 336, 371-72
Bayard, Adrien, 30-33, 350, 362
Bayle, Moïse (Moyse), 120
Beauvais-Préau, Charles Nicolas, 111
Bentabole, Pierre, 66
Bergoing (Bergoeing), François, 87
Berlier, Théophile, Comte, 91
Bertrand de la Hosdinière, Charles Ambroise, 87
Beurnonville, Pierre Riel, Marquis de, 130-31, 368
Beuvin, 24, 29
Bigot, 32
Billaud-Varenne, Jacques Nicolas: characteristics, 366; Committee of Public Safety, activity in, 93-95, 167, 367; Danton, responsibility for attack on, 209, 221; Daubigny, charges against, 332; Hébertist, 197, 202; Jacobin constitutional committee, member of, 65; police bureau, 230-31, 382; Saint-Just, appeal to, 379; Saint-Just, hostility to, 273, 279-81, 284-85, 287-89; Saint-Just, on, 202; terrorism, 234, 241, 373, 376
Biroteau, Jean Baptiste, 87
Bitche, 155-56, 158-61, 165
Blérancourt, 4-6, 8-10, 16-23, 29-30, 33, 51, 97, 249, 299, 328, 359-61
Bonaparte, Napoleon, 67, 132, 151, 229, 277

INDEX

Courtois (Edme Bonaventure) report, 297-98

Cousolre, 251, 254

Couthon, Georges Auguste: bureau of police, 230-32; Committee of Public Safety, activity in, 91, 93-95, 118, 206, 286, 345; Convention constitutional committee, member of, 75-76; fall, 236, 289-92, 294; hostage offer, 82; Jacobin constitutional committee, member of, 65-66; Robespierre, ally of, 273-74, 276, 280, 282; Saint-Just, friendship with, 215, 335; social policy, 383; terrorism, 226, 234, 241, 376-77; Thermidorian slanders, 295-96, 325-26, 336-37

Crosne, Thiroux de, 7, 15, 350

Cusset, Joseph, 156

D

Danton, Georges Jacques, 106, 130, 236, 368; Committee of Public Safety, member of, 91-93; constitutional committees, member of, 65; estimate of character, 216-17, 324, 342, 374-75; fall, 89, 207-22; hostage offer, 82; Indulgents, leader of, 179, 186, 191, 204

Daubigny, Jean Louis Marie Vilain, 31-32, 172, 328, 332, 336

David, Jacques Louis, 120, 219, 279

Decaisne, Emmanuel, 21-22, 361-62

Decize, 3

Delaunay d'Angers, Joseph, 186

Delmas, Jean François Bertrand, 83, 91, 168

Demaillot, 144

Dentzel, Georges Frédéric, 168

Departmental organization, 72-73, 78

Descharmes, Dubois, 7-8, 349

Desjardins, Jacques, 97, 248-49, 254, 257-59, 268, 378

Desmoulins, Camille, 236, 324; arrest, 210; defense, 218-19; Dillon plot, on, 87; execution, 222; Indulgents, member of, 179; Robespierre, break with, 209; Saint-Just's attack, 213-15; Saint-Just, early relations with, 10, 16, 17-18, 31; Saint-Just, epigram on, 34, 238

Desmoulins, Lucile, 217, 220, 222

Deville, Jean Louis, 130

Diedrichsen (Diederichsen), Jean Frédéric, 186

Dietrich, Philippe Frédéric, Baron de, 134

Dillon, Arthur, Comte, 83, 87, 214, 220, 222, 233

Du Barry, Marie Jeanne Bécu, Comtesse, 13

Dubois-Crancé, Edmond Louis Alexis, 66

Dumas, René François, 292-93, 296, 337

Dumouriez, Charles François, 82, 85, 117, 212-13, 215-17, 219, 247

Duplay family, 117-27, 254, 385

Duquesnoy, Ernest Dominique François Joseph, 118-19, 256, 380

Du Roy, Jean Michel, 91

E

Ehrmann, Jean François, 156, 163, 370

Enragés, 47, 53-55, 81

Épigramme sur le comédien Dubois, see Saint-Just, Louis Antoine

Esprit de la Révolution, see Saint-Just, Louis Antoine

Estaing, Charles Hector, Comte d', 85

Evry, Armand Jérôme Joseph Brunet, Chevalier d', 6-7, 350-51, 359

F

Fabre d'Eglantine, Philippe François Nazaire, 112, 131, 186-87, 189, 192, 212-15, 236

Faure, Balthasar, 163, 169

Federation, Festival of, 21-22, 27

Fleurus, 247, 264, 266, 270-71, 285, 287, 330

Foreign plot, 145, 179, 186-87, 198-99, 201, 203, 208, 212, 324

Fouché, Joseph, 273, 281

Fouquier-Tinville, Antoine Quentin, 220, 231-32, 234, 294, 325

Fragments sur les institutions républicaines, see Saint-Just, Louis Antoine

Fréron, Louis Marie Stanislas, 273, 289

Frey brothers (Junius; Emmanuel), 186-87, 212

397

INDEX

INDEX

W

Wattignies, 107, 132, 247

Wissembourg, 98, 132-33, 153, 156-57, 161-62, 166-67

Wurmser, Dagobert Sigmund, Reichsgraf von, 133, 136, 157, 162

Y

York and Albany, Frederick, Duke ot, 84, 89, 248

Ypres, 248-49, 261

Ysabeau, Claude Alexandre, letter to Tallien, 192

COLUMBIA UNIVERSITY PRESS
COLUMBIA UNIVERSITY
NEW YORK

FOREIGN AGENT
OXFORD UNIVERSITY PRESS
HUMPHREY MILFORD
AMEN HOUSE, LONDON, E.C. 4